UNDER THE SOUTHERN CROSS

OSPREY
PUBLISHING

UNDER THE SOUTHERN CROSS

THE SOUTH PACIFIC AIR CAMPAIGN AGAINST RABAUL

THOMAS McKELVEY CLEAVER

OSPREY PUBLISHING
Bloomsbury Publishing Plc
Kemp House, Chawley Park, Cumnor Hill, Oxford OX2 9PH, UK
29 Earlsfort Terrace, Dublin 2, Ireland
1385 Broadway, 5th Floor, New York, NY 10018, USA
E-mail: info@ospreypublishing.com
www.ospreypublishing.com

OSPREY is a trademark of Osprey Publishing Ltd

First published in Great Britain in 2021

© Thomas McKelvey Cleaver, 2021

Thomas McKelvey Cleaver has asserted his right under the Copyright, Designs and Patents Act, 1988, to be identified as Author of this work.

This paperback edition was first published in Great Britain in 2022 by Osprey Publishing.

A catalog record for this book is available from the British Library.

ISBN: HB 9781472838223; PB 9781472838230; eBook 9781472838216;
ePDF 9781472838193; XML 9781472838209

22 23 24 25 26   10 9 8 7 6 5 4 3 2 1

Maps by www.bounford.com
Index by Zoe Ross

Typeset by Deanta Global Publishing Services, Chennai, India
Printed and bound in Great Britain by CPI Group (UK) Ltd, Croydon, CR0 4YY

Every attempt has been made by the Publisher to secure the appropriate permissions for material reproduced in this book. If there has been any oversight we will be happy to rectify the situation and a written submission should be made to the Publishers.

Osprey Publishing supports the Woodland Trust, the UK's leading woodland conservation charity.

To find out more about our authors and books visit www.ospreypublishing.com. Here you will find extracts, author interviews, details of forthcoming events and the option to sign up for our newsletter.

CONTENTS

LIST OF MAPS

LIST OF ILLUSTRATIONS

Curtiss P-40Ns of 17 Squadron, RNZAF
P-40Ns of 14 Squadron RNZAF en route to Henderson Field
B-25D "Tondelayo" of the 500th "Rough Raiders" Squadron
F4U-1A Corsairs of VF-17 aboard USS *Bunker Hill*
Three B-25Ds strafe Wewak airfield on New Guinea
B-25Ds attacking Wewak airfield with parafrag bombs
A B-25J skip-bombs a Japanese patrol boat

FOREWORD

The "Germany first" strategy the United States had agreed to with Britain committed the US into supporting and winning the war in Europe before dealing with Japan. But Admiral Ernest King wasn't that good at waiting. Japan was running wild in the South Pacific, attacking shipping and capturing islands, and developing island fortresses. Its carriers, battleships and other combatants were formidable and combat-tested. Their aircraft and pilots were combat-honed.

This marvelous history picks up after the author's previous book, *I Will Run Wild: The Pacific War from Pearl Harbor to Midway*. On August 7, 1942 the US Navy landed the 1st Marine Division on Guadalcanal. Thus began the Solomons Campaign, which would become the bloodiest battle the US Navy ever fought. The Navy, Marines, Army Air Forces, and Allies worked together to confront the power of Japan, contain it, then diminish it, as they paid the awful price necessary to advance across the Pacific toward the Japanese home islands. You will see both sides of the Battle of the Eastern Solomons, the Battle of Santa Cruz, the Battle of Cape Esperance, the two Naval Battles of Guadalcanal, the Battle of Tassafaronga, and the Battle of Rennell Island – aircraft carrier and battleship battles unequaled before or since.

Ground operations include the landing at Guadalcanal, the Battle of Edson's Ridge, and the Battle of Henderson Field. The Japanese often fought to the death, and the Marines were determined to oblige them. You will also get your feet wet invading Tulagi, Gavutu and Bougainville.

Meet and grow to know and understand the key players on both sides. Listen in on the conversations, messaging and radio calls of the command staff, the ship commanders, and the pilots on both sides, as the author has sewn together an amazing narrative gleaned from interviews, ships' logs, squadron websites, and award citations, to tell the complete, fascinating story.

Look over Admiral Isoroku Yamamoto's shoulder as he tries to understand, predict and counter the growing US presence in the South Pacific. Sail with Admiral Tanaka, and fly with Japanese pilots, like Tetsuzo Iwamoto, Hiroyoshi Nishizawa and Saburo Sakai, as they fly against ever-improving US fighters and bombers.

But also enjoy views into the US leadership, with Admirals Ernest King, Chester Nimitz, and Bull Halsey. Meet larger-than-life characters that have been immortalized by movies like *PT-109*, and TV shows like *Baa Baa Black Sheep* and *McHale's Navy*. There are amazing stories of John F. Kennedy, Stanley "Swede" Vejtasa, Joe "The Coach" Bauer, Gregory "Pappy" Boyington, Marion Carl, Richard Bong and Tommy Blackburn. You will fly on combat missions to Simpson Harbor, Rabaul, Lakunai, Vunakanau, Rapopo and Wewak. Be amazed as Paul "Pappy" Gunn adds additional nose guns and cannon from scrapped airplanes to make the B-25 into a strafing gunship.

Following the South Pacific campaign, there would never again be massed air battles between forces of near-equal capability such as those seen over Rabaul between October 1943 and February 1944. The war in the south Pacific was won, and the US Navy, Marines and Army Air Forces would move on to the central Pacific, en route to the Japanese home islands.

Another pilot who was there was my dad, Bob Dosé, although he goes unmentioned by name. He was Commanding Officer of VF-12, flying the F6F Hellcat off USS *Saratoga*, as part of Task Force 38. They had been in combat since September 1943. On November 5, 1943, his log books show that he participated in a 4-hour "Raid on Rabaul – Shot down one Zero." He was in combat for six more months before VF-12 returned stateside. I was born a year later. 27 years after that, I was also a US Navy fighter pilot, in VF-92 flying the F-4J Phantom II on my second Vietnam War combat cruise aboard USS *Constellation*. On May 10, 1972, in a 2 F-4s vs. 7 MiGs fur ball over North Vietnam's Kep Airfield, I shot down a North Vietnamese MiG-21. This was the first of 11 MiGs shot down that day – the bloodiest air war day of the conflict. I believe my father and I are the only father-and-son both to have had aerial victories.

This book took me into the environments and battles in which my father flew, while presenting information I was not previously familiar with.

Thanks to the greatest generation for growing into the magnificent warriors and home support needed to change the course of World War II. Thanks to my dad, Captain Robert G. Dosé with whom I shared so much, who passed away in 1998. And thanks to Thomas Cleaver for researching and writing this amazing book. I thoroughly enjoyed it.

Commander Curtis R. Dosé, USNR (Ret)
Fighter Pilot

INTRODUCTION

In February 1942, the Japanese took control of the island of New Britain and its major port, Rabaul, situated at Simpson Harbor, the best deep-water anchorage in the South Pacific. From Rabaul, Japanese forces would move west to take New Guinea, and southeast to take the Solomons. Their goal was to cut off the continent of Australia from outside support. Rabaul became the most important Japanese base south of Truk, and the most important goal of the Allies to recapture or neutralize to obtain victory in the Pacific. The campaign would take two years from the day the Japanese first came ashore to the day their air forces were forced to abandon the base to its fate.

The loss of four aircraft carriers and the majority of the highly experienced aircrews in their air groups meant that the Imperial Navy would no longer undertake offensive operations in the Pacific War. Yet this was far from a spent force. While the surviving Japanese carriers other than *Shōkaku* and *Zuikaku* were not fleet carriers, they still outnumbered what the US Navy could bring to a fight, and their fliers were still the best naval aviators in the world. With *Shōkaku* repaired from the damage inflicted on her at Coral Sea, the Mobile Fleet was a dangerous opponent and one the American Navy took on with trepidation. With regard to surface warfare capability, the Imperial Navy was far better than its American opponent in the field of night combat, which would be the centerpiece of the majority of naval action in the year following Midway.

The US Navy was still forced to husband its forces and remain conservative in their deployment, since the "new navy" on which construction had begun in 1940 was still a year from entering the ring. However, events overwhelmed plans and the Navy was forced to go

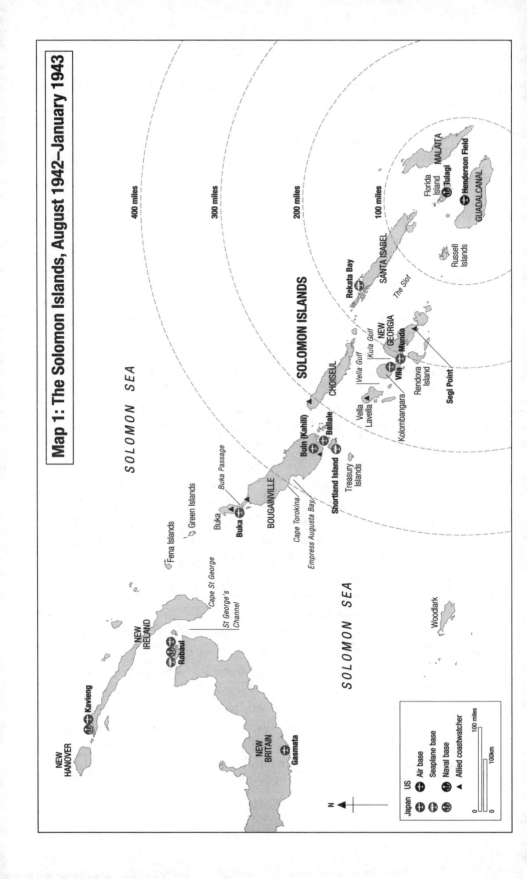

Map 1: The Solomon Islands, August 1942–January 1943

SOLOMON SEA

NEW HANOVER

Kavieng

NEW IRELAND

Rabaul

Cape St George

St George's Channel

NEW BRITAIN

Gasmata

Fena Islands

Green Islands

Buka Passage

Buka

Buka

BOUGAINVILLE

Cape Torokina

Empress Augusta Bay

Buin (Kahili)

Ballale

Shortland Island

Treasury Islands

SOLOMON ISLANDS

CHOISEUL

Vella Gulf

Kula Gulf

NEW GEORGIA

Vella Lavella

Vila

Munda

Kolombangara

Rendova Island

Segi Point

SANTA ISABEL

Rekata Bay

The Slot

Russell Islands

Florida Island

Tulagi

MALAITA

Henderson Field

GUADALCANAL

SOLOMON SEA

Woodlark

400 miles

300 miles

200 miles

100 miles

N

Legend

US
- Air base
- Seaplane base
- Naval base

Japan
- Air base
- Seaplane base
- Naval base

▲ Allied coastwatcher

0   100 miles
0   100km

on the offensive in the face of dangerous new developments in the South Pacific. That they were able to do so surprised the Japanese, who did not expect any US offensive action in the Pacific War before the spring of 1943. One hundred and forty days after the American victory at Midway, only USS *Enterprise* would remain of the carrier force so carefully built up in the years before the war. USS *Saratoga* had finally seen action at the Battle of the Eastern Solomons after being torpedoed shortly after Pearl Harbor, only to be torpedoed again within a matter of days of her air group's successful defense of the Guadalcanal invasion. Two weeks after that, USS *Wasp* would fall victim to another Japanese submarine, and five weeks after that, USS *Hornet*, the carrier that had launched the Doolittle Raid, would end in a watery grave at the bottom of the Coral Sea, 370 days after her commissioning. Until *Saratoga* could return to the South Pacific in the spring of 1943, *Enterprise* was the only American fleet carrier left.

In the meantime, events forced the United States to undertake an offensive far earlier than any American had expected. The discovery of Japanese air bases in the southern Solomons meant the sea route by which Australia was supplied and kept in the war was threatened. The invasion of Guadalcanal led to a six-month battle that at times seemed to carry inevitable US defeat, before the enemy was expelled from the island.

At the same time, another campaign undertaken with too few resources had broken out on the island of New Guinea during the spring of 1942. The Japanese attempt to reinforce their position there had led to the Battle of the Coral Sea in May. In the months after till the end of the year, American and Australian armed forces were only just able to prevent a Japanese conquest of New Guinea.

The end of 1942 saw the Japanese stopped in both the Solomons and New Guinea, but it would take another 18 hard-fought months in both places before Japan was forced to retreat from the South Pacific. The campaign would see high losses on both sides. For the Japanese, the Solomons and New Guinea became the graveyard of their best remaining units, chewed up in the meatgrinder Admiral Yamamoto, the only Japanese leader who had seen American industrial strength first-hand before the war, had predicted. The expulsion of Japanese forces from the region and the neutralization of Rabaul left them unable to respond with more than holding actions when the Allied

Pacific offensive began in November 1943 that would lead to near-total destruction of Japan two years later.

The story of the Allied campaigns in New Guinea and the Solomons is one of success against the odds. The battles that happened under the Southern Cross between August 1942 and February 1944 are well worth remembering. They were the foundation stones of victory in the Pacific War.

Thomas McKelvey Cleaver
Los Angeles, California

I

OPERATION *WATCHTOWER*

While the possibility of further Japanese offensives and expansion had died with the four sunken aircraft carriers at Midway, the Imperial forces were far from defeated and in fact still overshadowed the US Navy in both numbers and combat experience. However, events in the immediate aftermath of Midway forced American action, ready or not. The discovery of Japanese air bases in the southern Solomons that could effectively interdict the trans-Pacific supply lines to Australia required Allied action to neutralize them before the Japanese could begin such operations.

When the Japanese planners were developing their scheme for the Pacific War, they determined that an American counterattack in the Pacific could not take place before early 1943 and made their plans for war accordingly. However, American Chief of Naval Operations Admiral Ernest King never saw the Japanese plans and worked to his own relentless schedule. As early as March 1942, following the Japanese capture of Rabaul that both sides had seen as a crucial base for operations in the South Pacific, the admiral became a forceful advocate for an offensive operating from the New Hebrides to move through the Solomon Islands and the Bismarck Archipelago to eventually retake Rabaul, to start that summer. This call for action in the Pacific stood in direct opposition to the "Germany first" strategy the United States had agreed on with Britain, but King was determined the Japanese would not have the time to turn their Pacific conquests into formidable island fortresses while the US Navy stood idly by and put its effort into transporting the Army to England, and then waiting until the Nazis had been defeated to begin the rollback in the Pacific.

King had an ally whose desire for action in the Pacific was equal to his own. In the wake of the victory at Midway, General Douglas MacArthur, the Allied Supreme Commander in the Southwest Pacific area that included Rabaul, the Bismarcks, and the Solomons, proposed a lightning offensive to retake Rabaul, moving from New Guinea. The two competing proposals were resolved by consultation in mid-June between Admiral King and Army Chief of Staff General George C. Marshall, which created a three-task plan: Task One was the capture of Tulagi in the Solomons, which the Japanese had turned into an advanced air base capable of interdicting Allied convoys from the United States to Australia; Task Two was an advance by MacArthur's forces along the northern New Guinea coast; Task Three was the capture of Rabaul, which was foreseen as happening by late 1943.

The Joint Chiefs approved Task One on July 2, 1942. Operation *Huddle* would see the invasion and occupation of Santa Cruz Island in the southern Solomons, to be followed by Operation *Pestilence* which would take the Japanese base at Tulagi and the neighboring Florida Island. The word "Guadalcanal" did not appear anywhere in the plans the Joint Chiefs approved. This changed on July 8, 1942, when a B-17 of the 14th Reconnaissance Squadron returned to base with photographs of a major Japanese airfield under construction and nearing completion on Guadalcanal's Lunga Point. Japanese possession of such an air base would allow land-based bombers to interdict the crucial Allied supply line through the Coral Sea to Australia. Operations *Huddle* and *Pestilence* were quickly forgotten and Operation *Watchtower* was hurriedly planned to land the 1st Marine Division on Guadalcanal and take the airfield. Thus began the Solomons campaign, which would become the bloodiest battle the US Navy ever fought.

Before any action could be taken, however, an important matter of military bureaucracy had to be settled. According to the map, the Solomon Islands were firmly in General MacArthur's kingdom of the Southwest Pacific Theater, making him the overall commander of any operations there, though the Santa Cruz Islands immediately southwest of the Solomons were in Admiral Nimitz's Pacific Ocean Theater. Admiral King was not about to allow an Army general, who he viewed as seriously ignorant when it came to naval operations, to control the activities of the US Navy, the service that would provide all of the offensive force for the operation. Despite MacArthur's protests, Army Chief of Staff George C. Marshall, who knew MacArthur well from the previous 20 years and was no fan of the general, agreed with King. MacArthur's kingdom was subdivided; the boundary between the Southwest Pacific area and the Pacific Ocean area was shifted 360 miles to the west as of August 1, 1942, with the area including the Solomon Islands as far north as Bougainville, the New Hebrides, and Fiji carved out and assigned to a new theater command, the South Pacific Theater, which would be under the control of the US Navy. MacArthur was ordered to support the Solomons operation with his forces in New Guinea and to plan a campaign to retake the northern coast of New Guinea and the island of New Britain, in preparation for a two-pronged attack against Rabaul once Allied forces had retaken the Solomons. There would be no "lightning campaign" against Rabaul, but rather a long-term series of offensive actions to obtain position and isolate the base from Japanese support. Espiritu Santo in the New Hebrides was chosen as the headquarters for the new command.

The 1st Marine Division had been hastily organized in 1941 as the United States began its prewar military expansion. After Pearl Harbor the growing division trained at the new Camp Lejeune in North Carolina. The handful of "old salts," prewar Marines who were veterans of the Central American "banana wars" and China, were leavened with newly trained recruits graduated from nearby Parris Island. Among the veterans was freshly promoted Staff Sergeant (from Lance Corporal) James F. Eaton, a 21-year-old "Tientsin Marine," one of the last members of the 4th Marine Regiment to get out of China and all the way back to the United States in the summer of 1941. The new recruits included aspiring writer Robert Leckie, who had joined the Marines in the aftermath of Pearl Harbor and completed recruit training just as the division began its move to the Pacific.

By May 1942, the division was considered ready for operational use and the division commander, General Alexander Vandegrift, was told the unit would move to the South Pacific for eventual offensive use. At the time of the move to the Pacific, the division's 7th Regiment was still manning the defensive garrison in American Samoa, where they had been stationed since late January. In addition to the 1st and 5th Regiments, both the 1st Raider Battalion, which were currently stationed on New Caledonia, and the 3rd Defense Battalion now at Fiji, would rendezvous with the main party when the transport convoy from the United States stopped in Fiji en route to New Zealand.

The 5th Marine Regiment arrived in New Zealand in June, where they underwent final training. In early July, Vandegrift was informed that the 1st and 5th regiments would provide the tip of the spear for Operation *Watchtower*, which at the time involved taking Tulagi and the nearby Florida islands in the Solomons. At the time, the 1st Regiment was still en route and did not arrive in Wellington until July 11. On July 12, General Vandegrift was informed the entire division would invade the new focus of the operation, Guadalcanal. Their objective would be to capture and defend the airfield under construction on the Island.

Due to a strike of dockworkers in Wellington, the Marines loaded their own transports. At the time, no one knew how to "combat load" a ship to support an amphibious operation, and equipment was loaded without thought as to what had the higher priority for immediate use. This would become problematic when the transports were forced to depart the island early in the face of Japanese attacks before fully off-loading the division's equipment. On July 22, 11 days after the arrival of the 1st Regiment, the 16,000 Marines loaded aboard a convoy of 50 ships of Task Force (TF) 62 commanded by Rear Admiral Richmond Kelly Turner and departed Wellington, taking with them a 60-day combat load that did not include spare clothing, bedrolls, tents, typewriters, unit muster rolls, or pay clerks. Also unthought of at the time was insect repellent or mosquito netting. Because of a shortage of transport, all the 2.5-ton trucks, 155mm howitzers, and the equipment necessary for counter-battery fire were left behind. The division took part in landing rehearsals on Koro Island between July 28 and July 30, which General Vandegrift described in a message to the commandant of the Marine Corps as a "disaster."

The invasion convoy left New Zealand on July 31, steaming across the Coral Sea as it headed for Guadalcanal. The transports were protected by British Admiral Victor Crutchley's screening force, composed of the US heavy cruisers *Chicago* (CA-29), *Vincennes* (CA-44), *Quincy* (CA-39), *San Juan* (CL-54), and *Astoria* (CA-34) with the Australian heavy cruisers *Canberra*, *Hobart*, and Crutchley's flagship *Australia*, and the destroyers *Blue* (DD-387), *Monssen* (DD-436), *Buchanan* (DD-484), *Patterson* (DD-392), *Helm* (DD-388), *Wilson* (DD-408), and *Jarvis* (DD-393). The convoy was covered by the Navy's Task Force 61, commanded by Vice Admiral Frank J. Fletcher, considered after the battles of Coral Sea and Midway to be the Navy's most experienced carrier task force commander; the admiral's flag was in the recently repaired USS *Saratoga*, operating with the veteran *Enterprise* and the newly arrived USS *Wasp* (CV-7), which had been sent to the Pacific in June from her assignment with the Atlantic Fleet after the loss of *Yorktown* at Midway, despite being manifestly ill-equipped as regarded armor and defensive armament for combat against the Imperial Navy. *Saratoga's* polyglot Air Group 3 included Lieutenant Commander (LCDR) Leroy Simpler's 24 Wildcats of Fighting 5 (VF-5), Scouting 6 (VS-9), formerly part of the *Enterprise* air group, Bombing 3 (VB-3), and a reconstituted Torpedo 8 (VT-8). Among the pilots in the air group was Scouting 6's Ensign John Bridgers, survivor of the sinking of *Yorktown* at Midway. He later wrote that the sunrises and sunsets he saw while the ship cruised in the Coral Sea were "the most spectacular I ever saw in my life, completely belying the nature of our reason for being there."

Fortunately, storms and low clouds on August 5 and 6 kept Japanese patrol planes from discovering the fleet. The transports dropped anchor in Sealark Sound, which would soon be known as "Ironbottom Sound," at dawn on August 7, taking the Japanese on Guadalcanal and Tulagi by complete surprise. The Japanese had been aware of Allied movements in the region through signals intelligence, but had interpreted it as possible reinforcement of New Guinea. The Marines were ashore on all three islands by mid-morning. Florida was unoccupied by the enemy and was taken without opposition, while the main force went ashore on Guadalcanal at Lunga Point without encountering the enemy. Taking Tulagi became a preview of the no-quarter-asked-or-given fighting that would be a hallmark of the Pacific War.

Together, *Enterprise*, *Saratoga*, and *Wasp* fielded 99 F4F-4 Wildcat fighters, 103 SBD-3 Dauntless dive bombers, and 41 new Grumman TBF-1 Avenger torpedo bombers. Newly arrived *Wasp's* air group was the first to get into action when SBD-3 Dauntlesses of Scouting 71 (VS-71) struck the Japanese seaplane base at Tulagi shortly after dawn, sharing credit for destroying 21 moored H6K "Mavis" flying boats, F1M2 "Pete" floatplanes, and A6M2-N "Rufe" floatplane fighters with the Wildcats of Fighting 71 (VF-71). Standing patrols over the fleet were maintained throughout the morning, with *Saratoga*'s CAG, Commander Harry D. Felt, directing sorties from his SBD.

The surprised Japanese on Guadalcanal melted into the jungle as the Marines landed. Things would not be so easy at Tulagi, where the 1st Raider Battalion, led by Lieutenant Colonel Merritt A. Edson, known as "Edson's Raiders," and the 2nd Battalion, 5th Marines (2/5), commanded by Lieutenant Colonel Harold E. Rosecrans, landed, initially unopposed, at 0800 hours. The 886 Japanese defenders were led by a 310-man detachment of the 3rd Kure Special Naval Landing Force (SNLF), commanded by Masaaki Suzuki, and the Yokohama Air Group, commanded by Captain Shigetoshi Miyazaki. Miyazaki radioed Captain Sadayoshi Yamada at Rabaul that they were destroying their equipment and papers, signing off "Enemy troop strength is overwhelming. We will defend to the last man."

The Japanese defensive works on Tulagi were composed of dozens of tunneled caves dug into the limestone cliffs of what the Marines would come to know as Hill 281. The two battalions reached the main defense point at dusk after clearing the rest of the island and dug in for the night in expectation of taking the hill in the morning.

The SNLF troops attacked the Marine positions throughout the night. At times the fighting was hand-to-hand, but the Japanese failed to break the Marine positions. The next morning, the Marines, reinforced by the 2nd Battalion, 2nd Marines (2/2), surrounded the hill and attacked. They used improvised explosives to destroy each cave, where the defenders fought to the death. Organized resistance ended by mid-afternoon. While the Marines suffered 45 casualties killed and wounded, 307 of the 310 Japanese defenders were dead with three badly wounded taken prisoner.

The Marines believed the Japanese seaplane base on the small islands of Gavutu and Tanambogo was defended by fewer than 200 airmen of the Yokohama Air Group and the SNLF; in reality they faced 536 enemy fighters. The islands were connected to each other by a narrow causeway, dominated by Hills 148 on Gavutu and 121 on Tanambogo, where the defenders held positions in bunkers and caves, with each island able to provide fire support for the other.

The 397 Marines of the 1st Parachute Battalion landed on Gavutu at noon on August 7; they had been forced to land late since there were insufficient aircraft to provide cover for landings on Guadalcanal, Tulagi, and Gavutu simultaneously. The bombardment that preceded the landing damaged the seaplane ramp and forced the Higgins boats to go ashore at a more exposed location on a nearby small beach and dock, where defensive machine gun fire killed or wounded one in ten of the Marines as they tried to take a position that would get them out of the crossfire from Tanambogo; consequently, they became scattered and pinned down. A Navy dive bomber attack on Tanambogo lessened the fire and the invaders were able to reorganize. Two hours after hitting the beach, the Marines reached Hill 148 and climbed to the top, from where they began clearing enemy positions with explosive charges, grenades, and hand-to-hand combat. By midday Gavutu was secured.

A company from the 1st Battalion, 2nd Regiment, which was unneeded on Florida Island, was sent to land on Tanambogo, which the Marines believed was lightly defended. The Marines landed shortly after dusk and ran into fire from the 240 members of the Yokohama Air Group that defended the islet. Most of these men were unequipped for combat, but they were able to use machine guns to rake the five Higgins boats as they approached. Twelve men led by the company commander made it ashore despite the loss of three boats, but the position was untenable and the commander ordered the two surviving boats to evacuate wounded Marines while he and the men with him retreated across the causeway to Gavutu. Under the cover of heavy thunderstorms, the surviving Japanese attacked the Marines on Gavutu while General Vandegrift ordered the 3rd Battalion, 2nd Marines (3/2), who were still embarked on ships off Guadalcanal, to assault Tanambogo the next morning.

The 3rd Battalion landed on Gavutu at 1000 hours on August 8. They and the original invaders completed the destruction of the defenders there by noon. The Marines requested support from aircraft and naval gunfire for the assault on Tanambogo, but when the dive bombers bombed the Marines on Gavutu twice, killing four, further air support was canceled. Fortunately, USS *San Juan* (CL-54) accurately shelled Tanambogo for 30 minutes.

Then 3rd Battalion made the assault at 1615 hours by landing craft and crossing the causeway. Two Marine M3A1 Stuart light tanks provided support and at first the Marines made good headway against the defenders. However, one tank became stuck on a stump. Without infantry support, it was surrounded by about 50 Japanese airmen led by Lieutenant Commander Saburo Katsuta of the Yokohama Air Group, who set the tank afire; two crewmen were killed and the two surviving crewmen were severely beaten before the Japanese were killed by rifle fire. As the Marines moved across the island, methodically dynamiting the caves, Captain Miyazaki blew himself up inside his dugout late that afternoon. By 2100 hours, organized resistance was over, but the few surviving defenders made isolated attacks throughout the night. By noon on August 9, all resistance had ended. American casualties were 70 dead, while 476 Japanese defenders died. The 20 prisoners turned out to be Korean laborers from the Japanese construction unit. Some 80 defenders escaped from Tulagi and Gavutu–Tanambogo by swimming to Florida Island, where they were all hunted down and killed over the next two months. The Americans quickly went to work turning Tulagi anchorage, which was among the finest natural harbors in the South Pacific, into a naval base and refueling station.

On Guadalcanal, the main force captured the airfield by mid-afternoon of August 7, immediately naming it Henderson Field to memorialize Lieutenant Colonel Lofton R. Henderson, the commander of VMSB-241 who had been lost attacking the Japanese fleet at Midway on June 4. Fortunately for the invaders, they were able to capture the entire stock of Japanese food supplies on the island. Within weeks, the Japanese rice would be the Marines' main sustenance.

The Japanese surprise did not last long. The nearest Japanese air base was Rabaul, 600 miles away across the Bismarck Sea. Saburo Sakai's Tainan Kōkutai (Naval Air Group), part of the 25th Air Flotilla, had transferred there from their base at Lae in New Guinea four days earlier. A strike force of 27 G4M1 "Betty" bombers armed with torpedoes, nine one-way D3A1 "Val" dive bombers, and 17 A6M2 escorts was quickly organized following radio notification of the arrival of the US invaders. Among the fighter pilots in addition to Sakai were New Guinea aces Tadashi Nakajima and Hiroyoshi Nishizawa. After a four-hour flight, the Japanese arrived over the invasion fleet shortly after noon. The speed of the Japanese response and the ability to strike from a base 600 miles distant astonished the Americans. The attackers had been spotted by radar before they came into sight, and *Saratoga* had launched two divisions of F4F-4 Wildcats from Fighting 5 (VF-5), led by Lieutenant James J. "Pug" Southerland, a 1936 Annapolis graduate who had picked up his nickname from his pugnacity in the boxing ring, to reinforce the two airborne flights from *Wasp*'s VF-71 and *Enterprise*'s Fighting 6 (VF-6). Southerland's Wildcats were launched with enough time to climb to 12,000 feet before the Japanese formation arrived at close to 1300 hours, with the Bettys at 10,000 feet and the Zeros a few thousand feet higher.

The defending Wildcats fell on the Bettys just as the bombers dived to initiate the attack against the transports with their Type 92 torpedoes. At 1315 hours, Southerland spotted the enemy, radioing to the others, "Put gun switches and sight lamps on. Let's go get 'em boys." He dropped into a low side run and picked out the lead Betty, flown by Shisuo Yamada of the 4th Kōkūtai, and hit it solidly in an engine, setting it on fire. The bomber fell away, leaving a smoky trail across the sky before it hit the water, the first Japanese plane shot down in the Guadalcanal campaign. Southerland banked tight and hit the second Betty, which caught fire in an unprotected gas tank and fell away in a fatal dive.

As Southerland executed his attack, Japanese fighters fell on the Wildcats and scattered Southerland's division. Lieutenant (jg) Donald A. "Stinky" Innis managed to climb, scissor and trade head-on shots with five enemy fighters before he escaped into a cloud. Southerland's wingman, Ensign Robert L. Price, and Innis's section leader, Lieutenant (jg) Charles A. Tabberer, both went down under the enemy fire.

The second division was led by Lieutenant Herbert S. Brown with his wingman Ensign F.J. Blair, and section leader Lieutenant (jg) William M. Holt with wingman Ensign Joseph R. Daly. As Southerland attacked the Bettys, Brown's division was attacked by Zeros. Brown was seriously wounded in the fight, but managed to bring his Wildcat back to *Saratoga*, where he reported he had damaged at least one of the five Zeros which had attacked him. Brown's wingman, Ensign Blair, managed to elude the enemy by taking cover in a cloud, then attacked the enemy bombers and damaged one. He reported that either Lieutenant (jg) Holt or Ensign Daly, who failed to return, shot down two of the bombers, and that he had seen flames in the bomb bay of one of the bombers he attacked. Ensign Daly was rescued from the water by the cruiser *Chicago*, which was directing the air battle.

An air battle between the defending Wildcats and the Zero escort quickly developed in the cloudy skies over the fleet. Lieutenant Commander Tadashi Nakajima, leader of the Japanese fighters, found himself confounded when he attacked two Wildcats that responded with the maneuver known to the Americans as the "Thach Weave." As the wingman turned toward him from the side while he attempted to follow the leader, Nakajima was forced to dive away. The section leader Nakajima attacked was Lieutenant (jg) Holt, who fearlessly turned against the other Zeros in Nakajima's group, though he and his wingman, Lieutenant (jg) Daly, were outnumbered. Using the "Thach Weave," they engaged the enemy for several minutes, during which Holt managed to break away from the Zeros long enough to shoot down one Betty that exploded when he hit its torpedo, and damage another before the Zeros caught up with him and exploded his Wildcat; Daly managed to bail out, landing in the water near Red Beach on Guadalcanal where he was rescued by a whaleboat from *Chicago* and was returned to *Saratoga* later that afternoon. Holt was later awarded the Distinguished Flying Cross for his sacrifice, and USS *Holt* (DE-706) was named for him.

As the Bettys turned away to the north from their runs, with the formation still relatively intact, they were jumped by a division of Wildcats from VF-6. Defending Zeros engaged the Wildcats and a fight developed over Santa Isabel Island when six more Wildcats, led by VF-6 LCDR Lou Bauer, joined the first four. The Zeros knocked down four of the Fighting 6 Wildcats, in exchange for five Bettys and two Zeros.

Southerland pulled out of his attack dive and turned in on the tail of a Zero flown by Ichirobei Yamazaki. He lined up astern of the Zero, only to find his guns would not fire. Suddenly, tracers flew wildly past his Wildcat and two enemy fighters flown by Enji Kakimoto and Kazushi Uto skidded past him as they overshot and tried to kill their excessive speed. Southerland turned into the Zeros, which sent them scattering. As he turned to avoid them, he suddenly felt the impact of cannon hits in his rear fuselage. His attacker was Saburo Sakai, who had become momentarily separated from his two wingmen just before they engaged Southerland. When he saw his over-eager wingmen outmaneuvered by the Wildcat, Sakai quickly jumped into the fight and rolled in on a gunnery pass. "I snapped out a burst. At once the American snap-rolled away to the right, clawed around in a tight turn, and ended up in a climb straight at my own plane."

Both Southerland and Sakai knew the capabilities of their mounts. Turn for turn, climb for climb, dive for dive, they matched the other's every move. Sakai later described the fight as he experienced it. "Never before had I seen an enemy plane move so quickly or gracefully, and with every second his guns were moving closer to the belly of my fighter. I snap-rolled in an effort to throw him off. He would not be shaken. He was using my favorite tactics, coming up from under." After an extended battle in which both pilots gained and lost the upper hand, Sakai managed to put a burst from his two 20mm cannon into the Wildcat, which streamed smoke then leveled out.

Southerland pulled back his throttle and Sakai overshot, putting his Zero at the mercy of the American. Sakai braced for the deadly impact of bullets into his fighter's flimsy fuselage, but nothing happened. Surprised, he pulled up alongside the Wildcat, close enough that he could describe Southerland's features. His opponent waved at him and he saw the man had been injured.

I had full confidence in my ability to destroy him and decided to finish off the enemy fighter with only my 7.7mm machine guns. I turned the 20mm cannon switch to the "off" position and closed in. For some strange reason, even after I had poured about 500 or 600 rounds of ammunition directly into it, the airplane did not fall, but kept on flying. I thought this very odd – it had never happened before – and closed the distance between the two airplanes until I could almost reach out and touch the Grumman. To my surprise, the Grumman's rudder and tail were torn to shreds, looking like an old torn piece of rag. With his plane in such condition, no wonder the pilot was unable to continue fighting! A Zero which had taken that many bullets would have been a ball of fire by now.

Impressed by his enemy's coolness, Sakai executed a chandelle and came in again on the Wildcat's tail, aiming for the engine and hitting it solidly with his cannon. When he saw Southerland successfully bail out, Sakai found himself surprised to feel gratitude that his enemy had survived. "There was a terrific man behind that stick," he later recalled. Southerland also remembered the fight.

My plane was in bad shape but still performing nicely in low blower, full throttle, and full low pitch. Flaps and radio had been put out of commission and the after part of my fuselage was like a sieve. She was still smoking from incendiaries but not on fire. The ammunition box covers on my left wing were gone and 20mm explosives had torn some gaping holes in the upper surface. My instrument panel was badly shot up, the goggles on my forehead had been shattered, my rearview mirror was broken, my plexiglass windshield was riddled. The leakproof tanks had apparently been punctured many times as some fuel had leaked down into the bottom of the cockpit even though there was no steady leakage. My oil tank had been punctured and oil was pouring down my right leg. At this time, a Zero making a run from the port quarter put a burst in just under the left-wing root and good old 5-F-12 finally exploded. I think the explosion occurred from gasoline vapor. The flash was below and forward of my left foot. I was ready for it and I dove over the right side immediately, though I don't remember how.

Southerland parachuted into the Guadalcanal jungle, deep in the heart of enemy territory. He struggled through the thick vegetation, bleeding and exhausted. After more than a week spent avoiding Japanese patrols, he finally reached the coast, where he was found by Solomon Islander Bruno Nana, who fed him and treated his wounds, at risk of his life if they were found by the enemy. With Nana's assistance, Southerland was able to return to American lines and was evacuated on August 20, 1942 by the first PBY Catalina to land at Henderson Field.

Sakai, meanwhile, watched the plane crash into the jungle, then headed off to find other American planes to attack in the cloudy sky. Running low on fuel, he gathered Kakimoto and Uto in preparation to return to Rabaul and the three began climbing back to altitude. Suddenly, as they broke out of the clouds, Sakai found himself under attack as a string of bullets hit his Zero, with one that smashed a hole in his canopy missing him from behind by a matter of inches. Sakai quickly spotted his attacker and was surprised to discover it was an SBD-3 Dauntless dive bomber. The Dauntless was from *Wasp*'s VF-71, flown by Lieutenant Dudley Adams with his gunner, ARM3/c Harry Elliott. Sakai swung around and gave the audacious dive bomber a burst of 20mm fire that set it afire. Lieutenant Adams was able to bail out but his gunner was killed. The Dauntless was Sakai's 60th victory since he had shot down Colin Kelly over Clark Field two days after Pearl Harbor.

As the three Zeros flew on, Sakai spotted another American formation. Unfamiliar with the American Navy aircraft, he identified the aircraft as Wildcats and closed to attack from the rear. In fact, the eight planes he closed in on were a mixed flight of Dauntlesses from Bombing 5 and 6 (VB-5 and VB-6), whose gunners had spotted him at nearly the same moment he spotted them. Just as he tripped his triggers and hit two of the bombers that caught fire and fell out of the formation for his 61st and 62nd victories, the other six gunners opened fire on the attacking Zero. Caught in the crossfire, Sakai took several hits. His windscreen was shattered and a .30-caliber round clipped the top of his head, blinding him in the right eye and paralyzing the left side of his body. Stunned and disoriented by his wound, he instinctively pulled back on the stick and the Zero rolled inverted before it fell off into a dive, lost to sight by friend and foe.

Finally, the wind ripping through his shattered windscreen blew away enough blood from his uninjured eye that he was able to see well enough to pull out of the near-fatal dive. Badly wounded, he considered ramming an American warship: "If I must die, at least I could go out as a Samurai. My death would take several of the enemy with me. A ship. I needed a ship." As he flew aimlessly, the cold air blasting against his face finally revived him enough that he checked his instruments; his fuel supply was sufficient that he decided if he used the knowledge he had developed when training to fly from Formosa to Luzon and back, he might be able to return to Rabaul.

What followed is considered one of the great epics of aerial survival in the Pacific War. With his face and good eye covered in blood, blinded in his right eye and in constant pain, Sakai fought a grim battle to remain conscious. The wind blast tore away his first aid gear when he tried to treat his wound; eventually he managed to tear off part of his scarf and stuff it into his torn helmet to use as a bandage and stanch the bleeding.

Finally able to see, he set his throttle for minimum fuel consumption and took up a course across the open sea for Rabaul, some 600 miles distant. Over the next four hours and 45 minutes he lapsed in and out of consciousness as the Zero droned on. He thought about turning back to die attacking the enemy, but heard his mother's voice scolding him for thinking of giving up and turned back on course. Eventually Rabaul came into sight and he was able to overcome his paralysis enough to set up for landing and touch down without crashing. His friends lifted him from the cockpit to discover bullet or fragment wounds in his left arm, chest, and leg. He was evacuated to Yokosuka Naval Hospital in Japan, where he was told by his doctors that he was permanently blind in his right eye and would never fly again.

The nine "one way" Vals arrived over the fleet nearly an hour after the first attack. They were met by a Combat Air Patrol (CAP) of defending Wildcats from VF-5. In a running fight with the enemy dive bombers, Ensign Mark R. Bright shot down two of the Vals and shared credit for two others with his wingman. Altogether Fighting 5 shot down five Vals without loss, but Admiral Fletcher was concerned that he had lost nine Wildcats, ten percent of his fighters, and was worried about declining fuel reserves. He announced he would withdraw the three carriers and their escorts from the immediate vicinity of Guadalcanal the evening of August 8, with the admiral promising to provide "long range" support for the next three days. Before he did, the Japanese mounted another air raid the next morning, when 23 Bettys and their Zero escort flew at low level and managed to get within five miles of the fleet before they were spotted by radar, despite the fact their passage down the island chain from Rabaul had been reported by the Australian coastwatchers. They were intercepted at the last minute by three VF-6 Wildcats which shot down three bombers and a Zero. NAP (Naval Aviation Pilot) Aviation Machinist's Mate 1/c Don Runyon shot down the Zero and one of the Bettys to open his score against the Imperial Navy. Shipboard gunners managed to shoot down 13 more bombers, in exchange for hits on two ships, one of which was the destroyer USS *Jarvis*, which was seriously damaged.

Admiral Fletcher decided that the loss of 23 Wildcats to all causes over the two days meant that he did not have adequate air defenses for his carriers and announced that Task Force 61 would withdraw to maximum range. The unloading of the transports was proceeding more slowly than planned and Admiral Turner decided, as a result of Fletcher's decision, that he would have to withdraw the transports since they would not have adequate air cover. He announced the fleet would unload as much as possible before departing at dawn on August 9. Marine Sergeant Eaton, who had landed on Guadalcanal in the first wave that day, later remembered that when word the Navy was "turning tail" spread through the Marines ashore, "We felt we were being left to distract the enemy from chasing after the navy."

The attacks by the Tainan Kōkūtai and the rest of the 25th Air Flotilla were not the only Japanese response to the invasion. Vice Admiral Gunichi Mikawa, commander of the Eighth Fleet aboard his flagship the cruiser *Chōkai*, which was in Simpson Harbor at Rabaul with Rear Admiral Mitsuharu Matsuyama's 18th Cruiser Division composed of the light cruisers *Tenryū*, and *Yūbari* with the destroyer *Yūnagi*, ordered Rear Admiral Aritomo Gotō's 6th Cruiser Division, composed of the heavy cruisers *Aoba*, *Furutaka*, *Kinugasa*, and *Kako*, which were en route to Rabaul from Kavieng Harbor on New Ireland, to rendezvous with his force and strike the American invaders. The Japanese force rendezvoused near Cape St. George that evening and headed southeast toward New Georgia Sound, a body of water to either side of which the islands of the Solomons chain lay, that would soon come to be known to the US Navy as "the Slot." Guadalcanal lay at the far end. Mikawa's orders were to disrupt the invasion fleet. He ordered the ships to heave to off the east coast of Bougainville at the northern end of "the Slot" so they would transit the narrow waters commencing in the late afternoon, with an expected arrival at Guadalcanal shortly before midnight of August 8–9.

Mikawa's fleet was spotted by two different RAAF Hudson patrol planes flying from Milne Bay in New Guinea at 1020 and 1110 hours on August 8. They were misidentified in the first sighting as "three cruisers, three destroyers, and two seaplane tenders." The first Hudson's crew tried to make a sighting report to the Allied radio station at Fall River, New Guinea; when they received no acknowledgment, they returned to Milne Bay at 1242 hours and reported the sighting in person. The second Hudson failed to radio a report of its sighting and landed back at Milne Bay at 1500 hours, where the crew reported sighting "two heavy cruisers, two light cruisers, and one unknown type." The sighting reports were not relayed to the fleet off Guadalcanal until 1845 and

2130 hours, respectively, on August 8. By then, the Japanese were mere hours away from their objective.

Mikawa launched two floatplanes that morning to scout Guadalcanal; they returned by 1200 hours to report there were two groups of Allied ships, one off Guadalcanal and one off Tulagi. The admiral assembled his warships and headed toward Guadalcanal, passing near Choiseul Island at 1600 hours, at which time he communicated his battle plan to the fleet: "On the rush-in we will go from south of Savo Island and torpedo the enemy main force in front of Guadalcanal anchorage; after which we will turn toward the Tulagi forward area to shell and torpedo the enemy. We will then withdraw north of Savo Island."

Admiral Turner had requested Rear Admiral John S. McCain, Sr., the Allied air forces commander for the South Pacific (ComAirSoPac) to conduct extra reconnaissance missions over the southern Solomons that afternoon, but McCain had not ordered the missions and did not so inform Admiral Turner, who thus mistakenly believed the waters of the southern Solomons were under Allied air observation throughout the day. Admiral Mikawa became increasingly confident as night fell that his fleet had not been detected by the Americans and that his attack would be a surprise.

That afternoon, Admiral Crutchley divided his support force into three groups to protect the transports while they unloaded during the night. The "southern" group, composed of HMAS *Australia* and *Canberra*, with *Chicago* and the destroyers *Patterson* and *Bagley*, patrolled between Lunga Point and Savo Island in order to block the entrance to Sealark Sound between Savo Island and Cape Esperance on Guadalcanal. *Vincennes*, *Astoria*, and *Quincy* with destroyers *Helm* and *Wilson* comprised the "northern" group and conducted a patrol between Tulagi and Savo Island to defend the passage between Savo and Florida Islands. *San Juan*, HMAS *Hobart* and the destroyers *Monssen* and *Buchanan* guarded the eastern entrance between Florida and Guadalcanal Islands. The radar-equipped destroyers *Blue* and *Ralph Talbot* were positioned west of Savo Island to provide early warning of any approaching Japanese ships, with *Talbot* in the northern passage and *Blue* in the southern passage, 8–20 miles apart.

The Americans were unaware that the primitive radars on the two destroyers could be affected by a nearby landmass, which meant that the two destroyers were too far apart to provide full coverage to the west with their uncoordinated patrol patterns. Captain Howard D. Bode of *Chicago* ordered that ship's radar turned off at dusk in the mistaken belief its emissions could reveal his position, allowing a single sweep with the fire control radar every 30 minutes. The remaining seven destroyers were deployed with the transports for anti-submarine protection. The sailors aboard the Allied warships had been on constant alert and action for the previous two days, while the weather was hot and humid. In the words of naval historian Samuel Eliot Morison, it was a situation "inviting weary sailors to slackness." As night fell, the fleet went to "Condition II," with half the crews on duty while the other half rested in their hot and humid berthing compartments or above decks near their battle stations.

Admiral Turner called a conference on his command ship for 2130 hours with Admiral Crutchley and General Vandegrift to discuss Fletcher's departure and the planned withdrawal schedule for the transports. Crutchley, aboard *Australia*, left the southern group at 2055 hours to attend the conference. He placed Captain Bode in charge of the southern group, but did not inform the commanders of the other groups of his absence, which contributed to a further dissolution of command arrangements. When Captain Bode was awakened from sleep to receive the assignment, he decided not to place the cruiser in the lead of the southern group, the customary place for the senior ship, and went back to sleep. Turner, Crutchley, and Vandegrift discussed the reports they had received of the "seaplane tender" force and decided it would not be a threat since seaplane tenders did not normally operate at night. Vandegrift departed shortly before 2400 hours to inspect the transport unloading situation at Tulagi. Crutchley decided not to return to the southern force and stationed *Australia* outside the Guadalcanal transport anchorage, neglecting to inform the other ship commanders of his decision or location.

Nearing Guadalcanal shortly after 2300 hours, Admiral Mikawa launched three floatplanes for a final reconnaissance and to provide flare illumination during the coming battle.

Several Allied ships in Sealark Sound heard or observed these floatplanes, starting at 2345 hours on August 8, but none considered the presence of unknown aircraft to be an actionable threat, and the sightings went unreported to Crutchley or Turner. The Japanese fleet adopted a single column formation led by *Chōkai*, with *Aoba*, *Kako*, *Kinugasa*, *Furutaka*, *Tenryū*, *Yūbari*, and *Yūnagi* following. Between 0044 and 0054 hours on August 9, lookouts spotted the destroyer *Blue* about five miles ahead.

Mikawa ordered the fleet to slow to 22 knots so as to reduce their wakes and changed course to pass north of Savo Island. The warships held their course while covering *Blue* with more than 50 guns, ready to blow the destroyer out of the water at the first sign they had been spotted, but she continued on, failing to spot the enemy by radar due to the backdrop of the surrounding islands and reversing course less than a mile from Mikawa's fleet when she reached the end of her track. Four minutes after passing *Blue*, the lookouts spotted *Ralph Talbot* ten miles distant. Having determined that he had not been spotted, the admiral turned back to pass south of Savo as he increased the fleet's speed to 26 and then to 30 knots in preparation for the coming action. At 0125 hours, Mikawa released the rest of the fleet to operate independently of *Chōkai*.

At 0131 hours he gave the order "Every ship attack."

At 0132 hours, lookouts on *Furutaka* spotted the damaged destroyer *Jarvis* as she departed for Australia. *Furutaka* fired torpedoes at the destroyer, all of which missed. Passing within 1,000 yards of the American ship, officers aboard *Tenryū* could see there were no personnel on *Jarvis's* weather decks and the ship gave no indication of having spotted the Japanese as they passed her.

At 0134 hours, lookouts sighted the ships of the southern force 12,500 yards distant. Four minutes later, the cruisers launched torpedoes at the unsuspecting enemy. At the same time, lookouts aboard *Chōkai* spotted the northern force ten miles away. The flagship turned to face the new threat while the rest of the fleet followed.

The captain of the destroyer *Patterson* had taken seriously the reports of enemy warship sightings and the sighting of unknown aircraft earlier, and held his crew at readiness. At 0143 hours, lookouts on the destroyer spotted what was likely the cruiser *Kinugasa* 5,000 yards dead ahead. The captain immediately radioed the fleet: "Warning! Warning! Strange ships entering the harbor!", sending the warning also by signal lamp as he ordered the ship to full speed while his gunners fired star shells toward the enemy. His order to fire torpedoes went unheard over the sound of the guns.

As *Patterson* engaged the enemy, the Japanese floatplanes overhead dropped flares directly over *Canberra* and *Chicago*. *Canberra's* Captain Frank Getting ordered her speed increased and reversed the initial turn to port, keeping the cruiser between the enemy and the transport fleet. A minute later *Canberra* opened fire on the Japanese just as *Chōkai* and *Furutaka* opened fire on her; they scored several hits on the Australian cruiser while *Aoba* and *Kako* joined in. *Canberra* took 24 hits within three minutes and caught fire. Her gunnery officer was killed and Captain Getting was mortally injured while both boiler rooms were destroyed. Without power and unable to fire her guns or radio a warning to the rest of the fleet, *Canberra* came to a stop, unable to fight the fires or pump out water to correct the ten-degree list.

Chicago came to life when the flares exploded overhead and *Canberra* suddenly turned in front of her. Captain Bode, awakened from a sound sleep, ordered his 5-inch secondary battery to fire star shells at the Japanese column, but the shells were defective. Moments later, at 0147 hours, the cruiser was hit in her bow by a torpedo likely fired by *Kako*; the explosion sent a shock wave the length of the ship and damaged the main battery fire control director. An instant later, a second torpedo hit but failed to explode, while a shell hit the mainmast and killed two men. *Chicago* then steamed west for the next 40 minutes, leaving the transports behind. Captain Bode made no attempt to take command of the battle, though he was technically still in command, and gave no warning to the others as he headed away from the fight. With only her secondary batteries able to fire, she opened fire at the ships to the rear of the Japanese formation and may have hit *Tenryū*, causing only superficial damage. Eventually the damage control parties were able to make good the damage.

As *Canberra* and *Chicago* were being dealt with, *Patterson's* captain engaged in a gun duel with the enemy. She took a hit aft that caused moderate damage and killed ten crewmen. The destroyer continued to engage the enemy and moderately damaged *Kinugasa* before her lookouts lost sight of the enemy fleet as it headed northeast along the eastern shore of Savo Island and disappeared in the darkness.

The cruisers *Vincennes*, *Astoria*, and *Quincy* in the northern force were steaming quietly at ten knots with their captains asleep when the Japanese opened fire on the southern force. Although the cruisers received *Patterson's* radioed warning and the flares and gunfire south of Savo were plainly visible, it took precious minutes for the crews to go from Condition II to General Quarters. *Astoria*'s bridge crew called General Quarters upon sighting the flares south of Savo at 0149 hours. The Japanese fleet had already turned toward the northern force at 0144 hours; the light cruisers *Tenryū* and *Yūbari* in the rear inadvertently turned slightly to the west, followed by *Furutaka* as she maneuvered to avoid colliding with *Canberra*. This allowed the Japanese to envelop the northern force and attack from both sides. As they neared the American cruisers, the Japanese cruisers fired torpedoes, then turned on their searchlights at 0150 hours and opened fire on the three ships.

Two minutes later, as Japanese shells fell around *Astoria*, her main gun director crew spotted the enemy ships and opened fire. Captain William G. Greenman, awakened by the gunfire, ran to the bridge and ordered a ceasefire in the mistaken belief his ship was firing on friendly ships. It took a minute of incoming shells from *Chōkai* – all of which missed – to convince him otherwise, but Mikawa's flagship found the range with her fifth salvo, which ripped *Astoria*'s superstructure and started a fire amidships that quickly became an inferno following the sixth salvo that set the airplanes in their hangar afire, giving the Japanese a self-illuminated target. The next enemy salvo put turret number one out of action. *Aoba*, *Kinugasa*, and *Kako* joined *Chōkai* and between 0200 and 0215 hours they pounded *Astoria*, destroying her engine room and bringing the burning cruiser to a stop. A final shot from *Astoria* at 0216 hours missed *Kinugasa*'s searchlight, but hit *Chōkai* in her forward turret, putting it out of action and causing moderate damage. At approximately 0225 hours, *Astoria* lost steering control from the bridge and control was shifted to the central station. She began steering a zigzag course south, but before she had gone far the fires amidships found the engineering spaces and she lost all power.

Quincy had received *Patterson*'s warning and called General Quarters when the flares were spotted. The crew had just manned their battle stations when the Japanese searchlights came on. Captain Samuel N. Moore gave the order to open fire but the main battery crews were not ready. *Quincy* quickly came under a crossfire from *Aoba*, *Furutaka*, and *Tenryū* that set her afire. Captain Moore ordered the ship to turn toward the Japanese column; as she did so, she was hit by two torpedoes fired by *Tenryū* that caused severe damage. *Quincy* managed to fire four salvos, one of which hit *Chōkai*'s chart room 20 feet from where Admiral Mikawa was standing, killing and wounding 36 men though the admiral escaped injury. At 0210, a Japanese salvo hit *Quincy*'s bridge, killing or wounding all of her bridge crew, including Captain Moore. A torpedo fired by *Aoba* struck at 0216 hours and silenced her guns. *Quincy*'s assistant gunnery officer arrived on the scene minutes after and later reported that he found the bridge a shambles of dead bodies with only three men still alive. The quartermaster at the wheel in the pilot house was trying to check the swing to starboard and reported the captain had ordered him to beach the cruiser on Savo Island before he was hit. At that moment, Captain Moore straightened up and uttered a moan, then slumped over, dead. Stepping back onto the bridge, the assistant gunnery officer found the ship was heeling rapidly to port and sinking by the bow. At 0238 hours, *Quincy* slipped beneath the waves of Sealark Sound bow first.

Vincennes also sighted the flares and gunfire. Awakened with the news, Captain Frederick C. Riefkohl called for General Quarters and ordered the crew to battle stations. The cruiser was ready to open fire when the Japanese searchlights illuminated her, but Captain Riefkohl hesitated to open fire out of fear the searchlights might be friendly. Moments later, *Kako* took *Vincennes* under fire and Riefkohl ordered his main battery to return fire at 0153 hours. *Kako*'s salvos damaged the cruiser and set her afire; Riefkohl ordered speed increased to 25 knots to escape the attack. At 0155 hours, two torpedoes fired by *Chōkai* hit and caused heavy damage. *Kako* was joined by *Kinugasa* and the two pounded *Vincennes*. An American salvo hit *Kinugasa*, moderately damaging her steering engines. *Vincennes* then came under fire from the rest of the Japanese fleet, taking 74 hits by the time she was hit by a third torpedo fired by *Yūbari* at 0203 hours. With his ship afire at multiple locations and listing to port as she came to a halt with her boiler rooms destroyed, Captain Riefkohl ordered "abandon ship" at 0216 hours and *Vincennes* sank at 0250 hours.

The Allied fleet at Guadalcanal only escaped further catastrophe that night because of Admiral Mikawa's decision to withdraw as *Vincennes* sank. At that moment, the Japanese fleet was superior to what was left of the Allied force covering the invasion transports, which was now reduced to the cruisers HMAS *Australia* and *Hobart*, and USS *San Juan*, none of which was in an immediate position to oppose an advance by Admiral Mikawa, each of which would likely have suffered the fates of *Canberra*, *Astoria*, *Quincy*, and *Vincennes* if they had entered combat against the superior Japanese force.

Just as Captain Riefkohl was ordering his crew to abandon ship, Admiral Mikawa conferred with his staff as to whether they should turn east and try to sink the Allied transports. With his fleet scattered in the action, it would take time to regroup; additionally, the cruisers needed to reload their torpedo tubes, which was a time-consuming labor-intensive activity. Additionally, his ships had fired much of their ammunition and the Japanese did not know whether there were any surviving enemy warships, or where they might be if they had. Most importantly, the admiral knew the enemy was supported by aircraft carriers and that his fleet had no air cover. What he didn't know was that Admiral Fletcher had withdrawn the three carriers to maximum range, effectively removing them from the battle. Several of his officers urged him to gather the fleet and continue the attack, but the consensus was to withdraw before daylight to prevent loss of any ships to enemy aircraft.

While *Vincennes'* crew went into the water, Mikawa ordered his ships to cease fire. As they passed beyond range around the north side of Savo Island, *Furutaka*, *Tenryū*, and *Yūbari* ran across *Ralph Talbot*. Fixing the destroyer with searchlights, they heavily damaged her before she was able to escape into a nearby rain squall.

While the Japanese disappeared into the darkness, heading back up New Georgia Sound to return to Rabaul, the survivors began a fight to save themselves. Amazingly, *Astoria* was still afloat. By 0300 hours, nearly 400 of her crew, including about 70 wounded, had assembled on the forecastle deck. The cruiser had taken 65 hits. A bucket brigade was assembled to battle the fire in the secondary battery while the wounded were moved to the captain's cabin where the doctors and corpsmen improvised an emergency sick bay. Soon the deck became so hot that it became necessary to move the wounded back onto the forecastle. Making steady headway, the bucket brigade managed to drive the fire aft on the starboard side of the gun deck.

Ashore, every Marine had been awakened by the distant thunder of the ships' guns. Sergeant Eaton remembered that he first thought the sounds and the light flashes were thunderstorms over the sea: "It was the first time I had ever heard heavy artillery." Private Robert Leckie was able to see much of the battle from his position on a low hill and remembered later that when the ships exposed themselves by the flash of their gunfire, "the sea around them flattened and looked like it was made of obsidian."

While the recovery effort continued, *Patterson* came alongside *Canberra* to provide firefighting assistance. After an hour, the fires were almost under control. Admiral Fletcher had withdrawn his fleet to refuel, which left the transports without air cover. In the face of this situation, Admiral Turner decided to withdraw the fleet by 0630 hours and ordered the cruiser scuttled if she could not accompany the rest. The survivors were removed and the destroyers *Selridge* and *Ellet* sank her. *Canberra* took five torpedoes before she finally disappeared under the waves.

While *Patterson* fought *Canberra*'s fires, the destroyer *Bagley* came alongside *Astoria*'s starboard bow and managed to take off all the wounded by 0445 hours, evacuating them to another ship for further care. When *Bagley* returned at daylight, it appeared the cruiser could be saved and a salvage crew of 325 went back aboard. Another bucket brigade was quickly assembled. The destroyer *Hopkins* was able to secure a towline at 0700 hours and managed to swing *Astoria* around in order to tow her to shallow water.

While these efforts continued, General Vandegrift advised Admiral Turner that the Marines desperately needed more supplies unloaded before the fleet departed. Turner postponed the departure until 1500 hours and unloading proceeded. Unfortunately, due to the disorganized loading of the ships, much valuable and crucially needed equipment never came ashore before the fleet departed.

At about 0900 hours, the destroyer *Wilson* came alongside *Astoria* to pump water into the fire, but at 1000 hours both destroyers departed when word was received by the fleet from an Australian coastwatcher that a Japanese air strike was headed down from Rabaul. Shortly afterward, the destroyer *Buchanan* was ordered to assist *Astoria* and the fleet tug *Alchiba* was sent to tow her to safety. However, the below decks fire increased in intensity and several internal explosions occurred before *Buchanan* could arrive. *Astoria*'s list increased to ten degrees, then 15 and the stern sank while the bow rose. *Buchanan* arrived at 1130 hours but could not come alongside due to the list. Captain Greenman ordered all men out of the ship and they assembled on the stern, which was now awash. At 1200 hours, Greenman gave the order to abandon ship as she continued to settle. The men went into the water and *Astoria* rolled slowly over on her port beam and sank by the stern, slipping under at 1216 hours. *Alchiba* arrived just before the cruiser sank and assisted *Buchanan* in rescuing the men. None of the salvage crew were lost, but 219 men were listed missing or killed in the battle.

Fortunately, the expected air attack did not happen. It was not discovered until after the war that the Japanese strike had spotted the damaged *Jarvis* south of Guadalcanal and sank her with all hands. Admiral Turner ordered unloading resumed until nightfall, when the fleet departed and sailed to Nouméa.

A measure of revenge was exacted against the victorious Japanese the next morning. The submarine *S-44*, one of the ancient World War I-era submarines that had been sent to Brisbane that spring to reinforce the surviving submarines of the Asiatic Fleet, was on her third war patrol, hunting targets in the shipping lanes of the Bismarck Sea between Rabaul and Kavieng. The night of August 9, Admiral Mikawa had released *Aoba*, *Furutaka*, *Kako*, and *Kinugasa* to return to their base at Kavieng while he proceeded to Rabaul with *Chōkai*, *Tenryū*, and *Yūbari*. At 0750 hours on August 10, *S-44* came to periscope depth and sighted the four heavy cruisers 70 miles from Kavieng at a range of less than 900 yards. Tracking the enemy ships, the submarine fired four Mark X torpedoes at 0806 hours at the rear ship, which was only 700 yards distant.

Fortunately, the old Mark Xs were better performers than the defective Mark XIVs that equipped the more modern fleet submarines. The first torpedo struck *Kako* at 0808 hours, abreast the No. 1 turret on her starboard beam. The other three hit near the forward magazines and boiler rooms number one and two. In the heat and humidity, *Kako* had all of her portholes open; at 0813 hours, she rolled over to starboard and exploded when sea water reached her boilers. She sank bow first off Simbari Island at 0815 hours. *S-44* had sunk the largest Japanese man-of-war lost to date in the Pacific War. *Aoba*, *Furutaka*, and *Kinugasa* rescued Captain Takahashi and all but 71 of *Kako*'s crew and went on to Kavieng, their victory at Savo tarnished by her loss.

In its first night action involving heavy ship units with the Imperial Navy, the United States Navy had been thoroughly savaged. The Battle of Savo Island was the worst defeat ever suffered by the US Navy in a fair fight. As a result of the losses incurred in the battle, all supplies sent to Guadalcanal for the next few crucial months in which the Japanese would come close to reconquering the island would come by small convoys during daylight hours, when they could receive air cover. During that time, the Marines on Guadalcanal received barely enough provisions to survive, and just enough ammunition to withstand the repeated Japanese attempts to retake the island. Sergeant Eaton recalled the diet of Japanese rice and other enemy foodstuffs: "There wasn't that much to eat, and there were no fat Marines in the division when we were finally evacuated. During the four months I was there, I lost 45 pounds from an original weight of 178." The transports that Mikawa did not sink the night of August 8–9 were used many times to resupply the Marines. Had Mikawa gathered his fleet and gone after the transports, the outcome of the Battle of Guadalcanal might have been different.

As it was, the results of the battle rocketed through the Navy, landing quickly on Admiral King's desk at the Pentagon. That December, Admiral Arthur J. Hepburn, US Navy (Retired), formerly Commander in Chief of the United States Fleet, and at the time Chairman of the General Board of the Navy, was asked by Admiral King to lead an investigation into the battle and make recommendations for future action by the Navy. Hepburn spent more than four months, from December 23, 1942 to May 13, 1943, inquiring into the disaster. He personally questioned the principal commanders in the South Pacific and Southwest Pacific Areas, and the commanding officers still alive, while gathering an enormous amount of documentary evidence.

The final report recommended official censure for Captain Howard D. Bode of the *Chicago*, for his failure to broadcast a warning of approaching enemy ships. The report stopped short of recommending any formal action be taken against other Allied officers, including Admirals Fletcher, Turner, McCain, and Crutchley, and *Vincennes'* Captain Riefkohl. The careers of Turner, Crutchley, and McCain were not adversely affected by the defeat or their mistakes in contributing to it, which were dealt with in detail in the report. Captain Riefkohl never

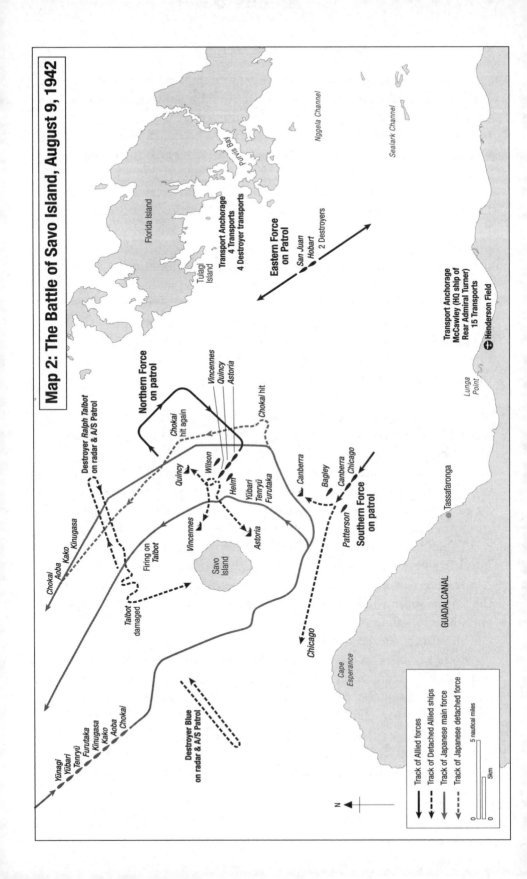

Map 2: The Battle of Savo Island, August 9, 1942

commanded a ship again. Upon learning he would be censured for his actions, Captain Bode shot himself in his quarters at Balboa, Panama Canal Zone, on April 19, 1943, and died the next day. In the spirit of Allied cooperation, Admiral Crutchley was awarded the US Legion of Merit in September 1944.

In his testimony, Admiral Turner assessed why his forces were so soundly defeated in the battle:

> The Navy was still obsessed with a strong feeling of technical and mental superiority over the enemy. In spite of ample evidence as to enemy capabilities, most of our officers and men despised the enemy and felt themselves sure victors in all encounters under any circumstances. The net result of all this was a fatal lethargy of mind which induced a confidence without readiness, and a routine acceptance of outworn peacetime standards of conduct. I believe that this psychological factor, as a cause of our defeat, was even more important than the element of surprise.

While the lethargy of peacetime was not completely shaken off until the Navy had absorbed more hard blows to its pride in the desperate battles around Guadalcanal, the service did pick itself up after Savo and make preparation for what would be the most savage combat in its history to that time. Admiral Hepburn's report led to many operational and structural changes in the operation of the fleet. In the ensuing months, every cruiser was retrofitted with emergency diesel electric generators to maintain power on board regardless, while all shipboard fire mains were changed to a vertical loop design that could function despite being broken. Many fires aboard the ships at Savo had been the result of hangars filled with gas, oil, and airplanes. Ships' boats, filled with gasoline, also caught fire. For the lost cruisers, these facilities were dead amidships and thus presented a perfect target at night. The explosion of ready ammo service lockers had added to the destruction; the report noted the lockers were never close to being depleted and contained more ammunition than needed. CO_2 cannisters were increased and placed near these stations.

For the ten days following the battle, Fletcher's fleet loitered southeast of the Solomons as they waited for the arrival of enemy carriers that intelligence claimed were en route. The Marines on

Guadalcanal expected land-based air cover to arrive on August 16, but the transfer was delayed. Beginning August 18, the Japanese 25th Air Flotilla began the aerial assault leading up to the first Japanese effort to land troops and retake the island with bombing raids that arrived each day around noon. With the only Japanese base in the region being 600 miles distant, these missions would not have been possible without the long range of the G4M1 bombers and A6M2 fighters.

2

BATTLE OF THE EASTERN SOLOMONS

The Allied offensive in the Solomons had taken the Japanese high command by surprise, given that the staff planners had been unanimous in supporting the idea that the Allies would not be in a position to respond offensively before the summer of 1943. The fact that the Allies had managed to go over to the offensive in the Solomons a year early upset many plans. This followed the rude awakening of Midway, in which Admiral Yamamoto's prewar prediction that he would "run wild for six months" had been proven incredibly prescient. The Midway defeat had resulted in an immediate decision by the Japanese military leadership to discard planned offensive operations and substitute a defensive line that was to be held at all costs. It was this policy that would drive Japanese actions over the six months following the arrival of the Marines at Guadalcanal on August 7, 1942.

While the Imperial Navy had lost the heart of their carrier striking force when *Akagi*, *Kaga*, *Soryu*, and *Hiryu* were sunk at Midway, what was left of the carrier fleet was still formidable in comparison with the carrier force the US Navy could put forward. The heart of Japanese naval aviation was now the First Carrier Division, composed of the fleet carriers *Shōkaku* and *Zuikaku* and the light carrier *Zuihō*, and the Second Carrier Division with the light carriers *Junyō*, *Hiryo*, and *Ryūjō*. *Shōkaku* and *Zuikaku* were comparable to the American carriers *Enterprise* and *Hornet*, while *Zuihō*, *Junyō*, and *Hiryo* were equivalent to the American light fleet carrier *Wasp* regarding capability and performance.

While the Japanese had planned to put the airfield on Guadalcanal to use as a bomber base from which to interdict the Allied supply lines in the Coral Sea, they had neglected to make any plans for other air bases in the Solomons. Thus, the only air base they had left after the American capture of Tulagi and Guadalcanal was at Rabaul, their main base in the region. However, since Rabaul was 600 miles distant, which kept many aircraft like the Val and Kate from entering the battle due to range considerations, construction began after the American invasion on an airfield located on northern Bougainville, the island in the Solomons chain closest to Rabaul, but the Japanese did not have the ability to construct an airfield quickly. The Imperial Japanese Navy Air Force (IJNAF) units based at Rabaul could make no more than one strike per day on the Americans, if they took off and landed in daylight. Without a weather-reporting capability in the Solomons, strikes were forced to abort many times when they encountered adverse weather, which could build quickly in the sub-equatorial climate.

Within the first month after the Allied invasion, the 25th Air Flotilla lost 18 Vals, the majority of which were due to running out of fuel as they attempted to return from their attacks. The best these crews could hope for was to crash-land on one of the other islands and make contact with friendly forces for rescue. In the first three days following the invasion, the Japanese listed 42 aircraft lost to all causes. This loss rate was unsustainable.

Furthermore, the replacements sent to Rabaul to make up for losses of the A6M2 Zeros as the fight for Guadalcanal went on were the new A6M3 Model 32, eventually known to the Americans as "Hamp." This Zero sub-type had an engine of increased power that improved performance against Allied fighters, but featured clipped wings and reduced fuel capacity, rendering it incapable of making the long flight to Guadalcanal until the bases on Bougainville could be completed, and even then their "combat time" over Guadalcanal was less than the earlier sub-type. Mitsubishi finally solved the problem of lack of range by restoring the extended wing of the A6M2 Model 21 to the A6M3, resulting in the A6M3 Model 22, but these fighters did not appear operationally until the end of the Guadalcanal campaign.

The airfield at Buka on northern Bougainville was completed by August 27, but it was small and had a limited basing capability. A second base at Buin on the southern end of the island was completed in mid-September, but was also limited in ability and could only operate fighters and single-engine bombers. To make up the numbers, the IJNAF was forced to rely on floatplanes that could be based in shallow lagoons of islands closer to Guadalcanal during the three crucial months between the invasion and mid-November. Chief among these was the A6M2-N, a floatplane development of the land-based Zero, known to the Allies as "Rufe." While the Rufe had nearly the same incredible maneuverability as its land-based cousin, the airplane was significantly slower, with a top speed of around 275mph as compared with the land-based A6M2's 332mph top speed. The F1M2 reconnaissance floatplane known as "Pete," a two-seat biplane, was even slower, but its maneuverability was such that Allied pilots who attempted to tangle with one did so at their own risk. Several Marine aces would fall victim to what they thought was an "easy kill."

Following the Guadalcanal invasion, the American offensive was seen as the first step of a direct threat to Rabaul, and opposing it thus became the Imperial Navy's top priority.

Japanese naval forces and the Army prepared a counteroffensive to drive the Americans out of Guadalcanal and Tulagi, named Operation *Ka*. The naval forces were responsible for destroying the US carriers in the South Pacific.

The campaign to retake Guadalcanal required the Imperial Navy and the Imperial Army to collaborate. The traditional rivalry between the two armed forces made this collaboration difficult and ultimately contributed to their defeat in the campaign. Following the landings on Guadalcanal, the Imperial Army's 17th Army, commanded by Lieutenant General Harukichi Hyakutake from his headquarters at Rabaul, was assigned responsibility for retaking Guadalcanal. The 17th Army, a corps-sized unit, was already committed to the New Guinea campaign and only a few units could be diverted to Guadalcanal. These included the 35th Infantry Brigade at Palau, the 4th (Aoba) Infantry Regiment in the Philippines, and the 28th (Ichiki) Infantry Regiment, en route to Japan from Guam. Being already at sea, the Ichiki Regiment would be the first to arrive on the island.

The Imperial Army underestimated the number of American troops on Guadalcanal as a result of an aerial reconnaissance mission flown with one of General Hyakutake's senior staff officers aboard, which sighted few US troops on the island and no shipping in Sealark Sound. The ensuing report led the general's staff to conclude that the Allies had withdrawn most of their troops following their defeat at the Battle of Savo Island. In fact, no troops had been withdrawn, and the reconnaissance mission had been flown on one of the few days that at least one or two transports did not arrive to quickly unload additional supplies.

On August 16, a three-ship convoy carrying 1,411 soldiers of the 28th (Ichiki) Infantry Regiment and the 5th Yokosuka Special Naval Landing Force departed Truk bound for Guadalcanal. The escorting warships were led by the redoubtable Rear Admiral Raizo Tanaka, while Vice Admiral Gunichi Mikawa's four heavy cruisers that had won the Battle of Savo Island provided the covering force. Tanaka planned to land the troops on Guadalcanal on August 24, in coordination with strikes by the Japanese carriers against Henderson Field which would prevent the American units there from attacking the convoy. General Hyakutake also ordered that a battalion of the Ichiki Force be landed on Guadalcanal by destroyers to immediately attack the Americans and retake the airfield. Regimental commander Lieutenant Colonel Ichiki and 916 of the regiment's 2,300 soldiers landed at Taivu Point, 22 miles east of the Marines' defensive line at Lunga Point at 0100 hours on August 19. The colonel had been ordered to scout the Marine positions and await the arrival of the rest of the regiment before taking any offensive action. Ichiki, however, was so confident of success that he wrote in his journal, "18 August, landing; 20 August, march by night and battle; 21 August, enjoyment of the fruit of victory." His plan was to march down the beach to Lunga Point and penetrate the American defenses. On the night of August 19, Ichiki advanced with 800 of his soldiers and took position in the jungle eight miles from the Marine positions by dawn of August 20.

On August 21, the main naval force, composed of the fleet carriers *Shōkaku*, *Zuikaku*, and the light carrier *Ryūjō*, and their screening force, under command of Vice Admiral Chuichi Nagumo in *Shōkaku*, departed Truk. The fleet's "vanguard force" of two battleships, three heavy cruisers, one light cruiser, and three destroyers, was commanded by Rear Admiral Hiroaki Abe, while an "advanced force" of five heavy cruisers, one light cruiser, six destroyers, and the seaplane carrier *Chitose* was commanded by Vice Admiral Nobutake Kondō. One hundred land-based bombers, fighters, and reconnaissance aircraft of the 25th Air Flotilla were at Rabaul for operational support.

Ryūjō was placed with the "advanced force" in order to act as bait for the Americans in the coming carrier battle. Once the Americans took the bait, *Shōkaku* and *Zuikaku*, which were positioned 60 miles to the north with full deckloads, would quickly close the trap and attack the US carriers. The Japanese objective was to sink or damage the American carriers in order to eliminate the air cover provided to Allied supply convoys, thus cutting Guadalcanal off from reinforcement.

The Marines had been warned of the Ichiki force by Solomon Islanders led by coastwatcher Martin Clemens, and were prepared for battle the evening of August 20 at a location they mistakenly called the Tenaru River (which was several miles further east). What was later called "Alligator creek" was actually a tidal lagoon separated from the ocean by a narrow sandbar. The 1st Marine Regiment dug in on the western side of this lagoon so that the Japanese would be forced to cross through the water and over the sandbar to get at their positions. The Japanese arrived at the other side of the lagoon shortly after midnight. At 0130 hours on August 21 they commenced their attack. Machine gun fire and cannister grapeshot rounds fired from the Marine positions slaughtered the Japanese troops as they attempted the crossing. The attack broke around 0200 hours when the Marines killed the few enemy troops who had made it across. Ichiki ordered a second attack at 0230 hours; nearly all the 200 Japanese troops were killed attempting to cross the lagoon. A third attack around 0500 hours was also blocked. At dawn, the remaining Japanese refused to retreat. The 1st Battalion, 1st Marines, moved inland around the lagoon and enveloped the enemy. As Japanese troops tried to escape down the beach, they were strafed by the newly arrived Wildcats of VMF-223. In mid-afternoon, five M3 Stuart light tanks attacked across the sandbar and ground their way through and over the Japanese position. All resistance ended by 1700 hours. When some wounded Japanese fired at Marines, the Marines went through the battlefield and shot every enemy soldier they came across whether dead or alive, except for 15 taken prisoner, while some 30 troops managed to escape to tell the tale to their comrades back at Taivu Point. When he later inspected the battlefield, General Vandegrift commented that the rear ends of the tanks "looked like meat grinders."

The battle alerted the Allied command to the threat of a Japanese offensive to retake the island and Admiral Fletcher's carriers turned toward Guadalcanal the morning of August 21. Between August 21 and 23 they flew search missions to find the enemy. An alarming number of Japanese submarines were spotted with some attacked and one claimed sunk; aboard the fleet, sailors who learned of the presence of submarines started calling the waters south of Guadalcanal "Torpedo Junction." The Japanese were also searching for the Americans, but neither found the other despite intense scouting efforts.

Finally, at 0950 hours on August 23, a PBY Catalina sighted Tanaka's oncoming convoy in "the Slot" despite the heavy rainstorms and poor visibility over the southern Solomons. In mid-afternoon, strike forces from *Saratoga* and Henderson Field took off to attack the convoy. However, following the sighting of his force, Admiral Tanaka had reversed course and thus eluded the strikes; he planned to reverse course again and continue south overnight, pushing the troop landings back to August 25. Despite flying a search pattern, neither US formation was able to find the enemy in the heavy storms and poor visibility. *Saratoga's* CAG, Commander Harry Felt, took his force of 31 SBDs and six TBFs in to Henderson Field for the night to avoid the bad weather.

With the Japanese carriers still undetected, Admiral Fletcher assumed the lack of contact meant the Japanese were still at Truk. At 1823 hours on August 23, the admiral, who always worried about his ships having sufficient fuel aboard, detached *Wasp* and the rest of her Task Force 18 for the two-day trip south toward Efate Island to refuel. With this move, he reduced his available force by one-third.

At 0145 hours on August 24, Admiral Nagumo ordered *Ryūjō* to attack Henderson Field, while *Shōkaku* and *Zuikaku* prepared to launch their strikes on short notice if the American carriers were located. Between 0555 and 0630 hours, *Enterprise* launched scout aircraft. At Henderson Field, *Saratoga's* strike force took off at dawn and landed back aboard the carrier at 1130 hours.

At 0935 hours, a patrolling Catalina sighted the *Ryūjō* force. At 1155 hours, another PBY made contact and sent in a more complete sighting report that put *Ryūjō* and the warships of Kondō's and Mikawa's forces heading south, 250 miles northwest of Task Force 61. Admiral Fletcher sensed the possibility that *Ryūjō* could be bait and delayed launching a strike while he waited for any sightings of the main force. When the lack of such reports led him to believe there were no other Japanese carriers in the area, he finally ordered a strike against *Ryūjō*.

At 1435 hours, Commander Felt led 13 SBDs from Bombing 3 (VB-3) and 15 Scouting 3 (VS-3) dive bombers, along with eight Torpedo 8 (VT-8) Avengers from *Saratoga* to attack *Ryūjō*.

In accordance with her orders, *Ryūjō* launched six B5N2 Kate bombers and 15 A6M2 Zeros to attack Henderson Field in conjunction with an attack by the 25th Air Flotilla from Rabaul. Unfortunately, the Rabaul aircraft encountered severe weather and returned to their base. The *Ryūjō* aircraft were detected on radar by *Saratoga* as they flew toward Guadalcanal. They arrived over Henderson Field at 1423 hours, almost the same time as *Saratoga*'s force was taking off to hit their carrier. The Marine fighters from Henderson were waiting at 20,000 feet; in the ensuing fight, VMF-223's pilots claimed 20, though actual losses were three Kates, three Zeros, and three Wildcats shot down with no significant damage to Henderson Field.

While *Saratoga*'s force was en route to their target, three *Enterprise* scouts spotted different elements of the oncoming Japanese main fleet. The first sighting was of *Ryūjō* and her escorts, made by Scouting 6's Lieutenant Stockton B. Strong and Ensign John Ritchey at 1510 hours. Strong repeated his sighting report several times over six minutes, but *Enterprise* failed to acknowledge. Unknown to Strong and Ritchey, another search team in a separate search quadrant also spotted the carrier at nearly the same moment.

The Guadalcanal campaign marked the first carrier operation of the Grumman TBF-1 Avenger that had replaced the hapless Douglas TBD-1 Devastator as the fleet torpedo bomber. *Saratoga*'s air group included the reconstituted Torpedo 8 that had been devastated at Midway, while *Enterprise* operated *Saratoga*'s Torpedo 3. In addition to the SBD scouts that were launched to search for the Japanese fleet, seven VT-3 Avengers were sent out on search missions. VT-3 commander LCDR Charles M. Jett and his wingman, Ensign R.J. Bye, thus also discovered *Ryūjō* at nearly the same time that Strong and Ritchey did. After sending a sighting report, Jett and Bye conducted the only level bombing attack against an aircraft carrier ever made by the Avenger, attacking from up-sun and leveling off at 12,000 feet over the carrier, where each dropped the two 500-pound bombs they carried. Just as they reached their drop point, the Japanese opened up on them with AA fire and their quartet of bombs hit the ocean in a cluster 500 feet astern of the carrier.

Lieutenant J.N. Myers and Midway veteran Chief Aviation Machinist's Mate H.I. Corl, who were searching in a different sector, sighted a Japanese cruiser and prepared to attack it. As they entered their bomb run they were suddenly intercepted by three Zeros. Though the enemy CAP scored no hits, the Avengers were forced to break off as the cruiser was also putting up an accurate AA barrage. Corl was pursued into a cloud by one of the Zeros, which hit the TBF with a solid burst of 20mm fire that killed Corl. His turret gunner, Aviation Radioman 3/c D.D. Wiley, managed to get out of the burning Avenger. After a seven-month South Seas adventure, he was returned by Solomon Islanders to Guadalcanal. Myers managed to get back to the fleet just as the *Zuikaku* strike arrived, and was badly shot up by a Zero, though he managed to trap aboard *Saratoga* despite the damage.

Commander Felt heard Strong's position report when his force was 55 miles south of the reported enemy position. Unfortunately, Strong's navigation had been slightly off, and when the *Saratoga* force arrived at the broadcast position, they had to spend precious minutes and fuel searching for the enemy, which were actually further west. At 1606 hours, Felt spotted *Ryūjō*, headed southeast at 20 knots. He ordered the 15 Scouting 3 and six of Bombing 6's SBDs to attack the carrier with five Torpedo 8 Avengers; among the VT-8 pilots was Ensign Bert Earnest, the only survivor of the VT-8 detachment that had fought at Midway. The dive bombers maneuvered to attack from different directions and break up the enemy's defensive fire while the Avengers broke into two groups, one of two planes and the other of three, to initiate a "hammer and anvil" attack on the enemy carrier.

At the time the *Saratoga* strike arrived overhead, *Ryūjō* was headed toward her pickup point for the strike launched against Guadalcanal. Despite the fact that the American attackers maneuvered for 15 minutes to get into position, the Japanese made no move to launch any defensive aircraft until 1620 hours, when the carrier turned into the wind to launch her remaining Zero fighters. By then the Dauntlesses were in their attack dives. Her turn to the right threw off the aim of the first attackers and Commander Felt watched from above with frustration as the first ten bombs came no closer than a few near misses. At that point, he directed the Bombing 6 SBDs he had held in reserve to attack the escorts to attack *Ryūjō*.

The remaining bombers were also unsuccessful in their attacks, with the six Zeros that had managed to get airborne attacking them in their dives and throwing off their aim. Despite the fact he had no wingman, Felt threw himself into the attack, diving through flak so intense that his radio mast was shot off, and planted his 1,600-pound armor-piercing bomb slightly port and aft of the flight deck's center. He strafed a destroyer as he pulled out and his radioman saw a torpedo explosion on the carrier's starboard bow just after his own bomb hit.

The Bombing 6 dive bombers had heard the order to change targets just as they pushed over in their dive on the cruiser *Tone*. Pulling out of their dives they regrouped and went after *Ryūjō*. All seven attacking pilots were Midway veterans, and they scored three direct hits and four close misses that were as damaging as torpedo hits. The attacking Avengers came in just before the VB-6 dive bombers and all launched their torpedoes within 900 yards of the target and claimed a hit on the starboard bow. The carrier reeled under the hits and caught fire as her attackers flew off. With 120 men killed in the attacks, the crew was unable to contain the fires and abandoned ship at nightfall; she sank soon after.

Unknown to the Americans, just at the moment *Saratoga* began launching her strike, a Japanese scout from the cruiser *Chikuma* sighted the American carriers and provided the final fix on the US fleet after it had been originally spotted by another scout that had been shot down at 1100 hours. The scout was spotted by the combat air patrol and shot down at 1430 hours, but not before getting off the sighting report. Upon receiving the message, Admiral Nagumo immediately ordered *Shōkaku* and *Zuikaku* to launch their strikes. The first wave of 27 D3A1 Vals and 15 Zeros from *Zuikaku* was on its way toward *Enterprise* and *Saratoga* by 1450 hours. *Shōkaku* and *Zuikaku* were finally spotted at 1530 hours by Bombing 6's commander, Lieutenant Ray Davis, and his wingman, Ensign R.C. Shaw, flying a search at 1,500 feet. The carrier he spotted was *Shōkaku*, which was in the middle of launching her strike. Davis immediately began climbing, broadcasting the all-important sighting report repeatedly. Unfortunately, his reports never reached Admiral Fletcher. By 1545 hours, the two Dauntlesses were at 14,500 feet and Davis could now see *Zuikaku* beyond *Shōkaku*. Davis opened his flaps and rolled into his 70-degree attack dive, followed by Shaw. The SBDs were coming down on the enemy from out of the sun. *Shōkaku* was beginning a turn to starboard as Davis plunged through 5,000 feet and antiaircraft fire opened up, the explosions bouncing the two attackers. Finally, 2,000 feet above the target, Davis and Shaw pulled their bomb releases and the two 500-pounders fell free, arcing toward the target. Unfortunately, while *Shōkaku*'s 70-degree right turn didn't throw off the Americans' aim by much, it was just enough that both bombs hit close alongside, causing negligible damage. As they initiated their pullout, the two Dauntlesses flashed through a group of enemy planes circling the carrier. They were low enough that Shaw's gunner, ARM3/c H.D. Jones, was able to count 20 planes on *Shōkaku*'s deck.

As the two Dauntlesses flew clear of the enemy task force, Davis once again radioed his sighting report. While *Enterprise* never heard either message, other ships picked it up and passed it on. When he finally saw the message, Admiral Fletcher tried to divert Felt's strike force from the *Ryūjō*, but Felt and his dive bombers had just completed their drops. The 27 Wildcats of VF-5 aboard *Saratoga* and the 28 of VF-6 aboard *Enterprise* were prepared to defend the fleet and the combat air patrol was augmented with fighters from both carriers. Fourteen VF-6 Wildcats were airborne, with 12 from *Saratoga*. Each carrier would handle its own fighter direction.

At 1602 hours, *Enterprise*'s CXAM radar picked up the first wave of 27 Vals and ten escorting Zeros from *Zuikaku* inbound. *Enterprise*'s 14 Wildcats were overhead at 8,000–15,000 feet, while *Saratoga*'s dozen were at 10,000–15,000 feet. The two carriers turned into the wind and each launched their remaining Wildcats. *Enterprise* launched four four-plane divisions beginning at 1637 hours, while *Saratoga* launched her 15 remaining fighters at 1645 hours.

In the meantime, *Enterprise*'s Air Officer, LCDR John Crommelin, ordered the remaining nine SBDs and seven TBFs on deck launched immediately after the Wildcats, with orders to fly north and hit any target they found. Crommelin's quick action likely saved *Enterprise*, since the fully fueled and fully armed dive bombers had been parked right where the ship would be hit only minutes after they got airborne. While the Wildcats engaged the enemy, the dive and torpedo bombers flew on north in an attempt to find and hit the remaining Japanese carriers.

The force of 53 Wildcats – 28 from VF-6 and 25 from VF-5 – were directed to intercept with enemy altitude estimated at 12,000 feet; 46 eventually made contact with the enemy, the largest fighter force yet to defend an American task force. Lieutenant "Chick" Harmer, VF-5's

XO, later remembered that, as had happened at Coral Sea and Midway, the high-frequency radio net was quickly inundated once the fight began, leaving the Fighter Direction Officers (FDO) unable to direct the defenders toward the oncoming enemy, while the primitive radar did not provide accurate height information. The escorting Zeros held off those Wildcats that did find the enemy, keeping all but a few from engaging the Vals before they began their attacks.

Chick Harmer's three division-mates were unable to stick with him as he initiated an attack on the Vals just before they entered their dives. He picked out the leading Val and stuck with it as it dived on *Enterprise*, shooting it into the sea before it could drop its bomb. He fired at the second Val and saw pieces fly off it before a Zero closed on him and loosed a burst that hit the Wildcat solidly and wounded Harmer in his left leg. He steepened his dive and got away from the enemy fighter, then found he could land on *Saratoga* since the carrier was not under direct attack, though he bounced when he touched the deck and went inverted into the barrier, suffering additional minor injuries in the crash.

The rest of Harmer's division managed to score three more Vals destroyed and a probable. The top scorers for VF-5 were Lieutenant Howard Jensen's Scarlet-Six division, which scored seven Vals and a Zero, including three Vals credited to Jensen. VF-5 claimed 14 Vals shot down and were credited with 13 since the last was hit by ship's AA as the pilot opened fire on it, in addition to three Zeros for a loss of three pilots and four Wildcats. Among the lost pilots was Lieutenant Marion Dufilho, who had been Butch O'Hare's wingman in their epic defense of *Lexington* off Rabaul the previous February.

Fighting 6 hit the attackers moments after Fighting 5 had waded in. NAP Aviation Electrician's Mate 1/c R.W. Rhodes claimed a Val, while NAP Aviation Machinist's Mate 1/c L.P. Mankin discovered how maneuverable the Val was when one turned inside him and peppered his tail. The pilots also got another lesson in how maneuverable the Zero was when six Wildcats tried to corner one at 17,000 feet that evaded all six with a series of elegant aerobatics before flying off. Ensign R.M. Disque didn't let the Zero's maneuverability bother him when he shot one off the tail of an SBD, then followed up with a second that tried to attack four other Wildcats.

Almost all of the attackers concentrated on *Enterprise*. Several defending Wildcats followed the Vals into their attack dives, disregarding the intense antiaircraft fire from *Enterprise* and her screen. At 1612 hours the first of 30 Vals banked into their dives at 20,000 feet. Below on the carrier, Marine Sergeant Joseph R. Schinka, commander of the number four 20mm antiaircraft battery, spotted a puff of smoke overhead as a Val was hit by a Wildcat. Schinka opened fire even though the attacking Vals were out of range. The tracers thrown up, however, guided the fire of the screening ships. In moments, a barrage of 20mm, 1.1-inch and 5-inch antiaircraft fire filled the sky over the fleet as *North Carolina*, *Portland*, *Atlanta*, and the escorting destroyers all came to the Big E's defense.

While the Wildcats were able to shoot down several Vals and the antiaircraft fire threw off the aim of others, four Wildcats were shot down by "friendly fire." The first nine attackers missed the carrier, but at 1644 hours, an armor-piercing, delayed-action bomb penetrated *Enterprise*'s flight deck near the aft elevator and passed through three decks before it detonated below the waterline, killing 35 and wounding 70, wiping out a damage control team that was stationed in the chief petty officers' quarters. The explosion ripped six-foot holes in the hull at the waterline and the carrier took on a list to starboard as seawater poured in. The blast tore huge holes through the steel decks overhead and the hangar deck bulged upwards a full two feet, which rendered the aft elevator useless. The concussion of the blast whipped *Enterprise* from stem to stern, upwards then side-to-side. Thirty seconds later, the 11th Val dropped its bomb which hit 15 feet from the first, igniting a large secondary explosion that started a large fire. The 12th Val, piloted by Kazumi Horie who was hit in his dive and crashed soon after dropping his bomb, hit *Enterprise* on the flight deck forward of the first two hits, creating a 10-foot hole and disabling the number two elevator, but caused no further damage. Had the last four Vals not diverted to attack the escorting *North Carolina* and instead hit the carrier, *Enterprise* might have been lost. The last of the attackers flew away by 1648 hours. With *Enterprise* so badly damaged, the VF-6 Wildcats and other aircraft of her air group still airborne diverted to *Saratoga*.

While the Japanese first strike hit Task Force 61, ten SBDs of Scouting 3 and three Bombing 5 tag-alongs rendezvoused after their attack on *Ryūjō* and took up a heading to return to *Saratoga*, climbing to 10,000 feet. Squadron commander, LCDR Lou Kirn, spotted 30 Japanese aircraft 2,000 feet below on the same heading. They were the second strike from *Zuikaku* and *Shōkaku*. After radioing *Saratoga* that the enemy was inbound, the Americans flew on, not having enough fuel to engage the enemy and still get home. By the time they arrived over the fleet, the first Japanese strike was going after *Enterprise*. Kirn spotted four Val dive bombers at 500 feet as the formation turned toward *Saratoga* and led the squadron in attacking the enemy dive bombers. Ensign Hanson hit one Val and set it smoking before it nosed into the water below. Lieutenant (jg) R.K. Campbell hit another of the Vals in its right wing tank and set it afire to leave a fiery streak across the sky into the water. Ensign H.R. Burnett, who had not participated in the strike, was returning from Inner Air Patrol when he caught the third Val and set it afire.

The Americans claimed 48 Japanese aircraft shot down, even though there were only 42 in the attack. Actual Japanese losses were 25 aircraft, including 18 of the 27 Vals and six of the ten Zeros. The surviving Japanese aircrews mistakenly reported that they had heavily damaged two carriers.

Just as the first blips of the second wave appeared on the task force radars, *Enterprise* lost steering control. The steering room had been sealed off after the first hit, to prevent the crew of seven being overwhelmed by smoke. Heat generated by the powerful electric steering motors pushed the temperature inside the compartment to 120 degrees, then 150, and finally to 170 degrees at which point men and machinery failed. At 1750 hours, *Enterprise*'s rudder swung right, then left, then right again before it jammed hard over to starboard. Radar showed the incoming Japanese were 50 miles away as the carrier narrowly missed slicing the destroyer *Balch* in half. In engineering, the screws were thrown in reverse, slowing her to 10 knots as the signalmen ran a breakdown flag up her truck. The rudder was jammed so far over that control was not regained even when the port screws were put to reverse with the starboard screws put to full ahead. *Enterprise* circled, helpless, for 38 minutes until damage control parties were able to fight their way into the steering compartment and start the second of the two steering motors. In the Combat Information Center, radar operators watched anxiously as the enemy planes passed 50 miles south, then reversed course as they turned to the northwest, missing the fleet entirely.

The dive and torpedo bombers that Crommelin had launched before the attack were led by Lieutenant Turner Caldwell. By the time they were in the vicinity of where *Ryūjō* had last been reported, the carrier had already sunk. Faced with approaching darkness and an uncertain fuel state, Caldwell led his SBDs and TBFs to Henderson Field where they landed after dark.

As darkness fell, Task Force 61 retreated to the southeast, to avoid any approaching Japanese warships. Admirals Abe and Kondō were steaming south in an attempt to catch the US carriers at night, but turned back at midnight without making contact. Admiral Nagumo's carriers, having suffered heavy aircraft losses in the battle and with their escorts low on fuel, also retreated northward.

That evening, Admiral Tanaka's troop convoy reversed course and headed back toward Guadalcanal in the belief the US carriers were out of action and that Henderson Field had been badly damaged. At dawn on August 25, the convoy was joined by five destroyers that had shelled the airfield the night before. At 0800 hours, the ships were 150 miles from Guadalcanal. Five minutes later, 18 Marine dive bombers from Henderson Field attacked out of the sun, damaging the cruiser *Jintsu*, wounding 24 of the crew and knocking the admiral unconscious. The SBDs also scored solid hits on the transport *Kinryu Maru*. Just as the destroyer *Mutsuki* maneuvered to come alongside *Kinryu Maru* to rescue her crew and troops, four B-17Es from Espiritu Santo made one of the most successful high-altitude bombing attacks on a ship in the entire war, dropping five bombs on or around *Mutsuki* and sinking her immediately. A badly shaken but uninjured Admiral Tanaka transferred from *Jintsu* to the destroyer *Kagerō*, ordering *Jintsu* back to Truk. He then ordered the convoy to alter course to the Japanese base in the Shortland Islands.

The first Japanese attempt to reinforce Guadalcanal and expel the Marines had failed.

The Battle of the Eastern Solomons has been called indecisive, since the Japanese lost *Ryūjō* and the US suffered major damage to *Enterprise*, without either fleet being forced to retire in defeat. Nagumo's carriers lingered near the northern Solomons, out of range from aircraft based at Henderson Field, before the ships finally returned to Truk on September 5. While the US Navy only lost seven aircraft, the Imperial Navy lost 61 aircraft and more than 100 irreplaceable experienced pilots and crew as well as the carrier *Ryūjō*, resulting in a tactical defeat for the Imperial Navy. Eastern Solomons was the only carrier battle of 1942 in which the US Navy lost no carriers; the fact that the Navy

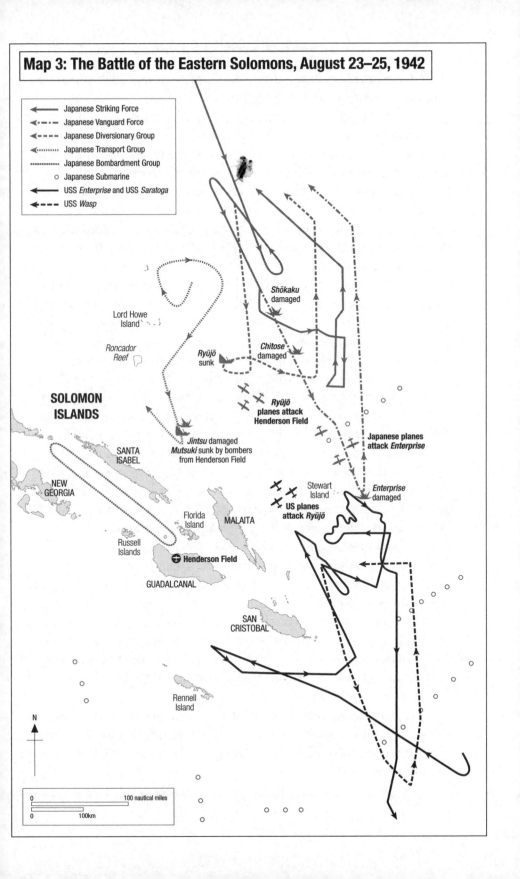

Map 3: The Battle of the Eastern Solomons, August 23–25, 1942

Japanese Striking Force
Japanese Vanguard Force
Japanese Diversionary Group
Japanese Transport Group
Japanese Bombardment Group
Japanese Submarine
USS *Enterprise* and USS *Saratoga*
USS *Wasp*

Shōkaku damaged

Ryūjō sunk

Chitose damaged

Ryūjō planes attack Henderson Field

Japanese planes attack *Enterprise*

Lord Howe Island

Roncador Reef

SOLOMON ISLANDS

SANTA ISABEL

NEW GEORGIA

Russell Islands

Jintsu damaged
Mutsuki sunk by bombers from Henderson Field

Florida Island

MALAITA

Stewart Island

US planes attack *Ryūjō*

Enterprise damaged

Henderson Field

GUADALCANAL

SAN CRISTOBAL

Rennell Island

N

0   100 nautical miles
0   100km

still retained the ability to reinforce Guadalcanal made the outcome a strategic victory for the United States.

The battle also demonstrated again that communications had to be improved. The failure of either *Saratoga* or *Enterprise* to pick up the scouting reports in time to divert the *Saratoga* strike from *Ryūjō* to the newly discovered *Zuikaku* and *Shōkaku* left the last two Japanese fleet carriers to participate with deadly effect in the coming Battle of Santa Cruz. The single high-frequency radio net meant that effective control of defensive fighters against an incoming strike would break down at the most important moment. This would not be changed until the "new" navy arrived on the scene the following year.

Enterprise needed to return to Pearl Harbor to have her damage repaired. She transferred 17 Wildcats and six Avengers to *Saratoga* as replacements before departing on August 25. She would be gone for seven weeks. Following the departure of *Enterprise*, *Saratoga* rendezvoused with *Wasp* the evening of August 26. On August 29, *Hornet* and Task Force 17 arrived to replace *Enterprise*.

The scuttlebutt about the operating area south of the Solomons in the Coral Sea being "Torpedo Junction" was proved right when *Saratoga* was torpedoed by the Japanese submarine *I-26* on August 30, the torpedo striking her starboard side, just aft of the island. Admiral Fletcher and 12 crewmen were injured, while one fireroom was flooded. The carrier took on a four-degree list while multiple electrical short circuits caused by the flooding damaged her turbo-electric propulsion system, leaving the carrier dead in the water for an hour while the heavy cruiser *Minneapolis* rigged lines to take her in tow. By noon, damage control parties had been able to correct the list and her electrical system was restored, allowing her to steam under her own power by late afternoon. On September 6 *Saratoga* dropped anchor at Tongatapu, where she stayed for six days while making temporary repairs. Escorted by the battleship *South Dakota*, cruiser *New Orleans*, and five destroyers, *Saratoga* departed for repair at Pearl Harbor. Task Force 11 entered Pearl Harbor on September 21; *Saratoga* entered dry-dock the following day for more permanent repairs.

Both sides licked their wounds while Admiral Yamamoto planned the next attempt to retake the island. The battle settled into seven weeks of stalemate as both sides made attempts to reinforce the troops they had ashore.

3

THE CACTUS AIR FORCE

On August 18, the escort carrier USS *Long Island* (CVE-1) departed Efate in the New Hebrides, headed to Guadalcanal. Marine Air Group 23 (MAG-23), which had only been formed the previous May, had been assigned a month earlier to provide air defense on Guadalcanal with the responsibility given to the group's forward echelon, 19 F4F-4 Wildcats of VMF-223 and 12 SBD-3 Dauntlesses of VMSB-232. Originally equipped with Brewster F2A-3 fighters, VMF-223 had been hastily re-equipped with Wildcats and given barely six weeks to learn combat flying and become carrier-qualified for their mission. Among the squadron's pilots were three survivors of VMF-221 who had flown at Midway: Marion Carl, Clayton Canfield, and Roy Corry. Eight pilots from VMF-212 at Turtle Bay airfield on Espiritu Santo had been traded for the eight least-experienced VMF-223 pilots. Carl had been named executive officer on his arrival in late June. Fortunately, gunnery was a fetish with squadron CO Major John L. Smith, who had a reputation in the corps as a tough, abrasive officer who was ambitious and determined; under his leadership, the squadron's pilots had concentrated their efforts on improving their fighting and flying skills. Unfortunately, the ground crews for the two squadrons had been put aboard the transport *W.W. Burrows* which would not arrive on Guadalcanal for another two weeks. The night of August 19, the pilots packed their planes with everything they could stuff inside: spark plugs, starter cartridges, tool kits, even spare tires.

While VMF-223 had transitioned to Wildcats, VMSB-232 had exchanged their hand-me-down SBD-2s for factory-new SBD-3s. They were the last available in the fleet pool at Ford Island, which left the squadron short by six of its authorized strength of 18 dive bombers. Skipper Lieutenant Colonel Richard H. Mangrum, who had learned the art of dive-bombing flying O2U Corsairs in Honduras as a young Marine aviator back in 1928, worked hard to bring his ten new second lieutenants fresh from flight school up to a combat-ready standard. While each had some 250 hours of flight experience, none had ever flown the SBD. He thanked the gods for having Captain Bruce Prosser report aboard at about the same time from having flown SB2U-1s with VMSB-241 at the Battle of Midway. As Mangrum later recalled, Prosser became the backbone of the squadron as they trained hard for war, beloved by the younger pilots. Once they'd received notice on July 5 that they would be going to war in 30 days, Mangrum and Prosser had led their youngsters in dive-bombing practice every day as they put the new pilots and the freshly arrived gunners through a frantic shakedown course. The night of August 19, the carrier support crews had loaded a 500-pound bomb on each Dauntless's shackle to supplement the small supply of bombs available at Guadalcanal. As with the fighter pilots, the Dauntless crews packed all the spare parts and tools they could jam into their cockpits.

The next afternoon, August 20, 1942, *Long Island* arrived at the launch point off the tip of San Cristobal Island, 200 miles south of Guadalcanal. While the ship steamed into the southeast trade wind, the Wildcats and Dauntlesses were catapulted into the air one at a time, after which they formed up and headed north. An hour and 20 minutes later, Guadalcanal came into view on the horizon. The Marines on the island had put the captured Japanese equipment to use during the preceding two weeks. Henderson Field was now a 3,800-foot strip 150 feet wide, covered with gravel, while the taxiway and parking area were dirt that would frequently become fields of mud in the many rainstorms. The airfield was surrounded by a tenuously held defensive line that extended from Point Cruz on the west to the Ilu River on the east and left the airfield only a quarter mile from a mile-long piece of high ground that would come to be known in Marine history as "Bloody Ridge." There were no protective revetments and aircraft maintenance would be a test of American ingenuity throughout their tour on the island. There would be a chronic shortage of oxygen bottles, all manner of parts and equipment, and even gasoline. Robert Sherrod, who had landed with the Marines to report for *Time* magazine, described living conditions as "appalling"; the sleeping choices were mud-floor tents or dugouts, with slit trenches close by. Malarial mosquitoes abounded; fortunately, the fliers were given Japanese mosquito netting, something the "mud marines" could only hope for.

The first night the aviators spent ashore, the newly landed Ichiki Battalion attempted to storm the Marine positions, and what became known as the Battle of the "Tenaru River" broke out. By morning, the 1st Battalion of the 1st Marines had killed over 800 attackers, many in hand-to-hand combat, before the surviving Japanese had retreated back into the jungle. Smith, Carl, and the other experienced pilots flew two strafing missions in the afternoon that convinced any enemy troops still alive to get away.

The day after MAG-23's arrival, Admiral Fletcher's carriers provided cover for two transports that slipped into Sealark Channel and unloaded more supplies. MAG-23's senior mechanics came ashore from the destroyer that had brought them up from Efate, a welcome addition. Major Smith's division of four Wildcats provided cover over the transports; during the noon hour they tangled with six Zeros. Smith found out quickly that the Wildcat was heavy enough that it could disengage from the superior Zeros by diving away, if it had sufficient altitude. In the fight, Smith's wingman, Sergeant John Lindsey, was hit, but managed to make it back to Henderson Field. The Wildcat was a write-off after he made a dead-stick wheels-up landing. Smith claimed a Zero shot down, and later that afternoon Second Lieutenant E.A. Trowbridge claimed two more in a second fight, but Japanese records indicated all planes returned to Rabaul. In the next two days, the squadron claimed two more Zeros for a total of five and proved they could stay in the same air with their more-experienced enemies.

For the fliers at Henderson, there was only the most basic maintenance of the most critical items in the aircraft. Aircrews and ground personnel both sweated under the tropic sun to fuel the planes manually from 55-gallon avgas drums the men carried by hand to each plane, then hand-pumped the gas. The gravel that covered the airstrip battered the undersides of the airplanes from prop wash. Only the ruggedness of the Wildcats and the Dauntlesses kept them operating. Sleep at night was fitful and often spent curled in a slit trench or foxhole while "Washing Machine Charlie," one of the Japanese floatplanes based in the Shortlands that owned the night sky over Henderson Field, dropped anti-personnel bombs and destroyed sleep between bombs with the sound of its engine.

The Marines were reinforced on August 22, when the first P-400 Airacobras of the USAAF's 67th "Fighting Cocks" Fighter Squadron arrived, flying up from Espiritu Santo. The squadron had endured many tribulations in becoming operational after they originally arrived in Australia in early March. They had then been shipped to New Caledonia to provide fighter defense for the French colony. Once there, they unloaded the 47 crated fighters that had accompanied them, to discover that these were ex-RAF P-400 Airacobras, which no one in the unit had ever seen before. Not only that, there were no erection manuals included. The squadron had ten sets of basic mechanic's tools, but none of the specialized tools necessary for assembling their fighters. The first task involved dragging the crated airplanes 35 miles from the port to their airfield, a primitive dirt strip at Tontouta, which took eight hours for each plane and was completed over a week.

Veteran line chief Master Sergeant Robert Foye got his mechanics together and built an A-frame assembly rig from old timbers. Piecing through the first plane, they managed to discover what went where, and after a week they began producing airplanes at the rate of one and a half a day. Foye remembered one plane in particular. "It evidently had the electrical circuit hooked up at the factory by a maniac. When you pressed the flap switch, the wheels would retract, press the wheel retraction and the guns would fire. It took a week to straighten it out."

By the time the squadron arrived at Henderson Field, the pilots had four months of flying experience. They would soon find out how badly outclassed the fighters they had struggled so hard to make flyable were when they entered combat.

The Marines' first real test came on August 23, when a PBY spotted Admiral Tanaka's transport force advancing down the Slot. A "maximum effort" strike of nine SBDs and 12 F4Fs was sent off, but by the time they arrived at the reported position, the wily Japanese admiral had reversed course and the ships were out of range of the Marine fliers. The weather was "dirty" with low-hanging clouds and rain that created near-zero visibility when the planes strayed into a thunderstorm, and the fliers had difficulty finding their way back to the island after reluctantly giving up the search for the missing enemy.

The big test for VMF-223 came the next day, August 24. While the Navy engaged in what would come to be known as the Battle of the Eastern Solomons, six B5N2 Kates and 15 Zeros were launched from the Japanese carrier *Ryūjō*; they rendezvoused over Florida Island with 20 Bettys of the 25th Air Flotilla. Forewarned by the coastwatchers on the islands up the chain, Smith had been able to lead 14 Wildcats to 20,000 feet.

Marion Carl's division struck first. Carl shot a Zero out of the sky in his first pass while Lieutenant Trowbridge also got one. Carl then spotted the carrier bombers and went after them, shooting down two Kates, while First Lieutenant Zenneth Pond claimed two Zeros and Sergeant Lindley shot a third enemy fighter out of the formation. With these three victories combined with his three scored at Midway, Captain Marion Carl became the first Marine Corps ace of the Pacific War. The Marines chased the surviving Japanese over Henderson Field. Their final claims were for 20, including seven Zeros; Japanese records credited them with three A6M2s, three B5N2s, and five G4M1s, for American losses of three pilots killed.

While the Marines were showing that even if the Wildcat was outclassed by the opposition, it could still mount an effective defense with the right tactics, the Army fliers of the 67th Squadron were discovering they could barely get to the fight in their P-400s. The first five pilots had spent August 23, the day after their arrival, flying patrols around the island's coast to learn the ropes. The next day, as the Marines went up against the enemy aircraft launched from *Ryūjō*, Captain Dale Brannon and Second Lieutenant Deltis H. Finscher managed to get airborne in their Airacobras just as the field was hit by a string of bombs. While the Marines shot down eight of the nine attacking enemy bombers, Brannon and Finscher ran across a careless Zero at low level and shared the victory as their gunfire set it aflame. The 67th was on the scoreboard.

The next aerial reinforcement of Guadalcanal was accidental. Lieutenant Turner Caldwell's Enterprise Flight 300, which the Big E had launched just before the Japanese strike arrived overhead at the Battle of the Eastern Solomons, had come to the end of their search for the Japanese carriers and Turner led them to Henderson Field since it was not possible to get back to their carrier which had retreated from the battle after being damaged. The eight Scouting 5 (VS-5) and three Bombing 6 (VB-6) SBDs were a welcome addition to the island's offensive force, since they doubled the number of Dauntlesses available. The Navy fliers, along with the Marine and Army fliers, spent the night in foxholes while five Japanese destroyers shelled the Marine positions for two hours.

While the destroyers shelled the field, Mangrum, Captain Iverson, and First Lieutenant Baldinus managed to lift their Dauntlesses off the field at 0230 hours in a fruitless attempt to attack the ships, but were unable to make effective attacks in the darkness, despite aiming at the flashes of gunfire. An hour before dawn, Coral Sea veteran Lieutenant Roger Woodhull, XO of Scouting 5, led Ensigns Walter Coolbaugh and Walter Brown on a mission to bomb the destroyers as they retreated up the Slot. They were unable to locate the enemy in the pre-dawn darkness, and Ensign Brown lost the first Flight 300 Dauntless when he ditched off Malaita, northwest of Guadalcanal, after running out of gas. He and his gunner were rescued by Solomon Islanders and returned to Henderson later that day.

An hour after sunrise, eight SBDs – five Marines led by Mangrum and four Flight 300 planes led by Caldwell – launched to go after the transport force that had been reported shortly after first light by a patrolling PBY. Admiral Tanaka was surprised by the appearance of the eight dive bombers as they burst through the clouds over the fleet. Mangrum led the dive on the old cruiser *Jintsu*, but discovered his bomb wouldn't release. His fledgling wingmen, Second Lieutenants Hise, Thomas, and McAllister, each scored near misses, while First Lieutenant Baldinus planted his bomb on the cruiser's forecastle between the two forward gun mounts, wounding Admiral Tanaka with shrapnel from the explosion. Lieutenant Caldwell missed the largest transport, *Kinryu Maru*, but his wingman, Ensign Christian Fink, put his bomb directly amidships, starting a fire that spread to ammunition that exploded and stopped the ship dead in the water. Admiral Tanaka transferred to one of the destroyers while the damaged *Jintsu* set course for Truk.

Mangrum ended the encounter by making a second dive on another transport and managed to yank the manual bomb release hard enough to drop it and set that transport afire also. As he flew off, he encountered an F1M2 "Pete" floatplane, but his guns wouldn't fire and he dodged into a cloud. The Dauntlesses ran across other Japanese floatplanes on the way back to Henderson and their gunners claimed two. That night, the Marine aviators got their first full night's sleep when the enemy left them alone.

On August 25, nine more P-400s, led by Captain John Thompson, showed up from New Caledonia in the middle of an air raid. They were quickly refueled so they could get clear of the field. With 14 fighters the USAAF categorized as interceptors, each heavily armed with a 20mm cannon and two .50-caliber machine guns in the nose with a further four .30-caliber weapons in the wings, the pilots looked forward to showing what they could do against the Japanese bombers.

On August 28 at 1700 hours, a pair of scouting dive bombers spotted four troop-carrying enemy destroyers a mere 70 miles from the island. The two attacked but scored no hits. Their frantic sighting report brought 11 Marine and Navy Dauntlesses to the ships within 30 minutes. Turner Caldwell led five Navy SBDs in first, and the sharp-eyed Ensign Fink drilled the destroyer *Asagiri* directly amidships with his 1,000-pounder. The ship blew up and sank in a matter of minutes. While the Marines badly damaged *Yugiri*, Caldwell hit the *Shirakumo* so badly she had to be towed by *Amagiri*, the one remaining undamaged enemy ship; she also managed to inflict the only American casualty when her AA fire hit Second Lieutenant Oliver Mitchell's SBD, which crashed into the sea with the loss of both pilot and gunner. They were VMSB-232's only fatalities during their tour.

The spirits of the "Fighting Cocks" fell on August 29 when 12 Airacobras took off to intercept the incoming raid, but could only circle helplessly at their maximum altitude of 14,000 feet while the Marines downed eight of the enemy in a battle several thousand feet above them. The next day 11 P-400s went up to intercept what they were told were enemy dive bombers. The "dive bombers" turned out to be 20 Zeros, which tore through the "Fighting Cocks'" formation with guns blazing, knocking down four Airacobras while the seven survivors limped back to Henderson riddled by enemy gunfire. Only Captain Thompson was able to claim a Zero, and he paid for his victory with 15 bullet holes in his fighter and one in his shoulder.

In the course of three days of combat, the 67th had gone from 14 to three serviceable planes, and the pilots now referred to the P-400s as "klunkers." As Captain Brannon put it, "We thought we were a fighter outfit, but if you got into combat with a Zero, you were done." General Vandegrift was so disappointed with the P-400s that he begged the USAAF not to send any more and condemned them in his diary as "practically worthless for any kind of altitude fighting." The next month would show the Airacobras could provide valuable service to the Marines in a way no one had expected.

The Army fliers weren't the only ones who had suffered loss. After only six days of combat, General Vandegrift recorded in his diary that 11 of the 31 Wildcats and Dauntlesses that had landed on August 20 were either lost or down for maintenance that could not be provided at the field, due to lack of spare parts and necessary tools. Nine of VMSB-232's Dauntlesses were operational, while two others were grounded awaiting the arrival of spare parts.

On August 30, *Long Island* again turned into the wind 100 miles south of Guadalcanal and launched the rest of Air Group 23's Wildcats and Dauntlesses. VMF-224's 19 Wildcats, led by Major Bob Galer, and VMSB-231's dozen Dauntlesses led by Major Leo Smith effectively doubled the Henderson force. Additional combat experience appeared in the person of Galer's Executive Officer (XO), Captain Elmer Glidden, another VMF-221 veteran of Midway. Shortly after their arrival, a Marine R4D transport delivered Brigadier General Roy S. Geiger, a World War I veteran of the Marine Northern Bombing Force in France who had led other Marine units through the banana wars of the interwar period, assigned as overall commander of what came to be called the Cactus Air Force. Two additional transports put into Sealark Channel that afternoon. They unloaded ammunition, aviation gasoline, spare parts, and the rest of the ground echelon for MAG-23. Over the course of the next few days, the would-be "hangar queens" on the field were repaired and brought up to operational status.

The battle for Guadalcanal had only just begun.

4

GREEN HELL

While the Navy was able to commence a limited offensive operation in the Solomons, the Allied forces in the Southwest Pacific area were still as limited and stretched as thin as they had been in the spring, with General MacArthur fighting as hard with Washington to obtain the necessary forces to oppose the Japanese as his men did fighting the enemy. The USAAF's primary focus in the Pacific during the second half of 1942, following the successful defense of Darwin in the spring and summer by the 49th Fighter Group, would move to New Guinea. The largest island in the world, New Guinea was rightly seen as the gateway to Australia if the Japanese were successful in their planned conquest. The newly established Fifth Air Force would fight there with limited force as the Air Force's new commander fought repeated battles with USAAF headquarters in Washington over the policy of placing air force priority on the struggle in the European Theater. This fight to obtain first-rate equipment with which to oppose the enemy was as important as the actual air battles themselves. In the overall scheme of Allied battle in the South Pacific to force the Japanese to retreat, the battles in the Solomons and New Guinea would become a pincer to neutralize Rabaul.

New Guinea is one of the most inhospitable environments for modern warfare on earth. The world's largest island, it is covered in heavy jungle. Located just south of the equator, the weather systems are unpredictable and fast-changing, with monster thunderstorms that are a greater threat to aircraft than the enemy forming quickly. New Guinea's spine is the forbidding Owen Stanley Range, with peaks as high as 15,000 feet and possessing a dangerous weather system all its own.

In 1942, many of the indigenous people of the island had never been in contact with Westerners, and several tribes were still headhunters and cannibals. A flier parachuting into this jungle faced the problem that he could be mere feet from a trail and not know it, while the humans in the jungle could stalk him without their presence being known. Survival in such a situation was not easy, with the odds strongly against the downed aviator.

The Far East Air Force still struggled to oppose the enemy as effort went in to rebuilding the force after the disasters in the Philippines and Netherlands East Indies that spring. The 19th Bomb Group struggled to maintain serviceability of its B-17s, many of which had survived the battles over Java and the Philippines in the earlier, darker days of the war. Formations of three or four B-17s managed to fly from Port Moresby to bomb Rabaul at night from April 1942 onward, though their numbers were too few to really inflict damage on the enemy.

The dwindling force of B-17s was reinforced over the summer and fall of 1942 with small numbers of new B-17Fs to replace the aging B-17Es, but the Flying Fortress had priority for groups headed to England. Even with the new planes, the old survivors continued to fly. B-17E 41-2417, another Pearl Harbor raid survivor which had been named "Monkey Bizz-ness" and had survived the Java campaign, was distinguished from other B-17s by her distinctive multi-color camouflage that had been applied by the Hawaiian Air Depot. The old bomber flew one of the most unusual missions of the war the night of March 22–23, 1943, when she dropped two 2,000-pound bombs into the Matupi Volcano outside Rabaul town in an unsuccessful attempt to cause an eruption and destroy the base. Hitting Rabaul would have to wait another six months until the campaign had seized bases that put the planes General Kenney managed to obtain in range of the base.

The fight for adequate resources was all-consuming. A shipment of 100 crated P-400s that had been on their way to the Philippines when it became clear the islands were lost had been diverted to Brisbane in March. The P-400 had originally been known as the Airacobra I when ordered by the RAF, but the airplanes had been spurned by the British in the fall of 1941 when the first squadron equipped with the aircraft had found the performance was not what Bell Aircraft had promised, and the fighter was found unable to meet the demanding high-altitude combat environment in western Europe. They differed from the standard Bell

P-39D Airacobra then serving in the USAAF in being equipped with a 20mm Oerlikon cannon in the nose rather than a 37mm cannon. Following their rejection by the RAF, the undelivered airplanes on the British order were seized by the USAAF, which designated them P-400 to differentiate from the standard P-39.

The first unit equipped with the P-400 was the 8th Fighter Group, which had already received some P-39s. They were able to move up to Port Moresby in late April where they were thrown into the thick of combat. The next to take on the P-400 was the 35th Group, which had originally been scheduled to move to the Philippines in the fall of 1941. The unit's 21st and 34th pursuit squadrons arrived shortly before the outbreak of war; both were lost in the desperate fight. The group headquarters was held at Pearl Harbor until early February, when they were sent to Australia, arriving on February 25, 1942. The 39th "Cobras" and 40th "Fighting Red Devils" squadrons were assigned to the group in March. In late April, they were equipped with P-400s. The pilots of the 39th Squadron had experience with the Airacobra, having been the first squadron equipped with the fighter in early 1941, and they assisted the 40th Squadron's pilots in the transition. The two squadrons flew to Port Moresby on June 2. They replaced two squadrons of the 8th Group, which had lost 20 P-400s in combat since late April. The 35th Group's tour was not as difficult, since the Imperial Navy units at Lae and Salamaua that had mauled the 8th Group's P-400s were pulled out in July and returned to Rabaul, replaced by less-experienced Japanese Army Air Force (JAAF) squadrons.

MacArthur was so hard-pressed to gain support for his efforts that when Congressman Lyndon B. Johnson, a naval reserve Lieutenant Commander, arrived in Australia on a fact-finding mission in late May, the general went out of his way to accord the congressman and his fellow fact-finders every deference, despite his initial suspicion that they had been sent by Roosevelt to find fault with him so he could be relieved and sent home. Johnson, an ardent prewar interventionist, had promised his constituents that if the country went to war, he would leave his congressional seat and enter active service, which he had volunteered for following Pearl Harbor. After several months on the west coast spent supervising shipbuilding contracts, he had convinced President Roosevelt to send him to the Pacific to personally see what the situation was. While he and the others visited various bases in Australia, Johnson repeatedly requested an opportunity to see combat. MacArthur finally decided to grant the request in hopes Johnson would return home with a positive account of how well the fliers were doing despite their lack of equipment, and Johnson was assigned as an observer for a mission by the B-26s of the 22nd Bomb Group to bomb Lae on June 9, 1942. Such a mission was actually quite dangerous, since the bombers flew without fighter escort and the enemy always opposed them.

Johnson had originally been assigned to fly with the crew of the "Wabash Cannonball," whose pilot was First Lieutenant Willis G. Bench. After meeting the crew and touring the plane, he felt the need to relieve himself before takeoff. Returning to the flight line, he found his seat on the plane occupied by Lieutenant Colonel Francis R. Stevens, another observer on the fact-finding mission. Johnson then asked First Lieutenant Walter H. Greer, pilot of "The Heckling Hare," if he could fly the mission in that plane; Greer agreed to bring him along.

The flight was uneventful until the bombers crossed the Owen Stanleys, where they were intercepted by Japanese fighters. The "Wabash Cannonball" was hit and crashed into the sea, killing all aboard. The "Heckling Hare" suffered failure of an electrical generator for one of its engines, which meant the propeller could not be controlled; the engine was shut down and the prop feathered as the B-26 aborted the mission, but not before it was raked by fire from an intercepting Zero. The bomber was met on its return by General MacArthur, who awarded Johnson a Silver Star on the spot, with a later citation that noted the congressman's "marked coolness despite the hazards involved," concluding that "his gallant action enabled him to obtain and return with valuable information." No one else on the crew was mentioned.

Johnson was at first embarrassed by the award, but when he was recalled to Washington following FDR's decision that congressmen should remain in office, he promised MacArthur that he would support sending additional supplies and units to the theater, which had been the general's purpose in making the award. Once returned, Johnson forgot his initial embarrassment over the award and made a point of publicizing his "combat service" in his future political campaigns, to the point where he embarrassed other military veterans who knew the truth. He was, however, good for his word and once back in Washington he did call for sending additional support to MacArthur's command throughout the rest of the war.

The Japanese threat to Port Moresby by amphibious invasion ended with the Battle of the Coral Sea, but there was still the possibility of the Japanese taking the base by an overland invasion through the Owen Stanley Mountains, and the airfields around Moresby were regularly raided by the Japanese beginning in April after they had taken the airfields at Lae and Salamaua on the northern coast. Boyd D. Wagner, recognized as the first American ace of the war during the fighting in the Philippines, had by April been promoted to Lieutenant Colonel and placed in charge of USAAF fighter units at Port Moresby. "Cyclone's Flying Circus," as the 8th Group was known for their commander, Major Emmett "Cyclone" Davis, was the first fighter unit to move from Australia to New Guinea, with 28 P-400s of the 35th and 36th Pursuit Squadrons arriving at 12-Mile 'Drome by April 27. On the afternoon of April 30, Wagner led 26 Airacobras on their first combat mission, a strafing attack on the Japanese airfields and fuel dumps at Lae and Salamaua. The Japanese had warning of their approach and the defending Zeros engaged the attackers in an intense dogfight. Four Airacobras were lost, but the Americans claimed three Zeros shot down.

The loss of the four P-400s was exacerbated by the fact that the next flight sent north was not as fortunate as those that had preceded it. On April 29, 11 P-400s left Woodstock airfield outside Brisbane, headed for Moresby with a stop for fuel at Horn Island before crossing Torres Strait. They were caught in a severe equatorial rainstorm 170 miles south of Horn Island. Without enough fuel to turn around and fly the 270 miles back to Woodstock, First Lieutenant George Green, the formation leader, elected to push on through the weather to Horn Island. By the time he and First Lieutenant Norman Morris arrived at Horn Island after crossing Cape York, Green realized the rest of the flight had gotten lost in the bad weather. The two had little fuel remaining; Morris ran out of gas on approach to the field but was able to make a successful forced landing. First Lieutenant Jack Hall and Second Lieutenant John Long were killed in the thunderstorms around Cape Grenville, while seven other Airacobras made forced landings on the coast of Cape York as they ran out of gas. Five remaining P-400s finally showed up at Horn Island. On May 1, a further flight of six Airacobras ran into bad weather and all were lost in forced landings on Cape York. Fortunately, all pilots other than Hall and Long were rescued.

Once the P-400 entered combat over New Guinea, it was found to be completely outclassed by the Zero. Lacking a supercharger, the airplane was virtually useless above 10,000–12,000 feet, which meant the enemy almost always used their height advantage to initiate combat. The inexperienced American pilots were also up against the experienced pilots of the Tainan Air Corps. The Airacobra's leakproof gas tank and rugged construction saved many pilots who managed to bring their damaged aircraft back to base, while the heavy firepower of a 20mm cannon and two .50-caliber machine guns in the nose meant that if they could fire on a Zero they had a chance of destroying it (most pilots removed the four .30-caliber wing guns to save weight, since they were not of particular use in combat). However, the superior maneuverability, greater acceleration, and higher ceiling of the Zero meant their opponents could initiate or avoid combat almost at will.

Only one prewar USAAF fighter was competitive with what the enemy had produced: the P-38 Lightning. Originally designed in response to a 1938 Air Corps request for proposals for a high-altitude point defense interceptor, the airplane was among the first capable of a top speed over 400mph. Experiments in the fall of 1941 with a P-38D equipped with two 160-gallon drop tanks had demonstrated the airplane's potential as a long-range fighter. The P-38 had only begun to enter service in June, 1941, when the 1st Pursuit Group received the first 13 pre-production YP-38s. Production ramped up with the 36 P-38Ds delivered that September, which were the first equipped with self-sealing fuel tanks and armor plate. A follow-on order for 210 P-38Es was still at the beginning of its delivery cycle when the United States went to war on December 8, 1941. On Friday, December 5, 1941, there were 69 P-38s of all sub-types on the AAF roster; none were combat-capable. At this point in its development, the P-38 was full of gremlins, not the least being an unfortunate tendency to tuck the nose under in a dive, as controls stiffened while the dive angle increased until the pilot was unable to pull out. When engaged in aerobatics, the Fowler maneuver flaps could deploy differentially with the airplane then going inverted without notice.

Following Pearl Harbor, the USAAF needed to create units to take the P-38 to England as rapidly as possible. The 1st Pursuit Group lost more than half of its trained pilots and ground crews between mid-December 1941 and early January 1942, as experienced personnel were assigned as cadre to the new 14th and 82nd Pursuit Groups. Second Lieutenant Robert Eby, who had been transferred to the 49th Squadron of the 14th Group, remembered January 7, 1942 as a red-letter day:

"That day, we transferred to Long Beach Airport to check out in P-38s. Of the other two squadrons in the group, one flew P-38s and P-43s, while the third was equipped with Vultee P-66 fighters, which were terrible." The 14th Group's motley collection of fighters went to Hamilton Field, north of San Francisco, on January 20. Eby recalled:

We trained new pilots and prepared for overseas duty. Twice a week the call came down from Fighter Command to ship a certain number of pilots overseas the next day, which was done by drawing names out of a hat. We were one of two groups defending the northern West Coast, with the other at Paine Field, Washington. In the meantime, we were averaging more than one crash a week in the P-38, with most of those being fatalities. Pilot morale was low.

Once the 14th Group arrived at Hamilton Field, the 78th Pursuit Group was formed from the unit. The two groups operated as one while their pilot ranks were fleshed out with new flight school graduates, most of whom had no twin-engine training. Newly promoted Captain Gene Reynolds remembered:

A high-time P-38 pilot in this period was one who could record his total P-38 time in low double digits. At this time, we were losing approximately a pilot a month to fatal crashes. One I had to investigate north of Hamilton Field had gone straight in from a vertical dive. The two engines required a backhoe to retrieve them from ten feet in the ground. A jellied mass the size of two basketballs was all that was identifiable of the pilot.

On May 6, 1942, 21-year-old Second Lieutenant Richard Ira Bong reported to the 49th Squadron. He had been fascinated by flying since age six, when he saw airplanes flying over the family farm in Poplar, Wisconsin, as they delivered mail to President Coolidge's Summer White House in nearby Superior. He became an avid model airplane builder and read everything he could find about the pilots of World War I. The boy convinced his father to take him to see Charles A. Lindbergh when he arrived in Milwaukee during his national tour in 1928 and became one of a future generation of pilots who were inspired by "The Lone Eagle." In 1938, while studying at Superior State Teacher's College, Bong enrolled in

73

the Civilian Pilot Training Program, the successful completion of which allowed him to skip basic training when he joined the USAAF on May 29, 1941. Following graduation from flight school on January 19, 1942, he had been assigned as a gunnery instructor pilot at Luke Army Air Field in Arizona. At the time, AAF gunnery training for future fighter pilots was so abysmal that Bong later recalled those three months as "the blind leading the blind." Bong had no twin-engine time when he arrived at Hamilton, but he was a good student and soloed within two weeks of his arrival.

Once they were turned loose to gain time in the P-38, the young pilots discovered there were Navy squadrons at Alameda Naval Air Station, just south of the Oakland side of the San Francisco Bay Bridge. Daily meetings between P-38s and F4F Wildcats ensued, giving the pilots experience in what would be known to a later generation of pilots as "dissimilar type training." The Army pilots were under strict orders not to fly under the Bay or Golden Gate bridges, while the Navy pilots had no such restriction. Thus, the Wildcat pilots knew they could always break away from a disadvantageous position by diving under the bridges, secure in the knowledge their competitors could not follow on pain of being grounded for 30 days.

For the P-38 pilots, the bridges were a temptation that some could not resist. On June 12, Bong became involved in a "hassle" with the Navy pilots and followed them under the Golden Gate Bridge. Now that he'd done it, he figured he might as well go all the way and looped the big P-38 over the bridge and under it again, then banked around to the San Francisco waterfront and flew up Market Street at an altitude so low it was reported people in second-story offices were looking down at him. He finished off by banking over Twin Peaks and disappearing out toward the ocean. Unbeknownst to Bong until he landed back at Hamilton Field, one of the cars that had been stopped in the traffic jam he'd created on the bridge was the base's commanding general. He was immediately called to the general's office where he received a chewing out that ended with a recommendation that he stock up on Second Lieutenant's bars since he would never be promoted past that lowly rank. He was also grounded, which kept him from accompanying the rest of the group to England in July.

Following the chewing out by his field commander, Bong was summoned to the offices of the Commanding General of the Fourth Air Force at The Presidio in San Francisco. There, he met Brigadier General George C. Kenney. Kenney was a one-of-a-kind Army Air Forces officer.

A New Englander born in Nova Scotia on August 6, 1889, while his family were vacationing there, he had left MIT after three years of study to work as an instrument technician with the Quebec Saguenay Railroad. Following the entry of the United States into World War I, Kenney enlisted in the Signal Corps where he was accepted for flight training and learned to fly under the instruction of legendary aviator Bert Acosta. Sent to France, Kenney flew the Salmson 2 reconnaissance-bomber in the 91st Aero Squadron, where he was credited with two victories over German fighters. After the war he remained in the service and flew reconnaissance missions along the US–Mexico border during the Mexican Revolution. After receiving a commission in the Regular Army in 1920, he attended the Air Corps Tactical School at Maxwell Field, where he became an advocate for tactical aviation, rather than becoming one of the strategic bombing advocates. Assigned as Assistant Military Attaché to the American Embassy in Paris in 1940, he witnessed the German Blitzkrieg that defeated France in five weeks and returned to the United States even more committed to the development of tactical aviation and battlefield interdiction.

By May 1942, Douglas MacArthur had become disenchanted with General Brereton, his Far East Air Force commander. Fortunately for the course of the war in the Southwest Pacific, Army Air Forces Chief General H.H. "Hap" Arnold chose Kenney as his replacement, ordering him to report to MacArthur by July 1. Kenney had gathered all the information he could find about New Guinea and was convinced the war there would be one primarily of tactical aviation, not a war of strategic bombers. He was also convinced that the P-38 was the airplane he would need to meet the Japanese on an even footing, and convinced Arnold to ship 50 P-38s to Australia that fall, along with some experienced pilots. When Lieutenant Bong arrived in his office for disciplinary action, Kenney was more interested in the fact he was the kind of P-38 pilot who would do the things he was accused of having done. In his later memoirs, Kenney wrote that he told Bong, "If you didn't want to fly down Market Street, I wouldn't have you in my Air Force, but you are not to do it any more and I mean what I say." It was the beginning of what would be a fruitful relationship over the next two years. Bong was still grounded when Kenney departed for Australia at the end of the month, but his orders to the Fifth Air Force were not long in coming. He arrived in the Southwest Pacific on September 1 and was assigned to the 9th Fighter Squadron of the 49th Fighter Group, which was still flying P-40E Warhawks at Darwin.

Once General Kenney arrived, officially taking command on August 4, his first act was a whirlwind inspection of the combat squadrons. Following that, he ordered a stand-down of combat operations to allow the maintenance crews to get the B-17s ready for a big mission. He informed MacArthur that he intended to send 16 B-17s to bomb Vunakanau airfield on August 7, where there were an estimated 150 Japanese aircraft, to divert the enemy's attention from the Marine landings that were to take place at Guadalcanal that day. The mission bears special note, since Captain Harl Pease, one of the 19th Group pilots who had survived the Japanese attack on Clark Field on the opening day of the war, and flown in every important mission since, was lost with his crew in circumstances that later brought him a posthumous award of the Medal of Honor.

The day before, Pease had flown a reconnaissance mission to Rabaul but suffered an engine failure that forced him to abort and return to Mareeba Field in Australia for an engine change. Despite having been taken off operations while his plane was repaired, Pease determined that he would participate in this vital mission regardless. There was a war-weary B-17E on the field at Mareeba, which had been declared unserviceable and was being used for spare parts to keep other bombers flying. The old plane was B-17E 41-2429, which carried the name "Why Don't We Do This More Often?" after a popular song of the time. She had an interesting history, being one of the 12 Flying Fortresses that arrived over Pearl Harbor during the Japanese attack and was later flown in the first trans-Pacific reinforcement mission to Australia in late December 1941 to join the 19th Group. After participating in the Java campaign, she was one of four B-17s sent to Mindanao in March 1942 to evacuate General MacArthur and his staff to Australia, a mission that was led by Pease in a different bomber. MacArthur had taken one look at the battered bomber, which had bullet holes covered with metal from cut-up C-ration cans, and refused to fly aboard her. Pease and his crew worked through the day to rearm the bomber and fit her with long-range fuel tanks in the bomb bay with a hand pump for fuel transfer. In the last light of day, he took off with his crew – who had all volunteered to accompany him in the old bomber – and touched down at Port Moresby at 0100 hours on August 7.

After only a few hours' rest, Pease took off with the rest of the force, led by Lieutenant Colonel Ralph Carmichael. One B-17 crashed on takeoff, while two others turned back because of mechanical problems. Despite losing an engine during the flight, Pease managed to keep up with the formation. When they were 40 to 50 miles from the target, they were intercepted by more than 30 Japanese fighters. 41-2429 was on the side of the formation that bore the brunt of the hostile attack, but with accurate shooting by the crew, they succeeded in knocking down several Zeros. The remaining 13 B-17s went over Vunakanau at 22,000 feet, still under attack from enemy fighters, and dropped their bombs on the airfield. Simpson Harbor was filled with ships, and crews later reported that antiaircraft fire was heavy. After 25 minutes of aerial combat, the formation dived into cloud cover and the Zeros finally broke off. However, Pease's bomber had lost a second engine and fallen behind the rest of the group. The last sight the others had of "Why Don't We Do This More Often?" was when the old bomber caught fire while under attack by the Zeros and Pease dropped the flaming bomb bay tank.

No one saw the final action, but it was later learned that Pease and another crew member had been able to bail out before the Flying Fortress went down in flames. Both were captured and taken to the POW camp at Rabaul. On October 8, 1942, Pease, along with three other American and two Australian POWs were forced to dig their own graves before being beheaded. After the war, the remains of three of his crew were recovered and identified, but his remains and those killed with him were not found. Word of what happened got out of the camp with an escaped prisoner who was picked up by the coastwatchers on New Britain. Informed of Pease's death, Douglas MacArthur endorsed General Kenney's recommendation for the award of the Medal of Honor and it was presented by President Roosevelt to Pease's parents at the White House on December 2, 1942.

While the 49ers' 7th Squadron moved to New Guinea in September, followed in October by the 8th Squadron, the 9th remained at Darwin for the time being. General Kenney's plan for the 50 P-38s he had been able to convince General Arnold to give him was that they would equip a squadron in each of his three fighter groups. The 9th Squadron had been picked to become the 49ers' P-38 unit. As things turned out, Kenney was forced to lobby for additional P-38s to make up for training and combat losses in the first squadron to receive P-38s, which led to delays in equipping the other squadrons until early 1943.

The first squadron in the Pacific to re-equip with P-38s was the 39th Cobras of the 35th Group. They had been notified of their good fortune after their return from Port Moresby on July 26, and the twin-tail fighters had started showing up later in August after they had been cleaned up from "cocooning" for overseas shipment. Several of the P-38 pilots General Kenney had brought with him were assigned to the squadron to assist in the transition. Once they had received their full complement of 24 fighters, the squadron decided to paint tiger mouths over the radiator intakes of each engine similar to what the American Volunteer Group had used on their P-40s, as their squadron insignia. By late September, after experiencing several losses in training while the P-38s were modified to meet the requirements of the theater, the 39th was considered combat-capable. They flew to Port Moresby on October 18, 1942, where they were based at a new airfield recently hacked out of the jungle and known as "14-Mile 'Drome" for its distance from the town of Port Moresby.

While the 49ers' 9th Squadron awaited the delivery of its new fighters, several of the pilots were sent on to New Guinea in late November on temporary duty to gain combat experience with the 39th Fighter Squadron. Bong was one of those picked – after refresher training on the P-38, he and the others arrived at 14-Mile 'Drome on November 14. At the same time, the rest of the 9th Squadron arrived in New Guinea with their P-40Es to relieve the 7th Squadron.

General Kenney visited the 39th Squadron shortly after Bong's arrival, and promised the award of an Air Medal to the first P-38 pilot to shoot down an enemy plane. Over their first few weeks of operations, the P-38s had failed to encounter any Japanese fighters, since the Japanese had avoided the new fighters when they were spotted. On November 26, four P-38s were sent to make a ground strafing and bombing attack on Lae Airdrome. Once over the enemy field, the Americans taunted the Japanese on the radio, daring them to come up for a fight. Shortly thereafter, an enemy fighter was spotted taking off. Lieutenant Ferrault banked out of formation and initiated an attack. Just before he was ready to open fire, he remembered he still had his bombs, and quickly dropped them. The bombs fell in the water at the end of the runway and exploded, just as the enemy pilot lifted off and flew into the explosion, crashing in the bay. Back at their base, General Kenney kidded the young pilot that he had not actually been the first to shoot down an enemy airplane, but he still awarded him the medal.

Once in New Guinea, the 49th Fighter Group made up for lost time as compared with the other two fighter groups. On December 7,

1942, the first anniversary of Pearl Harbor, the 7th and 9th squadrons intercepted 18 G3M bombers, escorted by 12 Zeros as they approached Port Moresby. Employing the tactics they had developed over Darwin of avoiding combat with the fighters while attacking the bombers only from a height advantage that gave their heavy P-40s the speed to dive through the escorts, the 49ers shot down six of the bombers for no losses.

After numerous patrols during December while the ground forces fought to take Buka, the P-38 pilots finally got to show what they could do on December 27, 1942. Twelve P-38s were on alert at Laloki, an advanced airfield used by fighters for refueling, when word was received that a Japanese formation had been spotted headed for Port Moresby. The P-38s took off, led by Captain Thomas Lynch, who had already scored two enemy aircraft while flying the P-400. His wingman was Second Lieutenant John H. Mangas, with Dick Bong flying as element lead with his wingman, Second Lieutenant Kenneth Sparks. The other eight fighters took off minutes later. Lynch's flight spotted a 35-plane formation over Dobodura – Val dive bombers escorted by Zeros. The four P-38s had an altitude advantage and Lynch led them in a dive into the enemy formation.

Bong became separated from the others and found himself surrounded by enemy planes. He managed to shoot down a Val and a Zero before diving out of the fight. In the meantime, Lynch shot down three Zeros, while Mangas and Sparks each downed one. As the battle spread, the eight other P-38s following joined the fight, which lasted a good 20 minutes – a lifetime in air combat. On their return, the pilots submitted claims for a total of 15 enemy aircraft shot down. They were credited with nine Zeros and two Vals. It was the most decisive American air combat victory in the Southwest Pacific Theater in the war to date and confirmed to General Kenney that he needed more P-38s.

The day before Bong and the other P-38 pilots scored their victory, First Lieutenant John D. Landers, a 9th Squadron veteran of the 49ers' early days at Darwin, discovered just how dangerous New Guinea could be for a pilot forced to bail out over the jungle.

Unknown to the Allies at the time, the Imperial Navy had found itself stretched too tightly with responsibility for defending both the Solomons and New Guinea. On December 18, 1942, the first unit of the Imperial Army Air Force, the 12th Hiko-dan comprising the 1st and 11th sentais, arrived at Vunakanau airfield on Rabaul. The units had brought 60 Ki.43-I "Hayabusa" (Peregrine Falcon) fighters known to the Allies as

"Oscar" with them from Truk. Many pilots in the unit were aces from the fighting in Burma, including Lieutenant Tomoari Hasegawa and warrant officers Naoharu Shiromoto, Haruo Takagaki, and Tokuyasu Ishizuka.

The 1st Chutai of the 11th Sentai flew from Rabaul to Lae on December 20, and entered combat over New Guinea on December 26 when 15 Oscars strafed Dobodura airfield. They were surprised by four 49er P-40s, one of which was flown by Landers. That morning, he was Red Leader for a patrol by the squadron over newly captured Dobodura airfield, the first airfield taken by the Allies on the north side of the Owen Stanleys, flying his P-40E named "Big Doll." Just before the squadron was due to be relieved from a patrol that had to that point proved monotonous, with the enemy failing to make an appearance, an enemy formation of Zeros (which were actually the Ki.43 Oscars of the 1st Chutai) was spotted flying at low level and heading for Dobodura for a strafing attack. Landers called Blue Flight to join his Red Flight as they dived toward the enemy formation.

Landers' flight hit the "Zeros" while the others went after the Vals. The P-40s were unseen by the enemy, who continued on as Landers curved in and exploded the wingman of the enemy leader, then turned his guns on the leader, who finally spotted the oncoming nemesis and banked away to the right, but not before Landers hit his engine. Landers grimly hung on the enemy fighter's tail and poured in a second burst. The fighter never completed its turn, as it fell into a dive straight into the jungle-covered mountains below. The two were victories five and six for Landers, making him an ace.

When Landers leveled off 100 feet above the jungle, tracers suddenly flashed past and he took hits in his right wing. Glancing back, he spotted the enemy fighter on his tail. At low altitude, there was no chance for him to use the P-40's weight to dive away from the enemy fighter, which was easily capable of out-turning him in the kind of fight he was now in. Landers threw "Big Doll" first left, then right, trying to throw off the enemy's aim, but the enemy pilot hung on his tail and continued to pour fire into the P-40. Hit in the engine, Landers' fighter began smoking as he turned over the jungle and tried to work his way up the mountainside to escape through the pass to the southern side of the mountains. The enemy pilot closed in again and opened fire. This time, the P-40's Allison engine was hit solidly and black smoke poured from beneath the cowling. Landers was now at 6,000 feet, and just below the crest of a ridge. He pushed the throttle to maximum and the engine responded with its last power. He crested the ridge with 50 feet to spare and the clouds right above him. A valley opened beyond. The enemy pilot didn't follow as Landers plunged into the dead-end valley. There was no place below where he could safely crash-land.

A moment later, the engine seized and quit. Landers was only 1,000 feet above the jungle when he unstrapped, slid back his canopy, and leaped into space. The rudder flashed past him and he yanked the D-ring on his parachute. The canopy spread above him an instant later. He swung once before the tree tops rushed past him and he went into the limbs and branches. Suddenly he was jerked to a stop as the parachute canopy tangled in the trees. Pulling himself up the shroud lines, Landers climbed back to where the parachute was caught. Pulling his machete, he cut the canopy and then fashioned a rope from the canopy and shrouds so he could lower himself safely to the ground 50 feet below. He still had his map, but had no idea where he was.

Once down, he began hacking his way through the thickly tangled undergrowth toward a stream he had spotted while in his parachute. The distance was less than 100 yards away, but it took him 40 minutes to hack his way to where he could catch sight of it. Fifteen minutes of hard work later, he finally got to the stream, where he rested for half an hour before deciding to head upstream in search of a trail, scrambling through the water over the wet rocks. After four hours' hiking in the exhausting heat and humidity, he found a footpath and decided to follow it. Twenty minutes later, he found himself surrounded by nine Papuan natives. Fortunately, they recognized him as an American. They then took him to a path that led downhill, only 20 feet from the stream he had struggled up for four hours.

After a day, the native group arrived at a village, where Landers was introduced to a guide who spoke enough English that they could communicate. Over the next two days, they made their way over the Kokoda Trail, past the rotted remains of Japanese, American, and Australian soldiers, till they reached the coast near Buna and he found an American food dump. The GIs guarding the dump radioed Moresby and, the next day, an Australian coastwatcher arrived to take him to an airfield where he was picked up and returned to the squadron in time to take part in the New Year's festivities as 1942 turned into 1943. Other pilots would not be as lucky as Landers.

Allied fighter pilots would continue to mistake the Ki.43 for the Zero throughout the Pacific War. The two aircraft shared a similarity of planform, with low wings and "bubble" canopies. To add to the confusion, at the outset of the JAAF's involvement in the fighting over New Guinea, there were times when both IJNAF formations of Zeros and JAAF formations of Oscars were involved in the same air battle against the Allies, as happened on December 28 when the 1st Chutai, along with a squadron of Zeros, made a second attack on Dobodura, where they were caught by P-38s of the 49ers' 9th Squadron, claiming five P-38s shot down though there were no US losses. On December 31, Lieutenant Hasegawa – who had first become an ace during the 1939 Nomonhan Incident in which forces of Japan and the Soviet Union had faced off in combat – was shot up by a P-38 off Lae and he made a forced landing at Gasmata, returning to Lae several days later. During the same fight, future 11-victory ace Lieutenant Hironojo Shishimoto made his first victory claim for a P-38 destroyed.

While the three fighter groups struggled to contain their Japanese opponents, the bomber forces available were inadequate to change the situation strategically. There were too few bombers available, with only two squadrons of the 22nd Bomb Group's B-26A Marauders, the 13th Squadron of the 3rd Bomb Group with B-25C Mitchells, and the B-17s of the 19th and 43rd bomb groups.

In March 1942, 14 B-25Cs that had arrived in Australia bound for the Dutch air forces in the Netherlands East Indies had been seized by the USAAF following the Dutch surrender and sent on to the 3rd Bomb Group to supplement their A-20C Havoc attack bombers. By August, three more Mitchells had arrived in Australia. Dubbed a "luxury liner" by its crews, the Mitchell could carry a 4,000-pound bomb load over the Owen Stanleys on bombing missions against the bases at Lae and Salamaua.

The Japanese bases were the major targets of the bombers throughout the fighting in 1942. In a mission flown against Lae on May 16, 14 B-25s and four B-26s set fire to fuel dumps, destroyed buildings, and damaged grounded aircraft. Despite the continual bad weather of the monsoon, five B-25s, 11 B-26s, and two B-17s bombed Lae through an overcast on June 9, followed by a raid on June 16 in which nine B-25s, ten B-26s, and three B-17s scored hits on runways and buildings. Due to the unfavorable weather and the Japanese skill with camouflage, it was difficult to be sure of what damage had been done. Photographic reconnaissance showed the bombs often fell wide of the target.

Despite the Allied raids, the Japanese were able to expand the airfields at both places. While there were never more than 40 fighters at these bases during the spring and summer of 1942, they were enough to maintain a successful defense. On May 24, the Zeros scored a significant victory over eight unescorted B-25s of the 13th Squadron led by squadron commander Captain Herman F. Lowery. The Mitchells attempted to attack from the sea by sweeping wide of Salamaua before turning toward Lae from the east. The bombers were met by 12 Zeros over Huon Gulf. In the first enemy pass, Captain Lowery's B-25 burst into flames and dived into the ocean. As the others flew on, four other B-25s were shot down one by one as the Zeros made repeated passes. A sixth shot-up bomber crash-landed when it touched down at Moresby, leaving only two battered survivors able to fly the next day.

All the bombers remained based in Australia, using the airfields at Port Moresby for a staging and refueling point, since the distance to Rabaul from Townsville was 1,300 miles. After the Battle of the Coral Sea, the B-26s of the 22nd Group were used for attacks on Rabaul, since the heavy bomber groups were reduced to less than half their assigned strength. A mission to Rabaul took three days: on the first day, the Marauders flew up to Moresby, where they refueled and prepared for the 1,000-mile round trip from Moresby to Rabaul the next day, returning to Moresby for fuel before flying back to Australia the following day. The distance was such that the bombers had to put an extra 250-gallon gas tank in their forward bomb bay, reducing the bomb load to only four 500-pound bombs. Formations never exceeded six aircraft – frequently only two or three bombers would get to Rabaul, with the others aborting due to mechanical difficulties or the extreme equatorial weather. Such missions were merely pinpricks that accomplished little more than to remind the Japanese the Americans were still around. Morale in the unit suffered since losses were heavy from weather, mechanical aborts, and enemy action, for such little result.

Between April 6 and May 24, the 22nd Group flew 16 missions against Rabaul. The mission of May 24 was the last flown by medium bombers to Rabaul until October 1943. Despite the small numbers of B-17s, the heavy bombers were at least able to carry a bomb load double that of the Marauders. Due to the small formations, which were limited to four

B-17s at maximum, the raids were flown at night since the Japanese had no effective night defenses. Between June and August, the 19th Group carried out 18 missions against Rabaul. Unfavorable weather and darkness usually prevented any accurate assessment of results.

While the Far East Air Forces claimed more than 80 Japanese planes shot down in the period between the Battle of the Coral Sea and the invasion of Guadalcanal in August, the command suffered air combat losses of 61 fighters and 22 bombers during this period, with an additional ten bombers and a fighter destroyed on the ground at Port Moresby from enemy bombing. The loss of 54 fighters and 23 bombers to accidents demonstrated that weather and difficult operating conditions were at least as dangerous to fliers as the enemy. The discouraging fact that there were constant delays in the arrival of reinforcements and replacements contributed to an overall low morale. Many personnel who had survived the fall of the Philippines and the Indies experienced fatigue, while those who had arrived in the late spring were disillusioned by the meager results they obtained. Promotions were slow in coming considering the risks the aircrews were taking. This was one of the first problems General Kenney dealt with, creating a policy of spot promotions for demonstrated accomplishments that had an immediate effect in raising morale after his arrival.

The Far East Air Force became the Fifth Air Force in August with the arrival of General Kenney. His can-do attitude and willingness to dispense with military bureaucracy whenever it impeded operational efficiency was at least as responsible for the turnaround in accomplishment that began in the fall of 1942 as was the increased arrival of men and equipment he cajoled from his superiors in Washington.

Within a month of the general's arrival, a story circulated through the units about a photo technician who had been installing cameras in the bomb bay of a B-25 for a recon mission. While inside the bomb bay, he was unable to see anyone nearby. When a voice asked him how he was doing, he responded, "I'd be doing a helluva lot better if you could hand me those wrenches there in my tool box." A moment later, a hand appeared under the edge of the bomb bay door, holding the wrenches and the voice said, "Let me know if there's anything else you need." Finishing the installation, the sergeant ducked out of the bomb bay intending to thank his helper, to discover it was General Kenney standing there. Kenney's career leading the Fifth Air Force would demonstrate that personal leadership was at least as important as a regular supply line.

5

MARINE AVIATION'S FINEST HOUR

While the USAAF squadrons battled the Japanese to hold onto Port Moresby, the fighting at Guadalcanal became more desperate. The crucial period between the arrival of VMF-223 at Henderson Field on August 20 and the defeat of the Japanese reinforcement transports by the Cactus Air Force, 87 days later on November 15, has come to be known as "Marine Aviation's finest hour."

After the battles of August following the American invasion of the southern Solomons, there was an eight-day respite from Japanese attacks between September 1 and 8 as the enemy aviation units at Rabaul provided air cover for the Japanese Army forces fighting on New Guinea in the Kokoda Track Campaign. The engineers took the respite from bombing to finish a second airfield, "Fighter One," half a mile from the main strip at Henderson Field. The hastily scraped-out dirt field would soon become known to the fighter pilots as "the Cow Pasture." Due to the heavy losses the Marine aviators had taken following their arrival in late August, Admiral McCain sent reinforcements on September 4 in the form of Lieutenant Commander Leroy Simpler's 24 Wildcats of Fighting 5 and six SBD-3s of Scouting 6 that had been left behind at Espiritu Santo by *Saratoga* before she departed to Pearl Harbor after her torpedoing – among the Scouting 6 pilots was the doughty Ensign John Bridgers and his best friend, Ensign Niles Siebert, with whom he would become "closer than brothers" during their stay on the island. All of Marine Air Group 23 finally assembled on the island when Major Bob Galer brought VMF-224's 19 Wildcats, accompanied by VMSB-232's 12 Dauntlesses, up from Espiritu Santo on September 8, accompanied by nine VMF-212 fighters sent up to become replacements in the Henderson squadrons.

Bridgers later remembered that the morning after their arrival:

We were standing at the flight line when Washing Machine Charlie came over at dawn. We were on one end of the runway while the bombs were dropping on the opposite end. Even at a distance, the exploding bombs seemed close enough for concern and everyone jumped into a large sandbagged foxhole near the operations tent. A *Life* magazine photographer who had come up to the island with us was the last one in and landed atop the squadron members packed beneath him in the revetment. This cameraman was a stout fellow of nearly 300 pounds and, though we were well missed by the bombs, several of us suffered bruises and painful backs. While the news he and the reporter had come to cover was slow for the few days they were there, they made the most of being with us, and went on what we thought of as a "milk run" raid the next day. The next spring, just before I finally departed the Solomons, the April 12, 1943 issues of *Time* and *Life*, in both the stateside and the miniature "battlefield editions" featured accounts of our mission. For our visiting journalists, this was the only story in town thus it was that our "milk run" raid received notoriety far beyond its importance to the conduct of the war. At the end of the war, I was probably best remembered by the folks at home for having my picture in *Life* magazine than for the considerable and significant combat action I saw later in the war. For me, my memories of Guadalcanal are mainly of being fallen on by an overweight photographer and the food, which was even worse than what we had been getting back in New Caledonia.

A combat schedule had developed during late August as a result of the fact the Japanese could only fly a large formation of bombers down from Rabaul in daylight. Weather allowing, the bombers and their escorting fighters would take off from their air bases at Rabaul by 0800 hours, though delays were caused by early morning build-ups of weather over the Solomon Sea that could delay departure until as late as 1000 hours. As the Japanese formation flew down the Slot, the aircraft were spotted by the Australian coastwatchers on the various islands, who radioed their sightings to Cactus Control at Henderson Field. By the time they passed Munda, the defenders on Guadalcanal would man their fighters and take off. The Wildcats needed every minute of warning they could get, since it took around 45 minutes for the airplanes to get to 20,000 feet. The enemy formation would finally arrive between 1100 and 1300 hours. Given the variability of weather, there were a few times where the clouds over the Slot prevented the coastwatchers from spotting the oncoming Japanese in time to give sufficient warning.

Fortunately, during the break in the Japanese attacks, a radar set had been installed at Henderson Field on September 2, which allowed the defenders to be vectored to the oncoming Japanese from an advantageous position. Marion Carl recalled a typical combat:

> We would be orbiting the island at 20,000 feet when ground control would finally get a radar vector on the incoming formation. The bombers were generally flying at 12,000–13,000 feet with the escorts 1,500 feet higher. We had learned not to try and stick around, but to dive on them, take a shot, and then if possible zoom back up for another chance. The entire fight would be over inside 20 minutes.

The G4M1 "Betty" bomber lacked armor and self-sealing tanks, and more than lived up to its reputation with Japanese aviators as "a flying cigar." If a Wildcat could put a two-second burst into either engine and that wing, the bomber would generally catch fire quickly. Another target was the pilot's cockpit, just ahead of the wing. Fortunately, the Wildcat was heavy enough that it could dive faster than the lighter Zero, which allowed the Marines to escape.

The Marines weren't always able to outrun the Zeros. When the Japanese resumed their attacks on September 9, Marion Carl replaced squadron CO John L. Smith to lead 16 Marine and Navy Wildcats to intercept 36 Bettys inbound over the Slot. Carl managed to hit two and knock them down in his first pass, but a Zero slipped in behind him when he slowed his dive to go after the second bomber, and shot out his Wildcat's oil lines. With his engine on fire, Carl bailed out, falling free for what seemed an eternity before he felt safe in pulling his ripcord. Moments later, he dropped into Ironbottom Sound, shucking his parachute harness as his feet touched the water. He then treaded water for four hours before he was spotted by a passing native in a canoe, who pulled him aboard. Unfortunately, the native didn't speak

English and Carl didn't know enough Pidgin to communicate that he wanted to be taken back to the Marine positions on the island. Instead, the native put him ashore on the northern end of Guadalcanal, which meant he would have to find his way through the Japanese to get home. He spent September 10 and 11 hiding from Japanese patrols, during which time he met a Fijian medic named Eroni who worked with the coastwatchers and offered to lead him to the Marine lines. They were thwarted in their attempt on September 12, narrowly missing discovery by a Japanese patrol. After hiding in the jungle for a third night, the next morning they found a dilapidated motorboat which they managed to get running. They sailed out into Ironbottom Sound that night, and finally arrived back at the Marine lines the next morning, September 14. Carl found that after a five-day absence, all his personal gear had been doled out to his squadron mates and his bunk assigned to a recently arrived replacement.

While the Wildcats had managed to hold off the enemy air attacks, the Army pilots of the 67th Fighter Squadron, whose P-400 Airacobras had proven themselves woefully inadequate in air combat, found success in the air support role, where their good low-altitude performance, heavy armament of 20mm cannon and .50-caliber machine guns, and ability to carry a 500-pound bomb on the centerline rack, turned them into a very effective fighter-bomber in ground attack missions against the relentless enemy.

Their first opportunity to shine came when Japanese troop-carrying barges were discovered off the village of Tasimboko shortly after dawn on September 6. Newly promoted Major D.D. Brannon led four Airacobras, each carrying a 500-pound bomb, to attack the barges. After dropping their bombs, the P-400s circled around and strafed the enemy troops wading ashore. Once their ammo was expended, the pilots flew back to Henderson Field to rearm and refuel while other Airacobras replaced them. Brannon's P-400s were back over Tasimboko two hours later. The relentless attacks by the Army fighters left the Japanese with little to show for their reinforcement effort. Back at Henderson Field at the end of the day, one pilot reported that he and his wingman had cut a "bloody X" on the water with their strafing. With this success, the P-400s became flying artillery for the Marines, with their ground crews loading bombs and high-explosive ammunition every morning in anticipation of a quick response to enemy action.

The squadron became known as the "Jagstaffel," a corruption of the German term for "fighter squadron." Sometimes flying as many as five missions a day, the 67th maintained armed patrols to counter Japanese barge traffic as the enemy continually worked to keep a stream of reinforcements coming to the island. Throughout early September, the "Tokyo Express" made nightly missions to unload troops. While close air support missions were unglamorous and definitely dangerous to fly, the 67th Squadron gained a new sense of purpose. When supplies of bombs ran out as they frequently did, the squadron armorers devised contact fuses that allowed the fighters to drop depth charges on the enemy.

On September 12, coastwatcher Donald Kennedy on Bougainville alerted Henderson Field that 25 Bettys and 15 Zeros were on their way from Rabaul. Guided by the newly installed radar, 20 VF-5 and 11 Marine Wildcats shot down four Bettys and one Zero, while the ground defenses shot down two additional bombers. One Navy pilot died attempting to land his damaged fighter dead-stick following the action; VF-5 suffered five pilots killed, wounded, or missing in three days of combat. That night, Henderson was shelled by the Japanese cruiser *Sendai* and three destroyers to support an attack by the Imperial Army forces in what became known as the Battle of Edson's Ridge in which the Marine Raiders anchored the defenses along the Lunga River and kept the enemy from overrunning the airfield. Two pilots from VMSB-232 and one from VMSB-231 were killed in the shelling, but fortunately no aircraft were hit and the airfield did not sustain any serious damage.

That evening, Dauntlesses of the Scouting 6 detachment discovered and reported three groups of enemy ships steaming down the Slot. The most important – and dangerous – was the cruiser *Tenryū* and her three escorting destroyers, which were obviously headed for Guadalcanal to shell the Marine positions. There was not enough daylight left to mount an attack on the force.

Shortly before 2200 hours, Edson's Ridge was lit by flares dropped by "Washing Machine Charlie" in preparation for the Japanese assault. The *Tenryū*-led Tokyo Express arrived and began shelling Edson's Ridge, which was only 2,000 yards from Henderson Field at 2200 hours. Several "shorts" landed in the aviators' bivouac area, killing three and wounding two; two of the dead and one of the wounded were pilots in VMSB-232. Shortly after midnight, the "Kawaguchi detachment" of the 35th Infantry Regiment began their assault. The 1st Marine Raider Battalion and 1st Parachute Battalion held against these attacks. At dawn, the enemy retreated back into the jungle. Lt. Colonel Edson advised General Vandegrift, "They're testing, just testing. But they'll be back."

An hour later, the 19 Wildcats of VMO-251 that had been launched from *Hornet* and *Wasp* to reinforce the island arrived at Henderson Field. While the pilots expected to only deliver the airplanes and then return to Espiritu Santo for more training, they would be quickly introduced to combat. Within an hour of their arrival, two C5M2 "Babs" reconnaissance aircraft escorted by nine Zeros arrived over Guadalcanal to see if the Army had captured the airfield. The enemy aircraft had been spotted on radar and 12 Wildcats from VMF-223 and 224 and the newly arrived VMO-251 intercepted the formation. The Zeros managed to protect the two reconnaissance planes, but lost four of their number to the Wildcats while shooting down two F4Fs and damaging two others that crashed on landing back at Henderson, killing their pilots. The daily noon raid failed to appear until 1400 hours, when 27 Bettys and 12 Zeros were intercepted by Wildcats from VMF-212 and VF-5. The defenders shot down two Bettys and damaged two others. This time, six Japanese aircrew bailed out of the Bettys and were pulled from Ironbottom Sound to become POWs. VMF-212 and VF-5 each lost a Wildcat with its pilot.

Late in the afternoon, two Rufe floatplane fighters from the unit operating at Rekata Bay in the Shortland Islands caught an SBD from VMSB-231 over Lunga Point as it returned from patrol and shot it down as it was on final approach to Henderson. Second Lieutenant O.D. Johnson and his gunner were killed when the Dauntless hit short of the runway and exploded. Just before dusk, the last of *Saratoga's* air group – 18 Wildcats from VF-5 along with the last 12 Scouting 6 SBDs and six Torpedo 8 TBF Avengers – arrived from Espiritu Santo as reinforcements.

Colonel Edson had been right. The Japanese resumed their attack the night of September 13. Artillery and mortars hammered the enemy, but their attack was relentless and the Marines were forced to retreat halfway back across the ridge. Vandegrift fed in the last reserves and prepared for the worst. If Edson's Ridge fell, the airfields could be taken and the Marines driven from the island. At 0300 hours on September 14, the 67th's Captain John Thompson was awakened and told to report to the Pagoda, the remaining Japanese building that had been turned into headquarters for the air units. Waiting for him was a Marine officer from Edson's unit. Thompson later recalled, "He grabbed a pencil and a scrap of paper and drew a rough diagram of the ridge showing the positions of both sides. He said the Japanese were expected to make a big push at daybreak." The squadron had only enough fuel for three airplanes. At dawn, Thompson and Lieutenants B.E. Davis and Bryan Brown took off, circled the field, and made their attack. Thompson related, "We came in low over the trees, pulled up and saw the Marine positions. In the clearing below were hundreds and hundreds of Japanese, ready to charge. I lowered the nose, pressed the trigger and just mowed right through them. The next two pilots did the same thing."

Enemy ground fire damaged Brown's P-400, but he was able to use the momentum of his dive to pull up and manage a dead-stick landing at the Cow Pasture. Thompson and Davis came around for a second run, during which Thompson took a hit in his radiator and was forced to break off and execute an emergency landing at the Cow Pasture while Davis repeated his strafing runs until he ran out of ammunition. The desperate mission managed to break up what was to be the final assault on the ridge. Marines later counted 600 dead below the ridge, most of them the result of the Airacobras' gunfire. That evening, General Vandegrift called Thompson to his headquarters and told him, "You won't read about this in the newspapers, but you and your flight of P-400s just saved Guadalcanal." He then handed Thompson a fifth of Scotch, which he later shared with the rest of the squadron. Brown and Davis were awarded the Silver Star for the mission, while Thompson became one of only 11 USAAF pilots during the war to be awarded the Navy Cross.

The Cactus Air Force had one of its most successful days on September 14. The Rekata Bay floatplane force made several attacks on Henderson throughout the day, sending a total of 24 A6M-2N Rufe fighters and F1M2 Pete bombers over the island – the Wildcats shot down eight with no losses. Around midday, seven Second Air Group Zeros from Rabaul appeared over Lunga Point, losing one Zero and its pilot to the defenders, who also caught a C5M "Babs" reconnaissance plane over Cape Esperance and shot it down. The only American loss was a VMF-223 Wildcat that went out of control on takeoff, seriously injuring the pilot in the resulting crash. An R4D Skytrain arrived just before dusk to pick up the pilots from VMO-251 and return them to Espiritu Santo. They had experienced an eventful 24 hours on the island.

Between the first opposed raid on August 31 and mid-September, the Japanese had mounted 12 raids in which they lost 31 bombers and fighters, with seven Bettys returning to Rabaul heavily damaged. During the same time, the Cactus Air Force defenders lost 27 aircraft with nine pilots killed in action.

The 67th Squadron's history soon noted that, "Every airplane in commission soon became an example of the ground crew's ingenuity and resourcefulness." Routine maintenance to keep the airplanes flyable was difficult, since the mechanics still lacked proper tools and manuals to service the Airacobras. Lacking any replacement parts for the orphaned P-400s, wrecked planes were turned into a source of replacement parts. However, as the weeks wore on, the need for operational aircraft became so crucial that the ground crews were forced to take extraordinary measures to maintain the force. When one Airacobra cracked up on landing, the crews decided to rebuild the airplane rather than scrap it. The crumpled left wing was replaced by one taken from another wreck, while the mechanics managed to turn the bent propeller blades into a balanced replacement by pouring molten lead in them until they felt right. Renamed "The Resurrection," the battered P-400 operated over Guadalcanal for the next two crucial months. Throughout this period, the squadron was able to keep between six to eight Airacobras in good enough shape to sustain their mission of strafing and bombing the ubiquitous barge traffic.

For the Army pilots as well as the Marine and Navy fliers, conditions on Guadalcanal were hellish. The poor food combined with tropic diseases took an increasing toll. Huge rats on the island carried typhus, while the millions of mosquitoes brought malaria. The steady diet of cold rice and tinned sardines brought with it a crippling dysentery. The fetid environment meant that clothing, boots, and equipment quickly rotted. The tropic sun pushed daytime temperatures into the high 90s with accompanying high humidity that quickly enervated anyone undertaking any physical effort. The driving tropical rainstorms that came nearly every day turned foxholes and trenches into ponds that bred even more mosquitoes, while living quarters, roads, and airfield taxiways became muddy quagmires. It was observed that Guadalcanal was "the only place on Earth where you could stand up to your knees in mud and still get dust in your eyes."

During the month Scouting 6 was on Guadalcanal, John Bridgers had an opportunity to experience the strangest wartime food he found during the war.

Throughout the war, the food product manufacturers back in the States were constantly working to improve the foodstuffs they provided the armed forces. One such attempt I encountered during this period was called "canned butter," which had been formulated to withstand melting in the fierce heat of the tropics. It looked like the real thing. When a gallon container was put before us in the mess tent, we all tucked into it. The trouble was that it had a wax base and when a generous layer was slathered on a piece of bread, it simply coated the hard palate with an immovable layer of wax. No one ever explained to me how, if it didn't melt in the tropical heat of over 95 degrees, it was expected to liquefy at normal body temperature of 98.6 degrees. Anyway, I did momentarily forget my problems with spam while struggling to free the roof of my mouth of this so-called "butter."

Fortunately for Guadalcanal's defenders, a strong storm system swept over the northern Solomons and the Solomon Sea beginning the afternoon of September 14. The rain over the next two weeks kept the Japanese on Rabaul from mounting any raids until September 27, which gave the Henderson Field fliers respite to get as many airplanes operational as they could by cannibalizing those that had been damaged beyond repair and bringing in replacements, while the field was drenched from rainstorms spreading from the system over the northern Solomons. By the end of September, the Japanese provided the 26th Air Flotilla with 72 new G4M1s, 60 Zeros, and eight C5M2 reconnaissance planes, to their units at Rabaul, while 23 fighters and bombers arrived to reinforce Henderson Field.

On September 15, the Allied forces suffered a major reverse. USS *Wasp* was 150 miles southeast of San Cristobal Island, accompanied by the battleship *North Carolina*, carrier *Hornet*, light cruiser *Helena*, heavy cruiser *Salt Lake City*, and destroyers *Laffey*, *Lansdowne*, *O'Brien*, *Mustin*, *Farenholt*, and *Anderson*. Task Force 18 was escorting transports carrying the 7th Marine Regiment to Guadalcanal from New Caledonia. The skies over the Coral Sea were a clear blue. Aboard *Wasp*, Signalman 3/c Tom Curtis remembered the sea was "like glass" when he went below after morning flight operations were completed. *Wasp* was the "duty carrier," responsible for launching anti-submarine patrols to protect Task Force 18, which constituted the sum total of warships the Navy had in the South Pacific. Several enemy submarines had been spotted in the days since the fleet left Nouméa, and the waters were known as "Torpedo Junction." At 1215 hours, radar picked up a "bogey" 30 miles out. Minutes later, a Wildcat pilot in the combat air patrol above the fleet spotted and shot down a Kawasaki H6K Type 97 "Mavis" flying boat. At 1230 hours, *Wasp*'s crew went to watch condition 2, with the air department at flight quarters.

The Americans didn't know it, but just over the horizon the fleet submarine *I-19*, commanded by LCDR Shogo Narahara, was on the lookout for them. The veteran submarine had been victorious in previous attacks on Allied naval forces. At 1345 hours, Captain Narahara was called to the control room by a report from the officer of the deck manning the periscope that he had spotted smoke on the horizon. Narahara took a quick look for himself that confirmed there was more than one source to the wisps of smoke on the northern horizon. He gave orders to close on the target.

At 1420 hours, *Wasp* maneuvered away from the fleet into the wind and launched eight Wildcats and three Dauntlesses to relieve the midday search patrol. Once the planes were airborne, *Wasp*'s Landing Signal Officer (LSO), Lieutenant David McCampbell, quickly recovered the 11 planes waiting to return.

Watching through his periscope, Captain Narahara saw the enemy carrier heel slightly as she turned to starboard to rejoin the rest of the enemy fleet. At 1443 hours he fired the first of six Type 95 torpedoes from a distance of 1,000 yards.

With lookouts screaming their warnings of inbound torpedoes, Captain Forrest P. Sherman ordered the carrier to turn "hard a' starboard," but it was too late. Two of the six torpedoes passed ahead of *Wasp*. Lookouts on *Helena* saw them pass astern of the cruiser. At 1445 hours, *Wasp* staggered under the blows of three hits, all in the vicinity of the aviation gasoline tanks and the ship's magazine. At 1451 hours, the destroyer *O'Brien* was hit by one of the first two torpedoes as she maneuvered to avoid the other, while the destroyer *Lansdowne* managed to maneuver and narrowly avoid the sixth torpedo at 1448 hours. At 1450 hours, *Mustin* spotted it as the torpedo penetrated *North Carolina*'s screen – the battleship was hit at 1452 hours just forward of the number one gun turret, creating a hole 32 by 18 feet, 20 feet below the waterline. Five men were killed in the explosion but the ship avoided disaster through skillful damage control that quickly righted a 5.6-degree list and she was able to continue in formation at 26 knots.

Narahara's spread of six torpedoes was the most successful shot taken by a submarine of any side during the war.

In the aftermath of the torpedo hits, fiery blasts ripped through *Wasp*'s forward area. Aircraft on the forward flight deck were tossing about like toys. Below in the hangar deck, spare airplanes stored in the overhead broke free and dropped with such force their landing gears snapped off when they hit the deck. The planes in the hangar deck caught fire and the flames were sucked below through open hatches. The heat of the fires detonated ready ammunition stored near the forward antiaircraft guns on the starboard side and the number two 1.1-inch gun mount was blown overboard. The corpse of the gun captain was thrown through the air onto the bridge, spattering Captain Sherman with blood when it landed next to him.

In minutes, *Wasp*'s condition became even more desperate. Firefighting crews in the forward section lost their fight when the main pumps failed and cut off their water. Unchecked, the fire set off ammunition and bombs when it reached the magazines, forcing the evacuation of the central damage control station when the sound-powered phones went dead at 1452 hours. The aviation gasoline tanks were breached at 1455 hours, adding to the fire. *Wasp* took a 15-degree list to starboard as water flooded through her gaping wounds. She was surrounded by fires on the water as oil and gasoline spread from her ruptured tanks.

Having lost the ability to fight the ship's fires, Captain Sherman slowed the carrier to 10 knots and ordered a turn to port, hoping to get the wind onto the starboard bow to blow the flames to port. At 1508 hours there were three major gasoline vapor explosions. Captain Sherman realized they must abandon ship and notified Task Group commander Rear Admiral Leigh Noyes, who agreed with his decision. At 1520 hours Sherman ordered "Abandon Ship" and the crew began going overboard as the escorting destroyers maneuvered nearby to pick them up. David McCampbell, who had been a diving champion at

Annapolis, considered doing a fancy dive off the fantail, but when he saw the wreckage in the water below, "I grabbed the family jewels in one hand and my nose in the other and jumped like a kid going into a pool." Captain Sherman found a mattress in the water and managed to climb onto it before he was rescued by the *Farenthold*.

Wasp drifted as the flames spread; the rest of the fleet could not stop while she sank. *Lansdowne* was ordered to sink her, and fired two torpedoes that did not explode when they hit the carrier. The torpedomen then disabled the magnetic exploders and set the remaining three torpedoes to run at ten feet. All three exploded on impact, but *Wasp* refused to sink until 2100 hours, taking 193 dead with her. Twenty-five of 26 airborne aircraft landed on *Hornet*, while 45 went down when she sank.

O'Brien survived her torpedoing but the destroyer had suffered severe structural damage. After she reached Espiritu Santo on September 16, emergency repairs were carried out and she departed for San Francisco on October 8. She arrived at Suva in the New Hebrides on October 13 and departed three days later. By October 18, she was leaking badly and the crew jettisoned as much topside weight as possible. *O'Brien's* hull split open at 0600 hours on October 19 and her crew abandoned ship at 0630 hours; *O'Brien* sank at 0700 hours.

North Carolina also made temporary repairs at Espiritu Santo before departing for Pearl Harbor two weeks later. Once at Pearl Harbor, the battleship went into dry-dock for major repairs to her hull. She returned to the South Pacific in early January 1943.

As the storms continued in the Solomons throughout the last half of the month of September, the Imperial Navy took advantage of the bad weather to make further runs of the Tokyo Express to bring reinforcements to Guadalcanal. The destroyers would depart their base in the Shortlands each afternoon, carrying up to 1,000 troops on their decks. They would arrive at the 200-mile range of Guadalcanal-based aircraft around 1800 hours, which gave the defenders time to mount one strike against the force if they were discovered in time, before darkness would prevent further attacks. Maneuvering destroyers were the hardest naval target for any bomber to hit, and even the experienced Navy and Marine SBD crews frequently claimed a destroyer hit or sunk where nothing had been accomplished. The destroyers would increase their speed with darkness and arrive off Guadalcanal around midnight. The usual unloading point was just across the Matanikau River, 8–10 miles west of Henderson Field. Unloading was usually coordinated with a visit by "Washing Machine Charlie" to distract the Marines, or a shelling of the airfield by one or two escorting destroyers. Attempts were made to get SBDs airborne to attempt to glide bomb the destroyers while they were off the beach, but there never was a successful attack and several aircraft and crews were lost attempting this. By 0300 hours at the latest, the destroyers would finish the unloading and head northward at high speed, so that by daylight they were beyond range. By mid-October, this effort had landed as many as 28,000 Imperial Army troops on Guadalcanal to participate in the planned offensive to finally take Henderson.

On September 22, the advance section of VMSB-141 arrived to replace the worn-out aircrews of VMSB-232. The rest of the squadron, led by skipper Major Gordon Bell arrived on October 5. The two-week respite came to an end on September 27 when the coastwatchers were late spotting 18 Bettys and 38 Zeros in the broken clouds. When the warning arrived on Guadalcanal, the attackers were only 100 miles north and there was no time for the Wildcats to claw their way to 20,000 feet before the enemy appeared overhead in their bombing runs. Smith's and Galer's fighters went for the bombers almost directly over the airfield. Marion Carl was able to down one Betty and share a second with his wingman before the two Marines had to high-tail it at low altitude across Ironbottom Sound until the pursuing Zeros were forced to break off as they approached Tulagi. VF-5's 18 Wildcats had their hands full dealing with the Zeros and managed to shoot down two. While only one SBD was lost in the bombing, four others and three TBFs were damaged beyond the limited repair capability at Henderson. The next morning, there were only 18 SBDs and two Avengers available for operations. An R4D flew up from Espiritu Santo during the day and took aboard the survivors of Scouting 6 and Flight 300 to evacuate them back to the rear area after their month of combat. The Navy fliers were replaced the next day by six of the survivors of Wasp's VS-71; the other eight VS-71 Dauntlesses, led by squadron leader Lieutenant Commander John Eldridge, arrived two days later.

Clear weather the next day allowed plenty of warning from the coastwatchers which gave 33 Wildcats time to get to altitude, where they intercepted 27 Bettys escorted by 44 Zeros. In the wild battle that ensued, the Marines claimed 23 of the 27 bombers shot down, their biggest score to date. VMF-223 claimed seven including one each by Smith and Carl, while Bob Galer's VMF-224 claimed eight with Galer himself responsible for three. Lieutenant Colonel Harold W. "Joe" Bauer, commander of VMF-212, was up from Espiritu Santo to see conditions on the island for himself and claimed his first victory. VF-5 claimed nine Bettys. The Japanese admitted to only seven Bettys missing, but the inability of the escorts to hold off the defending Wildcats led to a change in tactics.

After two days of rain, the Zeros returned on October 2, with 36 fighters escorting nine Bettys that again turned away when they sighted Guadalcanal. The coastwatchers had missed the sweep in the post-frontal weather and the enemy pilots found 33 Wildcats still struggling for altitude. VMF-223 lost two Wildcats in the first pass and John Smith was forced to hide in a cloud. When he popped back out, he found himself behind three A6M2s and shot down one, but the other two nearly got him. His engine failed on return to the Cow Patch and he crashed six miles short while trying to land dead-stick. Fortunately, though he was behind enemy lines, he was able to hike back through the jungle without encountering any Japanese. The Zeros returned to Rabaul claiming six Wildcats down over Ironbottom Sound for a loss of one of their own. In fact, the Zeros had tangled with VF-5's Wildcats, which had claimed four Zeros, including one by squadron CO Leroy Simpler, but the defenders had lost the battle, six to four.

The Japanese returned on October 3. The coastwatchers gave a better warning and the Wildcats were able to get up in time. Marion Carl led six that hit the 27 Zeros. In a hard-fought fighter-versus-fighter battle, Marion Carl scored what would turn out to be his last victory before his guns jammed, bringing his score to 16.5. Wingman Ken Frazier shot down two before being shot up and forced to bail out, running his score to 12 to take third place in VMF-223's "ace race." First Lieutenant Floyd Lynch of the newly arrived VMF-121 scored a Zero, but Colonel Bauer's four down was the top score of the day, making him an ace. The Japanese records admitted the Marine claims of nine were accurate.

At mid-afternoon of October 3, a pair of scouting SBDs spotted the enemy seaplane tender *Nisshin*, escorted by six destroyers, 200 miles northwest of Guadalcanal. *Nisshin* was carrying tanks that were to be offloaded that evening. The two scouts were jumped by ten Zeros but managed to escape after making their report. Three more destroyers were spotted at 1600 hours. The size of the force meant they had to be dealt with before darkness fell. At 1620 hours, a strike force of eight SBDs and three TBFs departed Henderson. They spotted *Nisshin* and her escorts at 1730 hours. Heavy enemy flak and wild maneuvering by the ships prevented any hits. The enemy force was again spotted off Cape Esperance at 2230 hours. Despite the darkness, a strike force of four Dauntlesses from four different squadrons took off, led by VS-71 skipper Eldridge. In the darkness, only Eldridge and one other managed to spot the enemy, but their bombs missed. After unloading the tanks and troops, the ships left before daylight.

On October 7, the pilots and ground crews of the 67th Fighter Squadron received a welcome boost when 11 P-39N Airacobras arrived from Espiritu Santo. These fighters outperformed the wretched P-400s on all levels. They could operate effectively at altitudes up to 18,000 feet and could even get as high as 27,000 feet, which could enable them to perform interceptions with the Marine Wildcats. However, what was really useful about these airplanes was the 37mm cannon they carried in their nose. This weapon was devastating when strafing barges and the ships of the Tokyo Express, and could take out an Imperial Army tank with one shot when the rare enemy targets were spotted. The Army pilots remained in the ground support role, but now they not only had airplanes that were not held together with baling wire, but a shipment arrived the next day with a full selection of spare parts, spare engines, proper tools, and proper maintenance manuals. The squadron war diary recorded that "morale is sky high now."

On October 9, the rest of VMF-121 was launched from the escort carrier *Copahee*. Among them was their Executive Officer, Captain Joseph J. Foss, who had fought a six-month battle with the authorities to obtain an assignment to a fighter squadron after being deemed "too old" for fighters at age 27. Squadron commander Major Leonard K. Davis led the 20 Wildcats in to land at the Cow Pasture. None knew at the time that they would write a record as the most successful squadron of the latter Guadalcanal campaign.

The exhausted pilots of VMF-223 flew their last mission from Henderson Field on October 10 when John Smith led seven Wildcats escorting SBDs and TBFs to New Georgia where Japanese ships had been spotted. On the way, Smith looked back and spotted some 15 Rufe and Pete floatplanes closing on the Marine formation. Smith reversed course as he radioed a warning and the other six fighters followed. The Japanese also turned back, but the Wildcats caught up with them and shot down six Petes and three Rufes, with Smith scoring his final victory for a total of 19 to become the leading Marine ace to that point in the war.

When they departed Guadalcanal for Espiritu Santo on October 12, VMF-223 had claimed 110 victories, including 47 Zeros and 47 Bettys in the course of their nine-week tour. Squadron CO John L. Smith shot down ten Bettys while XO Marion Carl claimed eight, more Japanese bombers than any other Marine pilots during the war. Of the 19 pilots that had landed at Henderson Field on August 20, ten had paid the ultimate price. The day before their departure, Bob Galer's VMF-224 pilots scored the biggest victory of their tour on Guadalcanal, claiming seven Bettys and four Zeros.

Following the failure to take Henderson Field in the Battle of Edson's Ridge, the Imperial High Command ordered preparations for a second offensive, and set the date at October 20. To reinforce Japanese forces on the island, the 2nd and 38th infantry divisions with 17,500 troops were transferred from the Dutch East Indies to Rabaul, from whence they would be transported to Guadalcanal. The Tokyo Express made several runs between September 14 and October 9, to deliver the troops of the 2nd Infantry Division as well as overall commander General Harukichi Hyakutake. While troops were primarily transported aboard cruisers and destroyers, the seaplane carrier *Nisshin* delivered heavy equipment including tanks and heavy artillery. Support for the Imperial Army by the Imperial Navy included increased air attacks on Henderson Field and the use of warships to bombard the American positions before the offensive.

While this enemy activity was taking place, Major General Millard F. Harmon, the commander of United States Army forces in the South Pacific, managed to convince Vice Admiral Robert L. Ghormley, Commander South Pacific, that the Marines needed immediate reinforcement if they were to defeat the next expected Japanese offensive. The 2,837 men of the 164th Infantry Regiment of the Army's Americal Division boarded transports at New Caledonia on October 8, with a planned arrival at Guadalcanal on October 13.

The night of October 11–12, the Navy fought the Battle of Cape Esperance, the first time the US Navy managed to defeat the Imperial Navy in a night engagement. This was the second of four major night surface engagements that took place during the three and a half months of the hardest-fought period of the Guadalcanal campaign. The battle occurred at the entrance to the strait between Savo Island and Guadalcanal, just off Cape Esperance, the northernmost point on Guadalcanal.

Rear Admiral Norman Scott, commanding Task Force 64 – composed of the heavy cruisers *San Francisco* (CA-38) and *Salt Lake City* (CA-25), the light cruisers *Boise* (CL-47) and *Helena* (CL-50), and the destroyers *Farenholt* (DD-491), *Duncan* (DD-485), *Buchanan* (DD-484), *McCalla* (DD-488), and *Laffey* (DD-459) – was ordered to intercept any enemy ships in the vicinity of Guadalcanal that threatened the convoy. Scott was an experienced surface warfare commander who had led the fire support group in the August invasion. Having seen Japanese night combat capabilities at Savo Island, he spent several days drilling the task force and conducted a full-scale night battle practice on October 8. While not possessing the experience of his opponents, Scott's task force would be the best-trained of any US Navy combat unit to fight in the Guadalcanal campaign. Task Force 64 took station south of Guadalcanal near Rennell Island on October 9.

The Imperial Navy's Eighth Fleet, commanded by Vice Admiral Gunichi Mikawa, the victor at Savo Island, was ordered to make a supply run to Guadalcanal on the night of October 11–12. Rear Admiral Takatsugu Jojima commanded the "Reinforcement Group" which included seaplane carriers *Chitose* and *Nisshin* that were to deliver 728 soldiers along with four large howitzers, two field guns, one antiaircraft gun, and a supply of ammunition, along with six destroyers – *Asagumo*, *Natsugumo*, *Yamagumo*, *Shirayuki*, and *Murakumo* transporting additional troops, covered by *Akizuki*. The veteran heavy cruisers *Aoba*, *Kinugasa*, and *Furutaka*, commanded by Rear Admiral Aritomo Gotō, were to bombard Henderson while the troops and their equipment were landed. Gotō's cruisers were screened by the destroyers *Fubuki* and *Hatsuyuki*. None of the Japanese commanders expected any opposition from the US Navy, which had made no effort to interdict operations by any Tokyo Express mission since the campaign had commenced.

Admiral Jojima's reinforcement group departed the Shortlands anchorage at 0800 hours on October 11 and began their 250-mile run down the Slot to Guadalcanal. Admiral Gotō departed the Shortlands at 1400 hours that afternoon. The approach was covered by the 11th Air

Fleet, with two air strikes against Henderson Field from bases at Rabaul, Kavieng, and Buin.

Just after midday on October 11, a sweep of 17 A6M3 Zero fighters known to the Allies as "Hamps" and believed to be a different type rather than a Zero sub-type due to their clipped wingtips, flew down from Buin. Identified as a fighter sweep by the coastwatchers, the mission failed to entice any defenders into the air. Forty-five minutes later, a second strike of 55 Bettys and 30 Zeros did meet opposition. The Guadalcanal defenders shot down one G4M in return for the loss of two defending Wildcats. While the attacks failed to inflict any serious damage, both missions prevented the launch of scouting flights that could have discovered the oncoming fleets. The ships were covered by revolving flights of Hamps from Buin, with the last flight of the day ordered to remain on station until sunset, then ditch their aircraft and wait for pickup by the reinforcement group's destroyers. While all six did as ordered, the destroyers only found and recovered one pilot in the dark waters.

While scouting flights from Henderson had been delayed, a PBY did spot Jojima's reinforcement force at 1445 hours, 210 miles north of Guadalcanal between Kolombangara and Choiseul islands. The sighting report identified the enemy ships as two "cruisers" and six destroyers. Unfortunately, Gotō's force was not sighted. When he received this report at 1607 hours, Admiral Scott turned his task force toward Guadalcanal to intercept the enemy. He had developed a simple plan for the engagement, operating in column formation with the destroyers at the front and rear of the cruisers. *Helena* and *Boise* would search a 300-degree arc with their superior SG surface radar to gain position advantage when the enemy approached. The cruisers would launch their SOC Seagull aircraft in advance, to find and illuminate the enemy with flares. Once engaged, the destroyers would illuminate the targets with searchlights and fire their torpedoes while the cruisers opened fire at any available targets without awaiting orders.

When Task Force 64 neared Cape Hunter at the northwest end of Guadalcanal, the floatplanes were launched at 2200 hours. One crashed on takeoff, but the other two patrolled Savo, Guadalcanal, and Ironbottom Sound. Just after passing Cape Esperance at 2233 hours, Scott ordered the force to assume battle formation. *Farenholt*, *Duncan*, and *Laffey* were in the lead, followed by Scott's flagship *San Francisco*,

Boise, Salt Lake City, and *Helena,* with *Buchanan* and *McCalla* in the rear. Each ship held position at 500 to 700 yards' distance between each other. Visibility in Ironbottom Sound was poor with no ambient light and no visible horizon due to the moon having already set.

At almost the same time, Jojima's force passed around mountainous Cape Hunter, and neither force sighted the other; Jojima radioed Gotō at 2220 hours, informing him there were no American ships. Later, as they unloaded the troops, men aboard Jojima's ships heard the American floatplanes, but the admiral failed to inform Gotō.

Gotō's force picked up speed to 30 knots as they approached Guadalcanal to commence the bombardment of Henderson Field. The ships passed through several rain squalls in the sound during the approach. Gotō's flagship *Aoba* led, followed by *Furutaka* and *Kinugasa,* with *Fubuki* to starboard of *Aoba* and *Hatsuyuki* to port. At 2330 hours, the force emerged from the last rain squall and were picked up on radar by *Helena* and *Salt Lake City.* Admiral Gotō remained unaware of the American presence.

San Francisco's SOC spotted Jojima's force off Guadalcanal at 2300 hours and reported them to Scott, who continued course to the west side of Savo, believing more enemy ships were likely approaching. Scott ordered the column to turn southwest at 2333 hours and take a heading of 230 degrees as a column movement. However, at this moment, the lack of American experience of night combat led the fleet to make a mistake. As the three lead destroyers executed the movement correctly, *San Francisco* incorrectly turned simultaneously, her captain having misunderstood. *Boise* followed *San Francisco,* which threw the three van destroyers out of formation. *Helena's* radar showed the enemy 27,700 yards distant at 2332 hours. *Boise* and *Duncan* picked up the enemy on radar at 2335 hours. *Helena* and *Boise* reported the contacts to Scott at 2342 and 2344 hours respectively. The admiral, believing the cruisers were tracking the three destroyers, radioed *Farenholt* to ask if she was attempting to resume station. *Farenholt* replied, "Affirmative, coming up on your starboard side," which confirmed the admiral's belief the radar contacts were friendly.

Farenholt and *Laffey,* still unaware of the approaching enemy warships, increased speed at 2345 hours to resume station at the head of the line. *Duncan* had the enemy on radar; her captain, thinking *Farenholt* and *Laffey* were starting an attack, increased speed to launch a solitary torpedo attack without telling Scott what he was doing. Finally, *San Francisco*'s SC radar spotted the enemy, but Scott was not informed. Gotō's ships were only 5,000 yards from Scott's force and visible to lookouts aboard *Helena* and *Salt Lake City*. At this point, Scott's formation was in position to cross the enemy's "T," providing a significant advantage. Believing Scott was aware of the rapidly approaching enemy, *Helena* asked permission to open fire at 2346 hours, using the general procedure request, "Interrogatory Roger" ("Are we clear to act?"). Scott answered, "Roger," meaning the message was received, not confirming the request to act. Upon receipt of Scott's "Roger," *Helena* opened fire, quickly followed by *Boise*, *Salt Lake City*, and – to Scott's surprise – *San Francisco*.

Gotō's cruisers were taken by surprise. *Aoba*'s lookouts had sighted Scott's force at 2343 hours, but the admiral had assumed they were Jojima's force. At 2345 the lookouts identified the ships as American, but Gotō directed his ships to flash identification signals. As *Aoba* executed the order, the first American salvo smashed into her superstructure and she was quickly hit by up to 40 shells from *Helena*, *Salt Lake City*, *San Francisco*, *Farenholt*, and *Laffey*. Her communication system was damaged and two main gun turrets and the main gun director were demolished. Several large-caliber projectiles passed through the flag bridge without exploding, but the force of their passage killed many men and mortally wounded Gotō.

Scott ordered a ceasefire at 2347 hours, still fearing his ships were firing on each other. Ordering *Farenholt* to flash her recognition signals, he finally realized the destroyers were almost back in position and ordered fire resumed at 2351 hours. *Aoba* took more hits before she turned to starboard to get away and began to make smoke, which led the Americans to believe she was sinking; they shifted fire to *Furutaka*, just behind *Aoba*. *Furutaka*'s torpedo tubes were hit at 2349 hours, igniting a large fire that attracted more shellfire. She was hit in her forward engine room by a torpedo fired by *Buchanan* at 2358 hours. *San Francisco* and *Boise* sighted *Fubuki* 1,400 yards away and raked her with gunfire. *Fubuki*, heavily damaged, began to sink. *Kinugasa* and *Hatsuyuki* turned to port and escaped immediate attention.

During the exchange, *Farenholt* took several damaging hits from both Japanese and American ships, killing several crewmen. She crossed ahead of *San Francisco* and passed to the disengaged side of the

American column, escaping further damage. While *Duncan* executed her solo torpedo attack, she was also hit by gunfire from both sides, set afire, and turned away to escape the crossfire.

Scott's task force tightened formation as Gotō's ships attempted to escape and pursued the retreating enemy. At 0006 hours, *Kinugasa* fired two torpedoes that barely missed *Boise*. *Boise* and *Salt Lake City* then turned on their searchlights to help target the enemy, which gave *Kinugasa's* gunners clear targets. *Boise* was hit in her main magazine between turrets one and two by two shells from *Kinugasa* at 0010 hours. The magazine's explosion killed nearly 100 men and threatened to blow *Boise* apart, but seawater rushing in through rents in her hull opened by the explosion stopped the fire before it exploded the powder magazines. Immediately after, *Boise* sheered out of the column and retreated. *Kinugasa* and *Salt Lake City* each hit the other several times. *Kinugasa* suffered minor damage while one of *Salt Lake City's* boilers was damaged which reduced her speed.

At 0016 hours, Scott ordered the force to turn to 330 degrees to pursue the fleeing enemy but the Americans quickly lost sight of the Japanese and all firing ceased by 0020 as the American formation began to scatter. Henderson Field was safe.

Jojima's reinforcement group completed its unloading while the battle raged and began its return journey using a route passing south of the Russell Islands and New Georgia. Though she was damaged extensively, *Aoba* joined *Kinugasa* in retiring north through the Slot. At 0050 hours, *Furutaka* lost power and she sank at 0228 hours, 22 miles northwest of Savo Island. Her survivors were picked up by *Hatsuyuki*, which then joined the retreat. Admiral Jojima sent *Shirayuki* and *Murakumo* to assist *Furutaka* and *Asagumo* and *Natsugumo* to rendezvous with *Kinugasa*.

At 0240 hours, *Boise* was able to extinguish her fires and rejoined the task force at 0305 hours. *Duncan*, which had been set afire, was abandoned by her crew at 0200 hours. Unaware of her fate, Scott detached *McCalla* to search for her, then ordered the rest of the force to retire toward Nouméa, where they arrived the afternoon of October 13. *McCalla* discovered the burning *Duncan* around 0300 hours and attempted to save her but was forced to abandon the effort at 1200 hours on October 12, when *Duncan* finally sank. *McCalla* and boats from Guadalcanal picked up 195 survivors from *Duncan*. They also found 100 *Fubuki* survivors who initially refused all rescue attempts but eventually allowed themselves to be picked up and taken prisoner the next day.

Shortly after dawn, the Cactus Air Force sent out 16 SBDs to search for any straggling enemy ships in the aftermath of the battle. At 0700 hours, VS-71's Lieutenant Commander Eldridge spotted three destroyers, north of the Russell Islands 30 miles from the site of the battle, two of which were assisting a third that had been damaged. His six Dauntlesses attacked, but only one scored a near miss on *Murakumo*. At 0800 hours, VS-3's CO, Lieutenant Commander Lou Kirn, led a strike force of SBDs from VS-3, VS-71, and VMSB-241, and TBFs from VT-8, with a strong Wildcat escort. Spotting the destroyers *Murakumo*, *Asagumo*, and *Natsugumo*, the Wildcats strafed the enemy ships before the dive bombers attacked. *Murakumo* was near-missed by three bombs that set her up for the Avengers. One torpedo hit the destroyer and brought her to a stop; she sank later that afternoon. *Asagumo* and *Natsugumo*. were attacked by another group of 11 SBDs and TBFs escorted by 14 fighters at 1545 hours. An SBD placed its bomb almost directly amidships on *Natsugumo* while two more near misses created severe damage. After *Asagumo* took off her survivors, *Natsugumo* sank at 1627 hours. The Americans also scored several more hits on the stationary *Murakumo*, setting her afire. She was scuttled by a torpedo from *Shirayuki* after her crew abandoned ship.

In the battle's aftermath, Captain Kikunori Kojima, Gotō's surviving chief of staff, claimed two American cruisers and one destroyer sunk. Although the bombardment mission failed, Jojima's reinforcement convoy successfully delivered the men and equipment. *Aoba* returned to the Imperial Navy base at Kure, Japan, where her repairs were completed on February 15, 1943.

Admiral Scott claimed Task Force 64 sank three enemy cruisers and four destroyers. The victory claims were widely publicized in American newspapers. *Boise* was damaged sufficiently to require a trip to the Philadelphia Naval Shipyard for repair, where the press dubbed her "the one-ship fleet" for her exploits. She was under repair until March 20, 1943.

While Cape Esperance was an American tactical victory, it had little strategic effect on the situation. The Navy was still unaware of the range and power of the Type 95 torpedo, the effectiveness of Japanese night optics, and the fighting ability of Japanese destroyer and cruiser commanders. With the battle perceived as a victory, the perceived lessons learned led to a belief that radar-directed American naval gunfire was superior to Japanese torpedo attacks. A junior officer aboard *Helena* later wrote of the battle, "Cape Esperance was a three-sided battle in which chance was the major winner."

On October 13, the pilots of VMF-121 scored their first victories when Lieutenants Freeman and Narr each got a Betty, though the day was a bad one for the Cactus defenders since the Japanese changed tactics, sending two missions rather than the usual one per day, with the first being missed in the poor weather by the coastwatchers. The Bettys in the first got through and damaged both airstrips, tearing gashes in the PSP (Pierced-Steel-Planking) runways and setting fire to 5,000 gallons of avgas. Two hours later, while the Wildcats were still being refueled by hand, the enemy returned, with 15 Bettys lining up to bomb the helpless aircraft on the ground.

Joe Foss led a dozen Wildcats to intercept 32 enemy bombers and fighters. In his first combat, he failed to spot the enemy as the rest of his squadron peeled away from the attacking enemy fighters. Foss was suddenly alone in the midst of the enemy. When the leader pulled out of his gunnery pass right in front of him, he scored his first victory with a quick burst that disintegrated the Zero. Instantly, three more were on him, and his engine was badly shot up. He barely made it back to "Fighter One," with his Wildcat dripping oil from the windmilling engine. Realizing he was lucky to be alive, he declared, "You can call me 'Swivel-Neck Joe' from now on."

That night, the Marines experienced the most devastating Japanese artillery attack in their time on Guadalcanal. At 1830 hours, the enemy shelling began when the 150mm guns that had been landed two nights before opened up from their position on the north end of the island. At approximately 1930 hours, "Washing Machine Charlie" made his appearance over the field and dropped flares for the continuing artillery barrage. At 0130 hours on October 14, "Louie the Louse," as a Japanese seaplane flown from Rekata Bay had become known, arrived overhead and dropped anti-personnel bombs on the field before dropping a red flare over the west end of the field, a white flare in the middle, and a green flare over the eastern end. Unknown to the Americans, a task force commanded by Vice Admiral Takeo Kurita consisting of the battleships *Kongō* and *Haruna*, was offshore in Ironbottom Sound.

Each ship carried a main armament of eight 14-inch naval cannons and a secondary battery of 6-inch guns (eight in the case of *Kongō* and 16 for *Haruna*). The battleships were armed with special high-explosive ammunition. At 0138 hours, they opened a barrage that would last a terrifying 97 minutes. Their 14-inch guns wreaked destruction throughout the Marine lines as they fired 900 shells into the airfield, accompanying that with fire from their secondary batteries. The earth shook and palm trees were splintered. Burning buildings crashed down and the fuel dump was set afire. The airfield seemed to be a sea of flame. Sergeant Jim Eaton later recalled the event as the most horrific in his 20-year Marine career. "Those shells sounded like express trains as they came in, and the ground shook like an earthquake with each explosion." More than 40 Marines were killed in the event, which was known forever after as "the Bombardment." After the battleships departed around 0300 hours, the Army artillery which had already been named "Pistol Pete" resumed fire.

Dawn revealed wreckage greater than anyone had imagined possible. Henderson Field was a shambles, the PSP runway reduced to twisted, tangled steel. The Pagoda was so badly damaged it had to be bulldozed. Fortunately, the battleships had concentrated on Henderson and left Fighter One alone. There were 30 Marine fighters at the Cow Pasture that were still operational, but 39 SBDs on Henderson Field were either destroyed or so badly damaged they were unflyable, with only seven others in flyable condition, while all the Avengers were gone. VMSB-141's commander, Major Bell, his executive officer, the senior division leader, and two other pilots were among the dead, leaving no pilot in the squadron over the rank of Second Lieutenant alive, while VS-71 lost Lieutenant W.P. Kephart. Radio communications were out and nearly all the avgas had been burned; the only fuel available was in the tanks of three badly damaged B-17Es from the 11th Bombardment Group that had arrived on the field the day before.

Over the next two days, R4Ds of VMJ-253 flew in fuel, ten 55-gallon drums at a time, while the destroyer-seaplane tender *McFarland* was loaded with avgas and sent from Espiritu Santo. YP boats brought over 200 gallons of avgas from the PT boat base on Tulagi.

Worse was on the way. Two enemy task groups, a transport force of six ships with destroyer escorts, and a bombardment force of two heavy cruisers with two destroyers, were heading down the Slot to finish off the work begun the night before by the two battleships. The Navy servicing unit had four of the damaged SBDs in condition to fly with the seven survivors by 1500 hours. The transports were well defended by AA from the destroyers and no hits were scored. Lou Kirn led nine Dauntlesses that had been gassed up with fuel scavenged from the B-17s to attack the transports at dusk but failed to score any hits, and the SBDs were lucky to be able to land on the damaged runway after dark without further loss.

The only other dive bombers available in the South Pacific were eight VB-6 SBDs that had been left behind at Espiritu Santo when *Enterprise* had been forced to leave after Eastern Solomons. During the day of October 14, an R4D was sent up to Henderson Field to collect pilots to fly the SBDs back to the island, giving a total force of 17 dive bombers to meet the enemy. *Hornet*, now the only surviving carrier in the region, was not in position to take part in the fight. The night of October 14/15, the Tokyo Express paid a return visit and the cruisers *Chōkai* and *Kinugasa* shelled the field again, dropping 752 8-inch shells. Dawn found the Tokyo Express unloading five transports off Tassafaronga. Major Joe Renner, the air operations officer at Henderson, worked to get the three surviving Dauntlesses ready for a do-or-die mission against the transports. The first of the three ran into a bomb crater on the runway and crashed on takeoff. Renner and Lieutenant Joe Patterson drove the length of the runway spotting craters. At 0500 hours, Patterson tried to take off, but he hit a crater and wrecked the second bomber. He and his gunner were unharmed and he volunteered to try again. He made it into the air, to discover that the landing gear wouldn't retract and the dive brakes were inoperable. He continued on, and dived through the enemy flak to score a direct hit on one of the transports.

After several hours' work, there were ten SBDs capable of being flown. Gassing the planes with 350 gallons of fuel found in a dump that had been forgotten, the Dauntlesses, with seven surviving P-39s, got airborne and strafed the enemy troops that had been put ashore, making several more attacks through the day in which the new P-39s demonstrated their knockout punch against ships. At 0700 hours, Lieutenants Waterman and Finch bombed the ships with their SBDs, while VMF-121's Major Davis led six Wildcats in a strafing attack. General Geiger finally stopped the piecemeal attacks and organized a strike. Despite the presence of 30 Zeros overhead, 12 SBDs were bombed-up by 1000 hours and the general's personal PBY-5A that had arrived the night before carrying two torpedoes went out to hit the enemy. Geiger's personal pilot, Jack Cram, made a torpedo run with the ungainly Catalina against a transport, hitting it with one torpedo before he was set on by Zeros as he returned to Henderson. First Lieutenant Roger Haberman of VMF-121 shot down one of the Zeros as Cram attempted to land while Haberman was approaching for an emergency landing himself. By the end of the day, the *Kyushu Maru, Sasako Maru,* and *Azumasan Maru* had been beached after they were bombed and set afire, which destroyed most of the artillery ammunition they were carrying. The other three transports were still in good-enough shape to be withdrawn. Approximately 4,500 troops of the 2nd "Sentai" Division had gotten ashore. (The rusted remains of the three ships were still visible on the beach as of 2019.)

The Japanese weren't through. That night, the heavy cruisers *Myoko* and *Maya* pumped out 1,500 shells over 60 minutes between 0025 and 0125 hours of October 16, but the bombardment was not as successful as the two previous had been. Bob Galer flew his last mission that morning, to strafe the beached transports. VMF-224 finally saw the end of their time on Guadalcanal come later that afternoon, when the squadron's surviving pilots and those of Leroy Simpler's Fighting 5 were evacuated. Galer's pilots had scored 56 victories for a loss of seven, with Galer scoring 14 victories. Fighting 5 had scored 40 victories during their time on the island, for a loss of five pilots killed in action and three wounded. The fact their losses were so comparatively light was a testament to the rescue work performed by Australian coastwatchers and the Solomon Islands natives who worked with them, who put out into the waters of Ironbottom Sound and the Slot in their canoes to search for downed American fliers and get them ashore where they could be picked up.

As the evacuees took off headed for Espiritu Santo, they saw the old four-piper destroyer *McFarland* drop anchor off the island. The ship was carrying 40,000 gallons of avgas and more bombs. Barges from the island unloaded the ship as quickly as possible, but before they could complete the work, a flight of Vals arrived overhead while a fully filled fuel barge was still close by. The stationary *McFarland* made a good target and one of the dive bomber pilots managed to land his 1,250-pound bomb directly on the fuel barge, which erupted like a volcano, staggering *McFarland*

and nearly sinking her. Just as the barge exploded, Major Joe Bauer's 19 VMF-212 Wildcats arrived from Espiritu Santo. The Wildcats were nearly out of fuel when they touched down at the Cow Pasture. Bauer didn't worry about his fuel state as he tore into the Vals and dropped four in a long firing pass through the enemy formation.

On October 23, Joe Foss proved he had become "Swivel-Neck Joe." He led his two flights into a formation of Zeros escorting bombers and shot down four, two on his first pass, after which he zoom-climbed to regain his altitude advantage and returned to shoot down the second pair. He was now an ace. Foss was one of the few Marines on the island who managed to fly a particular fighter. He had his plane's six guns bore-sighted in a particular manner, with the two inner guns set for 250 yards, the next two at 300 yards, and the outer two at 350 yards. While most pilots disliked the armament of the F4F-4, in which the six guns had the same ammunition supply as the four guns of the F4F-3, which reduced total firing time by 30 seconds – a lifetime in combat – Foss was of the opinion that with the defective ammunition being delivered, a pilot using six guns had a 50 percent better chance of keeping enough of his guns working to do the job.

On November 7, Foss tied John L. Smith's score of 19 in a fight with the Shortland Islands Rufes and Petes during which he knocked down two of the difficult Petes and set a Rufe on fire. However, following his victory over the Rufe, he suddenly found himself alone. In that situation, the rule was to head home. However, due to a series of squall lines between the location of the fight and Guadalcanal, Foss missed his landmarks and failed to check his compass. When he did, he discovered he was 30 degrees off course. He was also out of fuel. Ditching off Malaita, the big island just north of Guadalcanal, he was picked up by Solomon Islanders working for the local coastwatcher, with whom he spent the night before General Geiger's PBY appeared in the morning to pick him up and return him to Henderson.

The pace of combat was such that the VMF-212 pilots were relieved due to exhaustion and returned to Espiritu four days after Foss's adventure. Foss's squadron wasn't in much better shape. Four pilots were lost in a fight on November 11. VMF-112 arrived to replace 212 that afternoon.

The most violent four days over Guadalcanal coincided with the two naval battles on the nights of November 12/13 and 14/15.

When Admiral Turner's transports arrived on November 12, the Marine aviators were warned by Bougainville coastwatcher Paul Mason that 25 Bettys with eight Zero escorts were heading down the Slot. Foss and six other pilots managed to climb to 29,000 feet in time to meet the enemy, who failed to show up as they always had before. Cactus radar lost the incoming raid 30 miles out near the eastern tip of Florida Island when the bombers dropped off the screen as they dived to make a torpedo attack on the transports. Foss spotted them through a break in the clouds and led his pilots on a wild dive to catch them. As the fighters dived into warmer air, their canopies glazed with frost. Foss's wild dive created terrific pressure that blew out the plexiglass of his canopy and peeled the walk strips off the Wildcat's wings. He dropped into position behind the enemy bombers just as they began their torpedo run, pulling in 100 yards behind the trailing Betty and set its right engine afire, then flashing over it as it careened into the water below.

Other Wildcats from VMF-112 and P-39 Airacobras of the 67th Squadron got to the attackers before they could release their deadly torpedoes, and more big green bombers splashed into Ironbottom Sound. One Betty struck the stern of the cruiser *San Francisco*, starting a fire. Just as Foss lined up a second Betty, he was interrupted by a Zero that he turned on and exploded just above the water. With these two victories, he was the leading American ace of the war, with a score of 21. In the wild fight over the transports, the Marines shot down 17 Betty torpedo bombers and five Zeros for the loss of three Wildcats and an Airacobra. The transports were safe and continued unloading.

For the Allies in the South Pacific, there was doubt that the Marines could hold Guadalcanal against the coming Japanese offensive. The Japanese fleet was known to be on the move from Truk. The enemy was prepared to make a maximum effort to retake the island. What was left of the US Navy was badly outnumbered by their Imperial Navy opponents.

6

ALL IN

Following the loss of *Wasp*, Admiral Nimitz wrote bleakly of the situation in the Solomons a month later on October 15: "It now appears that we are unable to control the sea in the Guadalcanal area. Thus our supply of the positions will only be done at great expense to us. The situation is not hopeless, but it is certainly critical."

By now, Nimitz had lost confidence in the man he had appointed Commander South Pacific Theater (COMSOPAC), Vice Admiral Robert L. Ghormley, who had held several responsible commands between the wars, being promoted to Rear Admiral in 1936 when he became chief of staff to the Commander in Chief, US Fleet. In 1938, after completing the senior course at the Naval War College, he was appointed Director of the War Plans Division and Assistant Chief of Naval Operations, followed by promotion to Vice Admiral on October 1, 1938. In this position, he had become close to President Franklin D. Roosevelt, who felt a special closeness with the Navy from his time as Assistant Secretary of the Navy during World War I. Admiral Ghormley had been sent to the United Kingdom as a Special Naval Observer for the president after the defeat of France and had been instrumental in pushing for the agreement in which the United States transferred 50 World War I destroyers to the Royal Navy in exchange for American bases in the British New World colonies. He had in fact been senior to Nimitz, who had only been promoted to Rear Admiral in 1938 and then been promoted to full Admiral after Pearl Harbor over admirals like Ghormley and Halsey to take command of the Pacific Fleet.

Nimitz, who owed his position to the relationship he had established with the president while serving in Washington for the three years before his promotion to command the Pacific Fleet, had given command of the new South Pacific Theater to Ghormley at the behest of Chief of Naval Operations, Admiral Ernest J. King, who believed Ghormley's friendship with FDR would be of value in keeping the president in favor of the new offensive operation in the Pacific despite it violating the "Germany First" strategy he had agreed with Churchill would be the dominant feature of Allied war fighting strategy. Unfortunately, Ghormley had not proven equal to the task. His last sea command had been the battleship *Nevada* in the mid-1930s, and he had no experience of carrier operations or understanding of carrier warfare. In the face of the reverses suffered since the invasion of Guadalcanal, his performance had become lackluster and pessimistic, as reflected in his reports to Nimitz. Admiral King had directed Ghormley to "personally oversee" the effort in the Solomons and expected him to place his headquarters on Guadalcanal or aboard ship in the immediate area. However, the admiral had moved his headquarters to Nouméa, 900 miles from Guadalcanal. It had been noted that he had failed to set foot on the island since the Marines had landed or to "make himself visible" to the Allied forces for morale. More importantly, he had failed to resolve the differences between Admirals Fletcher and Turner before the invasion regarding how much time the carriers would provide cover to the landing forces and supply fleet. Fletcher's concern with the fuel state of his fleet was seen as over-cautious and Ghormley was blamed for not laying down the law with more offensively minded operational orders. Increasingly, the admiral was seen as weak and indecisive, two traits that were not looked on favorably in a commander of a combat theater. Both Nimitz and King were concerned with the precarious state of Allied forces in the theater and Ghormley's ability to command soundly.

The day before writing his bleak assessment of the situation in the South Pacific, Nimitz ordered Vice Admiral William F. Halsey, Jr., who was now out of the hospital after an attack of shingles (some thought brought on by nervous exhaustion from his service following Pearl Harbor) that had kept him from command at Midway, to pay a visit to Ghormley's headquarters and provide a personal assessment of the situation. Halsey flew to Nouméa on October 16, 1942, and over the next two days interviewed Ghormley and his staff. In the aftermath of the Bombardment at Guadalcanal and the desperate situation the forces on the island now found themselves in, Halsey's messages made it quickly apparent to Nimitz that Ghormley and his staff did not have answers to the serious questions that were in need of quick answers. In a curt message on October 18, Nimitz informed Ghormley he had been relieved of command and would turn over his duties to Halsey. It was one of the most important decisions he made during the Pacific War.

Placing Halsey in command was precisely what was needed at this moment. "America's Fightingest Admiral" quickly and took command, bringing his decisiveness and aggressive personality to the tasks before him. Word shot through the fleet and the Marines ashore on Guadalcanal like a shot of adrenaline. His fighting reputation sent American morale skyrocketing. His first act was to fly to Henderson Field, where he personally assured General Vandegrift that the Navy would provide all possible support.

Halsey faced an immediate crisis. There was no serious air power left on Guadalcanal and every effort needed to be put into resupplying the island as quickly as possible. In the face of the expansion of the Japanese military force with the successful landings at Cape Esperance, he needed to find reinforcement for the Marines. Most important, a fleet had to be cobbled together to face the Japanese, since it was now apparent their carriers were at sea and that plans were afoot for them to provide support for an offensive by the Imperial Army that could come any day. Fortunately, the US Army's Americal Division had arrived at Nouméa at the end of September. Halsey overrode those who followed the rules, who said he did not have the authority to alter the assignment of the regiment to defending an airfield under construction in Fiji, and Admiral Turner mounted a special convoy that landed the 164th Infantry Regiment on Guadalcanal on October 20.

The Japanese now moved to end the stalemate that had existed on Guadalcanal since the Marine victory at the Battle of Edson's Ridge on September 14. The Imperial Army had prepared a major ground offensive now that 15,000 troops had been landed between October 1 and 17. The battle to take Henderson Field would start on October 20 with victory predicted by October 25. There was a fatal flaw in the Army's plan, since their intelligence estimated there were only 10,000 Marines on the island when in fact there were 23,000, nearly two-and-a-half times the force the Japanese expected to fight. Admiral Yamamoto's plan to provide support for the Army's attack involved moving the Imperial Navy's carriers and other warships into position near the southern Solomons to block any American attempt at reinforcement, with the ultimate hope of engaging the Allied naval forces that responded to the ground offensive and defeating them as had been expected at Eastern Solomons back in August.

On October 20, the 17th Army began their offensive when the main force moved out to position itself for the attack on the Marine positions, scheduled to start the night of October 23. Due to difficulty in positioning the attack force by the planned date, General Hyakutake pushed the attack back 24 hours to October 24. Unfortunately, word of the delay did not make it to the forward units. Two battalions of the 4th Infantry Regiment, supported by nine tanks of the 1st Independent Tank Company, attacked the Marine position at the mouth of the Matanikau River at dusk on October 23. The Americans had no warning of the Japanese approach, but their positions were well laid out and Marine artillery and small arms fire destroyed all nine tanks, killing most of the attacking soldiers while suffering only light casualties themselves in what became known as The Battle of the Matanikau.

The main force under Major General Maruyama hit the Marine positions on the Lunga River late in the evening of October 24, though they did not have the naval gunfire support that had been planned. Over the nights of October 24/25 and 25/26, the Japanese launched several frontal assaults on the positions defended by the 1st Battalion of the 7th Marines, commanded by Lieutenant Colonel Lewis B. "Chesty" Puller, and the Army's 3rd Battalion of the 164th Infantry Regiment, led by Lieutenant Colonel Robert Hall, as the two sides battled in a driving downpour. The fighting came so close that 37mm anti-tank guns fired cannister grapeshot directly into the attacking enemy, and some units held their ground in hand-to-hand fighting. In the two nights of battle, over 1,500 Imperial Army troops were killed, while the Marines and soldiers suffered only 60 casualties. A few small groups of attackers did break through the American line, but were hunted down and killed over the following two days. During the daylight hours, the American positions had been supported by strafing Wildcats and Airacobras that risked taking off from muddy Fighter One and finding their way to the battle lines through the poor weather.

Unaware of the Imperial Army's failure, the Tokyo Express came south on the morning of October 24 to apply the *coup de grâce* to the airfield. As rain pelted Guadalcanal, six VMSB-241 pilots managed to take off. One spotted three enemy destroyers 40 miles from the island. A second found a larger force of five destroyers led by the light cruiser *Yura* 100 miles up the Slot. Five SBDs that had been pieced together in the days following the Bombardment took off at midday, led by VS-71's John Eldridge to deal with the larger force. They spotted *Yura* and the destroyers 50 miles north at 1300 hours. Eldridge led the attack and planted his bomb in the cruiser's main deck, followed by two near misses that brought the ship to a stop. A flight of bomb-carrying P-39s attacked the force while the SBDs went back to refuel and rearm. Bombing 6's Lieutenant Commander Ray Davis with two SBDs were back over the enemy ships at 1500 hours. Davis bombed the destroyer *Akizuki* while his wingmen hit *Yura* again. Eldridge was back at 1630 hours with four SBDs, four P-39s, and three F4Fs. One Army pilot hit *Yura* once more while *Akizuki* took two more near misses. The old cruiser finally sank while the surviving destroyers escorted *Akizuki* back north. There would be no shelling of the airfield.

Despite the Army's failure on Guadalcanal and the loss of *Yura*, Vice Admiral Nobutake Kondō kept the Mobile Fleet south of the Solomons in hopes that the plan to force a fleet action with the Americans might still happen. Kondō led the Advanced Force aboard the cruiser *Atago*, the carrier *Junyō*, battleships *Kongō* and *Haruna*, and their escorts. Vice Admiral Chuichi Nagumo, commander of *Kido Butai* at Pearl Harbor and Midway, commanded the main force, composed of the veteran sister ships *Shōkaku* and *Zuikaku*, and the light carrier *Zuihō*. The Vanguard Force was led by Rear Admiral Hiroaki Abe aboard the battleship *Hiei* with her sister *Kirishima*, accompanied by three heavy cruisers, one light cruiser, and seven destroyers.

On October 24, *Enterprise*, which had departed Pearl Harbor on October 16 following completion of repairs, rendezvoused with *Hornet* and her task force, 273 miles northeast of Espiritu Santo. The new fast battleship *South Dakota* (BB-57) accompanied *Enterprise* as replacement for the damaged *North Carolina*. Operating in accordance with prewar carrier doctrine, each carrier task force operated some ten miles apart and would thus fight separate, uncoordinated actions as the battle developed. Rear Admiral George Murray commanded Task Force 17 from his flagship, *Hornet*, while Task Force 16 was led by Rear Admiral Thomas Kinkaid aboard *Enterprise*. Kinkaid had participated in the Battle of the Eastern Solomons, and was in overall command of the combined groups as Commander Task Force 61/ senior officer present afloat (SOPA). The cruisers *Portland* (CA-33), *Northampton* (CA-26), *Pensacola* (CA-24), *San Juan* (CLAA-54), *San Diego* (CLAA-53), and *Juneau* (CLAA-52) and 14 destroyers escorted the carriers. *San Juan*, *Juneau*, and *San Diego* were a new type of light cruiser, each carrying 16 5-inch dual-purpose guns in eight mounts, specialized for antiaircraft defense.

Task Force 64, commanded by Rear Admiral Willis Lee in the battleship *Washington* (BB-56), included the cruisers *San Francisco* (CA-38), *Helena* (CL-50), and *Atlanta* (CLAA-51), with six destroyers, and was stationed to the south of Guadalcanal to intercept any Imperial Navy transports. In the event, none were sighted and Lee withdrew his force for fueling on October 24, playing no part in the battle.

On October 26, 1942, 40 days after the loss of *Wasp*, American and Japanese carriers met in the fourth and last carrier battle of the opening phase of the Pacific War, the Battle of Santa Cruz, which would prove everything learned in American fleet exercises of the 1930s regarding the deadly speed of carrier warfare.

The Japanese carrier force was spotted at 1103 hours on October 25 by a PBY, approximately 355 miles from Task Force 61, just beyond strike range. Knowing he had been spotted and not knowing the enemy's location, Nagumo turned north to remain beyond range. Kinkaid ordered the fleet north at top speed on receipt of the sighting report to close the range and attack. At 1425 hours, *Enterprise* launched 23 aircraft, but they returned a few hours later, having been unable to find the enemy.

Nagumo reversed course at 0250 hours on October 26. At dawn, the Japanese were 200 miles from Task Force 61. Both Japanese and American carriers launched scouts at first light, and each side discovered the other at almost the same time. Scouting 10 commander LCDR James R. Lee and wingman Ensign William E. Johnson spotted the Japanese carriers at 0645 hours. After making their report, Lee and Johnson attempted to make an attack but eight defending Zeros intercepted them. Lee's and Johnson's gunners shot down three and they escaped with only a

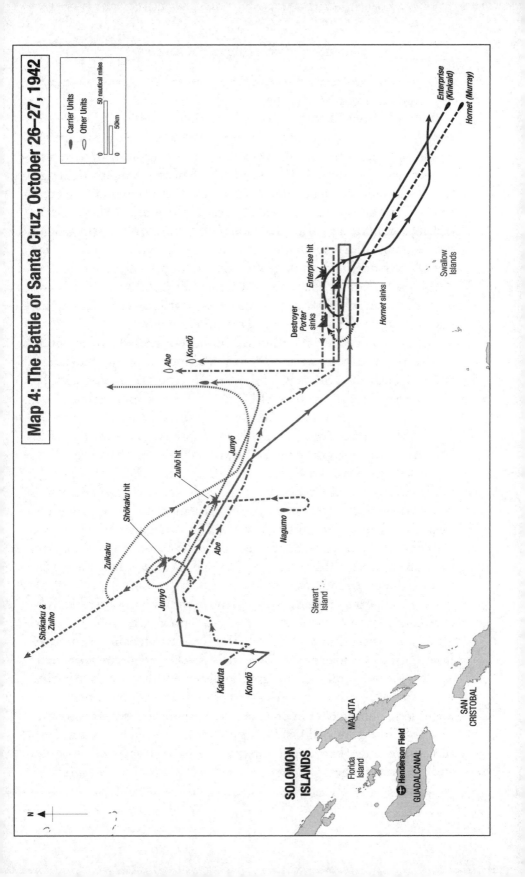

Map 4: The Battle of Santa Cruz, October 26–27, 1942

roughing up. As the VS-10 Dauntlesses evaded the Zeros, a *Shōkaku* Kate spotted *Hornet* at 0658 hours.

Both sides knew that the force that struck first would likely win, and each launched immediate strikes. *Zuikaku*, *Shōkaku*, and *Zuihō* launched 64 aircraft including 21 Vals, 20 Kates, and 21 Zeros at 0740 hours. Shortly after, Scouting 10 pilots Lieutenant Stockton Strong and Ensign Charles Irvine – who had found *Shōkaku* at Eastern Solomons – spotted *Zuihō*. They quickly made their reports and then attacked the carrier while her combat air patrol chased other scouts. Their two 500-pound bombs damaged *Zuihō*'s flight deck, putting her out of action for the rest of the battle, though they were too late to prevent her launch. At 0810 hours, *Shōkaku* followed up with a second strike of 19 Vals and eight Zeros, while *Zuikaku* launched 16 additional Kates at 0840 hours, putting 110 aircraft headed toward the American fleet.

The US carriers launched individual, uncoordinated strikes, rather than operating as the Japanese did in a combined force. At 0800 hours, *Hornet* launched 15 SBDs, six TBF-1s, and eight F4F-4s. Ten minutes later, *Enterprise* sent off three SBDs, seven TBF-1s, and eight F4F-4s. At 0820 hours, *Hornet* followed up with a second group of nine SBDs, eight TBF-1s, and seven F4F-4s. The extreme range meant the strike aircraft couldn't take the time and waste valuable gasoline assembling the strike force. Combined with communications difficulties due to the limited number of HF frequencies, the result was a disorganized action.

Twenty minutes later, the opposing formations flew within sight of each. *Zuihō*'s nine Zeros attacked the *Enterprise* group while they were still climbing for altitude. Four Zeros, three Wildcats, and two Avengers went down, while two Avengers and a Wildcat were so badly damaged that they returned to *Enterprise*.

At 0850 hours, *Hornet*'s strike sighted the Vanguard Force; they continued on and found the main force carriers ten minutes later. Three Zeros from *Zuihō*'s CAP hit the Wildcats, drawing them away from the 15 Dauntlesses that were then attacked by another 20 Zeros which shot down four of the dive bombers. At 0927 hours, *Shōkaku* was attacked by ten Dauntlesses that scored six hits and wrecked her flight deck, putting her out of action. The destroyer *Teruzuki* was near-missed by the 11th SBD, suffering minor damage. The six Avengers turned back after having gotten separated from the rest of the strike and attacked the heavy cruiser *Tone* unsuccessfully. The five surviving

Enterprise Avengers missed the carriers and made an unsuccessful attack on the heavy cruiser *Suzuya*. *Hornet's* second strike also missed the carriers but attacked the heavy cruiser *Chikuma*, causing heavy damage. The *Enterprise* and *Hornet* strikes went into the record books as the least-successful strike missions flown by Navy aircrews in the Pacific War. Only ten of 75 strike aircraft attacked and damaged *Shōkaku*, while two scouts damaged *Zuihō*.

The incoming Japanese strike was picked up on radar at 0830 hours. Unluckily, *Hornet* was spotted by an enemy scout at 0852 hours, just after *Enterprise* entered a rain squall. At 0855 hours radar reported the enemy force was 35 miles from the fleet and 37 Wildcats on CAP were vectored to engage. The single high-frequency radio net was swamped with calls within minutes and only a few defenders engaged the enemy. *Hornet* and her escorts opened fire at 0909 hours when the untouched 20 Kates and 16 Vals commenced their attacks.

At 0912 hours, a Val's 551-pound semi-armor-piercing bomb hit *Hornet* dead center on her flight deck across from the island. The bomb penetrated three decks before it exploded, killing 60 men. A moment later, a high-explosive bomb hit the flight deck and detonated on impact, creating an 11-foot hole and killing 30 men. At 0913 hours, a second armor-piercing bomb hit near the first and also penetrated three decks before exploding, causing severe damage.

At 0914 hours, a Val was hit and set afire by *Hornet's* defensive fire. The pilot continued his dive and hit the carrier's stack, killing seven while burning fuel spread over the signal bridge.

The deadly Kates could attack at 250mph and drop their torpedo from 2,500 feet. With the defenders positioned to stop an American-style low-level/low-speed attack, the Kates were impossible to catch before they dropped their torpedoes. They maneuvered for a classic "hammer and anvil" attack from ahead. Defensive fire from the fleet knocked down several of the Kates, but two Type 95 torpedoes hit *Hornet* in her engineering compartments at 0913 and 0917 hours which knocked out all power and brought her to a stop. A burning Kate deliberately crashed into the hangar deck, starting a fire near the main aviation fuel tanks. At 0922 hours, the surviving enemy planes departed. *Hornet* was dead in the water and on fire.

Enterprise was spotted by a departing attacker as she and her escorts emerged from the rain squall. She immediately began landing the CAP fighters from both carriers while the flight deck crew worked to launch a second strike as soon as possible.

At 1030 hours, *Enterprise*'s radar spotted the second Japanese strike, 40 miles out. She ceased landing operations and ordered the remaining airborne planes out of the area. By now, *Hornet*'s fires were under control with firefighting assistance from three destroyers which had also taken aboard her wounded. Despite the impending attack, *Northampton* continued her preparations to take the carrier under tow.

The enemy arrived overhead at 1105 hours. With *Hornet* judged to be sinking, they concentrated on *Enterprise* at 1108 hours. Radar had missed the enemy altitude and the defending Wildcats were unable to get high enough before the attackers reached *Enterprise*. Two Vals were shot down as they initiated their attack, but *Enterprise* was soon hit by two 551-pound bombs with a third a near miss. Two SBDs were blown overboard while 44 men were killed and 75 were wounded. Worse, the midships elevator was jammed in the "down" position, stopping flight deck operations. Fortunately, the American antiaircraft defense was stronger than had been the case in the previous battles, since *Enterprise*'s and *South Dakota*'s 1.1-inch "Chicago Piano" antiaircraft guns had been replaced by faster-firing 40mm Bofors cannons. Many of the attackers were shot down as they pulled out of their dives.

At 1123 hours, Pearl Harbor and Coral Sea veteran Lieutenant Commander Shigeharu Murata arrived with 15 Kates. Lieutenant Stanley "Swede" Vejtasa, who had just shot down two escaping Vals, spotted Murata's force racing toward *Enterprise* at 250 knots, ten miles out. With his wingman, Lieutenant Harris, Vejtasa dived on the Kates, shooting down five while Harris shot down a sixth before they ran out of ammunition, while another three were shot down by other Wildcats. In so doing, Vejtasa had just set the Navy record to date of seven enemy planes in a single day. The pilot of one Kate that was set afire deliberately crashed into the destroyer *Smith*, setting the destroyer afire and killing 57. *Smith* was saved when her captain steered her into *South Dakota*'s enormous wake, which put out the fires on her bow.

The six surviving Kates went after *Enterprise*. At 1144 hours, they lined up for a "hammer and anvil" attack. The planes to starboard dropped first. Captain Osborne Hardison ordered full right rudder and *Enterprise* combed the torpedoes. He then ordered full left rudder to miss *Smith* and more torpedoes. Moving at 28 knots, the Big E's stern shuddered with each radical turn. She then came in line with five other Kates that were forced into a long turn to get into position. Three of the five were shot down by *Enterprise* and *South Dakota*, while the fourth tried to drop its torpedo while in a stall off the stern; torpedo and bomber fell harmlessly into the sea. The last Kate managed a good drop, but Captain Hardison paralleled the torpedo as it ran past 50 feet away.

The attack was over at 1159 hours. *Enterprise* steadied on course and prepared to land the planes collecting overhead, despite the damaged midships elevator creating a huge hole in the deck. LSO Lieutenant Robin Lindsey had only brought a few aboard before the guns roared back to life. Lieutenant Maseo Yamaguchi's 18 Vals and 12 Zeros, launched belatedly from the carrier *Junyō*, had finally arrived. The Vals scored a near miss on *Enterprise*, while *South Dakota* was hit on the heavily armored number two 16-inch gun turret, which caused minor damage from shrapnel, killing one and wounding 50, including Captain Thomas Gatch. A bomb struck *San Juan* that went completely through her before it exploded under the hull, damaging the rudder. Only six of the Vals escaped to return to their ship.

In the course of the three attacks, *Enterprise*'s VF-10 claimed 17 shot down against seven Wildcats lost and four pilots killed. *Hornet*'s VF-72 claimed 28 for five pilots killed and ten Wildcats lost. *South Dakota* shot down 26, while *Enterprise* gunners claimed 46, the record for any American carrier in the Pacific War. The Japanese recorded the return of nine Zeros from the second strike, returned in serviceable condition, while only two of the 27 Vals and Kates that attacked *Hornet* returned. *South Dakota*'s original claim of nearly 100 attackers shot down was initially believed, and had the unfortunate effect of that belief determining that battleships would be seen primarily as antiaircraft defense for carriers for the rest of the war.

Junyō's air staff officer, Lieutenant Commander Masatake Okumiya, described the return of the strike groups:

We searched the sky with apprehension. There were only a few planes in the air in comparison with the numbers launched several hours before. The planes lurched and staggered onto the deck, every single fighter and bomber bullet-holed. As the pilots climbed wearily from their cramped cockpits, they told of unbelievable opposition, of skies choked with antiaircraft shell bursts and tracers.

The fliers claimed to have sunk three carriers, one battleship, one cruiser, one destroyer, and one "unidentified large warship" while the fleet claimed 79 American aircraft shot down.

At 1235 hours, *Enterprise* turned into the wind and commenced recovering aircraft. In the finest performance ever by an LSO, Robin Lindsey brought in plane after plane at 30-second intervals. They were carefully pushed past the open elevator, though it was impossible to take them below because the forward elevator had been jammed "up." Lindsey refused three orders to stop and brought 95 planes from both carriers aboard. The last 12 had to catch the first or second wire to avoid crashing into the full deck ahead. The last trapped aboard at 1322 hours with its engine dying of fuel starvation on touchdown.

With her deck full, *Enterprise* couldn't conduct air operations. Surmising correctly that the enemy was still capable of launching strikes, Admiral Kinkaid ordered a withdrawal. *Hornet*'s task force was ordered to retreat as soon as they could. Kincaid was right. At 1300 hours, while the damaged *Zuihō* and *Shōkaku* returned to Truk, Admiral Kondō ordered the Advanced and Vanguard Forces to head toward the last reported American position in hopes of a night engagement. At 1306 hours, *Junyō* launched seven Kates and eight Zeros, while *Zuikaku* launched seven Kates, two Vals, and five Zeros. *Junyō* followed with a final launch of four Kates and six Zeros at 1535 hours.

At 1445 hours, *Northampton* commenced towing *Hornet* at five knots. The carrier was on the verge of restoring partial power, but there was no chance she could be towed successfully in the face of continued enemy action, with the fleet so far from a friendly naval facility.

Thirty-five minutes later, *Junyō*'s second strike found the carrier. Six torpedoes missed but *Hornet* was hit amidships at 1523 hours. The sea flooded into the gaping hole and she took on a 14-degree list while the newly repaired electrical system failed. Admiral Murray agreed the cause was hopeless and *Hornet* was given up for lost. As her crew went into the water, *Zuikaku*'s third strike arrived and inflicted the final hit at 1720 hours. Radio intelligence spotted the approaching enemy fleet and Admiral Halsey reluctantly ordered *Hornet* scuttled. Despite destroyers *Mustin* and *Anderson* firing multiple torpedoes and more than 400 5-inch shells, she remained afloat. With the enemy only 20 minutes away, they abandoned the burning hulk at 2040 hours and the Japanese surrounded her at 2220 hours.

When Admiral Kondō realized this was the carrier that had launched the Doolittle Raid, he considered taking her as a war trophy, but it was impossible to take her under tow. The destroyers *Makigumo* and *Akigumo* fired four Type 93 torpedoes at her and *Hornet* finally sank at 0135 hours, October 27, 1942. The Japanese could not continue to pursue the retreating Americans due to fuel shortage. Turning north, the fleet met oilers north of Bougainville and dropped anchor in Truk lagoon on October 30. (*Hornet* was discovered in 17,000 feet of water in February 2019 by the research vessel *Petrel*, which has also discovered the remains of the first *Lexington* and *Wasp* in the Coral Sea.)

The US Navy was now reduced to one damaged carrier afloat in the South Pacific. Over ten and a half months of combat, only *Enterprise* and *Saratoga* were left of the seven carriers so carefully created over the previous 15 years. *Hornet* had lasted 371 days from her commissioning. She would be the last American fleet carrier sunk by enemy action.

Admiral Kincaid reported to Admiral Nimitz that two Shōkaku-class fleet carriers had been hit with bombs and eliminated. The summary report of damage to the enemy included hits to a battleship, three heavy cruisers, a light cruiser, and possible hits on another heavy cruiser. The American claims were as wide of the mark as were the Japanese.

While the Battle of Santa Cruz was a tactical victory for the Imperial Navy, it was a pyrrhic victory. *Shōkaku* and *Zuihō* had suffered such severe damage that *Shōkaku* remained under repair until March 1943. She was not reunited with *Zuikaku* at Truk until July 1943. *Zuihō* returned to Truk in late January 1943. Though undamaged, *Zuikaku* was forced to return to Japan because she did not have sufficient trained aircrew to man the air group. The elite fliers of the Imperial Navy's air force had lost 148 pilots and aircrew members, including two dive bomber squadron leaders, three torpedo squadron leaders, and 18 section or flight leaders, a greater loss than the total from the previous three carrier battles. With these losses, 409 of the 765 elite aviators who had flown in the attack on Pearl Harbor were dead. Their loss would never be replaced. The losses signaled the long decline of the Imperial Sea Eagles.

Admiral Nagumo was reassigned to shore duty in Japan. In his report to Admiral Yamamoto, he stated: "This battle was a tactical win, but a shattering strategic loss for Japan. Considering the great superiority of our enemy's industrial capacity, we must win every battle overwhelmingly in order to win this war. This last one, although a victory, unfortunately, was not an overwhelming victory."

Historian Eric Hammel summed up the significance of the Battle of the Santa Cruz Islands thus: "Santa Cruz was a Japanese victory. That victory cost Japan her last best hope to win the war."

Enterprise arrived at New Caledonia on October 28. The crew had erected a large sign on her flight deck: "Enterprise vs. Japan." Emergency repairs were made to the ship over the next two weeks.

The loss of *Hornet* was such a serious setback that, despite the fact Admiral King was a notorious Anglophobe, he went hat-in-hand to the Royal Navy and requested a British aircraft carrier as temporary reinforcement. HMS *Victorious*, known by her code name "USS Robin," crossed the Atlantic in December 1942 and, after being modified with American equipment, she joined USS *Saratoga* at Nouméa in March 1943. The two carriers provided crucial air support for the invasion of New Georgia in June. As a result of these combined operations, both sides learned important lessons from the other. The Americans adopted the British system of fighter direction for air defense, which was crucial in the Central Pacific campaign and the later battle against the kamikazes, while the British learned modern carrier air operations with their emphasis on the speed of the "operation cycle," knowledge that was put to use in creating a British Pacific Fleet whose carriers would be capable of operating successfully in the final battles of the Pacific War.

Marine Air Group 11 arrived at New Caledonia on October 30 and began feeding pilots and planes into Guadalcanal two days later when Major Joe Sailer's 18 SBDs of VMSB-132 arrived at Henderson on November 1. The next day, Major Paul Fontana and nine pilots of VMF-112 arrived in an R4D. By November 12, all of VMF-112, VMF-122, and VMSB-142 were operational at Henderson. VMSB-131, commanded by Lieutenant Colonel Paul Moret, was the last to arrive, flying the TBF-1 Avengers they had converted to during 22 days in Hawaii in mid-October.

Despite the defeat in the Battle of Henderson Field, the Imperial Army maintained its determination to defeat the Marines and expel them from the island with another attack in November. However, before this could happen, further reinforcements were needed. Admiral Yamamoto provided 11 large transports to bring the 7,000 troops of the 38th Infantry Division with ammunition, food, and heavy equipment from Rabaul to Guadalcanal. On October 9, the battleships *Hiei* and *Kirishima* were assigned to provide support with a second heavy bombardment of Henderson Field the night of November 12–13 to destroy the aircraft there so that the transports could unload safely the next day. Admiral Hiroake Abe commanded the support force from his flagship, *Hiei.*

In the meantime, Admiral Turner continued his small-scale attempts to resupply Guadalcanal. Due to the constant threat posed by enemy aircraft and ships it was difficult to run these convoys, which were forced to arrive shortly after dawn and depart before darkness. In early October, Allied intelligence deduced from radio traffic analysis of the Imperial Navy and from decoded Imperial Army radio messages that the enemy was preparing for a further round on Guadalcanal. In the face of this threat, Halsey demanded an all-out resupply effort. Admiral Turner brought Task Force 67, a large reinforcement and resupply convoy split in two groups that arrived at Guadalcanal shortly after dawn on November 11. The convoy was covered by two task groups commanded by Rear Admirals Daniel J. Callaghan and Norman Scott and given air cover by aircraft from Henderson Field. The ships were attacked twice that day by Japanese aircraft based at Buin on Bougainville, which delayed the unloading Turner had hoped would be completed by dusk. Unloading continued that night, with many ships empty by dawn, but more air attacks were expected with daylight, making it impossible to complete unloading before that evening.

Throughout the daylight hours of November 12, the fleet was at battle stations as waves of enemy planes attacked. That afternoon, Admiral Callaghan's flagship, the heavy cruiser *San Francisco* (CA-38), and destroyer *Buchanan* (DD-484) were both hit, with a total of 30 deaths and 50 wounded. *San Francisco*'s gunners hit a Betty on its torpedo run, setting it afire; the pilot deliberately crashed into the ship on her after machine gun platform, starting a fire. Boatswain's Mate 1st Class Reinhardt Keppler took charge of firefighting and also saw to treatment of the wounded and supervised removal of the dead, saving several lives in the process. Over November 11 and 12, a total of 12 enemy aircraft were shot down by antiaircraft fire from the ships or by fighters from Henderson.

Late the afternoon of the 12th, COMSOPAC warned that a large Japanese fleet had been spotted headed down the Slot. This was the force Allied intelligence had been tracking. Admiral Abe's warships had come through Indispensable Strait into the Slot, while the transports, under the command of the redoubtable Admiral Tanaka, had departed the Shortlands. The enemy force would arrive at Guadalcanal shortly after midnight. Admiral Turner combined his two cover forces into Task Group (TG) 67.4, with Rear Admiral Callaghan in overall command. This was unfortunate, because Rear Admiral Norman Scott had been the victor at the Battle of Cape Esperance in October and had the experience to command in the kind of battle that was expected. However, Callaghan was senior in rank by two days, though his previous experience had been as Chief of Staff to Admiral Fletcher and he had never held a combat command. The force included Callaghan's flagship *San Francisco* with the heavy cruiser *Portland* (CA-33), the light cruisers *Helena*, *Atlanta*, and *Juneau*, supported by the destroyers *Aaron Ward*, *Barton*, *Cushing*, *Fletcher*, *Laffey*, *Monssen*, *O'Bannon*, and *Sterett*. Callaghan's orders were to stop the Japanese at all costs.

Hiei and *Kirishima* were supported by the light cruiser *Nagara* and 11 destroyers, *Samidare*, *Murasame*, *Asagumo*, *Teruzuki*, *Amatsukaze*, *Yukikaze*, *Ikazuchi*, *Inazuma*, *Akatsuki*, *Harusame*, and *Yūdachi*. The destroyers *Shigure*, *Shiratsuyu*, and *Yūgure* were in the Russell Islands as a rear guard during the foray into what the Imperial Navy called "Savo Sound." Fortunately for the Americans, both battleships were only armed with high-explosive shells, for their planned bombardment of Henderson Field. Tanaka's transport force was some 75 miles to the warships' rear.

The night of November 12–13 was the dark of the moon with rain squalls and thunderstorms in all quadrants, perfect weather for what the Imperial Navy planned. The American battle line was led by the older destroyer *Cushing* (DD376), followed by *Laffey* (DD-459), *Sterett* (DD-407), and *O'Bannon* (DD-450). Admiral Scott's flagship, the light cruiser *Atlanta* (CL-51), led the main force followed by Callaghan's flagship *San Francisco*, heavy cruiser *Portland* (CA-33), *Helena* (CL-50), with *Juneau* (CL-52) at the rear of the cruiser line. The destroyers *Aaron Ward* (DD-483), *Barton* (DD-599), *Monssen* (DD-436), and *Fletcher* (DD-445) brought up the rear. The inexperienced Callaghan had placed *Helena* and the brand-new destroyer *Fletcher*, the two ships equipped with the newest SG radar that was less affected by the weather, at the rear of the formation. The rest were equipped with the temperamental

SC radar that would be blinded at important moments by the lightning that surrounded the force. Outside of Scott's ships, none of the fleet had operated or trained together for combat, and Admiral Callaghan did not provide any guidance through a battle plan. At 0124 hours, *Helena's* radar picked up the oncoming Japanese but the weather affected radio communications and she was unable to pass the word quickly to Callaghan, who – when he did get the word – wasted more time in an attempt to reconcile the information reported by radar with his limited sight picture. *San Francisco*, like the other ships, had no Combat Information Center (CIC) to quickly process and coordinate incoming information. Thus, the radar reported ships not in sight while Callaghan tried to coordinate the battle visually from the bridge.

During their approach, Abe's fleet passed through an intense rain squall. His fleet was in a complex formation, and the admiral's confusing orders split the formation into several groups just before they emerged from the storm into "Savo Sound" from the west side of Savo Island rather than directly from the Slot. They thus entered the battle zone from the northwest, rather than the north as the Americans had expected.

While the forces closed, each unseen by the other, Callaghan ordered a turn north to cross the Japanese "T" as Scott had done at Cape Esperance. Both formations then stumbled into rain squalls that affected the American radar and kept Callaghan uncertain of his fleet's positions when *Cushing* confirmed the radar contacts were enemy. The admiral's uncertainty led him to refuse to give the order to open fire in fear that the targets reported were American when *Cushing* requested permission to do so. His indecision was fatal.

Suddenly both formations emerged from the squalls, with Admiral Abe surprised to find an unexpected American fleet practically within point-blank range. Like Callaghan, Abe hesitated, unsure if the ships he saw were not some of his own. The American formation began to fall apart, which delayed Callaghan's order to open fire as he tried to ascertain his ships' positions. The delay by both admirals meant the two formations started to overlap as individual captains on both sides awaited permission to commence fire. At 0148 hours, both *Akatsuki* and *Hiei* turned on their searchlights, illuminating *Atlanta*, which was only 3,000 yards distant. At the same time, ships in both forces simultaneously opened fire and the two formations disintegrated completely.

Map 5: The First Naval Battle of Guadalcanal, November 13, 1942

Samidare

Murasame

Asagumo

IRON BOTTOM SOUND

Teruzuki

Amatsukaze

Kirishima

Yukikaze

Hiei

Yudachi

Nagara   Harusame

Ikazuchi

Cushing

Laffey

Sterett

Inazuma

O'Bannon

Atlanta

Akatsuki

San Francisco

Portland   Helena

Juneau

N

Aaron Ward

Barton

Monssen

Fletcher

| 0 | 2500 yards |
| 0 | 2500m |

Realizing his force was nearly surrounded by the Japanese, Callaghan ordered, "Odd ships fire to starboard, even ships fire to port." What happened next was described by one of the surviving officers on *Monssen* as "a barroom brawl after the lights had been shot out." The two fleets intermingled and fought each other in an utterly confused close-range melee in which the Imperial Navy's superior optic sights and 20 years of night battle training proved their superiority. Unfortunately for the Americans, the 13 Japanese destroyers were all armed with the deadly Type 93 torpedo and almost all the American losses in the battle would come from this weapon.

Cushing, in the lead of the American formation, took fire from the cruiser *Nagara* and several destroyers. Hit heavily, she stopped dead in the water. *Atlanta* was hit by gunfire and torpedoes from *Nagara* and the destroyers *Inazuma*, *Ikazuchi*, and *Akatsuki*, which caused heavy damage. A torpedo hit cut all engineering power and she drifted into *San Francisco*'s line of fire. The hits from *San Francisco* caused even greater damage, killing Admiral Scott and many of the bridge crew. Powerless and unable to fire her guns, *Atlanta* drifted out of control, taking more fire as the enemy passed her by until she drifted out of the battle.

Laffey, which had only been commissioned the previous March 31 and had arrived in the South Pacific in early September in time to rescue survivors of *Wasp* and participate in the Battle of Cape Esperance, would live up to her namesake, Seaman Bartlett Laffey, an Irish-born US Navy sailor who received the Medal of Honor for manning a howitzer at the Battle of Yazoo City in 1864, despite the rest of the crew being killed, thereby turning back the Confederate assault before he was killed by a rifle shot. The destroyer narrowly missed a collision as she passed 20 feet from *Hiei*, which couldn't depress her batteries low enough to hit her. *Laffey* raked *Hiei*'s superstructure with 5-inch and machine gun fire, damaging her bridge, wounding Admiral Abe, and killing his chief of staff. The battleship was also hit from close range by *Sterett* and *O'Bannon*. *Laffey* was hit by fire from an enemy destroyer that knocked out her number three gun mount. With *Hiei* on her port beam, *Kirishima* on her stern, and two destroyers on her port bow, *Laffey* fought with her three remaining main battery guns in a no-quarter duel at point-blank range in which she was hit by a 14-inch shell from *Hiei*. One of the enemy destroyers fired a torpedo that hit her fantail and put *Laffey* out of action. As her captain, Lieutenant Commander William

B. Hank, gave the order to abandon ship, a violent explosion ripped her in two and she sank immediately. Of her 247-member crew, 59 were killed, including Captain Hank, with 116 wounded. *Laffey* was later awarded the Presidential Unit Citation. When oceanographer Robert Ballard discovered her forward hulk in Ironbottom Sound in 1995, her two forward guns were still aimed out.

As *Laffey* sank, *San Francisco* passed 2,500 yards from *Hiei* and the battleship – along with *Kirishima, Inazuma,* and *Ikazuchi* – concentrated fire on her. *San Francisco* took 15 major hits and 25 lesser ones in two minutes. The bridge was turned into swiss cheese by the hits and Admiral Callaghan, Captain Cassin Young, and most of the bridge crew were killed. Fortunately, *Hiei's* and *Kirishima's* first shots were the special fragmentation bombardment shells and *San Francisco* was saved from being sunk outright. In return, *San Francisco* landed at least one shell in *Hiei's* steering gear room, flooding the compartment and shorting out the power steering generators, which severely inhibited the battleship's maneuverability. *San Francisco's* crew was plunged immediately into a fight to save their ship that is best described in the citations for the three Medals of Honor awarded for actions taken by the crew which saved her.

Command devolved within five minutes to Lieutenant Commander Herb Schonland, the damage control officer. His citation reads:

> For extreme heroism and courage above and beyond the call of duty as damage control officer of the U.S.S. San Francisco in action against greatly superior enemy forces in the battle off Savo Island, 12–13 November 1942. In the same violent night engagement in which all of his superior officers were killed or wounded, Lt. Comdr. Schonland was fighting valiantly to free the San Francisco of large quantities of water flooding the second deck compartments through numerous shell holes caused by enemy fire. Upon being informed that he was commanding officer, he ascertained that the conning of the ship was being efficiently handled, then directed the officer who had taken over that task to continue while he himself resumed the vitally important work of maintaining the stability of the ship. In water waist deep, he carried on his efforts in darkness illuminated only by hand lanterns until water in flooded compartments had been drained or pumped off and watertight integrity had again been

restored to the San Francisco. His great personal valor and gallant devotion to duty at great peril to his own life were instrumental in bringing his ship back to port under her own power, saved to fight again in the service of her country.

Wounded Marine Gunnery Sergeant Tom MacGuire was able to climb down from his battle station on the signal bridge where he was the only survivor and enter the navigating bridge. He recalled the scene of devastation in an interview 50 years later: "There was blood everywhere, the bulkheads looked like swiss cheese. The Admiral died as I touched him. Then I saw someone stir, and I went to him." It was Lieutenant Commander Bruce McCandless, the Communications Officer, who had been knocked unconscious when he was thrown against a bulkhead by an explosion. McCandless recovered and sent MacGuire to ascertain the situation, since all internal communications were knocked out. McCandless's citation reads:

For conspicuous gallantry and exceptionally distinguished service above and beyond the call of duty as communication officer of the U.S.S. San Francisco in combat with enemy Japanese forces in the battle off Savo Island, 12/13 November 1942. In the midst of a violent night engagement, the fire of a determined and desperate enemy seriously wounded Lt. Comdr. McCandless and rendered him unconscious, killed or wounded the admiral in command, his staff, the captain of the ship, the navigator, and all other personnel on the navigating and signal bridges. Faced with the lack of superior command upon his recovery, and displaying superb initiative, he promptly assumed command of the ship and ordered her course and gunfire against an overwhelmingly powerful force. With his superiors in other vessels unaware of the loss of their admiral, and challenged by his great responsibility, Lt. Comdr. McCandless boldly continued to engage the enemy and to lead our column of following vessels to a great victory. Largely through his brilliant seamanship and great courage, the San Francisco was brought back to port, saved to fight again in the service of her country.

While *San Francisco* continued her out-of-control death ride through the enemy fleet, Boatswain's Mate Keppler, the man who had led the fight to put out the fire caused by the crash of the Betty earlier that day, continued his heroic actions, as detailed in the citation for his posthumous medal:

> For extraordinary heroism and distinguished courage above and beyond the call of duty while serving aboard the U.S.S. San Francisco during action against enemy Japanese forces in the Solomon Islands, 12/13 November 1942. When a hostile torpedo plane, during a daylight air raid, crashed on the after machine-gun platform, Keppler promptly assisted in removal of the dead and, by his capable supervision of the wounded, undoubtedly helped save the lives of several shipmates who otherwise might have perished. That night, when the ship's hangar was set afire during the great battle off Savo Island, he bravely led a hose into the starboard side of the stricken area and there, without assistance and despite frequent hits from terrific enemy bombardment, eventually brought the fire under control. Later, although mortally wounded, he labored valiantly in the midst of bursting shells, persistently directing fire-fighting operations and administering to wounded personnel until he finally collapsed from loss of blood. His great personal valor, maintained with utter disregard of personal safety, was in keeping with the highest traditions of the U.S. Naval Service. He gallantly gave his life for his country.

Marine Sergeant James Eaton, ashore and seeing the battle from a hilltop, described it 30 years later: "It was the most terrible fireworks display you could ever see. In the middle of the lightning flashes all around were the bursting star shells and the bright lights of explosions as a ship was hit. The Bombardment scared me nearly to death; I can only imagine how awful it was on those ships."

Writing at the time, correspondent Ira Wolfert described the scene:

> The action was illuminated in brief, blinding flashes by Jap searchlights which were shot out as soon as they were turned on, by muzzle flashes from big guns, by fantastic streams of tracers, and by huge orange-colored explosions as two Jap destroyers and one of our destroyers blew up. From the beach it resembled a door to hell opening and closing, over and over.

Nagara and the destroyers *Teruzuki* and *Yukikaze* came upon the drifting *Cushing*. They pounded the wounded destroyer with gunfire, knocking out all systems. Unable to respond, the order to abandon ship was passed and *Cushing*'s crew went into the water. She sank several hours later.

Portland opened fire on the destroyer *Akatsuki* along with *Sterett*; their combined fire hit the enemy's magazines and *Akatsuki* blew up. Minutes later, *Portland* was hit by a torpedo from the destroyers *Inazuma* or *Ikazuchi* that caused heavy damage to her rudder, which was jammed over. Forced to steam in a circle, as she completed the first loop *Portland* spotted *Hiei* and hit her with four salvoes. Her crew was then fully occupied with getting the cruiser back under control and she took no further part in the battle.

Cruiser *Juneau* and the four destroyers at the rear of the American formation came under attack from the destroyers *Yūdachi* and *Amatsukaze*, which used their deadly Type 93 torpedoes with terrible purpose. *Barton* was hit by two torpedoes from *Amatsukaze*, which blew her up; she sank nearly immediately with most of her crew. *Amatsukaze* also torpedoed *Juneau* when she found the cruiser engaged with *Yūdachi*. The hit was ultimately fatal, breaking *Juneau*'s keel and knocking out most systems. The fatally damaged cruiser slowly crept away to the east. *Monssen* managed to avoid the wreck of *Barton*, but was spotted by *Asagumo*, *Murasame*, and *Samidare* just after they sank *Laffey*. The three opened fire and overwhelmed *Monssen*. The damage was so severe *Monssen*'s crew was forced to abandon ship.

While *San Francisco* had survived her out-of-control plunge through the enemy fleet, she was not out of danger. *Amatsukaze* spotted her and approached with torpedoes ready. Concentrating on the helpless target, no one aboard the destroyer saw *Helena* until she opened fire with a 15-gun broadside, following up with several more that seriously damaged *Amatsukaze*. Before *Helena* could finish, she was distracted by the busy *Asagumo*, *Murasame*, and *Samidare*, which allowed the badly damaged *Amatsukaze* to generate smoke and escape.

Helena was able to chase off her new attackers with a well-aimed radar-directed barrage of 6-inch shells that damaged all three enemy ships.

Yūdachi steamed through the explosion-laced darkness and failed to sight the approach of *Aaron Ward* and *Sterett* until both destroyers hit her simultaneously with gunfire and torpedoes. Heavily damaged, *Yūdachi's* crew abandoned ship. Minutes later, *Sterett* was ambushed by *Teruzuki* and hit badly, forcing her to withdraw from the battle area to the east. At nearly the same time, *Aaron Ward* was spotted by *Kirishima* and engaged in a close-in gunfire duel that she lost with heavy damage. Attempting to withdraw, *Aaron Ward* soon came to a stop when her damaged engines failed.

After close to 40 minutes of the kind of brutal, close-quarters ship-versus-ship fighting that hadn't been seen since the Age of Sail, the fleets broke contact and ceased fire at 0226 hours when Captain Gilbert Hoover of *Helena,* the senior surviving US officer, gave orders to disengage. On the American side, only *Helena* and the destroyer *Fletcher* could offer resistance, while *Kirishima, Nagara,* and the destroyers *Asagumo, Teruzuki, Yukikaze,* and *Harusame* were only lightly damaged, with *Inazuma, Ikazuchi, Murasame,* and *Samidare* damaged enough to somewhat impair their fighting ability.

At that moment, it appeared that the do-or-die effort by Callaghan's fleet had failed, since the enemy fleet was still capable of continuing on to bombard Henderson Field and finish off what American naval force was still in the area, which would allow Tanaka's fleet to land the troops and supplies safely in the morning. Admiral Abe, however, ordered his fleet to retire. While the decision has been compared with Admiral Kurita's decision to retire during the Battle off Samar two years later, when he could have proceeded to destroy the invasion fleet in Leyte Gulf, Admiral Abe faced a different situation. *Hiei* was badly damaged and both she and *Kirishima* had expended much of the special bombardment ammunition, which meant the fleet might not destroy Henderson. This would leave them vulnerable to an air attack at dawn. Because of *Hiei's* damaged communications, he did not know the extent of American losses, while his ships were scattered and would take some considerable time to reform for a bombardment. As the Imperial fleet turned back, *Kirishima* attempted to take *Hiei* under tow, but water flooded the damaged battleship's compartments and her rudder was jammed hard over, making it impossible. *Yukikaze* and *Teruzuki* remained behind to assist *Hiei's* withdrawal, while *Samidare* found and picked up *Yūdachi's* survivors at 0300 hours before retiring.

The rising sun revealed a terrible sight in Ironbottom Sound. *Portland, San Francisco, Aaron Ward,* and *Sterett* were badly damaged but their crews were eventually able to restore power and they were able to withdraw successfully for later repair. Unfortunately, the badly damaged *Atlanta* sank later that night at 2000 hours. Once the fleet was ready to limp away, *Helena's* Captain Hoover, the senior surviving commander, ordered the ships to prepare for withdrawal to Espiritu Santo at 1200 hours.

At 1100 hours, the badly damaged *Juneau* was steaming on one screw at her maximum possible speed of 13 knots, 800 yards off *San Francisco's* starboard forward quarter, down 13 feet at her bow with waves washing over her forecastle. At that moment, the Japanese submarine *I-26* spotted the fleet and fired two torpedoes at *San Francisco*. Both passed ahead of her and one struck *Juneau* in the same place where she had been torpedoed the night before. In an enormous explosion, the cruiser broke in two and disappeared in 20 seconds. Aboard *Helena*, Captain Hoover wrongly concluded there were no survivors from the sinking. Fearing a second submarine attack, he ordered the fleet to leave without stopping to try to rescue anyone.

However, more than 100 of *Juneau's* 697-man crew had survived, including at least two of the five famous Sullivan brothers of Boston, who had gained considerable publicity before the war when they all joined the Navy and were assigned together aboard *Juneau*. The survivors were left in the open ocean for eight days before the ten who had survived the elements and shark attacks were spotted in separate rafts five miles apart by passing aircraft, and USS *Ballard* (DD-267) effected their rescue on November 20.

Word of the loss of the five Sullivan brothers made it into the American press, along with the statement by one of the survivors that he had been with the last of the brothers until only days before their rescue. Captain Hoover's decision to depart in order to save the fleet was bitterly criticized both in the press and the Navy, and he was relieved of command by Admiral Halsey. Writing after the war, Halsey criticized his own decision, stating that Hoover's decision to save the fleet, when stopping to search would have exposed them to further attack, was right.

In the aftermath of the battle, the Navy announced the force had sunk an estimated seven enemy ships, and proclaimed that the Japanese withdrawal indicated a significant victory. Only when the Imperial Navy's records became available after the war did the Navy discover it had actually suffered a crushing tactical defeat, one of the worst in the service's history. Despite this, the outcome of the battle was as strategically important as the victory at Midway. The significance was described by historian Eric Hammel: "On November 12, 1942, the Imperial Navy had the better ships and the better tactics. After November 15, 1942, its leaders lost heart and it lacked the strategic depth to face the burgeoning US Navy and its vastly improving weapons and tactics. The Japanese never got better while, after November 1942, the US Navy never stopped getting better."

The badly damaged *Hiei* was discovered by planes from Guadalcanal shortly after dawn on November 14, circling to starboard at five knots accompanied by her two escorts. Later that morning, B-17Es of the 11th Bomb Group that flew up from Espiritu Santo attempted unsuccessfully to bomb her. At 1130 hours, two of VMSB-131's newly arrived Avengers successfully torpedoed the battleship but she refused to go down. Over the rest of the day, shuttle missions of dive and torpedo bombers from Henderson attacked, turning the ship into scrap with repeated hits. Finally, at dusk, her captain ordered the crew to abandon ship and the destroyers picked them up before finally heading north after torpedoing her again. *Hiei* eventually sank sometime in the night of November 13–14, the first Japanese battleship lost in the Pacific War. In 2019, the research vessel *Petrel* found her, upside down in Ironbottom Sound, at a depth of 900 feet.

Rear Admiral Norman Scott, the victor at Cape Esperance, who – with Admiral Callaghan – was one of only two American admirals killed in action during the Pacific War, was awarded the fourth Medal of Honor related to the battle, in recognition of his leadership in the first battle and for what might have been otherwise had he and not Callaghan commanded in the second fight. His citation reads:

> For extraordinary heroism and conspicuous intrepidity above and beyond the call of duty during action against enemy Japanese forces off Savo Island on the night of 11–12 October and again on the night of 12–13 November 1942. In the earlier action, intercepting a Japanese Task Force intent upon storming our island positions and landing reinforcements at Guadalcanal, Rear Adm. Scott, with courageous skill and superb coordination of the units under his command, destroyed 8 hostile vessels and put the others to flight. Again

challenged, a month later, by the return of a stubborn and persistent foe, he led his force into a desperate battle against tremendous odds, directing close-range operations against the invading enemy until he himself was killed in the furious bombardment by their superior firepower. On each of these occasions his dauntless initiative, inspiring leadership and judicious foresight in a crisis of grave responsibility contributed decisively to the rout of a powerful invasion fleet and to the consequent frustration of a formidable Japanese offensive. He gallantly gave his life in the service of his country.

The sacrifice by Callaghan, Scott, and their men had only delayed the Japanese by a day. Furious over Abe's poor performance, Admiral Yamamoto immediately removed him from his command and directed Admiral Kondō to resume the mission. Kondō was described by other officers he had served with as an "English sort of officer, very gentlemanly, and good with his staff, but better suited for training command than battle." He was well-respected by the "battleship faction" of the Imperial Navy, and was the senior admiral in the South Pacific. Admiral Gunichi Mikawa's cruiser force from the Eighth Fleet that had been originally assigned to cover the troop landing on November 13 was ordered to rendezvous with *Kirishima* and her escorts to finish the bombardment of Henderson Field. Mikawa's fleet included the heavy cruisers *Chōkai*, *Kinugasa*, *Maya*, and *Suzuya*, the light cruisers *Isuzu* and *Tenryū*, and six destroyers.

That afternoon, after having turned back with Abe's decision to withdraw, Admiral Tanaka's 11 transports and their escorts turned to again head for Guadalcanal with plans to land the troops early in the morning of November 14.

The evening of November 13, with the remains of the US fleet having withdrawn, Mikawa's force entered Ironbottom Sound uncontested. At 0155 hours on November 14, *Suzuya* and *Maya* bombarded Henderson for 35 minutes while the rest of the force stood off Savo Island to cover them if the Americans attempted to intervene. The bombardment caused some damage to aircraft and field facilities but Henderson was not put out of action. The Japanese withdrew toward Rabaul.

At dawn on November 14, as *Enterprise* sailed through squalls, low clouds, and rain, she launched ten SBD scouts to find the enemy. At 0915 hours, Lieutenant (jg) Robert D. Gibson reported spotting two battleships and two cruisers. He had actually found Admiral Mikawa's force, 230 miles north of Guadalcanal. After shadowing the force another 15 minutes, he broke out of the clouds and executed an attack on *Kinugasa*. Dropping his 500-pound bomb on the cruiser from 1,000 feet at 0930 hours, his bomb hit forward of the cruiser's bridge, killing the captain and executive officer. *Kinugasa* soon took on a ten-degree port list.

Shortly after Gibson's attack, Ensigns R.A. Hoogerwerf and P.M. Halloran showed up and pounced on *Maya*. Halloran held his dive too long and on pullout he clipped *Maya*'s mainmast, crashing into her port side, igniting 4.7-inch shells from her secondary battery. The crash and explosions killed 37, but the cruiser was able to maintain position and speed with the others. At 1045 hours, 17 more dive bombers appeared over the fleet in response to Gibson's sighting report and initiated attacks. Heavy cruiser *Chōkai*'s boiler room was flooded by near misses, while light cruiser *Isuzu*'s steering was knocked out. Other near misses knocked out *Kinugasa*'s engines and jammed her rudder. At 1122 hours, *Kinugasa* capsized and sank, taking 511 of her crew with her.

Bombers from *Enterprise* and Guadalcanal also spotted and made repeated attacks throughout the afternoon on Tanaka's transport force, sinking six transports and damaging a seventh so badly it was forced to turn back, later sinking. The four remaining transports continued on, stopping after nightfall to await the results of the second naval battle that developed that night.

Admiral Kondō, aboard the heavy cruiser *Atago* and accompanied by the heavy cruiser *Takao*, light cruisers *Nagara* and *Sendai*, with the destroyers *Asagumo*, *Hatsuyuki*, *Shirayuki*, *Shikinami*, *Uranami*, and *Teruzuki*, rendezvoused with *Kirishima*, *Samidari*, and *Inazuma* the evening of November 13, but remained out of range of Henderson's aircraft on the morning of November 14 while they refueled. The American submarine *Trout* (SS-202) spotted the ships and attempted to attack them unsuccessfully. Late in the afternoon, Kondō's force headed toward Guadalcanal and came under an air attack that failed to stop them. The submarine *Flying Fish* (SS-229) spotted the fleet shortly after the air attack and managed to fire five torpedoes but failed to score. Her contact report informed Admiral Halsey that Guadalcanal was still under serious threat.

In the face of the threat, Halsey ordered the battleships *Washington* and *South Dakota* to leave *Enterprise* on November 13 to reinforce Callaghan, but they were unable to reach the Solomons in time. It was a dangerous move on Halsey's part because the two battleships and *Enterprise* were his last capital ships, and he was unable to give what was considered proper support, since there were only four destroyers available, *Walke* (DD-416), *Benham* (DD-397), *Preston* (DD-379), and *Gwin* (DD-433). None of the American ships had ever operated or trained together. Task Force 54 was commanded by Rear Admiral Willis A. "Ching Chong" Lee, considered the Navy's leading gunnery expert and known as a chain-smoking, approachable commander who relieved tension by reading lurid novels or swapping sea stories with the enlisted men standing watch duty on the bridge. The next morning, when the oncoming Japanese were spotted, the two ships were 100 miles south of Guadalcanal. Halsey ordered them to proceed and enter Ironbottom Sound to stop the Japanese bombardment. Following an evening meal in which Lee briefed the ship's officers on their mission and went over his expectations of how they would fight the battle, the force entered Ironbottom Sound and arrived off Savo Island at dusk.

Shortly after 2200 hours, Kondō's ships entered the sound. The admiral split his force, sending *Sendai* and destroyers *Shikinami* and *Uranami* to sweep the east side of Savo Island while *Ayanami* swept the southwest side of the island to scout for Allied ships. Lee's force was spotted at 2300 hours, though the battleships were misidentified as cruisers. Kondō then ordered *Sendai* and her destroyers to join *Nagara* and the destroyers *Asagumo*, *Hatsuyuki*, *Shirayuki*, and *Teruzuki* to engage the enemy force before he brought his bombardment force into position off Guadalcanal. Lee's ships spotted the *Sendai* force on radar but failed to detect the others. Using radar-directed fire control, *Washington* and *South Dakota* opened fire on *Sendai* and her destroyers at 2317 hours. At 2322 hours, Lee ordered a ceasefire when the enemy ships disappeared from the radar. Unknown to the Americans, *Sendai*, *Uranami*, and *Shikinami* were undamaged.

As the battleships ceased firing, the four American destroyers engaged *Ayanami* and the *Nagara* group. The enemy responded, hitting *Walke* and *Preston* with gunfire and torpedoes. At 2336 hours, Commander Max C. Stormes, *Preston*'s captain, gave the order to abandon ship. *Preston* rolled over on her starboard side a minute later, then hung with her bow in the air for ten minutes before she sank, taking 117 men and her captain with her. *Gwin* took a hit in her engine room at 2332 hours that put her out of the battle. As *Walke*'s captain, Commander Thomas E. Fraser, prepared to fire torpedoes, the destroyer was hit by a Type 93 torpedo at 2338 hours in the number 2 magazine. The explosion blew off her bow. As the fires spread, power and communication failed. Fraser ordered abandon ship minutes later and four rafts were launched before she went down. As she sank, her depth charges exploded, killing 80 men in the water including Captain Fraser. Another torpedo hit *Benham* and blew off her bow, forcing her to withdraw before sinking the next day. Despite their losses, the American destroyers had successfully screened the battleships.

Washington steamed through the wreckage of *Walke* and *Preston*, drowning many of the few survivors as she took *Ayanami* under fire with her secondary battery and set the enemy ship on fire. *South Dakota*, which was close behind, suddenly suffered a series of electrical failures when her chief engineer locked down a circuit breaker in violation of safety procedures. The circuits repeatedly went into series, and her radar, radios, and almost all her gun batteries became inoperable. She followed *Washington* toward the western side of Savo Island until *Washington* changed course left to pass to the south behind the burning destroyers at 2355 hours. As she tried to follow, *South Dakota* was forced to turn starboard to avoid *Benham*, putting her between the fires and the enemy, thus silhouetting her.

Having received reports that the American destroyers had been destroyed, Admiral Kondō brought the bombardment force into Ironbottom Sound as he headed toward Guadalcanal in the belief the Americans had been defeated. Unknown to the admiral, his force and the two American battleships were now on a collision course.

Just before midnight, Kondō's ships sighted the silhouetted *South Dakota*, and *Kirishima* opened fire on her while the destroyers also opened fire and launched torpedoes. Nearly blind and unable to effectively fire her guns, *South Dakota* managed a few hits on *Kirishima* while taking 26 hits that knocked out her communications and what was left of her fire control while fires broke out on her upper decks, forcing her to turn away at 0017 hours on November 15.

As they concentrated their fire on *South Dakota*, the Japanese failed to detect the approach of *Washington*. At a range of 9,000 yards,

Admiral Lee determined the target he was tracking was not *South Dakota* and opened fire on *Kirishima* at exactly midnight, hitting her with at least nine and possibly 20 16-inch shells and 17 5-inch hits from the secondary battery, most of which hit below the waterline. The hits disabled all of *Kirishima's* main battery, caused major flooding, and set her on fire while her rudder was jammed, forcing her to circle to port, out of control.

Kondō ordered all ships that were able to converge and destroy the enemy at 0025 hours, but the force could not locate *Washington* in the darkness since they had no radar. Lee headed toward the Russell Islands to draw the enemy away from Guadalcanal and *South Dakota*. Kondō's surviving ships spotted *Washington* at 0050 hours and the destroyers launched several torpedo attacks which Lee avoided as he withdrew from the battle. Believing the way was now clear for the transport convoy, Kondō ordered his fleet to break off at 0104 hours. By 0130 the Japanese had departed.

Kirishima, badly battered, was still afloat. Like *Hiei*, her boilers and engines still worked, but the rudder was jammed ten degrees to starboard. Her commander, Captain Sanji Iwabuchi, fought to save his ship but the flooding was beyond control. He ordered the magazines flooded as fire spread through them but that only worsened the ship's condition. *Nagara* rigged a tow. *Kirishima* limped behind, listing to starboard. At 0300 hours Captain Iwabuchi ordered the emperor's portrait transferred to *Asagumo*. At 0325 hours, *Kirishima* rolled over and sank northwest of Savo Island. She was the second battleship the Imperial Navy had lost in two days and the first enemy battleship sunk by an American battleship since the Battle of Santiago Bay in the Spanish–American War. The badly damaged *Ayanami* was scuttled by torpedoes from *Uranami* at 0200 hours, after which *Uranami* rescued *Ayanami's* survivors. *Kirishima's* survivors were rescued by *Asagumo*, *Teruzuki*, and *Samidare*. *Kirishima* was found in 1995 by Robert Ballard, upside down at a depth of 3,000 feet.

The badly damaged *Gwin* escorted *Benham*, which staggered with a severely fractured hull. At 0300 hours her captain, Lieutenant Commander John B. Taylor, evacuated the forward half to reduce strain on the keel and radioed his situation to Lee, who ordered the two to head for Espiritu Santo. By mid-afternoon of November 15, *Benham* had lost headway and the crew was evacuated to *Gwin*. An attempt to

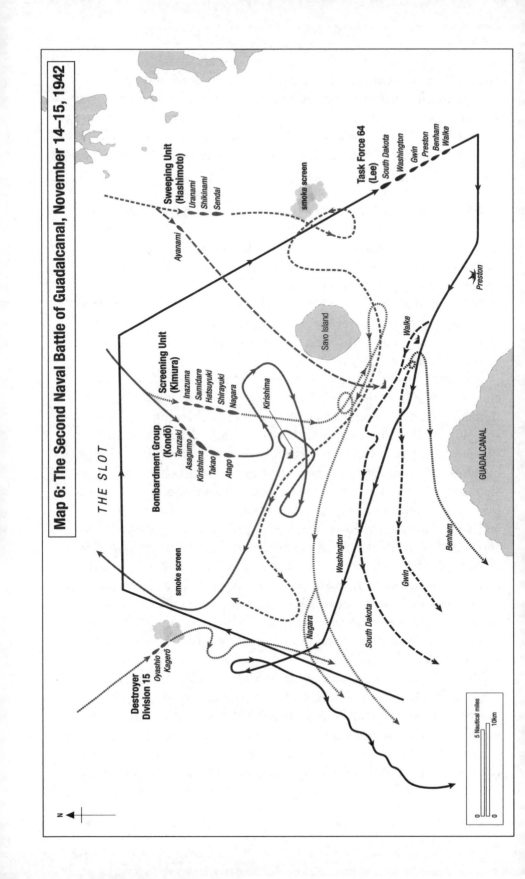

Map 6: The Second Naval Battle of Guadalcanal, November 14–15, 1942

N

THE SLOT

Destroyer
Division 15
Oyashio
Kagerō

smoke screen

Bombardment Group
(Kondō)
Teruzaki
Asagumo
Kirishima
Takao
Atago

Screening Unit
(Kimura)
Inazuma
Samidare
Hatsuyuki
Shirayuki
Nagara

Sweeping Unit
(Hashimoto)
Uranami
Shikinami
Sendai

Ayanami

smoke screen

Savo Island

Kirishima

Nagara

South Dakota

Gwin

Benham

Walke

Preston

Washington

Task Force 64
(Lee)
South Dakota
Washington
Gwin
Preston
Benham
Walke

GUADALCANAL

5 Nautical miles
0

10km
0

scuttle *Benham* was made when *Gwin* fired two torpedoes that failed. She then shelled *Benham* until a 5-inch round hit *Benham*'s magazines at 1735 hours and she sank. The badly wounded *Gwin* continued on to Espiritu Santo at 10 knots.

The four transports that had survived the attacks by the Cactus Air Force the afternoon of November 14 beached themselves at Tassafaronga at 0400 hours on November 15. Admiral Tanaka and the escort destroyers departed after unloading the troops they carried and raced back up the Slot toward safer waters. The beached transports were attacked, beginning at 0555 hours, by aircraft from Henderson Field, and by field artillery from Marine ground forces on Guadalcanal. Later that morning, the destroyer *Meade* (DD-602) crossed Ironbottom Sound from Tulagi and spent almost an hour blasting the four beached transports with several hundred rounds of 5-inch fire. *Meade*'s concentrated gunfire set them afire, destroying all equipment that had yet to be unloaded, and turned them into twisted wreckage wracked by internal explosions. In the end, only 2,000–3,000 troops made it onto Guadalcanal, where they offered little reinforcement since most of their ammunition and food had been lost.

Once she ceased firing at the transports, *Meade* cruised the waters between Savo Island and Guadalcanal, rescuing 266 survivors from the sunken destroyers *Preston* and *Walke*.

The Japanese failure to land the troops successfully with their equipment meant that there would not be another offensive mounted to take Henderson Field. From November 15 on, Admiral Tanaka's Tokyo Express could only deliver ever-dwindling supplies by destroyer, dropping them in waterproof cannisters to drift ashore.

After the Naval Battle of Guadalcanal, the US Navy was able to supply the island. Two fresh divisions of Army troops relieved the exhausted 1st Marine Division at the end of November and the Marines were evacuated to Sydney, Australia.

The Imperial Navy would never replace its losses at Guadalcanal. Within a year, a new United States Navy would appear in the Pacific, stronger and better-organized than the fleet that fought at Guadalcanal, but it was the prewar navy that held the line in the South Pacific in the darkest days of the war, making possible all that would come after.

7

THE END OF THE BEGINNING

The US Navy took from the Battle of Cape Esperance and the two naval battles of Guadalcanal the lesson that, while the Japanese were good at night fighting, radar-directed American naval gunnery could keep them at bay and even defeat them. In the afterglow of the victory in the Second Naval Battle of Guadalcanal, the Navy discounted the power of the Type 93 torpedo carried by every Japanese cruiser and destroyer, despite the majority of American losses at these battles having been the result of this weapon. While no one in the Navy breathed easy after Admiral Lee's hair's-breadth victory, the belief that the measure of the Japanese had been taken led to a certain complacency in thinking about future combat in the Solomons. Two weeks after Lee's victory, the Navy discovered just how mistaken this view was, when an American cruiser force came up against destroyers of the Tokyo Express commanded again by the redoubtable Admiral Raizo Tanaka. The Battle of Tassafaronga, sometimes referred to as the Fourth Battle of Savo Island or, in Japanese sources, as the Battle of Lunga Point, took place on November 30, 1942, and virtually disproved every "lesson learned" by the US Navy at this point in the struggle.

During the ten days following the Battle of Guadalcanal, the enemy seemed to have abandoned the troops on Guadalcanal to a slow but inevitable extinction. The level of shipping in the Buin-Faisi area fell rapidly during this period. General Vandegrift's reports for the latter part of November noted only minor encounters with enemy troops as the Marines dislodged small enemy units from their positions threatening Henderson Field. The Marines crossed the Matanikau River and moved westward under cover of naval bombardment during the last week of November as they passed beyond Point Cruz.

By early November, the six Naval Air Corps at Rabaul and Bougainville had only a total of 30 Zero fighters and 66 Betty and Nell bombers between them. Had they been fully equipped, there would have been over 250 Zeros in total. The units had never been at full strength, but over the course of fighting since the American invasion, the Japanese admitted the loss of 78 Zeros and 42 Bettys and Nells, along with 54 Val dive bombers, the majority of which had been lost due to fuel starvation since they were operating beyond their maximum range until the airfields at Bougainville became operational in September. The strain of the air war was showing in the IJNAF.

On November 14, Cactus Fighter Command could muster 14 airworthy Wildcats, three P-39s, and seven newly arrived P-38s, the first Lightnings to operate at Guadalcanal. That day, *Enterprise* launched 24 Wildcats of VF-10 commanded by Commander Jams "Jimmy" Flatley along with the last eight SBDs left aboard, with orders to land at Henderson following their mission against the Japanese transports headed for Guadalcanal. The Fighting 10 pilots got into a fight over the enemy ships as the dive bombers attacked. Ensign Ed Coalson, "tail-end Charlie" of the Wildcats as they made a strafing run, was jumped by two Zeros, with two more coming in on him. Pulling a loop, Coalson came around and shot down one Zero, then dived away and escaped the others.

November 14 saw the loss of Major Joe Bauer. "The Coach" was flying with VMF-121 commander Paul Fontana and exec Joe Foss, when he was jumped from the rear by two Zeros while the three were making a masthead strafing run on the transports. He turned into the enemy and shot down one while Fontana and Foss chased away the other. When they came back, Bauer was nowhere to be seen until Foss spotted an oil slick on the water and saw Bauer wave to him. Foss flew back to Henderson, where he and Major Joe Renner took the Grumman J2F "Duck" used for air-sea rescue and flew back to the scene of the fight. With the sun going down, they were unable to spot "The Coach," who was never seen again. His status as an ace was less important than the fact that he had provided the necessary "final training" down at the Turtle Bay airfield on Espiritu Santo for most of the pilots who came to Guadalcanal, ensuring they would be fully prepared to meet the enemy.

Throughout the day, reinforcements were flown up from Espiritu Santo while the battle of the transports went on. By the end of the day, Cactus could count 24 operational Wildcats, 23 P-39s, 16 Dauntlesses, seven TBFs, and nine B-26 Marauders available from all sources. With the victory of USS *Washington* that night, the crisis had passed for the island. In three months of fighting, six Wildcat-equipped fighter squadrons – five Marine and one Navy – had flown from Henderson Field against the enemy. The Marine squadrons claimed 305 enemy aircraft shot down, while VF-5 added another 45; admitted Japanese losses for the period were 260. Even against the admitted Japanese losses, the American pilots had a victory ratio of approximately 2.5:1, proof that the saying "Grumman saved Guadalcanal" wasn't hype.

Following the naval victory in mid-November, Japanese attempts at reinforcement changed. Because of the threat to any Japanese force from Guadalcanal-based aircraft, the PT boats operating from Tulagi, and a cycle of bright moonlight due to good weather during the second half of November that provided cloudless skies at night which made interception of surface ships easier in the bright light of the moon and stars in the clear night sky, the Imperial Navy could no longer use slow surface transports to deliver provisions to the Imperial Army forces on Guadalcanal. Instead, troops and supplies were delivered by destroyers and light cruisers that could make the trip down the Slot to the point they came in range of American aircraft on Guadalcanal then move to Guadalcanal, land the troops and supplies, and return to the area of the Slot beyond range of air attack in a single night. Also, beginning on November 16 and continuing for the next three weeks, 16 submarines made nocturnal deliveries to the island, avoiding interception by running submerged. Each could deliver 20 to 30 tons, about one day's worth of food, for the 17th Army. At the same time, there was no way of transporting additional ammunition or other heavy supplies, or any substantial number of troops, by this transportation method. Additionally, the difficult task of transporting the food supplies by hand to the front-line units limited their value. At the same time, the Japanese tried to establish a chain of three bases in the central Solomons on New Georgia, Choiseul, and Kolombangara, that could be used as staging sites and hiding places for small boats making supply deliveries to Guadalcanal. Damaging air strikes from Guadalcanal-based aircraft against these bases forced abandonment of this plan.

On November 26, the 17th Army on Guadalcanal notified newly arrived theater commander, General Hitoshi Imamura, that it faced a critical food crisis. General Hyakutake reported that many front-line units had not been resupplied for as many as six days and that rear-area troops were on one-third rations. The situation was critical if there was to be another offensive against Henderson Field, and forced the Imperial Navy to return to bringing supplies by destroyers.

The Japanese devised an ingenious plan to reduce the exposure of the destroyers in the vicinity of Guadalcanal. Large oil drums were cleaned out, then filled with medical supplies and food, with enough air space left inside to provide buoyancy. These drums were then tied together and loaded aboard a destroyer. When the ship arrived at Guadalcanal, it would make a sharp turn, during which the drums would be cut loose and put over the side to drift ashore on the tide. A swimmer from shore could bring the buoyed end of the rope to land, where working parties could then haul in the supplies.

Eighth Fleet commander Admiral Mikawa ordered the Guadalcanal Reinforcement Unit to make the first of five runs to Guadalcanal using the drums the night of November 30/December 1. Six destroyers – *Kuroshio, Oyashio, Kagerō, Suzukaze, Kawakaze,* and *Makinami* – would carry 240 drums each, making it the largest attempted shipment since November 11. Admiral Tanaka's flagship, the destroyer *Naganami*, and the destroyer *Takanami* were escorts. The six drum-carrying destroyers left their reloads of Type 93 torpedoes at their base, leaving each ship with eight torpedoes in their tubes, while *Naganami* and *Takanami* each carried reloads. All of the destroyers were Solomons combat veterans.

The US Navy had lost 18 ships in the surface actions around Guadalcanal since the August invasion. Following the successes in holding off the Imperial Navy in the two naval battles of Guadalcanal, Admiral Halsey was able to prevail on Admiral Nimitz to make a new commitment of combat units. On November 24, Rear Admiral Thomas C. Kinkaid was ordered to form Task Force 67 at Espiritu Santo, composed of the heavy cruisers *Pensacola* (CA-24) and *Northampton* (CA-26) that had arrived shortly after the mid-November battles, and the now-veteran destroyer *Fletcher*. On November 27, the heavy cruisers *Minneapolis* (CA-36) and *New Orleans* (CA-32), the light cruiser *Honolulu* (CL-48), and their escorting destroyers *Drayton* (DD-366), *Maury* (DD-401), and *Perkins* (DD-377) arrived from Pearl Harbor.

Admiral Kinkaid had prepared a set of operation orders but, before he could go over them with his captains, he was relieved on November 28 by Rear Admiral Carleton H. Wright, who had arrived in *Minneapolis*.

Wright, who had graduated 16th in the Annapolis class of 1912, was a well-regarded officer who had commanded the cruiser *Augusta* when she took President Roosevelt to his first meeting with Prime Minister Churchill at Placentia Bay, Newfoundland, in August 1941. Wright had been promoted to Rear Admiral the previous May. As an experienced surface warship commander, great things were expected of him in his first combat command.

Importantly, only *Fletcher* was a veteran of surface action against the Imperial Navy; all the cruisers were newcomers to a surface-battle task force, having spent their time since Pearl Harbor as escorts for aircraft carriers with their combat experience limited to providing antiaircraft support. Admiral Wright was also a newcomer to night surface action against the Japanese. The day after assuming command, with the task force on 12-hours' notice to get underway, Admiral Wright held a conference, attended by Admiral Tisdale, his second in command, and the commanding officers of the nine ships, during which Admiral Kinkaid's operation plan was briefly discussed, but Wright made no overall orders to accommodate Kinkaid's plan, pending a conference set for the next day. The next day, Wright decided to adopt Kinkaid's decision to divide the task force into one destroyer and two cruiser units, with at least one ship in each unit equipped with SG radar and one ship with CXAM or SC-1 radar. Wright would be in command of the unit including *Minneapolis*, *New Orleans*, and *Pensacola* while Admiral Tisdale led the second unit composed of *Honolulu* and *Northampton*, while the four destroyers were under command of the Senior Officer Present, Commander William M. Cole, captain of *Fletcher*.

Fortunately, while Allied intelligence had been unable to read Imperial Navy radio messages since a series of changes in the enemy code had been made in the two months after the Battle of Midway, it was still possible to read Imperial Army messages since that code had been broken and the enemy would leave it unchanged through most of the war. General Imamura's headquarters at Rabaul radioed the 17th Army on Guadalcanal, alerting them to Tanaka's pending supply run on November 29. This message was broken the same day, and at 1940 hours Admiral Halsey ordered Admiral Wright to depart at the earliest possible moment, and to proceed at the best possible speed to intercept an enemy group identified as six destroyers and six transports off Guadalcanal; there would be no further planning conference before the task force entered combat. Just before 2400 hours on November 29, Wright and his force departed Espiritu Santo for Guadalcanal.

While en route, Wright received additional intelligence that the enemy force might be composed entirely of destroyers. He then informed the task force of the expected composition of the enemy force and directed the destroyers to concentrate two miles ahead of *Minneapolis* before entering Lengo Channel. The force would pass six miles from the Tassafaronga area of the northern Guadalcanal coast. Wright added that he expected gunfire to commence at a range of about 12,000 yards. As the force approached Lengo Channel around 1830 hours to enter Ironbottom Sound, their order was: *Fletcher, Perkins, Maury, Drayton,* followed by *Minneapolis, New Orleans, Pensacola, Honolulu,* and *Northampton.* Just before the ships entered the channel, they encountered three transports escorted by five destroyers that had just unloaded at Guadalcanal. The destroyers *Lamson* and *Lardner* were ordered detached from the transport force to reinforce TF 67. This meant that Commander Laurence A. Abercrombie, in command of the two ships, would become Senior Officer Present for the destroyers, though there was no time to communicate Wright's battle plan to him; the two destroyers took position to the rear of the formation.

The ships entered Lengo Channel at 2140 hours on November 30, at which point Wright ordered all ships to battle stations. They exited into Ironbottom Sound shortly after 2200 hours. Unlike the sky condition over the previous ten days, it was very dark with the sky completely overcast. Maximum surface visibility was less than two miles.

Tanaka's destroyer force had departed their base in the Shortlands at 0005 hours on November 30. Paul Mason, the Australian coastwatcher on southern Bougainville, reported the departure and his message was passed to Wright. During the day, Tanaka attempted to evade being spotted by air patrols from Guadalcanal by first heading northeast through Bougainville Strait before turning south to pass through Indispensable Strait shortly after sunset. The admiral informed his destroyer commanders he expected action that night. At 2240 hours, Tanaka's force passed south of Savo Island and slowed to 12 knots as they neared the unloading area. At the same time, TF 67 headed toward Savo. The leading destroyers took position slightly inshore of the cruisers.

At 2306 hours, *Minneapolis*'s SG radar picked up Tanaka's ships near Cape Esperance at a range of 23,000 yards. Moments later, *Fletcher* picked up two targets 14,000 yards off her port bow. Further tracking located five ships, four approximately a mile and a quarter off Guadalcanal, the fifth half a mile outside the second ship. At 2316 hours, with the enemy formation at a range of 7,000 yards, Commander Cole requested permission to launch torpedoes. Wright responded at 2318 hours that the range was too great. Cole immediately responded that the range was fine. Finally, at 2320 hours, Wright gave permission to fire. In the time between Cole's initial query and Wright giving permission to fire on the enemy, the targets escaped from an optimum firing setup ahead to a marginal position passing abeam, giving the American torpedoes a long overtaking run near the limit of their range. As the attack was made, *Drayton*'s radar became erratic, reporting the enemy speed as zero, while *Perkins*' SC radar saw nothing until 2315 hours. *Fletcher* fired two five-torpedo salvos, starting at 2320 hours. *Perkins* launched eight in one salvo while *Drayton* launched two and *Maury*, which never spotted the enemy, did not fire. All 20 American torpedoes missed.

New Orleans was 1,000 yards astern of *Minneapolis*, and did not spot the enemy on her radar until 2314 hours, at a range of 14,000 yards. *Pensacola* lacked SG radar and made no contacts until after *Minneapolis* opened fire. *Honolulu* spotted nothing on radar until moments before the flagship opened fire, while *Northampton* lacked radar and depended on the reports of the others. Neither *Lamson* nor *Lardner* were able to locate the enemy and took little part in the battle that followed. At 2321 hours, Admiral Wright ordered all ships to open fire, and the destroyers began firing 5-inch armor-piercing shells and starshells. *Fletcher* fired 60 rounds at the rear enemy ship before losing the target on radar. She ceased firing and retired to the northwest around Savo Island, with the other three destroyers following astern.

Firing starshells from her port 5-inch battery, *Minneapolis* fired four main battery salvos at what was finally identified as a "transport," though there were none present. The first salvo was over, but the next three were directly on and the transport "violently disintegrated" after the fourth salvo, after which *Minneapolis* checked fire. *New Orleans* opened fire a minute after the flagship, firing by radar on an enemy destroyer 8,700 yards distant, which apparently blew up after her fourth salvo.

Pensacola had difficulty in locating a target, but with the aid of starshell illumination from either *Honolulu* or *Northampton*, she opened fire on what was identified as a light cruiser 10,000 yards off the port bow. *Pensacola* fired starshells for better illumination after her first three salvos. *Honolulu* and *Northampton* also fired at the same target, which was seen to sink after Pensacola's fifth salvo landed. While gunfire and smoke made identification difficult, all on *Pensacola's* bridge believed the ship was a cruiser.

At 2224 hours, *Honolulu* spotted an enemy destroyer in the light from other ships' starshells and opened rapid fire with her 6-inch battery for 30 seconds, producing several hits. She then fired her own starshells to illuminate the target, and after another minute of fire observers saw the enemy destroyer break up and sink and the cruiser checked her fire.

Northampton's old CXAM radar was unable to pick up targets due to the land background from Guadalcanal. Finally she opened fire toward the fall of shot from the other cruisers. She ultimately located a target and took it under aimed fire. All the cruisers engaged in rapid fire of starshells and big gun salvos. The blinding flashes, smoke, and splashes around the enemy made it impossible to obtain a clear picture of the Japanese formation. By 2326 hours, unable to clearly identify the enemy, all the cruisers checked fire since the night was so dark, visibility so limited, and flashes and smoke in the target area so confusing that it was impossible to obtain a clear idea of what was taking place.

At the same time *Minneapolis* had initially spotted the enemy; Tanaka's ships split into two groups to shove the drums overboard. *Naganami*, *Kawakaze*, and *Suzukaze* headed for Doma Reef while *Makinami*, *Kagerō*, *Oyashio*, and *Kuroshio* headed for nearby Tassafaronga. *Takanami* reported a visual sighting of Wright's column at 2312 hours and, at 2316 hours, Tanaka ordered unloading halted.

When Wright ordered his force to open fire, *Takanami* was the target for most of the initial American fire. As she returned fire, she launched all eight Type 93 torpedoes just before she was set afire and destroyed. *Naganami*, Tanaka's flagship, reversed course to starboard, and began laying a smoke screen as she opened fire, while *Kawakaze* and *Suzukaze* reversed to port. At 2323 hours, *Suzukaze*, followed by *Naganami* and *Kawakaze*, each fired eight torpedoes in the direction of the American gun flashes. The four destroyers at the head of the Japanese column maintained their heading, which allowed Wright's cruisers to pass on the opposite course. Once they were clear, *Kuroshio* fired four and *Oyashio* fired eight torpedoes at 2328 hours.

Wright's cruisers maintained course and speed as 44 Type 93 torpedoes headed straight at them. *Minneapolis* had just fired her ninth salvo when she was hit by two torpedoes at 2327 hours. Her aviation fuel storage forward of turret one was hit, while the second knocked out three of her four firerooms. With the explosion of the avgas, her entire bow forward of turret one folded down at a 70-degree angle and *Minneapolis* lost power and steering. Fortunately, the explosions raised waves so high that, when they fell around the port side of the ship, they put out the forecastle fires, while flooding the navigating bridge. Luckily, the clouds of smoke and acrid fumes did not penetrate the pilot house. Fumes and flames from the burning gasoline and oil swept aft along the main deck over the fantail. Two sailors near the port 5-inch battery were blown overboard. As *Minneapolis* shuddered and rolled drunkenly from side to side, many crewmen suffered severe bruises when they were thrown against bulkheads. The entire bow tore loose at frame 22 and dangled from the rest of the hull. The water flowed aft past shattered bulkheads as far as No. 1 barbette. Firerooms 1, 2, and 3 were flooded, with all personnel inside drowned or suffocated.

Amazingly, despite the terrific damage, the three main turrets quickly resumed fire on the third target. Her speed had been greatly reduced, and her tenth salvo passed directly over the stacks of *Pensacola* as she raced past to port. However, power failed in all turrets after the 11th salvo. Steering control was momentarily lost as *Minneapolis* slowed rapidly. Effective damage control saved her from sinking while oil was pumped overboard to correct a four-degree list to port and all heavy objects above the main deck were jettisoned. With *Minneapolis* unable to continue the fight, Admiral Wright passed command of the task force to Admiral Tisdale in *Honolulu*.

At 2328, *New Orleans* took a hit beside turret one, which exploded the forward ammunition magazines and aviation gas storage and severed her entire bow forward of turret two. The cruiser received additional damage when the bow twisted to port and was wrenched free of the rest of the hull by momentum. The bow floated aft along the port side, tearing gaping holes in the hull at frames 130 and 136 just above the waterline. All the crews in turrets one and two were killed and *New Orleans* was forced to reverse course to starboard; she then lost steering and communications. Her main deck was wrecked back to frame 42. The second deck was completely missing forward of frame 31, and flooded aft to frame 42. Everything below the second deck forward of frame 31 had been blown out in the explosion.

Seaman Herbert Brown, whose battle station was in the plotting room, described the scene after the torpedo hit:

> I had to see. I walked alongside the silent turret two and was stopped by a lifeline stretched from the outboard port lifeline to the side of the turret. Thank God it was there, for one more step and I would have pitched head first into the dark water 30 feet below. The bow was gone. One hundred and twenty five feet of ship and number one main battery turret with three 8-inch guns were gone. Eighteen hundred tons of ship were gone. Oh my God, all those guys I went through boot camp with – all gone.

When she saw *Minneapolis* and *New Orleans* hit, *Pensacola* steered to pass to their port side, then returned to course. At 2329 hours, a torpedo hit her abreast the mainmast. The resulting explosion spread flaming oil through her interior and across the main deck, ripping away the port outer shaft and killing 125 men. The cruiser quickly took a 13-degree list as she lost power, communications, and steering.

Immediately behind *Pensacola*, *Honolulu* turned to pass *Minneapolis* and *New Orleans* on the starboard side. Her captain ordered her engines full ahead and she increased speed to 30 knots while she maneuvered radically and somehow managed to avoid taking a hit while she kept up fire at the disappearing enemy ships and transited the battle area into the darkness.

Northampton followed *Honolulu's* turn to pass the damaged cruisers to starboard, but she did not increase speed or maneuver to make herself a more difficult target. At 2348 hours, two of *Kawakaze's* torpedoes were seen close aboard on the port bow, traveling very close together, with one at a depth of ten feet and the other almost on the surface. *Northampton's* Captain Kitts barely had time to order hard left rudder before the cruiser took two hits so close together that many in the ship felt only one explosion. One torpedo hit frame 108 at the waterline, causing the ship to list ten degrees to port and catch fire. The other struck frame 98 ten feet below the waterline, exploding in the after engine room, which flooded and stopped three of her four propeller shafts. Shortly after, the angle of list increased to 20 degrees and Captain Kitts stopped the cruiser in the hope that she would right herself, but the list instead reached 23 degrees, at which point he ordered the bridge abandoned, the firerooms secured, and all personnel brought topside.

At 2344 hours, Tanaka ordered his destroyers to break contact with the enemy and retire. *Kuroshio* and *Kagerō* fired eight more torpedoes toward the Americans, but all missed. *Takanami,* the only Japanese warship hit by American gunfire and seriously damaged during the battle, was abandoned by her surviving crew at 0130 hours on December 1, but an underwater explosion as she slipped beneath the waves killed many; only 48 survivors of the crew of 244 made it to shore, where the Marines captured 19. Tanaka claimed to have sunk a battleship and two cruisers.

Northampton was abandoned at 0130 hours when the crew was unable to contain the fires. At 0140, *Fletcher* and *Drayton* rounded Savo Island and were ordered to rescue *Northampton's* survivors. The fires aboard the cruiser increased as steadily as her list, and the water supply at the fire mains fell off. The list reached 35 degrees at 0240 hours, forcing Captain Kitts and the salvage party to abandon ship. Just past 0300 hours, *Northampton* turned on her beam ends, rolled over, and sank stern first. By 0400 hours *Fletcher* and *Drayton* had rescued all 57 officers and 716 men.

At dawn, three fleet tugs put out from Tulagi and were able to take *Minneapolis, New Orleans,* and *Pensacola* under tow. They arrived at Tulagi shortly after 0800. *Pensacola's* fires were not out until shortly before 1200 hours, after burning for more than 12 hours before they were extinguished. Otherwise undamaged structurally, *Pensacola* departed on December 6 for Espiritu Santo and further repair. *Minneapolis* and *New Orleans* were camouflaged to prevent their discovery by the enemy while temporary bows made of coconut logs were constructed and attached to the ships. They departed for Espiritu Santo on December 12. All three cruisers required lengthy and extensive repairs back in the United States. *New Orleans* returned to action in August 1943, while *Minneapolis* returned in September, and *Pensacola* in October.

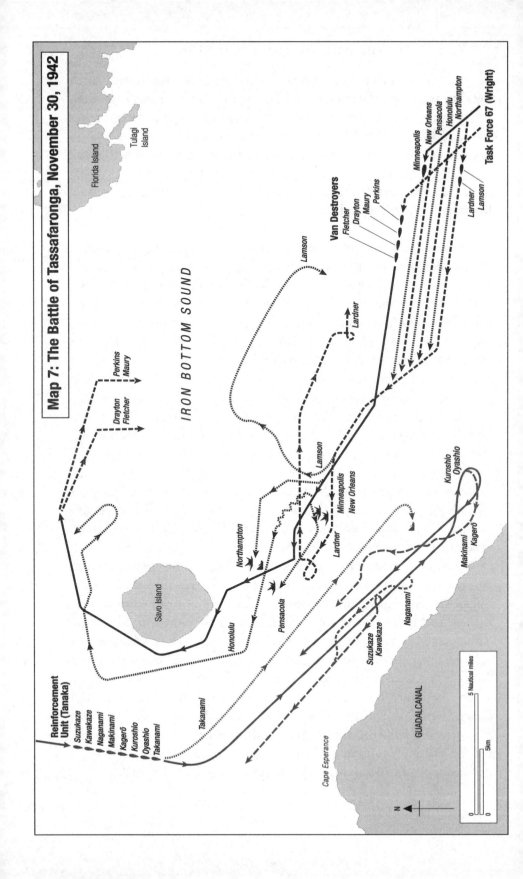

Map 7: The Battle of Tassafaronga, November 30, 1942

The Battle of Tassafaronga was the third-worst defeat suffered by the US Navy in World War II, after Pearl Harbor and the Battle of Savo Island. The Navy was temporarily left with only four operational heavy cruisers and nine light cruisers in the Pacific. Admiral Halsey placed much of the blame for the defeat on Commander Cole, determining that the destroyer squadron commander fired his torpedoes from too great a range to be effective and faulting him for circling around Savo Island instead of "helping" the cruisers.

Despite the heavy American losses, the Battle of Tassafaronga set the stage for the Imperial Navy's increasing difficulty in resupplying the troops on Guadalcanal. Wright's task force had prevented Tanaka from landing the desperately needed food supplies, though he was more successful on December 3, when he led ten destroyers back to Guadalcanal, where they successfully dumped 1,500 drums of provisions off Tassafaronga. However, the drums had not been brought ashore by dawn and strafing by American aircraft sank all but 310. A third attempt by 12 destroyers was turned back by PT boats off Cape Esperance on December 7. The next night, two PT boats spotted and sank the Japanese submarine *I-3* with torpedoes as it attempted to deliver supplies. Following this loss, the Imperial Navy informed General Imamura that they were stopping all destroyer transportation runs to Guadalcanal immediately. By this point, the Imperial Army on Guadalcanal was losing 50 men a day to starvation and tropical diseases for which they had no medicines for treatment. In response to Imamura's protest, the Imperial Navy organized one last run. Admiral Tanaka led 11 destroyers from his flagship *Teruzuki*. Five PT boats ambushed the force off Guadalcanal and torpedoed the flagship, severely damaging her and wounding Tanaka. *Teruzuki* was scuttled after the admiral transferred to *Naganami*. The Imperial Army was only able to recover 220 of the 1,200 drums released. Tanaka was relieved of command and transferred to Japan on December 29, 1942. On December 12, Admiral Yamamoto accepted the obvious and proposed abandoning Guadalcanal to establish a new defensive line in the central Solomons. While the Army opposed this, Imperial Headquarters agreed to the admiral's plan on December 31.

In early December, Fighter Two airfield at Kukum on the Lunga plain became operational, offering better drainage than Fighter One. Maintenance became improved as more ground personnel from squadrons back on Espiritu Santo were sent up to the island. Between the mid-November crisis and the end of December, the Henderson squadrons claimed an additional 31 victories. VMF-121 was given a two-week rest in Sydney, Australia, by which time exec Joe Foss had 23 victories, making him the top-scoring American pilot of the war at the time. On their return in late December, the men of VMF-121 went back to work under a new CO, Major Don Yost. He demonstrated his abilities on Christmas Eve, leading a four-plane division of Wildcats providing escort to nine SBDs on one of the first strikes against the new enemy airfield at Munda on the island of New Georgia. The Marines and 12 P-39s from the 67th Fighter Squadron tangled with 14 Zeros. Yost returned with a claim for four of the enemy fighters while his wingman claimed three. The limiting factor in reaching further up the Slot was the fighters' range. In December, a special shipment of newly developed 50-gallon drop tanks made of hemp, that Grumman had hastily developed, arrived at Guadalcanal to equip the Wildcats.

On January 15, VMF-121 put the new drop tanks to good use in a late afternoon mission to New Georgia where they and VMO-251's Wildcats put in claims for 20 enemy fighters shot down. Among the victorious Marines was Joe Foss, whose claim for three Zeros put his score at 26, making him the first American fighter pilot in World War II to equal the score of Eddie Rickenbacker, the World War I American Ace of Aces. By the end of January, VMF-121 had completed their second Guadalcanal tour, claiming a total of 161.5 victories since their arrival in October, gained at a cost of 20 pilots lost. The squadron was flown down to Espiritu Santo in R4Ds for transportation back to the United States.

The last naval engagement between American and Japanese forces in the Guadalcanal campaign happened on the night of January 29/30, 1943, in the sea between Rennell Island and Guadalcanal. Taking note of heightened Japanese radio traffic and air and sea activity, Admiral Halsey hoped to take advantage of what was believed to be an impending offensive to draw the Imperial Navy into battle, while at the same time landing replacement Army troops on Guadalcanal. On January 29, he ordered five task forces to cover the relief convoy and engage any Japanese naval forces they came across. Task Force 18, commanded by Rear Admiral Robert C. Giffen, newly arrived from having participated in Operation *Torch*, the invasion of North Africa, aboard the heavy cruiser *Wichita* (CA-45), commanded a fleet that included the heavy cruisers *Louisville* (CA-28) and the recently returned *Chicago* (CA-29), fresh from repairs after the Battle of Savo Island, the light cruisers *Montpelier* (CL-57), *Cleveland* (CL-55), and *Columbia* (CL-56), with air cover provided by the escort carriers *Chenango* (CVE-28) and *Suwannee* (CVE-27), supported by eight destroyers. A fleet carrier task force centered on *Enterprise* steamed about 250 miles behind the transports of Task Group 62.8 and TF 18, while a second task force centered on the newly returned *Saratoga* was 130 miles behind *Enterprise*.

Giffen's force was to rendezvous with destroyers from Tulagi the night of January 29 and conduct a patrol up the Slot on January 30 to cover the landing of the troops from the TG 62.8 transports. However, the escort carriers were too slow, so Giffen detached them and proceeded with his surface force. Wary of enemy submarines, TF 18 were organized for anti-submarine defense. However, they had been tracked by IJNAF flying boats operating from the Shortlands. At 1400 hours on January 29, 16 G4M Bettys from the 705th Air Group led by Lieutenant Tomō Nakamura and 16 G3M Nells from the 701st Air Group led by Lieutenant Commander Joji Hagai took off from Rabaul carrying torpedoes to attack Giffen's fleet. One Nell turned back, leaving 31 bombers in the attack force.

At sunset, TF 18 was 50 miles north of Rennell Island and 160 miles south of Guadalcanal when unidentified aircraft were detected on radar 60 miles west of the task force. At sunset, the combat air patrol over the ships returned to the CVEs. The attackers circled around to the south of TF 18 which allowed them to attack from the east out of the black backdrop of the eastern sky while the ships were silhouetted against the twilight of the western horizon. The Bettys attacked first at 1919 hours but all torpedoes missed and one Betty was shot down by the ships. Believing the attack was over, Admiral Giffen ordered the force to stop zigzagging and head on to Guadalcanal on the same course and at the same speed. Shortly thereafter, enemy aircraft began dropping flairs and floatlights, and Hagai's bombers roared in at 1938 hours. They hit *Chicago* with two torpedoes that stopped the cruiser and caused heavy damage. A third torpedo hit *Wichita* but did not explode, while Hagai's and another ship's Nells were shot down. Giffen ordered the ships to reverse course and cease firing at 2008 hours to conceal the fleet from the enemy aircraft, which departed by 2335 hours. *Louisville* managed to take the crippled *Chicago* under tow in pitch darkness and slowly head south, escorted by the rest of the task force.

Admiral Halsey took immediate steps to protect *Chicago*. The two escort carriers were ordered to maintain a continuous CAP over TF 18 from first light on January 30, with the *Enterprise* task force closing to augment the CVE's CAP flights. The fleet tug *Navajo* was dispatched to take over the tow from *Louisville*, which was accomplished at 0800 hours.

Throughout the day, enemy snoopers were spotted and the CAP vectored to chase them off. However, the scouts got a firm fix on *Chicago*'s position and reported it to Rabaul. At 1215 hours, a force of 11 torpedo-armed Bettys from the 751st Air Group that was based at Kavieng staged through Buka and were reported by coastwatchers, whose information fixed their arrival over the fleet at approximately 1600 hours. Halsey ordered the rest of the fleet to head for Efate in the New Hebrides, leaving six destroyers to protect the damaged *Chicago* and the *Navajo*.

By 1540 hours, *Enterprise* was 43 miles distant and the CAP she had launched to protect the cruiser shot down a snooping Betty. Fourteen minutes later, the incoming torpedo bombers were picked up on *Enterprise*'s radar and the carrier launched ten more Wildcats to augment the CAP. Over the next several minutes there was a question whether the Bettys were after the carrier herself, but at 1605 hours they turned toward *Chicago* when the *Enterprise* CAP attempted to engage them. Four other Wildcats chased them into the curtain of antiaircraft fire put up by *Chicago*'s escorts. Two Bettys were shot down before they dropped their torpedoes, but the six others that were also shot down had already released their weapons.

One Type 95 torpedo hit the destroyer *La Vallette* (DD-448) in her forward engine room, killing 22 and creating heavy damage. Four hit *Chicago*, one forward of the bridge and the other three in her engineering spaces. Her commander, Captain Ralph O. Davis, ordered the crew to abandon ship and *Chicago* sank stern first 20 minutes later. *Navajo* and the destroyers rescued 1,049 survivors from the water but 62 went down with their ship. A second enemy attack force failed to find the surviving ships, while *Navajo* took *La Vallette* under tow. The surviving ships made port at Espiritu Santo without further trouble.

Following the battle, the US Navy attempted for some time to conceal the loss of *Chicago*, the only survivor of the Battle of Savo Island. Nimitz was so strongly in favor of keeping the loss secret that he threatened to "shoot" any staff member who broke the silence. The Imperial Navy claimed to have sunk a battleship and three cruisers, which the Navy pointedly referred to as "more propaganda from Tokyo Rose." While both Halsey and Nimitz blamed Admiral Giffen for the loss of *Chicago*, he continued to lead surface combat forces in the Pacific until 1944 and was promoted to Vice Admiral. Wright, who had lost Tassafaronga, was also protected, leaving the Pacific to join the staff of the Chief of Naval Operations in Washington, though he never rose higher than Rear Admiral.

The Battle of Rennell Island marked the last time the F4F Wildcat would operate from a US fleet carrier in combat. Back in the United States, the first squadrons were being re-equipped with the new F4U Corsair, while Grumman's follow-on to the Wildcat, the F6F Hellcat, would appear in Fighting 9 in March 1943. The Wildcat would continue flying from escort carriers, and would participate in the Battles of Leyte Gulf in October 1944, with the last shoot-down of enemy aircraft by FM-2 Wildcats happening off the coast of the Japanese home island of Kyushu in June 1945.

The transports were able to unload the Army troops who replaced the 2nd Regiment, the last Marine unit on Guadalcanal, which had originally landed on August 7.

With Imperial approval for the evacuation of Guadalcanal, the Imperial Navy began its last major operation around the island, known as Operation *Ke*. On January 21, four H6K Mavis flying boats operating from Rekata Bay in the Shortlands flew a night bombing mission against Espiritu Santo to distract American forces. On February 1, five Vals with an escort of 30 Zeros got past the coastwatchers without being spotted and dive-bombed the destroyer *DeHaven* (DD-469) in Ironbottom Sound, sinking her at approximately 1605 hours. The attackers paid dearly when Wildcats of VMF-112 located them and shot down 21, including all the Vals, with Lieutenant Gilbert Percy scoring four and Captain Robert B. Fraser scoring three.

This attack was a diversion to cover the advance of 20 destroyers down the Slot. The force was spotted and attacked by SBDs and TBFs covered by F4Fs and newly arrived P-40Fs of the 44th Fighter Squadron. Three

SBDs were lost in the attack, which damaged the flagship *Makinami*. The remaining destroyers came on toward Guadalcanal, where *Makigumo* struck a mine and sank. That night, the surviving destroyers lifted the first of the remaining Imperial Army troops from the island. The Allies were unaware that this was the aim of the Japanese, concluding the effort had been a reinforcement for another offensive.

Three days later, a cruiser and 22 destroyers set out on an evacuation run. South of the Shortlands they were attacked by 33 SBDs and TBFs covered by 31 fighters. The defending Zeros lost 17 of their number while the bombers got through and disabled one destroyer while damaging three others, losing ten to the fleet's antiaircraft and defending fighters. The final evacuation run was made on February 7, impeded by a rain squall that covered the ships and prevented the 15 SBDs that made it through the stormy weather inflicting any damage. Ultimately, 11,406 Imperial troops were evacuated in the face of Allied superiority.

Admiral Yamamoto had conceded the hard-fought campaign to the Allies, with plans to establish a new defensive line centered on the island of New Georgia. For the Allies, the enemy's evacuation of a few thousand starving troops and the loss of one cruiser was a footnote to the securing of Henderson Field and Guadalcanal.

The results of the Battle of Tassafaronga included changes in tactical doctrine and the adoption of flashless powder. It would take another eight months, until Admiral Charles Lockwood had one of his submarines fire torpedoes against an underwater cliff in Hawaii where they could be recovered, before those on the front lines were able to convince the Bureau of Ordnance that the fault in US torpedoes was a design defect and not the failure of the operating forces to properly employ the weapon, as had been claimed. However, the Navy's leadership was still unaware of the range and power of Japanese torpedoes and the superiority of the Imperial Navy in night battle tactics. Admiral Wright even claimed his cruisers must have been attacked by submarines since the position of Tanaka's destroyers made it "improbable that torpedoes with speed-distance characteristics similar to our own" could have caused such damage. The Navy did not recognize the real capabilities of the Type 93 torpedo until well into 1943.

After the war, Admiral Tanaka was interviewed about his victory at Tassafaronga and said: "I have heard that US naval experts praised my command in that action. I am not deserving of such honors. It was the superb proficiency and devotion of the men who served me that produced the tactical victory for us."

The six-month battle for control of Guadalcanal had cost the Marines 1,044 killed and 2,894 wounded – a casualty rate that would pale in comparison with the battles to come in the Central Pacific – while the Army reinforcements suffered 550 dead and 1,289 wounded. The US Navy suffered greater losses in the battles around the island than the ground forces – 7,100 men killed and wounded, 29 ships sunk, and 615 aircraft shot down or otherwise lost – in the bloodiest and longest battle the service would ever fight. The Japanese on Guadalcanal lost 14,800 killed in action, 9,000 dead of diseases, and 1,000 taken prisoner of a total force of 36,000. Imperial Navy losses at sea were not officially counted, but were certainly close to those of the US Navy.

When he received the news that the Japanese were no longer on Guadalcanal, President Franklin D. Roosevelt stated, "It would seem that the turning point in this war has at last been reached." The longest, most stressful campaign of the Pacific War was over.

The new year, 1943, brought with it, from watery battlefields in the Pacific to the sands of North Africa, to the steppes of the Soviet Union at Stalingrad, a series of hard-won Allied victories that Prime Minister Churchill would describe thus: "Now this is not the end. It is not even the beginning of the end. But it is, perhaps, the end of the beginning."

8

WHISTLING DEATH

With the enemy having departed Guadalcanal, it was now possible for the Americans to turn the island into the major base they would use for the rest of the Solomons campaign.

Fighter One, which had been abandoned in December when poor drainage turned it into a swamp in the rain, became a major project for Henderson Field base commander Colonel William J. Fox. Coral had to be broken up and moved from fairly distant locations in order to get a quality base on the runway, taxiways, and revetments. The lack of proper equipment for airfield construction still slowed things. The four small Japanese road rollers that had been captured in August were still primary equipment six months later. By late February Guadalcanal's three airfields had a look of permanence about them.

In late December the first Allied aircraft arrived with the Lockheed Hudsons of 3 Squadron of the Royal New Zealand Air Force (RNZAF). These hardy reconnaissance aircraft would provide a new patrol capability as they ranged as far up the Solomons chain as Bougainville itself. The Kiwi forces would later expand with the arrival of P-40-equipped fighter squadrons in the spring.

Marine Air Group 11 at Turtle Bay airfield on Espiritu Santo had become the training and supply center, with newly arrived squadrons receiving last-minute operational training from recently returned Cactus veterans before they were put into the reinforcement chain to Guadalcanal. While there were far more aircraft available than had been the case in the dark days, there were still so few that squadrons did not retain their own aircraft. A tour of duty at Cactus was set at around six weeks, after which the pilots would be given a two-week liberty in Australia, generally in Sydney, before returning to Turtle Bay for refresher training and personnel changes. Ground crew and aircraft remained on Guadalcanal, where the newly arrived pilots of the relieving squadron would take over what had been left behind for their tour.

New aircraft types appeared. The 347th Fighter Group's 339th Fighter Squadron, now equipped with 18 new P-38G Lightnings, took up residence at Fighter Two, providing a very useful long-range capability to fighter escorts as the strike targets were more and more aimed at New Georgia, some 200 miles up the Solomons chain from Guadalcanal. Later that spring, the 44th Fighter Group would exchange their P-40s for P-38s, giving the newly formed Thirteenth Air Force two P-38 groups. That spring, the war-weary B-17s of the 11th Bombardment Group, which included at least three B-17Es that had seen service in the Battle of Midway and the entire Guadalcanal campaign, were replaced by the B-24D Liberators of the 5th and 307th bombardment groups, based on Espiritu Santo.

The Cactus Air Force had been an inter-service operation from the beginning, with Marine, Navy, and Army air units serving alongside each other in a single organization known as Aircraft, Solomons (AirSols) under the command first of General Geiger and then of Second Marine Air Wing commander, Brigadier General Francis P. Mulcahy. On February 13, 1953, all USAAF units in the South Pacific were organized into the Thirteenth Air Force. Two days later, Admiral Halsey established command of Solomons-based units under Commander, Aircraft, Solomons (ComAirSols). Rear Admiral Charles P. Mason assumed the command, leading the force until he was relieved at the end of March by Rear Admiral Marc A. "Pete" Mitscher, who would hold the command until the end of summer when he would turn over command to USAAF Major General Nathan F. Twining for the final campaign against Rabaul.

By mid-December, the enemy's new airfield at Munda on New Georgia was close to completion. Operating from this new forward airfield, every enemy aircraft type would now be capable of attacking the Allies in their southern Solomons bases, without the stress of a potential one-way mission as had been the case with Val dive bombers in the early days. With this new capability, the Japanese began planning for Operation *I-Go*, a heavy air assault against Guadalcanal that would overwhelm the defenders and which was the brainchild of Combined Fleet Commander in Chief Admiral Yamamoto himself. The land-based air force under the command of Vice Admiral Jinichi Kusaka had been increased to 190 aircraft by February 1943. The command was reinforced with 160 aircraft taken from the aircraft carriers *Zuikaku*, *Zuihō*, *Junyō*, and *Hiyo* at Truk, commanded by Vice Admiral Jisaburo Ozawa. This force contained what was close to the last of the prewar trained aircrews, and their first replacements who were not as well-trained as those they replaced, but were far superior to what would come later. The total of 350 aircraft of all combat types represented far more strength than had been available when the Americans first landed in the Solomons. Flying from their main base at Rabaul, this force would be thrown against the Allied forces in New Guinea as well as the Solomons.

The IJNAF would also be complemented by the arrival of the first Japanese Army Air Force units in the theater. In December, the first 100 JAAF aircraft and their veteran crews had arrived in Rabaul from the Dutch East Indies. They were first spotted by B-17s flying from Port Moresby when they attempted to intercept the American formation. On January 15, they entered combat over the Solomons when eight Ki.43 Oscars covering a mission of the Tokyo Express shot down five US fighters for the loss of three of their own. The first JAAF raid on Guadalcanal itself came on January 25, when a force of Ki.21 "Sally" medium bombers, misidentified as Bettys, escorted by Oscars that were misidentified as Zeros, were met by defending Marine and Army fighters that shot down three bombers and two fighters. The JAAF returned on January 27, when they lost ten bombers and fighters at a cost of three Americans, two of whom collided in combat.

On February 28, 1943, the Joint Chiefs of Staff set out the parameters for what would become the South Pacific campaign:

> Airdromes in southern Bougainville are required by South Pacific forces for operations against Rabaul or Kavieng and to support naval striking forces. Such bases exist in the Buin-Faisi area. Enemy airdromes in New Georgia… must be captured or neutralized prior to the assault on the Bougainville bases. With the enemy in possession of supporting airdromes at Kavieng, Rabaul, Buka and Buin-Faisi, it is improbable that amphibious forces can operate successfully in the New Georgia area prior to neutralization of rearward bases.

In mid-February, a strange new aeronautical shape appeared in the skies over the Solomons as the fighter that would have the greatest influence on the outcome of the campaign to neutralize Rabaul arrived in-theater. The F4U Corsair would be forever linked to the aerial battles in the Solomons as the airplane that broke the back of the Imperial Navy's air force. The first Corsairs and their pilots arrived just in time to face the new Japanese offensive.

In February 1938, the fighter desk at the Bureau of Aeronautics had put forward a request for proposals to create a single-engine fighter with a top speed over 350mph, a landing speed of 70mph and a range of 1,000 miles. Chance-Vought Aircraft's successful response, the V-166B, was accepted in June 1938 and a contract was signed for construction of a prototype designated XF4U-1, the fighter that was intended to be the Navy's fleet defense fighter for the Pacific war everyone knew was coming sooner or later. The airplane had a distinctive look unlike any other, due to the "inverted gull wing" configuration the designers had come up with to get sufficient ground clearance for the enormous 16-foot propeller, while keeping the landing gear short enough to retract into the wing. This design had the additional benefit of allowing the wing to attach to the fuselage at a 90-degree angle, thus obviating the need for fairings on the wing-fuselage join. It was also the largest naval fighter ever created at the time. The aluminum airframe was the first ever assembled by spot welding, which obviated the need for most rivets and resulted in a smoother surface.

Vought chief test pilot Lyman A. Bullard, Jr., first flew the new prototype on May 29, 1940, powered by the first Pratt & Whitney XR-2800-4 prototype engine, which had been designed specifically for the F4U and provided 1,800 horsepower. Given the emotive name "Corsair," which Vought had used for previous designs going back to the O2U-1 in the same way Curtiss had used "Helldiver," initial flight testing revealed the big fighter was the first carrier-based fighter with a performance superior to its potential land-based opponents. On July 11, 1941, 44 days after its first flight, the prototype was badly damaged when Vought test pilot Boone Guyton ran low on fuel returning to the Vought factory airfield in Stratford, Connecticut. Unable to raise any other nearby airfield on his radio, he made a forced landing on a golf course in Norwich. A former naval aviator, Guyton brought the plane in at minimum airspeed and planted it solidly on the fairway, but the grass was rain-slick and the big fighter skidded and then plowed into the trees at the end of the fairway, flipping the airplane onto its back and spinning it around, during which the right wing was torn off and the fuselage was damaged. Fortunately, Guyton was able to get out of the wreck safely, little more than bruised and shaken, due to the design's tough construction. Testing was delayed while the prototype was rebuilt, but Guyton was able to demonstrate its performance when he clocked a maximum speed of 404mph on October 1, making the XF4U-1 the first single-engine fighter in the world to fly this fast.

Manufacturer's testing was quickly completed and formal Navy acceptance trials began in February 1941. Based on initial tests, a letter of intent dated March 3, 1941 called for production of 584 F4U-1 fighters, with the order confirmed by a contract on June 30, 1941. The promise shown in flight tests was balanced by continuing difficulties with handling that included a nasty inclination of the XR-2800 engine to catch fire and to fail at high altitude. There were also some unpleasant handling problems, including bad recovery from developed spins, due to the inverted gull wing's shape interfering with elevator authority. It was also found the right wing could stall and drop rapidly without warning at the slow speed required for a carrier landing. Also, suddenly advancing the throttle during an aborted landing would result in the left wing stalling and dropping so quickly that the airplane could flip over from the rapid increase in power.

Originally, the XF4U-1 was armed with two .30-caliber machine guns in the nose, synchronized to fire through the prop, and one .50-caliber weapon in each wing, with an internal bomb bay outboard of each gun to carry 20 small 5.2-pound bombs that would be dropped on an enemy bomber formation. Early reports of European air combat convinced the Navy this was inadequate. Vought first proposed deletion of the nose guns and placing an additional .50-caliber gun in each wing, which was as much as could be done while keeping the fuel tanks in the wing. The Navy requested an increase in armament to three .50-caliber guns in each wing. This required a major redesign of the airframe in order to maintain balance, since the wing fuel tanks would have to be discarded to find room for these additional guns. The main fuel tank was moved to a position immediately aft of the engine over the center of gravity, which meant the cockpit was pushed back three feet. The result gave the airplane the sobriquet "Old Hose Nose" among naval aviators. The addition of 155 pounds of armor around the cockpit and the oil tank, plus an armor glass windscreen and self-sealing fuel tanks, required an uprated R-2800-8 Double Wasp engine with a two-stage supercharger and 2,000-horsepower takeoff power to handle the increased weight. Carrier landing was more difficult since the pilot could not see the landing spot on the carrier deck over the long nose while on final approach.

The first production F4U-1, BuNo 02153, first flew on July 25 and was delivered on July 31, 1942. At this point, the airplane had a maximum gross weight of 12,060 pounds, two tons more than the F4F-4. The fighter had a sea-level climb rate in excess of 3,000 feet per minute (FPM) with a service ceiling of 37,000 feet and a maximum speed of 415mph. Carrier trials began aboard the escort carrier *Sangamon* (CVE-26) on September 25, 1942 and proved difficult. The framed "birdcage"-style canopy provided a poor view for deck taxiing and the approach for landing. More important was the nasty tendency to "bounce" in anything other than a perfectly smooth touchdown due to overly stiff oleos, with the result that the plane could miss the arresting wire and slam into the crash barrier, or even go out of control. There was also the problem that the tail hook itself could bounce on hitting the deck and fail to engage an arresting wire. The danger of too-rapid application of power in the go-around and the tendency of the right wing to stall without warning during the approach if the pilot failed to keep his speed up made the Corsair the most difficult-to-land carrier-based airplane to date and early pilot reports doubted the ability of less-experienced pilots to operate the fighter successfully from an aircraft carrier.

By the end of 1942, Vought had produced 178 Corsairs. The F4U-1 was declared "ready for combat" on December 31, though it was only qualified to operate from land bases until the carrier qualification issues were worked out. The Marines had evinced interest in the new airplane from the outset and stated their willingness to participate in initial operational testing to work out problems. VMF-124 at Camp Kearney, California, became the first squadron assigned to equip with the airplane on September 7, 1942, with the first F4U-1s arriving at the end of the month. As with nearly every other pilot who became acquainted with the Corsair, the first impression the pilots had was the fighter's great size. In addition to being two tons heavier, the airplane was three feet taller than a Wildcat. The lack of a floor beneath the foot guides for the rudder pedals gave the space below the pilot the nickname "hell hole," and anything dropped was out of reach until the airplane was rolled upside down, at which time everything down there would cascade over the pilot into the canopy, to cascade back down on recovery to level flight.

Initial deliveries were slow. With the squadron scheduled to depart for the Pacific after the new year, by December 1 it seemed impossible they would have 24 Corsairs ready to go. Each airplane had to be inspected and modified to current production standards, which delayed acceptance. Air group commander Colonel Ridderhoff and Vought West Coast head of technical support Jack Hospers established a 24-hour-a-day operation that went 25 days straight in order to get the planes checked out in time, with the last one signed off on December 28. Because of this, the pilots had averaged only 20 hours of flight time in the airplanes when the squadron departed and some had never fired their weapons.

The second squadron formed was the Navy's Fighting 12 (VF-12) in October 1942, at NAS North Island in San Diego. Commanded by Lieutenant Commander Joseph J. "Jumpin' Joe" Clifton, their airplanes arrived even more slowly than the Marines to the north at Camp Kearney. By mid-January 1943, VF-12 had ten airplanes. Commander Fleet Air West decreed four planes a day would be delivered until the squadron was at full strength, which was accomplished on January 22. Carrier qualifications began on March 3, when Clifton and Lieutenant (jg) John Magda each made four landings aboard the escort carrier *Core* (CVE-13). Other pilots were qualified over the month and one airplane was lost, though the pilot was rescued. The squadron went to Hawaii in April aboard *Enterprise*, assigned to the *Saratoga*. In June, with 14 pilots having been killed in operational accidents during training, Clifton informed his superiors he would not take the Corsair into combat, and VF-12 re-equipped with Hellcats before going aboard *Saratoga* in July. From that point on, the Corsair was a Navy cast-off passed on to the Marines, who would come to love it and swear by it. The only Navy squadron that would take the Corsair into combat before 1945 was the third squadron to equip with what was now universally called "the bent-wing bird," Fighting 17, which managed to qualify aboard their carrier *Bunker Hill* (CV-17) but would be land-based in the Solomons when they went into combat .

On February 12, 1943, the green shape of Guadalcanal became visible on the distant ocean horizon as 17 F4U-1s of VMF-124 droned through the Pacific sky with their PBY-5 navigation escort, en route from Turtle Bay to Guadalcanal. While the island had been declared "secure" a week earlier, the position of American forces in the Solomons was far from secure. They held only Guadalcanal, while the Japanese controlled the rest of the island chain and had built a series of air bases on several, extending up the Slot to Bougainville, 300 miles distant. The Imperial Navy fliers were still a force to be reckoned with, with many experienced aces among their ranks. It could be said that at this point in February 1943, the campaign in the Solomons was just getting started for the long haul.

Among the pilots in the formation was Second Lieutenant Kenneth A. Walsh. At 26, he was one of the oldest and most experienced pilots in the squadron, having joined the Marines at age 17 in 1933, where he was first trained as a mechanic before being given the opportunity to learn to fly through the Naval Aviation Pilot program for enlisted personnel, pinning on his Wings of Silver in April 1937. A Master Sergeant NAP when Pearl Harbor was attacked, Walsh was promoted to gunner, the Marine equivalent of a warrant officer, in May 1942 and received his commission as a Second Lieutenant the following October. As he later recalled, "When we deployed to the Pacific, we had only averaged 20 hours in the F4U. We completed one gunnery hop, one altitude hop and one night flight, then we went. They needed us bad, and we would learn everything else by experience."

The big fighters landed at Fighter Two on Guadalcanal, with the pilots expecting to be given the opportunity to learn the lay of the land before going on operations. Instead, they were told they were scheduled for a mission in an hour, escorting a PBY to pick up two downed fliers rescued by the coastwatchers at Kolombangara Island, 200 miles north, who were now awaiting rescue at Sand Fly Bay on Vella Lavella. The two pilots were First Lieutenant Jefferson DeBlanc of VMF-112 and Staff Sergeant James Feliton of VMF-121. DeBlanc had been shot down two weeks earlier in a wild dogfight in which he had shot down five enemy dive bombers attempting to hit Guadalcanal, for which he would be awarded the Medal of Honor. Walsh flew that first mission and later recalled, "During that mission we were only 50 miles from a large Zero base. I hesitate to think what might have happened had they known we were coming up. Our pilots were so inexperienced and we were at low altitude. We could have lost most, if not all, of them, but we lucked out and didn't meet anybody." By the end of their first day, the pilots had nearly doubled their Corsair flight time.

There was still no time to get acclimated. The next day, they escorted USAAF B-24s to bomb Japanese shipping at Bougainville. Walsh led the fourth section with the callsign "13." He happened to be in F4U-1 BuNo 02350, numbered "13" in black below the cockpit. Though no one had a regularly assigned airplane, this would be the Corsair Walsh would fly the most during his first tour on Guadalcanal during late February and March, since most other pilots were superstitious about the number. Again, there was no combat and everyone returned safely.

The next day, February 14, VMF-124 got into the war for real, learning first-hand just how tough an opponent they faced. Again, the mission was bomber escort Bougainville, this time to bomb the Japanese airfield at Kahili. "The Zeros were waiting when we arrived. We lost our first two pilots that day, along with two PB4Y-1s, four P-38s and two P-40s. We got three Zeros, one the result of a head-on collision with one of our F4Us." This first introduction to combat was known ever after in the squadron as "The St. Valentine's Day Massacre."

With the arrival of the high-altitude-capable Corsairs to complement the P-38s, a Bougainville strike was generally organized as follows: the bombers, generally Army B-24s or Navy PB4Y-1s (the B-24 in naval camouflage), flew at 18,000–20,000 feet with P-40s providing close escort just above the bombers' level. The Corsairs flew at 20,000–30,000 feet, while the P-38s operated at 30,000–34,000 feet. The pilots quickly learned formation discipline. Enemy fighters would parallel the formation, coming no closer than 1,500 feet and refraining from an attack unless the Allied formation was broken. If an American fighter broke off to engage the enemy, he was swiftly pounced on by others waiting above. If a pilot straggled on the return, he could expect a possible ambush as far south as New Georgia.

Over the next month, the pilots of VMF-124 literally "wrote the book" on how to survive and thrive in combat with the Zero. They learned altitude was crucial, and they learned to use their plane's best performance to advantage. The Corsair could dive and zoom better than anything else in-theater. It had a good high-speed roll, which would be made even better in subsequent Corsairs by fitting balance tabs to the ailerons. They learned never to let their airspeed drop below 250mph when flying against the Zero, which meant the enemy pilot had difficulty deflecting his ailerons, canceling the Zero's famed maneuverability.

The American fighters had an easier time of making the long haul up the Solomons to Bougainville when the 33rd Construction Battalion (CB, later widely known as the "Seabees") completed airfields in the

Russell Islands, 60 miles north of Guadalcanal, which had been taken in an unopposed landing on February 21. Marine Air Group 21 took up residence there on April 4, 1943, with their F4F Wildcats tasked with interception of any enemy air units coming south to attack Guadalcanal. Eventually, the Russells bases would be important for providing a jumping-off point for the campaign against New Georgia that began in late May 1943. Imperial Navy staff officer Masatake Okumiya would later write that the American construction capability was the major reason for ultimate American victory in the theater. "We Japanese could not create an airfield in the region in three months, while the enemy could have their aircraft operating from a seized island within a matter of weeks."

Unknown to the Americans, the end of March and beginning of April would mark another major turning point in the Solomons campaign. Admiral Yamamoto had ordered Operation *I-Go*, his major campaign to destroy Allied air power in the region, to commence with the first attack on April 1, when 58 Zeros swept down the Solomons to attack Guadalcanal. The day happened to mark VMF-124's last mission of their first tour on Guadalcanal. Walsh and seven other Marines were patrolling over the Russell Islands, where the Seabees were hard at work constructing the airfield at Banika. The Corsairs completed their patrol and the formation turned south when eight P-38s of the 339th Squadron arrived to relieve them on patrol. The Marines were some ten miles away when the Zero strike force from Rabaul appeared overhead. The P-38s called for help as the enemy fighters overwhelmed them with numbers. Walsh demonstrated he had learned the lessons of air combat well when he heard the call for help and turned back with his wingman to assist the Lightnings. Wading into the wild fight, he quickly shot down three Zeros. The surprise arrival of the Marines gave the Army pilots the opportunity to dive away from the enemy after shooting down an additional three. The other 52 Zeros flew on to Guadalcanal, where they were intercepted in a fight that saw them shoot down six Americans while losing 18 of their number, with VMF-221's First Lieutenant William M. Snider equaling Walsh's performance with three of his own. Four days later on April 5, VMF-124 completed their tour and the pilots left for R&R in Sydney. Their place, and their airplanes and ground personnel, was taken over by the "Hellhawks" of VMF-213.

F-5 Lightning photo-reconnaissance planes spotted a vast increase in the number of enemy airplanes on Bougainville on April 6. Where there had been 40 at Kahili the day before, there were now 114, with 95 at Ballale when there had been none before. ComAirSols prepared to meet a major enemy attack.

Wildcat-equipped VMF-221 had only arrived at Henderson Field at the end of February. Among the squadron pilots was 22-year-old Second Lieutenant James E. Swett, who had enlisted in the Naval Reserve in August 1941, and become an aviation cadet that October. After winning his Wings of Gold at Corpus Christi in early 1942, he had chosen a commission in the Marines. He continued training at Quantico and San Diego before shipping out to Pearl Harbor in December 1942 and on to Espiritu Santo in January 1943. On arrival at Guadalcanal in mid-March, he had been assigned to VMF-221, which was operating its Wildcats out of Fighter Two.

On April 7, 1943, almost 400 aircraft from both the Japanese Army and Naval air forces, a larger force than that which struck Pearl Harbor, were ordered to attack Guadalcanal.

Swett had been assigned as division leader to fly a standard defensive dawn patrol with three other Wildcats. Gaining altitude, they flew over the Russell Islands and patrolled uneventfully for two hours. With fuel running low, they returned to Guadalcanal, where the word was passed from the coastwatchers that a major Japanese strike of 67 Val dive bombers escorted by 100 Zeros was on its way down the Slot. The squadrons on Guadalcanal prepared to launch 76 Wildcats, Corsairs, P-40s, and P-38s including the four Wildcats that had just landed. "Condition very red" was announced.

Quickly refueled, Swett's division was ordered to orbit over Tulagi Harbor to protect shipping from enemy dive bombers. As his foursome reached 15,000 feet, another pilot radioed, "Holy Christ! There's millions of 'em!" They continued their climb to 17,000 feet. Now over Tulagi, Swett spotted 20 planes heading right at him, which he quickly identified as D3A2 Val dive bombers. Swett's division closed on the Vals, but suddenly Zeros appeared above. It was a race to see whether the Wildcats would reach the Vals before they took aim on the ships below, before the Zeros engaged them.

Swett focused on the nearest Val. At 300 yards, he opened fire and hit the dive bomber, which started to smoke, burn, and twist out of control. Bombs exploded amid the ships in the harbor below. Swett dived after a second Val and fired a burst as soon as he was within range. The bullets hit solidly and the Val exploded. Now down to 2,000 feet, he closed quickly on a third Val. He hit it, but it refused to burn and pulled up. As he tried to stay close to the enemy bomber in its turn, he felt a heavy vibration; a gaping hole appeared in his left wing and the outboard gun stopped firing. Despite this, he stayed with the Val and continued to fire. Finally, it caught fire and hit the trees 500 feet below. Swett looked around and didn't spot any enemy fighters; he realized "friendly" antiaircraft fire had damaged his wing, though the Wildcat still responded to the controls.

Spotting seven more Vals attempting to escape over the harbor at low altitude, Swett flew into some clouds nearby and emerged almost in range of the rearmost of the seven Vals. He closed until the enemy aircraft filled his gunsight and opened fire. A long streak of flame appeared and the Val plunged into the water below. He closed on the rest of the formation. Moments later, he downed a fifth Val and accelerated after the others. The next was soon in range and he opened fire. It fell out of formation with the engine on fire and disappeared into the water. He pulled in behind the next in line, opened fire, and it too trailed smoke and dived into the sea. He turned to get the leader. Suddenly his canopy shattered as the rear gunner in the lead Val found his range. Swett returned fire, but he ran out of ammunition just as the Val began to smoke.

He turned to head back to Guadalcanal but soon the engine sounded bad and the oil pressure gauge registered zero. Moments later the engine ground to a stop. With no altitude to bail out, he ditched the Wildcat near Florida Island. As he set up to land, "friendly" flak bursts filled the sky around him. On impact, he banged his face into the gunsight and broke his nose. The Wildcat filled with water quickly, and he was dragged under. Struggling to free his life raft, Swett finally yanked it free and bobbed to the surface. Inflating the raft, he climbed in and fired his .45 to attract attention. Minutes later a Higgins boat pulled alongside and took him aboard, where he was treated to a combination of Scotch and morphine that made him sick. He ended up spending six days in the hospital at Henderson Field.

Swett faced initial skepticism when he claimed seven victories. After interviewing other witnesses, the intelligence officer awarded all seven; it was the record at the time for a single mission. American fliers claimed 39 victories on April 7, though five Vals hit the 14,500-ton tanker *Kanewha*, which sank that night. Additionally, the New Zealand corvette *Moa* went down in four minutes after taking two hits, while the destroyer *Aaron*

Ward had her engine room wrecked so badly that she sank while under tow to Tulagi Harbor. Allied claims by ship gunners and pilots were initially 100, but this was scaled back to 12 Vals and 27 Zeros. VMF-213 scored the squadron's first F4U victory, while VMF-221 was credited with an additional ten to Swett's seven, and the "Swashbucklers" of VMF-214 were credited with ten for their first outing in Corsairs. The enemy shot down seven Wildcats, but all pilots were rescued. The raid turned out to be the last major Japanese action of the Solomons campaign. The battle for control of the air over Guadalcanal was finally over.

VMF-213 got into their first really big fight with the enemy on April 25, when a division led by Major Monfurd Peyton returning from an escort to Bougainville spotted a large Japanese formation of 16 Vals and more than 20 Zeros headed south toward Guadalcanal. Despite the odds, the four Hellhawks dived headlong into the enemy formation. The fight was short and deadly, with two Corsairs going down after scoring two while Peyton and his wingman scored three and the Vals were routed. One of the two Marines shot down was rescued from the Slot by coastwatchers. Back at Fighter Two, Peyton counted over 80 holes in his Corsair.

The Marine squadrons at Guadalcanal were re-equipped with Corsairs as fast as the airplanes could be delivered to Espiritu Santo. Major Paul Fontana's "Wolfpack," as VMF-112 was now known, was next in line to re-equip after VMF-214. Pilots were flown down to Turtle Bay in R4Ds, where they received a fast checkout in the Corsairs. Most pilots flew back in their new planes with only some 15 hours in-type. Over the course of the summer, all Marine fighter squadrons in the theater would re-equip with the "Bent-Wing Bird." The Corsair would fly two-thirds of its wartime combat missions in the Solomons.

VMF-124 returned for their second tour on May 13. Twenty-five Zeros escorting two C5N Babs recon planes were picked up on radar and 15 Corsairs from the newly returned squadron and the recently re-equipped VMF-112 intercepted them near the Russells, led by 124's CO, Major Gise. In the fight, Gise was shot down and killed, while Ken Walsh scored two, to become the first Corsair ace with the three from his first tour. Just after scoring his second victory, Walsh spotted a Zero that barrel-rolled onto his tail and in an instant tracers were flashing past his cockpit. Walsh split-essed, firewalled his throttle, made a hard right turn, and dived away from the enemy. On return to Fighter Two, he discovered two 7.7mm "arrows" in his elevator. By this time, BuNo

02350 had been around for 90 days, long enough to be called "old and worn out," but Walsh had one of the squadron mechanics put five Japanese flag stickers on it and posed in the cockpit for photographers, preserving 02350 forever as "Ken Walsh's Corsair."

Captain Archie Donahue became VMF-112's first ace in the same fight when he shot down four Zeros to add to the one he had scored back in November during the squadron's first tour on the island.

On June 5, the two squadrons escorted 15 Navy SBDs and 12 TBFs of Air Group 11 to attack a Japanese destroyer, corvette, and transport that had been spotted off Buin. Walsh escorted CAG-11 Commander Weldon Hamilton who flew as strike director in a TBF. The bombers set the transport on fire and sank the corvette while the destroyer was badly damaged by Corsair strafing. Before the ships could be finished off, Zeros from Buin arrived on the scene. Walsh chased one off his wingman and shot it down within sight of its own airfield. With five American planes shot down for a dozen Zeros, Walsh escorted Hamilton's Avenger away from the fight. As they approached the Shortlands, a Pete floatplane popped out of the clouds and shot up the TBF. Walsh turned and pursued it through the clouds before exploding it. Turning back to Hamilton, he found an SBD had joined the CAG. The SBD's gunner called out a Zeke and Walsh turned on it to discover another Pete, but when he pulled his trigger his guns wouldn't fire due to a short circuit; the Pete dodged into the clouds and escaped.

The Japanese attempted to hit Guadalcanal twice in June. On June 7, 112 enemy planes were intercepted and 23 claimed destroyed, with VMF-112 claiming seven, for a loss of four F4Us and a RNZAF P-40N. During the fight, Lieutenant Gilbert Percy was surrounded by Zeros and badly shot up. When he went over the side at 3,000 feet with the Corsair heading down at 350mph, his parachute streamed behind him due to the speed and didn't open. He managed to stop spinning by holding his arms and legs out stiff. Without a parachute, he hit the water at terminal velocity for a human, about 100mph, feet first. The impact broke both ankles, his pelvis, and inflicted internal injuries as he went deep into the waters of the Slot. He managed to pop his CO_2 cannisters and his Mae West brought him to the surface, where he backstroked for 12 hours before ending up on a reef the next morning. Spotted by friendly natives who returned him to Guadalcanal, he spent the next year recovering in hospital.

The Marine and Army pilots were not the only ones now flying out of Guadalcanal.

The RNZAF had formed 14, 15, and 16 Squadrons on 80 P-40E-1 Kittyhawks in May 1942 and underwent training through the rest of the year. Among the pilots assigned to 14 Squadron that summer was Flight Lieutenant Geoff Fisken, now out of hospital from injuries received in combat over Singapore, where he had served with 243 Squadron and scored six victories flying the Brewster Buffalo before being wounded and evacuated in February 1942. In March 1943, the three squadrons were re-equipped with ex-USAAF P-40M-5 Warhawks and made ready to enter the war.

15 Squadron was the first to arrive at Henderson Field on April 8, 1943, the day after the last great Japanese raid on the island. The squadron flew escort for RNZAF Hudson reconnaissance flights in the Solomons, and scored their first success on May 6, when the squadron commander shot down an A6M-2N Rufe that he surprised during a rainstorm. After six weeks on Guadalcanal, the squadron was relieved by 14 Squadron after taking part in the great fighter air battle of June 7, when the Kiwis claimed four of the 23 Zeros shot down that day. 14 Squadron began its score on June 11 in the second big raid, when they claimed six of 25 Zeros shot down. Of the six claims, two were by Fisken, flying NZ3072 "Wairarapa Wildcat," which he had inherited on New Caledonia after it was repaired by a USAAF engineering unit that slapped the fighter with their "Wildcat" insignia, from whence it took its name. Five days later, in the largest of the three raids, 100 Zeros and Vals from the *Junyō* air group were intercepted by 74 Allied fighters; the Kiwis scored five when they dived into a big dogfight over Savo Island involving 33 Zeros.

With the invasion of New Georgia in July, the New Zealanders met the enemy on several occasions. On July 4, Fisken claimed two Zeros and a Betty, the only multi-engine Japanese aircraft claimed by a New Zealand pilot in the Solomons. With his Solomons score of five and his six previous victories over Singapore, Flight Lieutenant Geoff Fisken became the top-scoring Commonwealth fighter pilot in the Pacific War, with a total of 11 victories. Following the squadron's relief by 16 Squadron in August and their return to New Caledonia, Fisken's Singapore wounds, which had not fully healed, became infected and he was evacuated to New Zealand where he would be hospitalized for much of the rest of the war.

During the course of the Solomons campaign, the RNZAF Kittyhawks became the favorites of the Dauntless and Avenger crews to whom they provided close escort on the Bougainville raids, and later on missions against Rabaul. Unfortunately, their role as close escort did not allow much opportunity to score against the enemy, who opposed nearly every mission. When they were released for fighter sweeps on two occasions during the Rabaul campaign, they demonstrated their reputation for toughness, scoring strongly against the Japanese fighters despite the fact they were mounted in the "inferior" P-40. When they were withdrawn in 1944 to re-equip with the Corsair, the three squadrons had scored a total of 99 victories.

The last US Navy squadron equipped with the F4F Wildcat to enter combat was VF-11, "the Sundowners," which arrived at Guadalcanal on April 25, 1943. Organized at North Island the week of the Guadalcanal invasion, the squadron had trained at San Diego and then at Maui, under the leadership of Lieutenant Commander Charles R. Fenton, formerly commander of VF-42 aboard *Yorktown*. Fenton and fellow Fighting 42 alumnus Lieutenant William N. "Bill" Leonard had seen combat at Coral Sea together, with Leonard also serving with VF-3 at Midway. The squadron was mostly involved with escort missions for Dauntlesses and Avengers attacking targets in the mid-Solomons.

Finally, on June 7, the Sundowners met the enemy in the air when Lieutenant (jg) Gordon Cady's division ran across 24 Zeros ten miles south of Segi Point on New Georgia. With his division outnumbered 8:1, Cady evaded in the clouds and was chased by two Zeros. In the second section, Lieutenant (jg)s Terry Holberton and Ed "Smiley" Johnson were surrounded by Zeros after they shot down Lieutenant (jg) Daniel Hubler. Holberton was hit by enemy fire that punctured his oil cooler and hit him in his arm. He ducked in the clouds to get away and when he popped out, he was right behind a Zero on Johnson's tail, so close "I didn't need a gunsight." Unfortunately, his electrical system had been knocked out and his guns wouldn't fire. Then his engine gave out for lack of oil and he ditched in the lagoon between New Georgia and Vangunu islands. In the meantime, Section Leader Johnson escaped his pursuer in the clouds, but when he came out he was in the midst of three Zeros that turned on him. His engine was shot out and he bailed out over Vangunu. When he was just above the jungle, a Zero turned on a strafing pass at him, but he went into the trees before the enemy could open fire.

Dodging the enemy between the clouds, Cady, who was one of the squadron's best shots, came out of the clouds twice into situations where he could jump the enemy fighter he spotted, and he shot down two. Once back at Henderson Field, he organized a rescue for his three division-mates. Holberton was rescued that day by a J2F Duck, while Hubler was rescued by natives who returned him to Guadalcanal two days later in their canoe. Johnson spent 12 days evading the Japanese on Vangunu, with several close escapes before he located natives who were working with the coastwatchers. He was picked up by PBY from Segi Point and returned on June 19.

Also on June 7, a division led by Lieutenant "Sully" Vogel flew a strafing mission to Vila. On the way home, Lieutenant (jg) Robert Flath was bounced by two Zeros and badly shot up. Vogel shot one Zero off Flath's tail and then avoided the second as the Wildcats made their escape. VF-11 had come out even in the two air combats at 3:3, but lost no pilots.

On June 12, four divisions led by Bill Leonard were returning from a PBY escort when the Cactus fighter director reported a large "bogey." Leonard reported the Wildcats available and the 16 fighters spent the next 35 minutes following vectors until, at 1000 hours northwest of the Russells, they came across 36 Zeros stacked between 23,000 and 26,000 feet. The Sundowners were low on fuel and Leonard ordered, "Make one pass and head for home." Leonard downed two on his pass, but the others were drawn into fights with the enemy. Lieutenant (jg) Claude Ivie splashed a Zero but had to ditch out of fuel near the Russells. A flight of Marine Corsairs from VMF-121 with more fuel were drawn into the battle. Leonard's second section, Lieutenant (jg)s Vern Graham and Robert Gilbert, were drawn into the fight to support the outnumbered Corsairs and stayed as long as fuel allowed. Gilbert claimed three then broke off and rejoined Leonard. He had three gallons remaining when he landed back at Fighter One. Lieutenant (jg) Teddy Hull shot a Zero off the tail of his element leader, Lieutenant (jg) Les Wall, then shot down a second.

The best performance was put in by Vern Graham, who had become separated from Gilbert. He dived on a Zero rolling in on a Wildcat and blew it up. Seconds later he met a second head-on, which he hit in its belly as it rolled to get away and saw it hit the water below. Another instant later, a third came at him head-on and he blasted it, ducking when it exploded and the engine sailed over his Wildcat. He joined up with two Corsairs as they attacked four Zeros. One Corsair turned in front of him with a Zero on its tail and he exploded his fourth victory. Now worried about his fuel state, he turned toward the Russells but was attacked by a fifth Zero from "twelve o'clock high." He hit it as it dived past and caught fire. At that point Graham's engine quit from fuel starvation as two more Zeros came after him. Fortunately the Marines were still around and they shot down one and drove the other away. Graham glided for the airstrip on Russell Island to land dead-stick. Just as he realized he wouldn't make it, the engine caught on the very last bit of fuel and he managed to set down on the narrow strip. One landing gear collapsed from damage and he was knocked out, coming to several hours later in the hospital. Graham was the squadron's only "ace in a day," and this combat was the only time in his tour that he ran into the enemy. He was awarded the Navy Cross and sent home to recover from his injuries. Overall, in the battle on June 11, the Sundowners were credited with 14 victories for four Wildcats lost with all pilots recovered.

The Sundowners did even better five days later on June 16. Between 1310 and 1340 hours they scrambled seven divisions to take on an eventual 24 Vals and 70 Zeros intent on attacking shipping at Tulagi. Swinging wide to the southwest, the enemy avoided interception near the Russells and were finally spotted 25 miles south of Fighter One at 1400 hours. The Wildcats had a field day as each division scored against the enemy in the wild fight over Ironbottom Sound. The 20-minute fight saw the Sundowners and the other squadrons scrambled to meet the enemy claim 94 shot down of 120, with the Sundowners claiming 31. The victory came at a heavy cost to the squadron of four Wildcats and three pilots killed. All three died in collisions, two with each other and the third with a Kiwi P-40, a measure of how intense the battle was. Admiral Marc Mitscher sent VF-11 two cases of whiskey for congratulations.

On July 6, four Wildcats escorting TBFs to Kulaq Gulf were attacked by six Zeros and shot down four. In the last action of their tour on July 9, during a combat air patrol over Rendova eight Wildcats came across 40-plus Zeros, shooting down six for one Wildcat lost. After flying rescue CAPs over the next two days, the squadron finally departed Guadalcanal on July 12, having scored 55 – 37 Zeros, 17 Vals, and a Nell – for five pilots killed. Lieutenant (jg)s Charlie Stimpson and Vern Graham became aces with the squadron while Bill Leonard added two victories to his previous score to become an ace. By late August, VF-11 returned to San Diego where the pilots and their experience were spread through new squadrons headed for the fast carriers.

With the carrier *Enterprise* finally being withdrawn from the South Pacific for badly needed overhaul and repair in early May, *Saratoga* – which had returned to the South Pacific in late December 1942 following repair of the damage suffered in her second torpedoing in August following the Battle of the Eastern Solomons – and her Task Force 14 were the sole American carrier force in the theater. *Saratoga* was joined on May 17 by "USS Robin," the code name for HMS *Victorious*, the British aircraft carrier that had been sent as reinforcement following the loss of *Hornet* at the Battle of Santa Cruz.

John Bridger's Scouting 6 squadron, which had been redesignated Bombing 3 following their return from Guadalcanal, went back aboard *Saratoga*. In January, the air group sent the majority of the planes and pilots to Henderson Field, where they took part in the first missions flown against New Georgia.

With the addition of *Victorious* to Task Force 14, the two carriers provided distant cover for the coming landings on New Georgia. Since *Victorious* had difficulty operating the larger Avenger, most of the F4Fs of Fighting 3 were sent to the British carrier, which now operated the majority of the fleet's fighter defense. Out of this, the US Navy learned British fighter direction operation, which used a central fleet control and was superior to the system of individual ship control the Americans had been using, and it was consequently adopted throughout the US Navy for the coming Central Pacific campaign.

Bridgers, who was promoted to full lieutenant in May, later recalled that *Victorious* suffered from having a smaller storage capacity for food, and that *Saratoga* sent over provisions on two occasions.

On the request of the Brits, we loaded up a torpedo plane with dehydrated white potatoes and flew them over to the "Vic." A couple of days later a follow-up dispatch came requesting another planeload of dehydrated spuds along with a cook. When he returned, we learned that the British mess people had been unable to get the dehydrated potatoes to swell to their minimal consistency save by boiling them in a solution of Epsom salts. This, of course, greatly discommoded the officers and men.

Fortunately, the Imperial Navy made no move to contest the New Georgia operation. On July 26, Admiral Ramsay was relieved by Admiral Frederick Sherman and the force became Task Force 38. Air Group 3 was relieved on August 1 by Air Group 12. That same week, *Victorious* departed to return to Britain. The pilots of Air Group 3, including John Bridgers, traveled aboard as far as Pearl Harbor. Bridgers later recalled that, when they entered the harbor, he first laid eyes on USS *Essex* (CV-9), which was tied up to Ford Island. "Little did several of us know how intimately our lives were to become entwined with the history of that ship." From Pearl, the pilots traveled to San Diego, where Bridgers received orders sending him to commission Bombing 15 (VB-15), part of the new Air Group 15, as Senior Flight Officer following his leave. His good friend Niles Siebert also received orders to join the new squadron.

July saw the loss of perhaps the most legendary Solomons veteran of all, when the light cruiser *Helena*, which had survived the attack on Pearl Harbor and had fought the enemy in the darkest days of the Guadalcanal campaign, was lost in the Battle of Kula Gulf on July 6. The ship had returned to the Solomons in late March after undergoing an overhaul in Sydney, Australia.

Operating as part of Task Group 36.1 (TG 36.1), commanded by Rear Admiral Walden L. Ainsworth, *Helena* and the light cruisers *Honolulu* and *St. Louis*, plus four destroyers, had participated in a supporting shore bombardment in the early morning hours of July 5 off Vila on Kolombangara Island and Bairoko on New Georgia in preparation for the invasion that would go in at Munda's Rice Anchorage on New Georgia. Short of ammunition and in need of refueling after the operation, the task group was retiring to the Coral Sea for an underway replenishment when word was received that afternoon that the Tokyo Express was back in action with four troop-carrying destroyers escorted by six others headed for New Georgia. Despite the need for replenishment, the task group proceeded northwest of New Georgia Island to take up a blocking position near Kula Gulf.

The Imperial Navy force was commanded by Admiral Teruo Akiyama aboard the destroyer *Niizuki*. The 2,600 troops the destroyers carried were bound for unloading at Vila on Kolombangara, their staging point for a further move to Munda to reinforce the defenders there. Admiral Akiyama had divided his force, with three escorts in the lead, followed by the four destroyer-transports, with three other escorts trailing. They were picked up by American radar off Kolombangara at 0106 hours on July 6. The three American cruisers opened fire at 0157 hours, firing 612 6-inch shells in 21 minutes and six seconds, sinking *Niizuki* and killing Admiral Akiyama.

Helena's fire was so rapid and intense that the enemy later announced she must have been armed with "6-inch machine guns." Unfortunately, she had expended her flashless powder during the previous night's bombardment and was forced to use smokeless powder that produced immense flames when fired, illuminating the ship with every salvo. Seven minutes after she opened fire, at 0203 hours, *Helena* was hit by a Type 93 torpedo on the port side near frame 32, just below number one turret, which tore off her bow. Less than two minutes later at 0205 hours, two more Type 93s hit her port side near frame 82 and at about frame 85 under the second stack. These hits caused catastrophic, terminal damage. *Helena*'s forward movement, in addition to the massive structural frame damage, caused her to twist and jackknife around the damaged area as she passed her bow and began to take on water. The central part of the hull twisted 45 degrees to port and began sinking, dragging the rear section down until her stern was vertical. Helena sank about 0225 hours, 22 minutes after she was first hit.

The crew abandoned ship, going over the side after cutting all the surviving life rafts free. Due to the forward momentum, the survivors were scattered across several hundred yards of ocean at night, in the midst of a raging naval battle. Currents in the gulf separated the survivors even more by dawn. Many took refuge on the bow, which was floating vertically in the gulf.

The destroyer *Hatsuyuki* was badly damaged in the battle, while the *Nagatsuki* ran aground. The surviving enemy destroyers were forced to break contact after landing only 850 of the 2,600 troops. Both forces withdrew from the area, but *Amagiri* and the American destroyers *Radford* and *Nicholas* remained behind to rescue survivors. The two American ships picked up over 750 Helena survivors, and engaged *Amagiri* three times when they spotted her in the darkness. Finally, at about 0500 hours as the darkness turned to pre-dawn grayness, *Nicholas* spotted *Amagiri* clearly and the two ships exchanged gunfire and fired torpedoes at each other, all of which missed. *Amagiri* took several damaging shell hits and was forced to retire before she could pick up all the Japanese survivors. The crew of the beached *Nagatsuki* abandoned the ship at dawn, and she was bombed and destroyed by US aircraft during the day.

Afraid of an air attack while their decks were crowded with survivors, *Radford* and *Nicholas* turned south to deliver the rescued men to Tulagi. There were still around 275 survivors in the water they could not pick up. They left four boats manned by volunteers who gathered those still in the water. *Helena's* captain, Charles Purcell Cecil, gathered 88 men and organized a flotilla of three motor whaleboats, each towing a life raft, leaving behind some 200 men gathered around the now-sinking bow. They spent the day motoring to a small island some seven miles from Rice Anchorage and were rescued the morning of July 7 by the destroyers *Gwin* and *Woodworth*.

Disaster was avoided for those remaining with the bow when a PB4Y-1 Liberator sent to find survivors of the battle spotted them and dropped lifejackets and four rubber lifeboats. The wounded were placed in the rafts while the others surrounded them and worked to propel themselves toward nearby Kolombangara. However, wind and current carried them away and over the course of the day, many of the wounded died while search planes failed to spot them. They drifted past Kolombangara that night. The morning of July 7, they found themselves off Vella Lavella Island, which they managed to reach by midday, 165 men having survived the ordeal. Fortunately, they were spotted by Solomons Islanders working with the two coastwatchers on the island, and they were taken to the coastwatcher's camp, where the news of their survival was radioed to Guadalcanal. While they waited for rescue, they were forced to hide in the jungle to evade Japanese patrols.

Finally, on July 15, *Nicholas* and *Radford*, accompanied by *Jenkins* and *O'Bannon*, screened a rescue force of two destroyer-transports and four other destroyers. Over the night of July 15–16, the 165 *Helena* survivors, with 16 Chinese who had been in hiding on the island, were successfully brought aboard the ships. Of *Helena's* crew of 900, all but 168 were rescued. *Radford* and *Nicholas*, which had stayed behind to rescue survivors on July 6, were each awarded the Presidential Unit Citation for their work. On August 2 in Blackett Strait southwest of Kolombangara, the destroyer *Amagiri* rammed and cut in half *PT-109*, captained by future President of the United States John F. Kennedy.

On August 15, during the invasion of Vella Lavella, Ken Walsh led his section into a Japanese formation that outnumbered them 6:1. He shot down two Vals and a Zero, with his Corsair taking severe hits. On August 30, he suffered engine failure during an escort mission. He landed at newly operational Munda airfield where he grabbed another airplane, then took off and caught up with the squadron. Over Kahili, he found 50 Zeros forming up and attacked them single-handed. He managed to shoot down four before being hit so badly he had to ditch dead-stick in the Slot near Vella Lavella. In 1944, he was awarded the Medal of Honor by President Roosevelt for these two missions. Over the course of four tours, Walsh ran his score to 20, including 17 Zeros and three Vals.

Looking back on his Solomons combat, Walsh recalled:

> I shot down 17 Zeros and lost five airplanes as the result of combat. I was shot down three times, I crashed one that plowed into the line back at base and wiped out another F4U. I was shot up at least a dozen times. The times that I really got into trouble came about due to the Zero I didn't see, and conversely, I'm sure that most of the kills I got, they didn't see me.

The most well-known, and most controversial, Marine aviator to serve in the Solomons was Major Gregory Boyington, perhaps better known in later years by his nickname "Pappy," which was given to him by a war correspondent in a report written shortly before his loss in combat in January 1944. The younger fliers called him "Pops" due to his "advanced" age of 30 when he arrived in the Solomons in 1943. Boyington had fallen in love with flying at age six when he was given a ride by passing barnstormer Clyde Pangborn, who later became famous for flying from San Francisco to Hawaii in the Dole Race, and flying with Roscoe Turner in the 1934 MacRobertson Race.

That same year, Boyington graduated from the University of Idaho with a degree in aeronautical engineering. After a year working in the Boeing design department, he decided to join the new Naval Aviation Cadet program, but found he was disqualified due to being married. Raised all his life as Gregory Hallenbeck, he found when he obtained his birth certificate that his real father was Dr. Charles Boyington, who had divorced his mother during his infancy. With no record of a Gregory Boyington having ever married, he adopted his birth name and was welcomed into the service. During flight training, he was introduced to what would be his ultimate downfall, alcohol, and quickly became an alcoholic, which was little-understood at the time. Upon graduation from Pensacola on March 11, 1937, he took a reserve commission in the Marines, with a regular commission following on July 1. Promoted to First Lieutenant on November 4, 1940, he was assigned as a Pensacola flight instructor after two years' service with the fleet. He brought his family with him, whose existence he kept a secret. Attempting to support them on the minuscule pay of a Marine aviator, he quickly went into debt.

By 1941, Boyington's indebtedness of $4,000 ($65,000 in 2019) was brought to the attention of the Marine Corps by his creditors; failing to pay debts was grounds for dismissal as an officer, and it appeared that his career was over. He had found instructor duty not to his liking, and his reputation for drinking and brawling nearly canceled his record as an above-average pilot. In the midst of the situation, Boyington heard of the American Volunteer Group (AVG), which offered pay of $750 a month and a $500 bonus for every enemy airplane destroyed. Since the group was semi-officially sponsored by the US government, an officer could resign his commission to serve in the unit with permission to re-enter the service later. He took advantage of the opportunity to join in August 1941 before the Marines could take official action against him for "conduct unbecoming an officer." Despite the policy of readmittance to service, the Marine Corps' Director of Aviation, Brigadier General Ralph J. Mitchell, approved the resignation with an endorsement that he not be readmitted.

Boyington arrived in Burma with the other pilots in October, where he quickly failed to fit in and was not well-regarded by his fellow pilots. Charles Older, one of the first aces of the group, described him 60 years later as "unable to navigate his way around the breakfast table, let alone from one field to another." In his autobiography, *Baa Baa Black Sheep*, Boyington claimed he scored six victories with the AVG, though the group's official records credit him with two aerial victories, and three ground victories that had not been verified by the time he left. Claiming he was not being paid the agreed bonus for destroying enemy aircraft with regard to the claimed ground victories, he broke his contract with CAMCO, the company that organized the AVG, in April 1942 and returned to the United States, paying his own way with the money received for the two air victories.

Boyington managed to rejoin the Marines on September 29, 1942 and was given a wartime commission as Major on the strength of his unverified claim of being an ace with six aerial victories in the by then well-known

"Flying Tigers." In January, 1943, he arrived in New Caledonia aboard the former luxury passenger liner *Lurline*. After two months on the staff of Marine Air Group 11 (MAG-11), the unit responsible for final operational training for replacement pilots, he secured assignment to VMF-122 as executive officer, based on his experience flying the Corsair in training and his previous combat record, when the unit transitioned from the Wildcat. He soon clashed with squadron commander Major Elmer Brackett, who was transferred before he could make his views of Boyington known to his superiors. Following Brackett's departure, Boyington took over as CO of VMF-122. It was at this point, when speaking in an interview to a correspondent on Guadalcanal, that his claim of six victories scored with the AVG first made it into print in the subsequent article. Colonel Joe Smoak (whom he referred to as "Colonel Lard" in his autobiography) relieved him of command in late May.

By early August, Munda fell to the Allies. Within weeks, the Seabees had restored and expanded the coral airstrip there, and the first Corsairs landed on August 14 while the field was still being finished. On August 15, four battalions of Marines landed at Barakoma Beach on Vella Lavella. By mid-September, the Seabees had hacked out an entire new airfield there just a few yards from the water, and Corsairs began operating from the field.

In September 1943, the Marines needed to expand the existing fighter force in light of the planned invasion of Bougainville and the commencement following the invasion of a full-scale air campaign against Rabaul. VMF-214 had already served a tour on Guadalcanal, where the squadron was known as the "Swashbucklers." Following that tour, during which their CO Major William Pace was killed in action, the squadron returned to Turtle Bay, where the senior officers were reassigned back to the United States and the rest of the pilots went on leave to Sydney. Boyington, now without a command, learned of the planned expansion and talked his way into taking command of the semi-dormant VMF-214. Since casualties had not been as heavy as expected during the New Georgia campaign, there was a large pool of unassigned replacement pilots at Turtle Bay and it was from these men that the squadron took its personnel, making it the only Marine squadron formed in a forward area.

The new VMF-214 was ordered into existence on September 7, 1943. Pilot Fred Avey later described how the unit took the name "Black Sheep" during a party in their first days at Munda, when the pilots decided to call themselves "Boyington's Bastards," since they had been so hastily thrown together from replacements. The next day, squadron intelligence officer Captain Frank Walton was informed by a public relations officer that the nickname would not be acceptable for publication in newspaper accounts, so the name was changed to "Black Sheep." Walton later explained, "We were not raucous or anything. We were just looking for a name." In his autobiography published in the late 1950s, Boyington portrayed the pilots as having been "misfits" like himself. When the TV show *Baa Baa Black Sheep* made him and the squadron a cultural phenomenon in the 1970s, this "outlaw" portrait was contested by John F. Bolt, who had become a 12-victory ace in the squadron, and who was later the only Marine aviator to become an ace in the Korean War, in an article published in the widely read *TV Guide* magazine. Bolt pointed out that the only member who had not later found professional and personal success was Boyington himself. Far from being "outlaws" or "misfits," 15 of the original pilots had already flown a combat tour in the Solomons, while five were combat veterans with the RCAF in Europe.

VMF-214 flew up to Munda airfield six days later and commenced their first tour in mid-September after the pilots had been given transition training in the Corsair. On September 16, during their third mission, escorting SBD and TBF bombers in a mission to hit Ballale airfield at Bougainville, they met the enemy. Not being "up to speed" yet in the combat area, they initially found themselves in the midst of 40 enemy fighters. One enemy pilot who failed to recognize the Marine fighters flashed past Boyington and waggled his wings to "join up." Boyington quickly complied and shot the A6M3 Model 32 "Hamp" out of the sky. As the bombers pulled out of their attacks at low level, the enemy fighters fell on them. The Corsairs dived on the Zeros, and in the next few minutes of wild flying, Boyington added four more, confirmed by his wingman, to become the first Corsair "ace in a day." The rest of the squadron was credited with six destroyed and eight probables, for a loss of one pilot. The Black Sheep had "arrived." When they returned to Barakoma and word spread of their accomplishment, the unit quickly attracted the interest of war correspondents on the island, who soon took a liking to Boyington's charisma and his hard-drinking, hard-fighting reputation.

Over the course of the next six weeks, the Black Sheep added to their score and in so doing, their reputation. During their first 30 days, the squadron

A B-24D under modification with a replacement field-modification nose turret at the Townsville Modification Center. (USAF Official)

The Lockheed Hudsons operated from Henderson Field by the RNZAF were crucial in discovering IJN task forces heading for the island. (RNZAF Official)

The early F4U-1 Corsair was not compatible with an aircraft carrier, with its long nose limiting visibility on the final approach and its stiff landing gear guaranteeing a bounce into a landing accident on anything other than a perfect landing. (USN Official)

A VF-17 F4U-1 landing accident during carrier qualifications aboard USS *Bunker Hill* (CV-17) in June 1943. The squadron managed to "tame the beast" by de-bouncing the landing gear to successfully mate the Corsair with an aircraft carrier. This modification was later used on all Corsairs to go aboard carriers in 1945. (USN Official)

The first leaders of the Cactus Air Force: (left to right) Major John L. Smith, CO VMF-223; Lieutenant Colonel Richard Mangrum, CO VMSB-232; Captain Marion Carl, VMF-223. (USMC Official)

(Left to right) 339th Squadron commander John Mitchell, who led the *Yamamoto* interception; ComSoPac Vice Admiral William Halsey; and Major General Roy Geiger, Marine Aviator No.5, commander of air forces on Guadalcanal, and later the only aviator ever to command a ground campaign when he assumed command at Okinawa following the death of General Buckner. (USN Official)

Lieutenant Commander Thomas Blackburn, CO of VF-17 (left), with his F4U-1A, "Big Hog." (USN Official)

Left The legendary Lieutenant Colonel Greg "Pappy" Boyington, commander of VMF-214 "Black Sheep" during the Rabaul Campaign. (USMC Official)

Right Major Richard Bong, V Fighter Command (left), and Captain Thomas H. McGuire Jr., 433rd Fighter Squadron/475th Fighter Group (right). Bong became the US Ace of Aces with 40 victories, followed by McGuire with 38. Their "ace race" in the Southwest Pacific was the stuff of legend. (USAF Official)

Fisken with "Wairarapa Wildcat," at Guadalcanal, summer 1943. Fisken became an ace over Singapore in January 1942, then returned to combat in the Solomons in 1943, where his final score of 11 made him the Commonwealth Ace of Aces in the Pacific Theater. (RNZAF Official)

Captain Joseph J. Foss, USMC, the first US fighter pilot to equal Eddie Rickenbacker's World War I score of 26 victories. (USMC Official)

Captain Robert Hanson, the ace who wasn't. When commanders of AirNorSols stopped requiring independent verification of claims, Hanson – who had a verified score of 10 – began ditching his wingman over Rabaul, returning alone to claim false victories, bringing his "score" to 24. On what turned out to be his final mission, a special wingman was assigned, who stuck with him through all his evasion attempts, and proved what Hanson was doing. Unfortunately, by the time the wingman landed back at Bougainville, Hanson had been shot down while strafing the lighthouse at Rabaul harbor and the USMC proceeded to award "the leading Corsair ace" the Medal of Honor. (USMC Official)

Colonel Neel Kearby, CO 348th Fighter Group, who brought the unit to New Guinea and proved its value despite General Kenney's dislike for the fighter. (USAF Official)

Kearby, with his last "Fiery Ginger" P-47D. Scoring 22 victories before his death in action, he was the top-scoring P-47 pilot of the Pacific Theater. (USAF Official)

Lieutenant General George C. Kenney, commander of the Fifth Air Force in the Southwest Pacific Theater. Kenney was beloved by his men for his constant efforts on their behalf to obtain better equipment. (USAF Official)

Lt(jg) Ira C. Kepford, leading ace of VF-17, the "Jolly Rogers." (USN Official)

Major Thomas McGuire, CO 433rd Fighter Squadron, with Charles A. Lindbergh. Prevented from serving in the air force during the war because of his pre-war isolationist politics, Lindbergh went to the Pacific in 1944 as a tech rep for United Aircraft. He taught the pilots of the 475th how to operate their engines for maximum distance, doubling their effective range. (USAF Official)

First Lieutenant Vic Tatelman with his famous B-25D "Dirty Dora" of the 499th "Bats Outta Hell" Squadron/345th Bomb Group, February 1944. Tatelman was the only strafer pilot to fly two complete tours, finishing his wartime career by escorting the signed surrender papers ending the war from Okinawa to Tokyo on August 20, 1945. In his eighties, Tatelman regularly flew the restored B-25H "Barbie III" at air shows, making him the last World War II B-25 pilot to fly a B-25. (USAF Official)

Colonel Charles H. MacDonald, CO 475th Fighter Group (left), with his famous P-38J "Putt-Putt Maru." MacDonald was first the CO of the 433rd FS/475th, then became group commander in the summer of 1944. His personal score of 27 victories made him the fourth-ranked ace of the Pacific War, behind Bong, McGuire, and the Navy's Dave McCampbell. (USAF Official)

The pilots of Fighting 5 pose for a group portrait aboard USS *Saratoga* (CV-3) en route to the invasion of Guadalcanal, August 1942. (USN Official)

USS *Quincy* under fire from HIJMS *Kinugasa* during the Battle of Savo Island, August 8–9, 1942. (USN Official)

An IJNAF B5N2 "Kate" torpedo bomber flies near USS *South Dakota* (BB-57) at the Battle of Santa Cruz, October 25, 1942. *South Dakota* claimed over 70 enemy aircraft shot down – a gross overclaim that led to battleships becoming anti-aircraft escorts for the carriers for the rest of the war. (USN Official)

An IJNAF D3A1 "Val" dive bomber plummets toward USS *Hornet* (CV-8) at the Battle of Santa Cruz, October 25, 1942. *Hornet* was in commission for 11 months, during which time she took the Doolittle Raiders to Japan in April 1942, fought the Battle of Midway in June, and was sunk at Santa Cruz – the last American fleet carrier sunk by enemy action. (USN Official)

A damaged F4F-4 Wildcat at Fighter One airstrip, known as "The Cow Pasture," Guadalcanal, November 1942. (USMC Official)

Japanese aircraft attack cargo ships in Ironbottom Sound off Guadalcanal, November 12, 1942. (USN Official)

Left *Kinugawa Maru* – one of several Japanese ships of the "Tokyo Express" carrying troops to reinforce the Japanese Army on Guadalcanal – was beached on the night of November 13, 1942. The ship's remains are still there. (USMC Official)

HIJMS *Kirishima* was the first enemy battleship sunk by an American battleship since the Battle of Santiago in 1898. She rests upside down 6,000 feet under Ironbottom Sound. (USN Official)

The first F4U-1 Corsair of VMF-124 to land on Guadalacanal, February 1943. VMF-124 was the first Marine unit to take the Corsair into combat. (USMC Official)

B-17E "Typhoon McGoon II" of the 11th Bombardment Group at New Caledonia, January 1943. (USAF Official)

Ground crewmen and pilots of the 7th "Screamin' Demons" Squadron pose at Dobodura airfield, New Guinea, May 1943. (USAF Official)

Left Captain Bill Hennon of the 7th "Screamin' Demons" Squadron with his P-40E Warhawk at Darwin, Australia, 1942. (USAF Official)

P-40E Warhawk "Poopy II," belonging to Captain A.E. House, 7th "Screamin' Demons" Squadron at Dobodura airfield, New Guinea, May 1943. (USAF Official)

Curtiss P-40Ns of 17 Squadron, RNZAF on Guadalcanal, summer 1943. (RNZAF Official)

Left P-40Ns of 14 Squadron RNZAF seen from an accompanying Lockheed Hudson navigational leader en route to Henderson Field, June 1943. (RNZAF Official)

Right B-25D "Tondelayo" of the 500th "Rough Raiders" Squadron/345th "Air Apaches" Bomb Group, before the Rabaul mission of October 18, 1943, in which "Tondelayo" battled several Japanese fighters and lost an engine, but made it to an emergency landing on Kiriwina Island. (USAF Official)

Left F4U-1A Corsairs of VF-17 aboard USS *Bunker Hill*, September 1943. (USN Official)

Below Three B-25Ds of the 501st "Black Panthers" Squadron/345th "Air Apaches" Bomb Group strafe Wewak airfield on New Guinea, September 27, 1943. (USAF Official)

B-25D Mitchell bombers of the 500th "Rough Raiders" Squadron drop parafrag bombs during a low-level attack on Wewak airfield. (USAF Official)

A B-25J Mitchell of the 499th "Bats Outta Hell" Squadron skip-bombs a Japanese patrol boat, summer 1944. (USAF Official)

was credited with 47 victories over Bougainville. In combat around Kahili airdrome over two days at the end of September, they claimed 19 shot down and four probables, for no losses. On October 4, when a near-solid overcast resulted in the TBFs aborting their mission, Boyington led five other pilots over Kahili airdrome, looking for enemy fighters. Flying through the billowing clouds, they found nothing. Suddenly, a voice in unaccented American English asked over the radio, "Major Boyington, what is your position?" Boyington was quick to mis-inform the controller below that the Corsairs were at 20,000 feet over the Treasury Islands south of Buin. Minutes later, 30 Zeros popped out of the clouds, while the Black Sheep orbited 6,000 feet higher. The six F4Us hit the enemy fast as Boyington exploded the leader. In a port 360-degree turn, he sent two others down, while the other five submitted claims for probables.

The Black Sheep weren't the only Marine aviators finding success over Bougainville. The Hellhawks of VMF-213 also found the hunting profitable. Their leading ace was First Lieutenant Gus Thomas, who had a score of ten by September 23, when he added three in a wild fight to save two F4Us under attack. Unfortunately, he took hits in his oil line during the fight and his engine began to seize. He glided toward the Solomon Sea below, trying to put as much distance between himself and the island before leaving his Corsair. The engine finally quit some 20 miles offshore at 3,000 feet and Thomas took to his parachute. Other fighters from the squadron circled overhead as he shucked his parachute, inflated his raft, and climbed in. While the others departed, he settled in for what would turn out to be five hours of paddling, putting more distance between himself and the enemy. By 1500 hours, he was exhausted from the effort and fell asleep. Around 1630 hours, he was awakened by an albatross that landed on the raft. Several minutes later he saw a PBY above and fired his pistol to try to attract it with his tracers, to no effect. Around 2000 hours, in the last light of day, he saw another PBY and managed to make his presence known by spreading dye marker and again firing tracers. The Catalina dropped down and picked him up just before dark, returning him to Munda. Back in the air on October 11, he scored three Zeros in a fight over Bougainville, to take his score to 16. Four days later the Hellhawks finished their tour and Thomas arrived back at Turtle Bay, proclaimed the leading Marine ace still in combat. Questioned about his exploits by correspondents, he confessed he hoped he could get home to Kansas in time to not miss duck season.

Between October 15 and 30, AirSols mounted 60 different missions to Bougainville. Eight were fighter sweeps that claimed 47 victories for a loss of nine pilots. The Black Sheep were the top scorers at this time; when they completed their tour at the end of October, they were credited with 57 victories in six weeks of combat. Boyington now had a score of 20, counting the six non-existent AVG victories, and was within sight of matching the 26 credited to Eddie Rickenbacker in World War I and Joe Foss the year before at Guadalcanal. Lieutenant Colonel Raymond E. Hopper, commander of MAG-21 that included VMF-214, forwarded a recommendation to the First Marine Air Wing, nominating Boyington for the Medal of Honor, based on his "ace in a day" score and the squadron's repeated success "against superior numbers of enemy aircraft." Boyington arrived back in Turtle Bay to discover that AirSols Fighter Command had also commended him for his "brilliant combat record, readiness to undertake the most hazardous types of missions, and superior flight leadership." The nomination for the medal and the commendation both landed on the desk of the 1st Marine Aircraft Wing's commander, Major General Ralph J. Mitchell, the man who had recommended Boyington never be allowed back in the Marines two-and-a-half years earlier. In light of the Black Sheep's achievements, and the acclaim Boyington was now receiving in the press, General Mitchell had no problem changing his mind and approving both the medal nomination and the commendation.

The Corsair would go on to gain its greatest fame in the Bougainville–Rabaul campaign. By the time the Japanese evacuated their carrier squadrons from Rabaul on January 25, 1944, the Marine Corsairs had completed the destruction of trained Japanese aircrew that had begun at Midway. After the losses in the Solomons and at Rabaul, the IJNAF was a shadow of its former self. This fact should be taken into consideration when one compares the combat record of the Corsair and the Hellcat and their overall contribution to victory in the Pacific: the majority of Corsair victories – those before February 1944 – were against an enemy that was still a "worthy opponent," while the majority of Hellcat victories – which came after February 1944 – were against an enemy that, in the overwhelming majority of combats, lacked training and experience.

9

PAPPY GUNN AND THE SUNSETTERS

General George C. Kenney called Colonel Paul Irvin Gunn "one of the great heroes of the Southwest Pacific in World War II." The young fliers in the B-25s and A-20s called him "Pappy," for the fact he was then in his mid-40s, and thought of him as "The General's Uninhibited Engineer." To aviation history, he was the inventor of one of the most terrifying weapons used in the war, the "gunship," a medium or light bomber with its nose full of machine guns and cannons, capable of shredding any target from a building to a destroyer in a matter of minutes with up to 14 .50-caliber machine guns firing 600 rounds per minute. Admiral J.J. "Jocko" Clark, who knew him in the early 1930s when both were pilots for Admiral William A. Moffett, "the father of naval aviation," remembered Gunn – then an enlisted Naval Aviation Pilot – in his memoirs thus, "He was exceptionally able, always ready to go anywhere at any time, day or night. He had a cheerful and inspiring personality and a high sense of duty. On our team of pilots, he was universally regarded as the crack member." Kenney later wrote that he had noted in one of Gunn's efficiency rating reports, "This officer gets things done." The general went on to say, "I couldn't think of any higher compliment to pay him."

Born in Quitman, Arkansas, on October 18, 1900, Paul Gunn fell in love with the idea of flying at age ten, when one of the first airplanes in the South flew over his family farm. When the United States became involved in World War 1 in 1917, he changed the date of his birth to 1899 and enlisted in the Navy, where he was trained as an aircraft mechanic. Remaining in the Navy after the war, he volunteered for work as a mechanic to a local barnstormer in return for flying lessons, and had his own airplane by 1922, which he had rebuilt from a wreck. In September 1925, the Morrow Board appointed by President Coolidge to review the development of naval aviation recommended the Navy should increase the use of enlisted men as pilots, to reduce the demand for the limited number of officers. Legislation was passed in Congress in 1926, adopting a fixed ratio of 30 percent of total naval pilot strength as enlisted pilots, which constituted a significant increase in the ranks of Naval Aviation Pilots (NAP), the designation of enlisted pilots in the Navy. Gunn, who had re-enlisted in 1924 and had repeatedly requested assignment to flight training to be a NAP, took advantage of this new opportunity and by 1927 was a Chief Aviation Pilot with wings of silver rather than gold. When then-Lieutenant Commander Clark took command of the elite Fighting 2, known as "The Flying Chiefs" for the fact that all the pilots other than section leaders were NAPs, he made sure that Gunn followed him to San Diego to join the squadron. The enlisted pilots in the squadron were considered the best in the Navy.

Gunn retired from the Navy in 1937, and by 1939 he was working as the personal pilot for Andres Soriano, one of the richest men in the Philippines, living in Manila with his wife and two children. After listening to Gunn, Soriano created Philippines Air Lines (PAL), with Gunn in charge of the operation. The airline operated three twin-engine Beech 18s and one Sikorsky S-38 amphibian, flying throughout the archipelago. When war broke out in December 1941, Gunn volunteered his services to the Army and received a temporary commission as a Captain. PAL's airplanes were taken over by the Far East Air Force and he was now in charge of air transport. By Christmas Day, 1941, American air power was nearly non-existent in the Philippines. Gunn and his fellow pilot "Buzz" Slingsby were ordered to evacuate air force officers to Australia in the Beech 18s. Once in Australia, Gunn could not return to the Philippines; when Manila fell, his wife and children were interned by the Japanese at Santo Tomas University.

Gunn next saw action in Java, flying as navigation lead for the first USAAF P-40s sent to reinforce the Dutch and pioneering the route from Brisbane to Darwin that would become known as "The Brereton Route." From there, he flew on to Mindanao, where he reconnected with a fellow PAL pilot and they were able to repair one of the last B-17s on the island, which he then flew to Australia, overloaded with refugee Americans. Gunn first met the B-25 on April 11, 1942, when nine B-25Cs and three B-17Es led by Brigadier General Ralph Royce arrived at Del Monte airfield on Mindanao. His ability to keep airplanes flying in primitive conditions got him assigned as the group's maintenance officer. His experience was crucial for the unit successfully staging attacks in the central Philippines as they made the Mitchell's combat debut, hitting shipping and harbor facilities at Cebu, the harbor and airstrips at Davao, and Nichols Field on Luzon. When they returned to Darwin, Captain Gunn was among those they brought back with them.

Gunn finally met General Kenney on August 5, 1942, shortly after the general's arrival in Australia. By that point, he had been promoted to Major and had created a position for himself as group engineering and maintenance officer for the 3rd Attack Group, at the time a motley collection of nearly worthless A-24A dive bombers, B-25 Mitchell medium bombers that lacked spare parts to keep them in commission that had been "borrowed" from the surviving Dutch Air Force in Australia, and a dozen A-20C light attack bombers that had arrived in Australia lacking bomb racks and guns. Gunn had personally taken the B-25s, which had been shipped to Australia to equip the Netherlands East Indies Air Force (ML-KNIL), using forged orders directing the depot where the airplanes were being held to hand them over to the USAAF. Gunn had brought along 12 pilots with him, who immediately flew away with the bombers before higher authority could be contacted to confirm the validity of Gunn's paperwork. At the time of Kenney's visit, Gunn was in the midst of a project to turn the A-20s into ground strafers, mounting four .50-caliber machine guns taken from crashed P-40s in the former bombardier's nose position, and had completed and tested one successfully.

Kenney recalled that 3rd Group commander Colonel James "Big Jim" Davies took him to a tent where the armorers were at work building gun mounts for the A-20s. Gunn was working with the rest of the men. Davies introduced him to the general, saying, "This is our engineering officer, Major Gunn, who invents a new way to make life hard for the Japs every day." Kenney was immediately interested and Gunn gave him a tour of the completed A-20 gunship. As the man who had first put extra guns on an Army attack bomber to create the first "strafer," Kenney liked what Gunn was doing and ordered him to fix all the A-20s thus.

The two were each unorthodox and believed in doing what was needed to accomplish the mission with little regard for bureaucracy; both took an immediate liking to each other. Kenney informed Colonel Davies he could keep Gunn for another two weeks to complete the makeover of the A-20s, but that he would then become "Special Projects Officer" for the newly formed Fifth Air Force, reporting directly to the general. It would turn out to be Kenney's best personnel decision of the war. With the general's approval, Gunn set up shop at Townsville airfield outside Brisbane, bringing along with him the men he had chosen and trained at the 3rd Attack Group to become Fifth Air Force's experimental development department.

What ultimately became the B-25 medium bomber resulted from Circular 38-385, issued by the Army Air Corps in March, 1938, which called for a twin-engine bomber with performance that exceeded the single-engined types such as the A-17 currently in service, with a payload of 1,200 pounds, a range of 1,200 miles, and a top speed over 200mph. The primary goal of the new bomber would be battlefield interdiction. Responses were submitted by Bell, Boeing-Stearman, Douglas, Martin, and North American. Bell's Model 9 proposed an aircraft powered by two Allison in-line engines, but was withdrawn from competition before a prototype was built. Boeing-Stearman's Model X-100 was a three-seat high-winged monoplane with two untried Pratt & Whitney R-2180 radials. Martin's Model 139 was essentially a modernized B-10, a six-year-old design. The Douglas Model 7B was a high-winged monoplane using two 1,100hp Pratt & Whitney R-1830 Twin Wasp radials. North American's NA-40 had a five-man crew, unlike the competitors' three-man crews. The shoulder-mounted wings carried two Pratt & Whitney R-1830-S6C3-6 air-cooled radials rated at 1,100hp in underwing nacelles. Two rudders at the tips of the horizontal stabilizer behind the engines provided control in event of engine loss. Like the Douglas contender, it featured a tricycle undercarriage.

The NA-40 first flew on January 29, 1939. Early tests revealed severe tail shaking that worsened as speed increased, while the engines had cooling problems. With a maximum speed of 268mph at 5,000 feet, the general feeling was that the NA-40 was seriously underpowered. In February 1939, Wright R-2600-A71-3 Double Cyclone 14-cylinder air-cooled radial engines rated at 1,600hp were fitted and the prototype was redesignated NA-40B. The first flight on March 1, 1939 demonstrated a maximum speed of 287mph at 5,000 feet. The NA-40B arrived at Wright Field on March 12, 1939; however, it crashed on April 11, when the pilot lost control during an engine-out test. The crew escaped without serious injury, but the NA-40B caught fire in the crash and was a total loss. The basic design was not at fault, but the Air Corps awarded the attack bomber contract to Douglas in July 1939 for what became the A-20.

During the attack bomber contest, the Air Corps issued a specification for a medium bomber in March 1939 calling for a payload of 2,400 pounds, range of 1,200 miles, and maximum speed of 300mph. North American responded with the NA-62, which was ordered "off the drawing board" in September 1939 as the B-25 Mitchell, named for air power pioneer General Billy Mitchell. The B-25 was produced alongside the Glenn Martin Company design, which became the B-26 Marauder. The B-25 was powered by the same Wright R-2600s that had been fitted to the NA-40B, while Martin's bomber used the new Pratt & Whitney R-2800 Double Wasp. The two would be seen throughout the war as competitors for performance and the affection of their crews. John W. Young, who flew both types in the 319th Bomb Group in 1942–44, recalled the B-26 as being "like a Packard limousine," while the B-25 reminded him of "a tinny Model T." The B-25 never suffered the handling problems the B-26 faced and was considered far easier to handle following loss of an engine.

After limited production of the B-25A commencing in 1940 and the B-25B in 1941, the definitive B-25C/D arrived on the scene in the fall of 1941. The B-25C-NA was built at the Inglewood, California plant, where production began in January 1942, two months after the prototype's first flight. Inglewood produced 1,625 B-25Cs between January 1942 and May 1943. Initial changes from the B-25B were relatively minor, with engines changed to the Wright Cyclone R-2600-13, which had a different carburetor; on the B-25C the exhaust system remained a single pipe, exiting just behind the engine on the outer side of the nacelle, while on the B-25D the system changed to individual exhausts for the separate cylinders.

In late 1940, the Knudsen Commission recommended construction of additional aircraft factories in the Midwest where they would be safe from any potential enemy air attack and would utilize automobile production methods to meet increased wartime production demands.

North American began construction of a factory in Kansas City, Missouri (actually in Fairfax, Kansas, a suburb) at a location adjacent to the Fairfax Municipal Airport that was in Kansas City, Kansas. Formal ground breaking commenced on March 8, 1941. Five weeks later, on April 17, the first employees moved into their offices and the factory was declared ready that fall. Eventually 26,000 workers, the vast majority of whom had no previous experience in aircraft production, would turn out 6,883 B-25 Mitchells by the time production ceased in August 1945.

The first B-25D-NC bomber, christened "Miss Greater Kansas City," was completed on December 23, 1941, two weeks after Pearl Harbor. The airplane differed from the B-25C only in the location of its production and the chosen engine exhaust system, and was first flown on January 3, 1942 by chief North American test pilot Paul Balfour. Contract NA-87 authorized construction of 1,200 B-25D-NC bombers, the first 100 being constructed from B-25C-NA parts. Following cancelation of plans to also produce the B-29 in the factory, Contract NA-100 authorized an additional 1,090 B-25D-NC bombers. The first B-25D-NC was accepted by the Air Force on January 17, 1942. A total of 2,290 B-25Ds were produced at Kansas City by March 9, 1944, when production shifted over to the B-25J. Halfway through the production run, the lower turret was deleted, as it had proven problematical in operation and the upper turret was provided additional ammunition. Hardpoints for underwing bomb racks were added, with the outer wing strengthened to carry the extra weight. The flexible gun in the nose was increased from .30 to .50 caliber and a second .50-caliber gun was added, firing forward from the right lower side of the bombardier's compartment and controlled by the pilot. A 325-gallon fuel tank could be carried in the bomb bay.

Most of the additional changes in the B-25 would come as a result of the initial field modification work done by Colonel Gunn in Australia, where the majority of USAAF Mitchells would see combat.

Following the creation of the A-20 strafers, Gunn took on the project of turning the B-25 into an effective bomber for operations in New Guinea. He was put in charge of the maintenance depot at Townsville airfield outside Brisbane, where all B-25s delivered to the theater were modified before being sent on to the newly arrived bomb groups. Due to the fact that the "definitive" B-25 had only entered production in January 1942, delivery of aircraft to Australia was slow, because the majority of units being formed at Charleston Army Air Field in South Carolina to operate the bomber were initially designated for service in Europe. The Royce Detachment had brought six B-25s to Australia in February 1942, at about the same time the 12 Lend-Lease Dutch B-25s later stolen by Gunn had arrived. These were the only B-25s in the theater until August, 1942, when the 38th Bomb Group, the first group equipped with the B-25 to deploy overseas, arrived in Australia.

The 38th Bombardment Group, composed of the 69th, 70th, and 71st Bombardment Squadrons, was ordered into existence on November 18, 1940 and activated on January 15, 1941, at Jackson Army Air Base, Mississippi. The group was originally planned to be the second unit after the 22nd Bombardment Group to equip with the Martin B-26 Marauder, with those two units joined by the 42nd Bombardment Group. The squadrons initially trained on obsolete Douglas B-18 "Bolo" bombers, since the first production deliveries of the Marauder had only begun in February 1941. After two early landing accidents, the B-26 was grounded in April 1941 until the problem was traced to improper weight distribution since the dorsal gun turret had not yet been installed. The 38th Group only began to receive B-26s in the late summer of 1941 when production began on the B-26A. The airplane had quickly developed a reputation as a "hot ship," particularly when newly trained inexperienced pilots were behind the controls. The relatively small wing quickly resulted in the bomber gaining the nickname "Flying Prostitute," for "having no visible means of support." In November 1941, the group lost their first airplane in a crash when its vertical stabilizer and rudder separated from the aircraft at altitude. While the exact cause was never determined, the accident report considered the possibility a canopy hatch had broken off and struck the vertical stabilizer. For a time, pilots training on the airplane believed it could not be flown successfully on one engine until Colonel Jimmy Doolittle flew demonstration flights that featured single-engine takeoffs and landings at MacDill Army Air Field in January 1942, after which proper training techniques were developed which ended the stories of "one a day in Tampa Bay."

With the 69th and 70th squadrons nearing initial operational capability in early 1942, the unit was given orders to the Southwest

Pacific along with the 22nd Group, and the ground echelon moved to Australia in late January and February while the air echelon remained behind for further training. The air echelons of the 69th and 70th squadrons arrived in Hawaii in April 1942, where they were held back from further deployment to Australia due to the pending Battle of Midway. Two of the bombers formed half of the four-Marauder torpedo bombing mission against the Japanese aircraft carriers on June 4, 1942. One B-26 was shot down and the other never flew again after returning to Midway with severe battle damage. That July, the two squadrons were deployed to Fiji and New Caledonia in the South Pacific, where they were eventually detached from the 38th Group. By late 1942, the B-26 would be phased out of operations in the Pacific in favor of being supplied in quantity to units operating in the European Theater.

In the meantime, the group headquarters and the 71st Bomb Squadron had moved to Barksdale Field, Louisiana, where they were joined in April by the 405th Bomb Squadron, which had originally been the 15th Reconnaissance Squadron operating B-25s on anti-submarine patrol. The 71st Squadron commenced re-equipment from the B-26 to the B-25 with the unit receiving B-25Ds delivered straight from the Kansas City factory. Among the pilots who reported to Barksdale with the 15th Recon Squadron was First Lieutenant Ralph Cheli, who would become one of the group's leaders. Born and raised in New York City, he had enlisted as a flying cadet in February 1940. After receiving primary flight training at Tulsa, Oklahoma, basic flight training at Randolph Field, Texas, and multi-engine advanced training at Kelly Field, Texas, he graduated in November 1940 as a Second Lieutenant with orders to the 21st Reconnaissance Squadron in Miami, then equipped with the B-17. After a year with the 21st Squadron and the 43rd Bomb Squadron at MacDill Field, Florida, he was promoted to First Lieutenant in February 1942 and transitioned to the B-25 in the 15th Recon Squadron in February 1942. Cheli was one of the most experienced pilots in the group and was promoted to Captain in June, assigned as operations officer for the 405th Squadron.

In late June, the two squadrons were considered qualified on the B-25 and were given orders to finally join the group's ground echelon in Australia. Flying their airplanes across the United States to gain experience in navigation, they arrived at McClellan Air Base in Sacramento, California, where they were given three days' indoctrination in over-water flying, after which they moved to Hamilton Field, north of San Francisco, California, the last week in June, 1942.

On July 1, the first B-25s of the 71st Squadron took off at 2100 hours, headed for Hickam Field, Hawaii. Pilot Lawrence R. "Pop" Kienle, whose nickname came from his being 25, a whole three years older than the next-oldest pilot in the squadron, remembered that the flight took 12 hours and 30 minutes, during which neither he nor his co-pilot left their seats, and that they landed just before 1000 hours on July 2 with enough fuel for another 45 minutes.

After a 24-hour rest, the bombers took off shortly after dawn on July 3 for Christmas Island, 1,000 miles to the southwest. The flight was made in excellent weather, with broken clouds at 2,000 feet, and south-southwesterly winds. Flying by dead-reckoning navigation, when the scheduled ETA came, there was nothing below but water. The formation took up a square search, and 90 minutes later they found Christmas Island and landed. Over the next six days, they flew on to Samoa, Tutuila, New Caledonia, and arrived at Brisbane on July 9, 1942. Once in Australia, they discovered they had flown from a warm summer in the United States to what Kienle later described as the "bone-chilling cold" of mid-winter Australia at Eagle Farm Field outside Brisbane. They were the first group of medium bombers to successfully make the trans-Pacific flight.

Once all had arrived, the group was ordered north to Townsville, then inland 60 miles to Charters Towers airfield. The two squadrons then spent the next month training and bringing newly assigned crews up to standard. Kienle remembered that, during the briefings for training flights, the instructors emphasized, "Don't buzz the dry river beds" but never gave a reason why. A few days into training, a fighter pilot carrying his parachute showed up at the operations shack. Questioned what happened, he admitted he had buzzed the river bed, and had learned that, in the rural outback, cable lifts were used to cross rivers during the winter wet season. As Kienle put it, "Cables are hard to see at 200 plus miles an hour – 'nuff said." By mid-August the group's first squadrons were considered ready for combat and set off from Charters Towers for 17-Mile 'Drome at Port Moresby via Horn Island. During training the group as a whole had adopted the name "The Sunsetters," in honor of their west-bound flight to war. The 71st Squadron adopted the name "Wolf Pack," while the 405th became the "Green Dragons."

Photographer-gunner Tech Sergeant Hoyt D. Amos of the 405th, one of the original group members, remembered the first flight up to Port Moresby.

Shortly after we moved to Horn Island as an advanced echelon, I had the first of three narrow encounters with the Grim Reaper. I was assigned to Lieutenant Bill Pittman's crew. To protect our aircraft in case of an alert, we were instructed to rush to our aircraft for immediate takeoff, circle about 20 to 30 miles from the island and after the enemy left to return and land. While sitting around our plane, the upper gunner asked me to go to supply and get him a screwdriver he needed to work on his gun mount. Just as I reached supply, an alert sounded. I started running back as our plane taxied out. The gunner saw me and held the rear hatch open. I had closed to 30 feet when she picked up speed and I saw I couldn't make it. I watched it turn at the end of the strip and gun the engines for takeoff. To my horror, a P-40E was also taking off on the short strip to Lieutenant Pittman's right. They were on a collision course and at the point they met, neither had reached takeoff speed. Lieutenant Pittman jerked the plane up off of the runway and over the fighter. At about 50 feet altitude, he stalled and the left wing dipped and she nosed down. Pittman managed a slow turn, holding her flat and pancaked into the stumps and brush just off the runway. No one was hurt, but my rear compartment was completely squashed. Our plane became parts for our other aircraft.

Navigator First Lieutenant Ed Gervase of the 405th Squadron remembered their arrival at 17-Mile 'Drome.

Our tents were pitched about 100 yards south of the pierced steel plank runway. We were in mosquito-infested kunai grass about six feet high. Fortunately these conditions did not last long. We moved away from the runway onto higher ground with no grass, just clear ground. Shortly after we arrived, it was decided the 405th Squadron had a large number of highly qualified aircraft commanders, and there was a balancing of strength in the squadrons. My pilot, First Lieutenant Bill Tarver and our crew, were shifted from the 405th to the 71st.

The 38th Group flew its first mission on September 15, 1942, led by newly promoted Major Cheli. Gervase, who was not on the mission, remembered that the bombers failed to make rendezvous with their fighter escort, and that First Lieutenant Carey's crew was shot down by defending Zeros. Gervase's crew flew their first mission on October 5, a three-plane formation led by Captain Alden G. "Bud" Thompson, with First Lieutenant Larry Tanberg on left wing and Gervase's pilot, Lieutenant Tarver, on right wing. Gervase recalled:

> The mission was to search out and destroy Japanese shipping hiding out in the rivers emptying into the ocean off the north coast from Buna to Sanananda Point. We had no fighter cover. Weather was partly cloudy. We cleared the Owen Stanley Range and headed north along the coast. We finished the northward run, turned around and retraced our path. Suddenly the radio cracked, "Zeros!" The flight leader must have pushed his throttles through the firewall, because instantly the wingmen were left behind. Then Captain Thompson made a sharp turn to the right, leaving Lieutenant Tanberg hanging loose on his left. Next, he made a sharp turn to the left and we were left hanging on the right. The turret gunners were firing at the Zeros as the formation headed south over the coast. Captain Thompson kept zigzagging his flight path toward the south end of the Owen Stanley Range and we managed to figure out what he was doing and closed up. After about 15–20 minutes, the Zeros broke off the chase and we got home safely. Our plane had eight bullet holes in it, all through the mid-section of the plane. No one was injured.

Sergeant Amos remembered his second close call with the Grim Reaper, which happened on his sixth mission in late October.

> The 405th sent two B-25s on an armed recon "Search and Destroy" mission. Our pilot was Lieutenant Brandon, and the upper gunner was Jack Allan. We sighted a troop transport several miles off the coast of Buna. We started our bomb run at 5,000 feet. As soon as I saw the transport in my camera view finder, I started my strip of photographs. Unfortunately the bombardier pushed the wrong release switch, which dropped only one 250-pound bomb instead

of all six at one-second intervals. It hit about 100 feet in front of the transport. Had the correct switch been pushed, the transport would have been blown to smithereens with at least two or three direct hits. Lieutenant Brandon started a 360-degree turn to make another run when all hell broke loose. We nosed over and headed straight down. I thought we had been hit by heavy ack-ack. I had a chest pack harness but was sitting on the 'chute. I sailed up to the ceiling and floated around with the K-17 camera, which had come out of its mount, trying to find my chest pack so I could fasten up and bail out. What had happened was Lieutenant Brandon saw a Zero headed right at us and instinctively shoved the stick forward into a power dive. Everything not fastened down floated to the top of the aircraft. We went from about 5,000 feet to 500 feet before he and the co-pilot could pull out of the dive.

We were surrounded by Zeros. Unfortunately all the ammunition had come out of the cans and my waist gun had fallen out of its mount. The upper turret guns were in operating condition still in their containers. I remounted my gun in the rear window mount but could only fire out the right side. The radio-gunner was desperately working on his hopelessly jammed bottom turret. Two Zeros came in low on our blind spot and the upper gunner yelled that the fixed fire "scare gun" sticking out the rear did not react to his solenoid switch. I climbed back there and got 20 rounds out to scare off the Zeros. Back at my rear window, I fired at one on the right and Allan got the one on the left. Meantime, Lieutenant Brandon dropped the plane to 100 feet and put the engines in "High Blower." The Zeros could still fly faster, but could not turn into us without dropping back. I crawled back and got the "wobble gun" firing and we were able to get the Zeros off to the left or right where we could get to them. We sweated out climbing to cross the Owen Stanley Range with the last two Zeros finally turning back to Buna. The other B-25 and its crew were never seen again.

While the 38th was being introduced to combat that fall, Pappy Gunn was working to turn the B-25 into an effective weapon for the kind of war that was being fought in New Guinea. While the Mitchell had originally been designed to drop bombs from 10,000 to 12,000 feet, it was impossible to spot a target under the triple-canopy jungle from that altitude. Gunn removed the Norden bombsight. General Kenney had invented the "parachute-retarded bomb" during experiments in the 1930s, and these were manufactured in Australia as 100-pound fragmentation bombs known as "parafrags," which could be dropped at low altitude with the delay in their fall giving the bomber time to escape the explosion when they hit the ground. The crews of the 38th's two squadrons were pulled back one at a time in November and December and trained in low-level bombing.

Their ability in low-level bombing was now excellent in the anti-shipping role, but the parafrags were not what was needed to sink a ship. Major Bill Blenn of the 43rd Bomb Group's 63rd squadron had developed and refined the tactic that would become known as "skip bombing," in which an attacking aircraft flying at an altitude of 100 feet or so would drop a 500-pound bomb while flying at a speed of 250mph, causing the bomb to "skip" over the water like a stone thrown across a pond, hitting the target in the hull close to the waterline. Gunn immediately saw that this method of attack was better employed by the smaller and lighter B-25 than the B-17s flown by the 43rd. Once the crews had been trained in the tactic, it was possible to sink a ship as large as a destroyer with one bomb.

In the meantime, Gunn had transformed the former Dutch B-25s now in the long-serving veteran 3rd Attack Group into a larger version of the A-20 gunship the group had been the first to use. The bombardier's nose position was cleared out and mounts fitted for four .50-caliber machine guns with 500 rounds of ammunition for each gun. Additionally, "packages" of two .50-caliber weapons were mounted on the fuselage side below the cockpit, with the ammunition carried in wooden boxes behind and below the pilots' cockpit. In tests, the eight machine guns could fire all 4,000 rounds in a minute, creating such a hail of fire that any target was shredded. The only problem was that the vibration of the externally mounted guns cracked the surrounding skin. Pads were placed in the mounts, and special extra-strength structures were built inside on which to mount the external weapons.

With 12 B-25s so modified and the 38th Group's crews trained for low-level bombing attack, the new gunships and tactics were ready for their big test, the Battle of the Bismarck Sea that took place on March 2–4, 1943.

Following the loss of Buna in January, the Japanese needed to reinforce Lae on the northern coast. Despite increased Allied air power, a large convoy was to sail from Rabaul direct to Lae with 6,900 troops.

Imperial Army messages were decoded that revealed the operation, and plans were made to stop this convoy. The eight destroyer escorts and eight troop transports departed Rabaul on February 28, 1943, under cover of a storm. On March 1, a B-24 spotted them and the convoy was shadowed until it came within range of aircraft flying from Port Moresby. General Kenney threw in every plane he had in the Fifth Air Force, 130 bombers and fighter escorts.

Multiple sustained missions were flown on March 2. RAAF Beaufort torpedo bombers, Beaufighter long-range fighter-bombers, and A-20s flew along with the American gunship A-20s and the newly modified B-25s. On their first mission, the Mitchells attacked and sank four troop transports and two escorting destroyers in an attack lasting 15 minutes. Major Cheli led the 405th Squadron in a devastating masthead skip-bombing attack. 71st Squadron B-25 co-pilot, Second Lieutenant Garrett Middlebook, later described the results:

> They went in and hit this troop ship. What I saw looked like little sticks, maybe a foot long or something like that, or splinters flying up off the deck of the ship; they'd fly all around and twist crazily in the air and fall out in the water. Then I realized I was watching human beings. I was watching hundreds of those Japanese blown off the deck by all those machine guns in the planes. They spun around the air like sticks in a whirlwind and they'd fall in the water.

The final score was all eight transports and four destroyers sunk by fire from the gunships and masthead skip-bombing attacks by the Sunsetter Mitchells. The success of the gunship was solidly demonstrated. The next day, the aircraft returned and strafed the Imperial Army troops in the water. Middlebook later recalled that "the sea turned red." The Japanese never tried a major reinforcement again, sending troops in small flotillas which meant their reinforcements would never make up the losses as MacArthur's offensive moved along the northern coast of the island through the rest of 1943 until the last Japanese position at Hollandia was assaulted and taken in April 1944.

Following the success of the gunships at the Bismarck Sea battle, General Kenney traveled to Washington to discuss the progress of the war at the Pentagon with the USAAF leadership. Back in January, before the battle had proved the value of the gunship concept, Kenney had sent

General Hap Arnold a set of engineering drawings of the modifications made by Gunn to the B-25. The second day he was at the Pentagon, Arnold invited Kenney to a meeting with a group of engineering experts from the Air Materiel Division at Wright-Patterson in Dayton, Ohio. The experts had been given the drawings, which they had gone over in a detailed review. They proceeded to lecture Kenney for an hour on how the modifications would make the airplane nose-heavy and how it would therefore not fly properly. "I listened as patiently as I could," Kenney later wrote, "and then I informed them that 12 B-25s modified according to these plans had just played a rather important role in the destruction of a Japanese troop convoy at the Bismarck Sea battle, and that I was now remodeling 60 more in Australia and planned to modify every B-25 we received like that." Arnold dismissed the experts and told Kenney he wanted Gunn to come to the States "to teach my engineers something."

Gunn returned to the United States in April. He spent a week at Wright-Patterson where the engineering section was involved in making plans for creating gunships on the production lines. After a few days, he informed the assembled experts they didn't have the proper tone of activity in their offices, reminding them there was a war on and time was of the essence in accomplishing these plans. He did work with them to develop the requirements that North American would adopt in the later creation of the various B-25 gunships that would form the majority of B-25s produced after September 1943. He then flew to Los Angeles where he spent three weeks with North American's president, James H. "Dutch" Kindelberger, and his engineers going over in detail all the ways the B-25 could be turned into the devastating weapon it would become. Gunn's designs quickly became the B-25G, a modification of the B-25D with a solid "gun nose" and a 75mm cannon mounted in the former bombardier's crawlway under the cockpit, followed by the B-25H modification of the most-produced B-25 sub-type, the B-25J, with a similar cannon-armed nose and even more machine guns. The B-25J's factory-designed eight-gun nose made it the most heavily armed attack bomber of the war, with no fewer than 14 machine guns firing forward. North American also designed single-gun packs for the external weapons, which reduced vibration and structural damage, and were also more aerodynamic than Gunn's original two-gun "package."

Navigator Ed Gervase's B-25, "Pacific Prowler" was among the planes Gunn used for his experiment with a 75mm cannon armament. Gervase recalled:

> Bore sighting the gun was done by an Artillery Major. After three corrections, we flew missions with the gun. The pilot had all the firing controls on the wheel and the navigator did the gun loading from a rack of 21 shells. When the breech was closed and loaded, an electric circuit flashed a ready light on the control column. When the gun fired, the plane seemed to stop in mid-air; the vibration popped many rivets in the fuselage, and fire shot back from the breech, which meant you had to get up out of the way after loading each shell. On one mission, I was able to set off 12 rounds which was almost a miracle, though I don't think we did much damage. However, on a later mission we were near the back end of Lae strip close to the mountains, where we received machine gun fire. Lieutenant Tarver fired one shell but it was about 20 yards short. We circled around and lined up on the machine gun tracers and scored a direct hit. There was no more firing from the Japanese outpost.

The "Sunsetters" were completely re-equipped with B-25 gunships modified at Gunn's center at Townsville by June 1943. In May, the 822nd and 823rd squadrons had been formed from mid-level cadre in the 71st and 405th squadrons to bring the group to full four-squadron strength. Flying from the advanced airfield at Dobodura, the Sunsetters soon became the nemesis of enemy airfields and bases across northern New Guinea, as well as shipping in the Bismarck Sea.

On August 18, MacArthur's ground troops attacked the Japanese port at Lae. It was necessary to neutralize the enemy airfields at Wewak, some 300 miles to the west. More than 100 bombers and 90 fighters were based at Wewak and its satellite fields at But, Boram, and Dagua. The 500-mile flight was the deepest penetration into Japanese-held territory in daylight yet made by medium bombers.

The attack was preceded by a night attack with 50 heavy bombers on August 16–17, followed by a strike at dawn on August 17 by 32 B-25s, escorted by 80 P-38 Lightnings. Both attacks encountered intense antiaircraft fire but almost no fighter opposition. A third attack was mounted the morning of August 18 to strafe and bomb the fields from low altitude. The 3rd Attack Group was assigned to attack Wewak and Boram airdromes, while the 38th Group was sent further west to attack Dagua and But airdromes. Each B-25 was loaded with 12 three-bomb clusters of 23-pound "parafrag" bombs. The 405th Squadron would attack Dagua and the 71st Squadron the fighter field at But.

Major Cheli was assigned to lead the mission. The bombers encountered bad weather en route, which separated them from their P-38 escort. Mechanical problems forced one plane in each squadron to abort. As the 405th Squadron maneuvered at low altitude to attack the heavily defended airfield, 15 Ki.43 Oscar fighters attacked from above and made several passes at the formation over a ten-minute interval. Cheli's bomber was hit and its right engine caught fire two miles from the target. The fire quickly spread to the fuselage. Cheli's speed was such that he could have zoomed up and gained sufficient altitude for the crew to bail out, but doing so would have disorganized the formation just at the moment of attack. Cheli opted to fly on at minimum altitude, leading the squadron in a devastating bombing and strafing attack on the target. Once clear of the target, Cheli ordered his wingman to take lead, while he turned away and flew southeast, crash-landing in the sea two kilometers off Boram airdrome.

It was initially believed Cheli and his crew were killed in the crash, but postwar interrogation of Japanese officers at Rabaul discovered the major had been rescued and captured, then sent to the POW camp at Rabaul, where he was executed on March 6, 1944. With this additional information, Major Cheli was awarded the Medal of Honor, the only member of the 38th Group so honored. His citation reads, in part:

> ... Intercepting aircraft centered their fire on his plane, causing it to burst into flames while still two miles from the objective. His speed would have enabled him to gain necessary altitude to parachute to safety, but this action would have resulted in his formation becoming disorganized and exposed to the enemy. Although a crash was inevitable, he courageously elected to continue leading the attack in his blazing plane. From a minimum altitude, the squadron made a devastating bombing and strafing attack on the target. The mission completed, Major Cheli instructed his wingman to lead the formation, and crashed into the sea.

10

PEARL HARBOR AVENGED

Only two men have ever been specifically targeted as individuals for their roles in events that embarrassed the United States militarily. One, Osama Bin Laden, was hunted down and killed for organizing and directing "America's second Pearl Harbor," the attacks on the World Trade Center and Pentagon on September 11, 2001. The other, Admiral Isoroku Yamamoto, was killed in an act of revenge for organizing and directing the first "Pearl Harbor" on December 7, 1941, as commander of the Imperial Navy's Combined Fleet.

On April 14, 1943, Private Harold Fudenna, who belonged to a unit of the US Army's Military Intelligence Service (MIS) composed of Nisei (second-generation Japanese Americans) that specialized in translation of materials ranging from standard textbooks to captured documents, was given message NTF131755. This had been sent in the Japanese diplomatic code known as "Purple" by the Japanese Foreign Ministry to diplomatic personnel in the South Pacific, alerting them to a planned visit by Admiral Yamamoto to inspect all Imperial forces at Rabaul and Bougainville involved in Operation *I-Go*, the final Japanese attempt to wrest back control of Guadalcanal which had begun on April 7. The message outlined the admiral's itinerary and schedule of arrivals and departures. When Private Fudenna translated the message, it was at first met with disbelief that the Japanese would be so careless. However, other MIS linguists at stations in Alaska and Hawaii also intercepted it and confirmed the accuracy of Fudenna's translation.

It was fortunate the message was in the Japanese diplomatic Purple Code, which had been broken in the summer of 1941. The US Navy's codebreakers had been unable to read the Imperial Navy's JN-25 code since the end of May, 1942, the week before the Battle of Midway, because the Imperial Navy had changed the code three times between early June and the end of July, right after the battle. The translation was passed on to the Navy's cryptographers, who were astounded to read the details of the time of arrival of Yamamoto's trip, which included the number and types of planes that would transport and accompany him. On April 18, 1943, the admiral and his staff party would depart Rabaul aboard two G4M1 Betty bombers, one with the admiral and the other his staff, escorted by nine Zeros, with a scheduled arrival at Ballale airfield on Bougainville of 0945 hours local. The admiral was known for his punctuality. In the face of doubts, a young cryptography officer named John Paul Stevens vouched for Fudenna's skill as a translator and convinced his superiors to act on the message.

Events moved quickly. Some sources have claimed the order to "get Yamamoto" came directly from President Roosevelt to Navy Secretary Frank Knox, though no official record of such an order has ever been discovered. Secretary Knox was not a man who needed someone else to tell him what to do with the information once he saw it. He let Pacific Fleet commander Admiral Nimitz make the decision after consulting Admiral William F. Halsey, Jr., Commander, South Pacific. When Halsey read the message, he immediately saw the potential to decapitate the top command of the Imperial Navy. He made no bones about his attitude, naming the mission Operation *Vengeance*. It was coincidental that April 18, 1943, was the one-year anniversary of the Doolittle Raid which had provoked Yamamoto to attempt the invasion of Midway, which turned into the battle that reversed the course of the Pacific War. Nimitz gave the mission the go-ahead on April 17.

The Americans did not know that Japanese officers at Rabaul had tried to convince Yamamoto to cancel the Bougainville visit out of fear of ambush since he would be so close to the Americans. The admiral determined to go regardless, believing the men on Bougainville in the front-line units of the *I-Go* operation and the Army troops on the island needed the morale boost. His one concession to the potential danger was that he discarded his white dress uniform in favor of a khaki uniform.

The American mission would have to be flown outside the Solomons chain, to avoid premature detection by the Japanese. The only fighters with the range to fly such a round trip were the P-38G Lightnings of the 339th Fighter Squadron of the 347th Fighter Group, based at Fighter One on Guadalcanal. Flying south and then west of the Solomons to Bougainville was nearly 600 miles, 200 miles further than the direct distance between the two islands. Normally, the P-38s carried two 165-gallon drop tanks; for this mission they would carry one 165-gallon tank and a 330-gallon ferry tank, which would allow them to fly the 1,000-mile round trip.

Major John A. Mitchell, commander of the 39th Squadron, was assigned to lead the mission, which would be composed of 18 P-38s. One flight of four was designated the "killer" flight, while the rest – including two spares for the first flight – would fly cover at 18,000 feet to deal with the expected reaction by enemy fighters based at Kahili. While the 339th Fighter Squadron officially carried out the mission, ten of the 18 pilots came from the other two squadrons of the 347th Group. Using the itinerary, a flight plan was prepared that calculated an ETA of 0935 hours to catch the bombers ten minutes before landing at Ballale when they descended over Bougainville. The outbound flight would be flown at an altitude of 50 feet all the way to Bougainville, maintaining radio silence. At the mission briefing, the pilots were told the information had been obtained by coastwatchers, since "Magic" code breaking was top secret. This was done to provide cover in case anyone was shot down and captured.

The 18 P-38s lifted off from Fighter One at 0725 hours. Two P-38s assigned to the killer flight dropped out early on. One experienced a flat tire during takeoff, while the second aborted when its drop tanks failed to feed. Mitchell and his flight of four led the formation. The "killer flight" was now composed of first element Captain Tom Lanphier in number 122 "Phoebe," and First Lieutenant Rex Barber in number 147 "Miss Virginia," a P-38 normally flown by Captain Robert Petit, and second-element spares First Lieutenants Besby F. Holmes in number 100, the oldest P-38 in the unit, and Raymond K. Hine in number 102. Mitchell, flying number 110 "Squinch" since his regular aircraft was down for maintenance, managed to navigate entirely by dead reckoning on the longest interception mission of the war. His navigation was so skillful that the P-38s arrived at the intercept point at 0934 hours, one minute early. A moment later, Yamamoto's bombers and their six escorts descended into view in a light haze.

The P-38s dropped their auxiliary tanks, turned to the right to parallel the bombers, and advanced their throttles to make a full-power climb to intercept them. Unfortunately, Besby Holmes' tanks failed to separate, forcing him and Hine to turn out to sea while he tried to get rid of the tanks. Mitchell radioed Lanphier and Barber to engage. The nearest Zeros spotted the enemy fighters and dived toward the pair of P-38s. The two Bettys increased their dives, the pilots hoping to throw off the approaching Americans by flying low over the jungle. Lanphier immediately turned head-on toward the approaching Zeros while Barber went after the bombers. He banked steep and turned in behind the bombers, momentarily losing sight of them in the sun. When Barber regained visual contact, he found himself immediately behind one. He opened fire, hitting it in its right engine, rear fuselage, and tail. He aimed a second burst at the left engine, which immediately trailed heavy black smoke. The Betty rolled violently to the left and Barber narrowly avoided a mid-air collision. He turned to the right, looked back over his shoulder, and saw a column of thick black smoke rising from the jungle 200 feet below.

Barber then flew toward the coast at treetop level, searching for the second bomber. He soon spotted the second Betty, which carried Chief of Staff Vice Admiral Matome Ugaki and the rest of Yamamoto's staff. The bomber was low over the water off Moila Point, its pilot twisting and turning to evade an attack by Holmes, who had finally been able to release his drop tanks. Holmes' burst of fire hit the Betty's right engine, which immediately emitted a white vapor trail, but his high closure speed carried him and wingman Hine past the damaged bomber.

Barber then attacked the crippled bomber. His fire blew off debris that damaged his P-38 as the Betty crash-landed in the water. Ugaki and two others survived and were later rescued. Barber, Holmes, and Hine were then attacked by the nine Zero escorts. When he got back to Guadalcanal, Barber's P-38 had 104 hits. Holmes and Barber each claimed a Zero shot down, though the Japanese records record no losses. Major Mitchell and the top cover P-38s briefly engaged the enemy fighters without success.

Mitchell saw the column of smoke in the jungle from the crash of the first bomber. Hine's P-38 had disappeared in the fight, presumably shot down. The P-38s were all now low on fuel and were forced to break off contact. Besby Holmes was so low on fuel he was forced to land in the Russell Islands before returning to Guadalcanal.

Admiral Ugaki survived the crash of his plane, along with the pilot. The rest of the staff had been killed. The bodies of two of the crew washed ashore the next day. A Japanese search and rescue party led by Army engineer Lieutenant Hamasuna located the crash site of the first bomber the next day in the jungle north of the site of the former Australian coastal patrol post and Catholic mission of Buin, where they found Admiral Yamamoto, who had been thrown clear of the wreckage. He was still in his seat under a tree, his white-gloved hand grasping the hilt of his katana sword as his head tilted down as if deep in thought. After the body was returned to the main base at Ballale, a postmortem found two bullet wounds, one to the back of his left shoulder and a second that entered his left lower jaw and exited above his right eye. The admiral's death was publicly announced on May 21, 1943, though the details of his death were hidden from the Japanese public.

The Japanese never knew that the attack was a planned ambush, since the American announcement put out the official story that the bombers had been spotted by coastwatchers and the information had been passed to Mitchell's formation, which was coincidentally on patrol in the vicinity.

At this point, the story took an additional twist that would not be finally settled for 50-odd years: who shot down Yamamoto?

Tom Lanphier's actions during the battle after he turned toward the approaching Zeros were unclear and his account was later disputed by the other participants, including the Japanese fighter pilots who were interviewed after the war. The formation had broken after the attack and Lanphier was one of those who returned alone. As he approached Henderson Field, Lanphier radioed, "That son of a bitch will not be dictating any peace terms in the White House," which was a serious breach of security. Immediately on landing, Lanphier claimed he shot down Yamamoto. He wrote the only report of the mission, in which he stated that, after he turned to engage the escorting fighters, he shot the wing off one, then rolled inverted as he circled back toward the two bombers. He spotted the lead bomber circling below him, pulled out of his turn and fired, blowing off the right wing after which the Betty crashed into the jungle. He also stated that he witnessed Barber shoot down the second bomber, which also crashed in the jungle.

From Lanphier's report, intelligence officers believed three Bettys had been shot down, since Besby Holmes claimed a Betty that crashed into the sea. Since there were no formal post-mission interrogation procedures in use at the time, none of the other pilots were debriefed and Lanphier was officially credited with being the pilot who "got Yamamoto." However, many of the other pilots soon expressed skepticism about the official story. Over the summer, unauthorized details about the mission leaked in the press, and *Time* magazine published an article about the event in October 1943 in which Lanphier was mentioned by name. The Navy was outraged at what Halsey and Nimitz saw as a serious breach of security, with the result that the nomination of Major Mitchell for the Medal of Honor saw his award downgraded to a Navy Cross, which was subsequently awarded to all the pilots in the killer flight.

After the war, Imperial Navy pilot Kenji Yanagiya, who had been one of the escort pilots, told Mitchell he might have shot down Hine, since he had attacked and heavily damaged a P-38 escorting another P-38 that still had its fuel tanks. None of the escorting pilots made a claim for a P-38 that day and Hine is still listed as Missing In Action. Yanagiya also stated that none of the escorting fighters were shot down and that only one was damaged sufficiently to require a day of repair at Buin, which was a direct contradiction of Lanphier's claim. Japanese records did confirm that two G4M bombers had been shot down that day.

Eventually, the Air Force split the difference and officially awarded Lanphier and Barber a half credit each for the bomber that crashed in the jungle, with Barber and Holmes each receiving half credit for the second bomber that crashed at sea. A postwar inspection of the Yamamoto crash site validated Barber's account because "all visible gunfire and shrapnel damage was caused by bullets entering from immediately behind the bomber" not from the right. Despite the evidence, Lanphier maintained his claim for killing Yamamoto until his death in 1987, with the credit making it into nearly all the published obituaries. The fight for credit continued even after Lanphier's death, as Barber petitioned the Air Force Board for Correction of Military Records to have his half credit shared with Lanphier changed to a whole credit. The Air Force History Office advised the board in September 1991 that "enough uncertainty" existed in both Lanphier's and Barber's claims for both to be accepted, and Air Force Secretary Donald B. Rice ruled to retain the shared credit. Barber appealed to have the ruling overturned by the US 9th Circuit Court of Appeals, but the justices refused to intervene.

Barber contested Lanphier's claim, primarily in military publications, until his death in 2001.

Following Barber's death, the argument remained quiescent until May 2006, when *Air Force* magazine published a letter from one of the Operation *Vengeance* pilots, Doug Canning, who had escorted Holmes back to the Russell Islands. Canning, who had been friends with both Lanphier and Barber, stated that Lanphier had written the official report, the medal citations, and several magazine articles about the mission, and that until he gave Barber an unpublished article claiming he alone had shot down Yamamoto, Barber had been willing to share the half credit for the shoot-down. Canning further stated Barber had a strong case for his claim from the testimony of Kenji Yanagiya, who had stated he saw Yamamoto's plane crash 20 to 30 seconds after being hit from behind by a P-38. Furthermore, Canning stated categorically that the P-38Gs flown that day did not have aileron boost (which was not put on the fighter until the final P-38L model), making it physically impossible for Lanphier to have made the 180-degree turn he claimed he made to shoot down Yamamoto's plane. With this, the Air Force disqualified Lanphier's claim and his air-to-air victories were dropped from five to four. Today, Rex Barber is generally recognized as the man who killed the admiral who planned the Pearl Harbor attack.

More important than who actually killed Isoroku Yamamoto is what effect his death had on the Japanese conduct of the war. Writing after the war, Imperial Navy staff officer Commander Masatake Okumiya, who had served under Yamamoto, recalled that when he learned of the admiral's death he remembered what Yamamoto had said in his report to Imperial Headquarters presenting the plan for the attack on Pearl Harbor: "If this attack is approved, I will run wild for six months. After that I can promise nothing." The death was a severe morale blow to the Imperial Navy, and convinced officers like Admiral Soemu Toyoda, who would assume command of the Combined Fleet in 1944 following the death in a flying accident of Admiral Meinichi Koga who was Yamamoto's immediate successor in command, that the Imperial Navy's leadership had been right to consider a war with the United States unwinnable.

Those who replaced Yamamoto in command of the Imperial Navy were lesser men, none of whom possessed his force of personality and reputation, which might have allowed them to successfully argue against continuing the war after the defeat suffered in the Battles of Leyte Gulf, after which Japan was unable to take any offensive action against the enemy and was reduced to a war strategy of national suicide. Okumiya and every other officer who had served with and known Isoroku Yamamoto were unanimous in their belief he would never have taken such actions and would have fought to bring an honorable end to the war his successful plan of attack had brought on.

Following the postmortem, the surviving members of Yamamoto's staff cremated his remains at Buin, leaving a stone marker on the base at the site of the cremation. The ashes were then flown to Truk Atoll, where they were returned to Tokyo aboard the admiral's last flagship, the battleship *Musashi*. On June 5, 1943, Admiral Yamamoto was given a full state funeral and posthumously awarded the title of Marshal and the Order of the Chrysanthemum, 1st Class. On orders from Hitler, he was also awarded the Knight's Cross of the Iron Cross with Oak Leaves and Swords. A portion of his ashes were buried in the Tama Cemetery in Tokyo, with the remainder interred at the temple of Chuko-ji in Nagaoka City where he was born.

11

JAY ZEAMER'S EAGER BEAVERS

The B-17s that had been sent to the Southwest Pacific in 1942 continued to fly operations a year later. Never a large force, they were the only bombers capable of making a round trip to Rabaul from Port Moresby. With their high-altitude capability that made it difficult for the enemy to intercept them, and their overall performance and defensive armament that was superior to the Navy PBY Catalinas and the Lockheed Hudsons flown by the Australians and New Zealanders, they found increased usage in maritime patrol and reconnaissance as it became more obvious their numbers were insufficient to have an impact on enemy operations at Rabaul.

B-17E 41-2666, known as "Old 666," had been rolled out of the Boeing factory in Seattle in March 1942. It arrived in Hawaii that May and was flown to Australia over the trans-Pacific route shortly before the Battle of Midway. Following its arrival in Australia, the bomber was equipped with a trimetrogon camera array used in high-altitude topographical mapping, and assigned to the 8th Photo Reconnaissance Squadron (PRS), which was attached to the 19th Bomb Group. In November, 41-2666 was transferred to the 43rd Bomb Group. That December, it sustained damage on a mission that resulted in the bomber being grounded for need of parts. By April 1943, it was back with the 8th PRS, where it was transferred to the 65th Bomb Squadron, 43rd Bomb Group, at 7-Mile 'Drome at Port Moresby, with a reputation of being a "Hard Luck Hattie" for its record of odd accidents and damage. Once at 7-Mile 'Drome, the battered old bomber came to the attention of Captain Jay Zeamer, the squadron executive officer, who requisitioned the bomber for his use on photo-recon missions.

The 24-year-old Zeamer had first arrived in the Southwest Pacific as a co-pilot in the 22nd Bomb Group, the first unit to take the B-26 Marauder into combat, in the spring of 1942. He was remembered by the other pilots in the group as a quiet, affable, and unflappable man whose unruffled exterior belied a powerful need to excel, who kept his own high standards and was willing, if necessary, to go around the rules to do so. Born in Boothbay Harbor, Maine, he built his own boat at age ten and sailed it in the harbor before becoming an Eagle Scout at 14. He was remembered by his fellow scouts as being "determined to be his own man." In 1940, when he applied for acceptance in the Navy's AvCad program, he failed the eye exam. Over the next 90 days, he used self-help exercises in order to pass the vision test to be accepted for flight training in the Army Air Corps.

In the 22nd Group, his prospects for promotion to first pilot seemed limited. In August 1942 he requested transfer to the B-17-equipped 43rd Bomb Group, and arrived in the 403rd Bomb Squadron at Torrens Creek, Australia, that September. The second week he was with the squadron, he met and quickly became friends with bombardier First Lieutenant Joseph Sarnoski; both shared a desire to see combat and chafed at being in a unit now in the rear area.

The 403rd Squadron had more crewmen than planes. Over the next two months, Zeamer managed to check out in the B-17, and then to volunteer for every flight opportunity no one else wanted to do, becoming the "squadron errand boy." With tropic diseases affecting many of the squadron's pilots, by late November, he was rated as a first pilot on the Flying Fortress. He finally managed to fly a mission to Rabaul when the pilot scheduled was injured. The weather was poor and the other two bombers in the three-plane formation aborted for mechanical reasons, but Zeamer pressed on. The enemy was up and waiting when he arrived, and he eventually escaped the enemy by flying so low they couldn't attack him as he made his escape from the hornet's nest. On arrival back at Port Moresby, the belly gunner stated his refusal to ever fly again with Zeamer. Despite that negative review, his actions during the mission resulted in the award of a Silver Star and permanent assignment as a first pilot – if he could find a crew.

In December, Zeamer teamed with his friend Sarnoski, whose crew had been broken up after their pilot was lost in another airplane, to create a crew of their own. Most of the men they chose for the crew came from the 8th Photo Recon Squadron, while others came from crews that had broken up for various reasons. All shared Zeamer and Sarnoski's desire to come to grips with the enemy and fight the war. Once they were organized, Zeamer and his crew volunteered for difficult missions and soon had the nickname "the Eager Beavers." Still searching for a squadron where they could all fly together without having to beg for a plane, in March 1943 Zeamer wangled a transfer of the crew to the 43rd's 65th Squadron, commanded by a friend, which was on its way back to New Guinea for a tour at Port Moresby. He took the position of squadron operations officer. Over the course of the next few months, Zeamer and his crew gained a reputation for completing a mission regardless of difficulties, whether from the extreme equatorial weather, the poor physical condition of the aircraft, or the enemy.

When he spotted the old B-17 sitting off in the kunai grass near the end of the 7-Mile 'Drome runway, Zeamer considered "Old 666" to be just what he was looking for: an airplane no one else wanted, that "the Eager Beavers" could make their own, a bomber with which they could fight the war as they saw fit. Over the course of the following week, Old 666 had her worn-out engines replaced by lower-time powerplants scrounged from other wrecks, and a formidable armament was mounted: a twin .50-caliber mount in the extreme nose, with two other .50-caliber weapons in enlarged windows to either side of the nose compartment and a third such gun mounted overhead, firing directly forward, controlled by Zeamer. The single .50-caliber guns mounted in the radio compartment and either side of the bomber's waist were replaced with twin mounts in each position. The useless remote-control Sperry belly turret was removed and replaced with a ball turret scavenged from another wreck. When they were through, Old 666 now bristled with no fewer than 17 heavy machine guns, double the normal B-17E armament. In order to maintain performance, the bomb racks and other pieces of gear not needed in the photo-reconnaissance role were removed to save weight. Within a few weeks of completing their makeover of Old 666, the Eager Beavers established a record for getting the photos and getting home with a minimum of damage from the enemy.

That summer, the Allied forces in New Guinea and the Solomons were planning what would come to be known as Operation *Cartwheel,* the direct assault against Japan's major South Pacific base at Rabaul. MacArthur's forces were in the process of taking Japanese-held bases in northern New Guinea that would allow Rabaul to be directly attacked by medium bombers as well as heavies, with fighter escort, and believed they would be ready to start the campaign from their side by September. In the Solomons, Admiral Halsey's force had taken New Georgia. The former Japanese air base at Munda on New Georgia at last put Rabaul at extreme range of B-25s and B-24s escorted by P-38s and F4Us, but possession of the enemy airfields on Bougainville would mean every airplane in AirSols would be in range to put Rabaul under attack. One good photographic mission was needed to get photos of the proposed landing beaches and the airfields for use in planning the coming invasion.

Bougainville was well-defended; Navy PBY Catalinas and PB4Y-1 Liberators were hard-pressed to fly near the island, since the PBY was too slow and lightly armed, and neither it nor the PB4Y-1 could fly high enough to evade the intercepting Zeros. Only the B-17 had the altitude capability to make it hard for the enemy to get at it. Even then, the mission would be tough, because the photo plane would be over Bougainville for 20–25 minutes, in broad daylight, and would have to fly absolutely straight and level on the photo runs to ensure the necessary photos were obtained. Bougainville was 600 miles from New Guinea, too far to provide fighter escort. When they heard what was wanted, the Eager Beavers volunteered to fly the mission, with Zeamer pointing out that Old 666 was the only photo-recon airplane in the South Pacific with a chance of surviving the mission in such a dangerous location. Finally, in early June, the weather report was favorable. The mission, planned since April, was on for June 16.

The night of June 15 at 2200 hours, only four hours before the crew of Old 666 were scheduled to start preparing for the mission, Zeamer was awakened by a call from Fifth Air Force Bomber Command. A mission by the 8th Photo Squadron that day to get photos of the new Japanese fighter field on Buka, a small island off the northern coast of Bougainville, had been unsuccessful. Since the coming mission was scheduled to pass close to Buka, could Zeamer add in a run over the new airfield in addition to their photo-mapping of the proposed invasion area? His initial response was to refuse, due to the danger of the original mission; adding in more time, especially time spent over an airfield full of enemy fighters, made things too dangerous.

Zeamer started the engines on Old 666 at 0400 hours on June 16. As the bomber taxied toward the Milne Bay runway, it was stopped by a jeep and Zeamer was given a direct order to add in the Buka overflight. He again refused, and minutes later was airborne, heading toward the Solomon Sea and Bougainville.

After a four-hour flight, Bougainville came into sight 30 minutes early. The sun was too low yet and the light would not be right for the photo run over the invasion beaches before 0830 hours. Zeamer asked his crew if they wanted to make the Buka overflight while waiting for the main photo run. The unanimous response was "let's do it." As top turret gunner Johnnie Able later explained, "We thought so much of Captain Zeamer and had such trust in him and his ability that we didn't give a damn where we went, just so long as he wanted to go there. Anything okay by him was okay by us." Expecting the limited fighter response they had gotten on a previous mission to Bougainville, Zeamer circled to bring the B-17 over Buka from the northeast. What they didn't know was that, two days before, the enemy had brought in over 300 fighters to Rabaul, and had sent at least one additional squadron on to Buka in preparation for a major air strike against Guadalcanal scheduled for that very day.

As they made their run over Buka, the crew spotted some 50 enemy fighters on the field below, and saw 14 of them start up and take off for an interception. With the photo run completed, Zeamer turned toward Bougainville and the invasion beaches. At their altitude of 25,000 feet, they expected the now-climbing Zeros of the 251st Kōkūtai wouldn't be in position to make trouble for at least 20 minutes, which was more than enough time to make the run over the beaches and turn away. However, as they came to the end of the run, before they could turn away and climb higher to escape, five Zeros were spotted preparing for a coordinated attack, with three in front and two to the rear.

The three in front rolled inverted to aid their pullouts after their runs and opened fire. Bombardier Sarnoski returned fire with his .50-caliber gun while navigator First Lieutenant Ruby Johnston fired at the incoming fighters with the gun on the other side of the nose compartment. Bullets whistled through the compartment and Sarnoski went down an instant before Johnston crumpled to the deck, mortally wounded by a 20mm shell. Behind them, the cockpit took severe hits from 20mm cannon shells. Zeamer's left leg above and below the knee was shattered, his arms and calves slashed by shrapnel, and his left thigh ripped open. One rudder pedal was blown off while the other was bent 90 degrees and most of the instruments in the panel in front of him were blasted to bits. Sergeant Johnny Able, the assistant flight engineer substituting as top turret gunner for the mission, took a spray of shrapnel in his legs, and radioman Sergeant Vaughan in the compartment to the rear of the bomb bay got a bad grazing hit in his neck. In one pass, the Zeros had wounded or killed five of the ten-man crew. Co-pilot Lieutenant Britton had escaped injury by leaning forward in his seat just as shrapnel shredded it behind him. The two trailing Zeros managed to shred the rudder before they were driven off by tailgunner Sergeant Herbert "Pudge" Pugh.

When Zeamer looked out the cockpit, he saw a Ki.45 Nick twin-engine fighter bank into a second attack on the nose. In the forward compartment, Sarnoski managed to pull himself up and regain his gun in time to send a long burst into the enemy fighter that forced the enemy pilot to break off before he could open fire and finish them off. Radioman Vaughan discovered the oxygen tanks had caught fire and yelled a warning to Zeamer, who only had ailerons and elevators to control the big bomber, that he needed to get to a lower altitude if they were to survive without oxygen. With the altimeter shattered, Zeamer estimated altitude by the still-operating manifold pressure gauges and brought Old 666 level at 10,000 feet, where Vaughan and Able were able to beat out the flames with their flight jackets.

With all the forward guns knocked out or unusable and half the crew wounded, the Zeros surrounded the battered B-17, turning in to attack from ahead. Bullets ripped the fuselage again and again. In blinding pain, Zeamer and still-unwounded co-pilot Britton managed to throw the bomber left and right, up and down, in a desperate attempt to throw off the enemy's aim. When the Zeros pulled out of their attack runs, the rear gunners in the waist and ball turret raked them with fire. Four turned away, smoking, but the others bored in to attack again and again. Finally, after 40 minutes that felt like 40 hours, the enemy fighters ran out of ammunition and peeled away, flying back to Buka as the smoking B-17 turned west over the Solomon Sea. The engines were all working, but Zeamer had no rudder or flap. Fortunately the air speed indicator still worked and the magnetic compass had survived.

Co-pilot Britton, miraculously unwounded, took over care of the wounded while Sergeant Able took the controls to relieve Zeamer. In the nose, navigator Johnston wasn't as badly wounded as first thought, but Sarnoski died after ten minutes of treatment by Britton and Vaughan in the whipping airstream from the shattered nose, two days before he had been scheduled to go home.

Radioman Vaughan was able to contact their base and pick up the radio beacon from Dobodura airfield. Britton took the controls and turned to a new heading of 227 degrees magnetic, direct to the field. Over the two hours it took to get back, Zeamer succeeded in remaining conscious despite the blood loss from his wounds.

Their arrival at Dobodura was hair-raising. Britton managed to land without flaps or brakes, taking all 6,000 feet of runway to roll to a stop. When the medics climbed aboard, they questioned whether the badly wounded Zeamer was alive. The crew pulled him out regardless. He had lost nearly half his blood over the past four hours, but was kept alive overnight with plasma until he and the other survivors could be flown to Milne Bay the next morning.

Once word got around about the mission, and the fact that the crucial photos of the western beaches had been obtained, Zeamer and Sarnoski were nominated for the Medal of Honor by the end of June. Colonel Merian C. Cooper, a World War I aviator who had produced "King Kong," who was now on the Fifth Air Force staff, wrote up the paperwork for the medals. In his memoirs after the war, General Kenney stated the mission "still stands out in my mind as an epic of courage unequaled in the annals of air warfare." Sarnoski's Medal of Honor was given to his wife in December 1943, while Zeamer survived to be presented with his at the White House by President Roosevelt in January 1944. It was the only time two members of the same crew received the medal for the same mission in the Pacific War. The other members of the crew were all awarded the Distinguished Service Cross. The mission remains the most highly decorated in American aviation history.

With the crucial photos in-hand, Allied planners turned to working on Operation *Cartwheel*, the final act of the South Pacific campaign, the direct neutralization of Rabaul as the main Japanese base in the South Pacific.

Zeamer's mission took place 53 weeks after the victory at Midway, and ten months after the invasion of Guadalcanal. Four-and-a-half months after the final Japanese evacuation mission to bring out the surviving troops on Guadalcanal, the Allies were ready to advance through the central Solomons. Operation *Chronicle* would see Woodlark Island and Kiriwina invaded, following the Marine landing at Segi Point on New Georgia on June 21, while the Army took the rest of the island with an invasion on June 30. By the end of July, all of New Georgia would be under US control, with its airfields finally bringing Rabaul itself within maximum range of Solomons-based aircraft. Vella Lavella would fall in mid-August. By the end of September, all the Solomons airfields would be operational. American heavy construction technology and ability, honed in the creation of the Transcontinental Railroad and the Panama Canal, was an American weapon unmatched by any other ally or opponent in World War II.

A full-scale invasion of Kavieng and Rabaul was still contemplated, but only after the other operations had reduced the enemy forces through aerial attrition. However, when the British and American Joint Chiefs met with President Roosevelt and Prime Minister Churchill at the Quadrant Conference in Quebec that August, these two planned invasions were canceled in favor of aerial neutralization and bypassing both targets. Allied air power would finish what Japanese sea power had begun.

Zeamer's battle came at the end of B-17 operations in the Southwest Pacific. The 43rd and 19th bomb groups had never been able to maintain full strength throughout their time in the theater, since the Eighth Air Force in England had priority for the B-17, with nearly all new production being sent to groups training for deployment to Europe. The B-17 was loved by its crews who swore by its ruggedness in combat, the ease with which it could be flown, and its steadiness in formation. However, it had only a maximum bomb load of 4,500 pounds, scarcely more than that carried by the B-25 and the B-26, and even that load had to be reduced in order for the bomber to fly the distances involved in the Pacific.

The previous November, the 90th Bomb Group had brought their Consolidated B-24Ds to Australia, in replacement of the war-weary 19th. The group immediately suffered a run of nose gear failures that resulted in the grounding of all 48 Liberators until a cure was found for the problem. With that behind them, it soon became apparent the group had not been well-trained before its deployment, as they soon established a record of losses – including the group commander – that was such they were pulled off operations by General Kenney and put through additional training in night flying and navigation. Even after they returned to operations from this training period, the group suffered a high loss rate. After six months in the Southwest Pacific, the group had a record loss of 24 aircrews, of which only five were combat losses, another five being caused by crashes due to weather, and the remainder listed only as "missing"; therefore, Fifth Bomber Command commander General Ennis Whitehead felt the leadership of the unit should be entirely replaced.

While the B-24 had demonstrated that it was an airplane that was hard to fly due to the heaviness of its controls and was difficult to maintain in formation compared with the B-17, it was also faster at the altitudes most missions were flown from, capable of carrying a larger bombload than the Flying Fortress, and had a greater range. The operational conditions of the combat theater, combined with the difficulty of maintaining the 43rd at a strength that allowed them to mount meaningful missions, drove Kenney to conclude in May 1943 that the B-24 would be adopted as the Fifth Air Force heavy bomber. Thus, in June 1943, the 43rd began converting to the Liberator and the few Flying Fortresses remaining were relegated to VIP transport and squadron hacks. By the end of June, two squadrons in the group were declared ready for operations on the B-24. At the same time, Colonel Art Rogers assumed command of the 90th Group on July 11. Compared with their previous leader, Rogers was neither universally liked nor respected by the crews. Some saw him as a tough, no-nonsense leader they would follow into the gates of hell if the situation required it, while others contemptuously saw him as a glory-seeking martinet. All agreed that he was a capable pilot. General Kenney saw him as the firebrand the group needed. Within days of his arrival, the group finally had a nickname: "The Jolly Rogers," and the commander had the ground crews painting a skull and crossbones on the bombers' rudders. They would soon live up to the image. The 43rd, which had come to be General Kenney's favorite group since he had arrived, adopted the name "Ken's Men." While some later claimed the name honored Ken McCullar, their late beloved leader who had been genuinely popular with his men, others noted that Kenney was also genuinely popular with the airmen, and that he truly cared about their morale. Both groups would maintain a sometimes more than merely boisterous rivalry that led to improvement after improvement in their combat performance. Kenney later wrote of the rivalry, "Silly little things like that, which now sound like a species of insanity, were wonderful incentives to morale and set up a spirit of competition and a desire to outdo the rival organization that meant more hits on the targets, a quicker end to the war, and thereby a saving of American lives."

12

REINFORCEMENT

The summer of 1943 finally saw the Fifth Air Force begin to receive the desperately needed reinforcement and expansion that General Kenney had argued for since his arrival in Australia. With the outcome of the Battle of the Bismarck Sea having successfully demonstrated the use of gunships, the 38th Bomb Group was directed in May 1943 to split its two squadrons to create the third and fourth squadrons it should have had from the beginning, with all four squadrons receiving additional personnel and more B-25s as fast as Pappy Gunn's conversion center could create them. By the end of June, the group was at full strength, with the 822nd Bomb Squadron adopting the name "Black Panthers," and the 823rd calling themselves the "Terrible Tigers." With a full complement of 72 B-25s, all modified as strafers, Kenney's attack force was doubled.

Pappy Gunn's visit with North American that spring also began to bear fruit over the summer, as the new B-25G arrived in the squadrons. The new sub-type was developed from the B-25D and had a shorter "solid" nose with two .50-caliber machine guns and a 75mm pack howitzer that had been stripped and lightened, then mounted in the bombardier's "tunnel" beneath the cockpit floor. The weapon was serviced by the navigator; the nickname "cannigator" became common. Additionally, North American adopted the tail gun position that Gunn's technicians had developed, providing a raised canopy for a gunner armed with a single .50-caliber gun to take care of the most glaring defensive deficiency in the Mitchell. The B-25G was merely the progenitor of the B-25H, based on the new B-25J, which had a deeper rear fuselage allowing the tail armament to be doubled, while large waist windows immediately behind the wing provided beam defense with a .50-caliber weapon mounted to either side and operated by the radioman. The two-gun turret was moved from the rear to just behind the cockpit, still manned by the flight engineer. Gunn's two-gun "package" mounted below the cockpit on the fuselage side was replaced with two .50-caliber weapons, each mounted separately, which reduced vibration damage due to recoil to the fuselage structure, which was additionally "beefed up" to absorb the recoil. While the B-25J was still equipped with the bombardier's glass nose, the B-25H had a "solid" nose like the B-25G, with a total of four machine guns and the 75mm cannon. North American engineers were developing a factory-installed "gun nose" for the B-25J that would mount eight .50-caliber guns, with side panels easing access to them for the armorers. The first of these noses would appear as "kits" in the fall of 1943. Until the "gunship nose" became available, the bombardier-nose B-25Js were modified with the four-gun mount developed by Gunn's technicians for the B-25D.

Additionally, Douglas Aircraft began production of the A-20G Havoc light attack bomber in the spring of 1943. The airplane incorporated a factory-installed solid "gun nose" with a total of six .50-caliber weapons, while the hand-held .30-caliber rear defensive armament was replaced with a Martin turret mounting two .50-caliber machine guns. The airplane was a "factory produced" version of Gunn's original gunship.

Beyond new equipment for the existing groups, Fifth Bomber Command was reinforced by the arrival in June of the 345th Bomb Group. The group had been ordered into existence on September 6, 1942, established at Columbia Army Air Base on November 11, 1942, and was originally intended to operate in the European Theater with other B-25-equipped bomb groups in the Mediterranean. However, with the aura of victory from the success at Bismarck Sea, General Kenney was able during his Washington visit to convince Hap Arnold to send a second B-25-equipped bomb group. As a result, the 345th became the first fully organized bomb group sent to the Southwest Pacific since the beginning of the war. "The Air Apaches," as they called themselves, were composed of the 498th "Falcons," 499th "Bats Outta Hell," 500th "Rough Raiders," and 501st "Black Panthers" bomb squadrons. The group's original commander, Colonel Jarred V. Crabb, was remembered by the men as "not a very big man, but he made a big impression." The day the group officially came into existence, he announced to the newly assigned pilots, "Anyone can fly, but not everyone can be a combat pilot. I'm not only going to teach you how to fly in combat, but I'm going to teach you how to be an officer and a gentleman."

The group was fully equipped with brand-new B-25Ds delivered direct from the Kansas City factory in April 1943, making them "ready to go" when Hap Arnold acceded to George Kenney's request for another B-25 unit. By the end of the month, the aircrews were flying their Mitchells cross-country to McClellan Army Air Field in Sacramento while the ground crews packed up their equipment and went aboard troop trains headed for San Francisco. After a seven-day transcontinental trip, they arrived in Oakland, California, then went aboard the transport SS *President Johnson*. Originally the largest ship ever built in North America when she was launched in 1903 as the SS *Manchuria*, she had transported Doughboys to Europe in 1917–18, when she took her second name. Recalled to government service in 1941, she was remembered by the 345th's ground crewmen as "ancient, dank, dark, and very crowded." She pulled away from the San Francisco waterfront on May 1, 1943, loaded with 3,000 men from various units, bound for Brisbane, Australia. Five days out, the saltwater showers began to fail, and for the rest of the trip as many men as possible slept on the upper decks to get away from the miasmic odor of the crowded troop compartments. They finally docked in Brisbane on May 27.

In the meantime, the B-25s were fitted with long-range fuel tanks at McClellan to enable them to make the 2,100-mile flight to Hawaii. The week after the ground crewmen departed aboard the *President Johnson*, the 72 B-25s moved to Hamilton Field north of the Golden Gate, where they would begin their trans-Pacific voyage. From takeoff at Hamilton, they followed the same route taken the year before by the 38th Bomb Group and arrived in Australia a week before the ground echelon.

Among the pilots of the group was First Lieutenant Victor "Vic" Tatelman, assigned to the 499th "Bats Outta Hell" Squadron. Tatelman was born and raised in Indiana, where he became fascinated by airplanes and the thought of flying early on and had learned to fly at age 16, taught by a local pilot who owned an Alexander Eaglerock biplane and was willing to exchange flying lessons in return for Tatelman cleaning the airplane and the hangar it was kept in. By the time he graduated from high school in 1939, he had accumulated 50 hours of flying time. While at the University of Indiana, where he majored in aeronautical engineering, he also joined the Civilian Pilot Training Program and was the proud possessor of a Private Pilot's license with an additional 50 hours in his logbook when he left school and joined the Army Air Corps' Aviation Cadet program the week after Labor Day in September, 1941. He was sent to Fresno Army Airfield in California for basic training, being allowed to skip primary training due to his CPT experience. Graduating from basic training at the beginning of January, 1942, he opted for multi-engine advanced training. With his new gold bars and silver wings, he was sent to Columbia Army Airfield in South Carolina to transition to the B-25 in the fall of 1942, where he found himself assigned to the freshly created 345th Group. Although only a newly minted Second Lieutenant, his flying skills won him promotion to First Lieutenant and assignment to the left seat by the time the group received their orders to head west.

While the officers and men of the 345th Group admired and respected Colonel Crabb, they were in awe of the Deputy Group Commander, Lieutenant Colonel Clinton True, who had already been given the nickname "Fearless" before they departed for the Pacific. Born and raised in New Orleans, True was a West Point graduate in the class of 1937, where he had made a name for himself as an All-American playing football and lacrosse. On graduation, he had chosen the Air Corps. After graduation from flight school, he had been assigned to the first USAAF light bomb group to equip with the A-20A, before going to the 22nd Bomb Group with their B-26s. After a tour in New Guinea, he had returned to the United States where he was assigned to the new 345th Bomb Group. His personal reputation among the enlisted men was that of "hard-ass," but the aircrew recognized him as a leader who never asked anyone to do anything he had not done first. General Kenney was so impressed by Colonel Crabb that he promoted him to commander of Fifth Air Force Bomber Command in September, with True stepping up to take group command, just in time to demonstrate his personal courage and leadership in the Rabaul strikes. He was remembered by those he led as "stern, fair, and very efficient."

At the same time that the 38th Bomb Group was being brought to full authorized strength and the 345th Group was arriving in the Southwest Pacific Theater, General Kenney was thrilled to discover that his trip to Washington had paid off with a shipment of enough P-38s to bring the three existing P-38-equipped squadrons – the 80th Squadron of the 8th Fighter Group, the 39th Squadron of the 35th Group, and the 9th Squadron of the 49th Group – back to full strength, and to achieve his goal of one group fully equipped with Lockheed Lightnings. The 49ers' 7th and 8th squadrons were finally able to retire their war-weary P-40E Warhawks, replacing them with new P-40Ns, the final version of the venerable P-40 to see combat.

With 75 brand-new P-38H Lightnings just delivered from the factory in Burbank, Kenney called the 475th Fighter Group into existence on May 14, 1943, only the second fighter group to be completely created overseas after the American volunteers of the RAF Eagle Squadrons had become the 4th Fighter Group in England the previous September. The P-38H had a reputation in other units and other theaters for engine-cooling problems, but Kenney was happy to get any P-38s he could; in the meantime, he kept his plans for a completely new fighter group secret since other P-38 fighter groups already in combat in North Africa and the Mediterranean were screaming for replacement aircraft and the leaders of the Eighth Air Force were begging for P-38s to provide long-range escort in England. Originally, the unit – composed of the 431st, 432nd, and 433rd squadrons – was to be activated at Charters Towers in Queensland, but instead was established at Amberley Field outside Brisbane, located close to the supply depots. The group's first commander was Major George W. Prentice, who had formerly commanded the P-38-equipped 39th Squadron of the 35th Group. A fearless fighter pilot with an excellent combat reputation, Prentice was not a "natural" in combat leadership, and would leave the responsibility for combat unit leadership to his more capable squadron commanders; his organizational skills were second to none, and he would be extremely influential in creating the unit the 475th became. Prentice's deputy was Major Al Schinz, a combat veteran who had scored against the Japanese flying P-400s and P-39s in the 35th Fighter Group's 40th Squadron during the dark days at Port Moresby in the summer and fall of 1942. General Kenney had to find pilots and ground crews for the group within Fifth Fighter Command, and put out word to the commanders of the other fighter groups when he ordered them to send six pilots from each of their squadrons to the new group that he wanted no "deadheads" and would hold each group commander personally responsible if the order was not followed to the letter. Thus, the 475th was well on its way to becoming the premier fighter group of the Fifth Air Force from the beginning.

Among the veterans assigned to the group was First Lieutenant Harry Brown, who had shot down a Val during the Pearl Harbor attack while flying a P-36A and gone on to a second victory flying a P-38 with the 49th Group's 9th Squadron. Other pilots from the Seventh Air Force's 15th Fighter Group in Hawaii volunteered for duty in the Southwest Pacific for the promise of combat that was non-existent in their Hawaiian backwater. Major Franklin A. Nichols, who had achieved a measure of fame within the 49ers as the leader of the 7th Squadron's flight, "Nick Nichol's Nip Nippers," with which he had scored four victories, was appointed commander of the 431st Squadron, where he would continue as an outstanding combat leader during the group's initial operations, while four-victory ace Captain Danny Roberts from the 8th Group's 80th Squadron became his operations officer.

The 80th Squadron also provided leadership for the 432nd Squadron in the person of Major Frank Tompkins, who brought with him from the 80th Captain James Ince and First Lieutenant Noel Lundy. First Lieutenant John Loisel, who would become a leading ace and the final wartime commander of the 475th, transferred into the 432nd from the 8th's 36th Squadron.

The 433rd Squadron proved to be a "hard luck" unit initially, when squadron commander Captain Martin Low, formerly with the 35th Group's 40th Squadron, chose as First Sergeant a man who would become so universally detested in the unit that those who were there at the time would never mention his name in later years. The unit's morale dropped severely among the enlisted personnel forced to deal with this man, while morale among the pilots suffered when Low removed names from the promotion lists who he did not find personally "well-deserving." Low went home in October, replaced by Captain Roberts from the 431st Squadron, whose inspirational lead-from-the-front command style turned things around during the month he led the squadron before his unfortunate death in a mid-air collision moments after scoring his 14th victory on November 9.

Among the other newcomers who reported to the group was First Lieutenant Thomas Buchanan "Tommy" McGuire, Jr., who was transferred from the 49th Fighter Group's P-38-equipped 9th Squadron on July 20, a bit less than two weeks before his 23rd birthday. Five feet seven inches tall, he sported a big black mustache in an attempt to appear older. In McGuire's case, the 49ers were both following General Kenney's directive to send excellent pilots, and ridding themselves of a pilot they considered a misfit. By the time he came to the 475th, McGuire had acquired a reputation for being prickly and difficult to know, a man whose reputation was based on his skill in the cockpit of a P-38, not on his interpersonal skills. He had joined the USAAF as an aviation cadet on July 12, 1941. After graduation from flight school in Class 42-B on February 2, 1942, he trained as a fighter pilot with the 50th Pursuit Group at Key Field, Mississippi. From there, his first operational assignment was in the 54th Pursuit Group, based in Nome, Alaska, where he flew P-39s and honed his flying and shooting skills in the weeks following the Japanese invasion of Kiska and Attu, all the while making repeated transfer requests; his persistence finally resulted in his departing Alaska on October 16, 1942, assigned to P-38 training at Santa Ana, California. Mastering the big Lockheed twin, he received orders to the 49th Fighter Group and departed for Australia on March 14, 1943.

Shortly after his arrival in the 49th, McGuire met Dick Bong, already known as the hottest pilot in the Southwest Pacific; he was artless enough to let it be known that he now had the goal of matching Bong and then bettering him, an attitude that wasn't considered "socially acceptable" among fighter pilots. By July, the 49ers considered themselves well rid of him when he was given orders to join the 475th's 431st Fighter Squadron. Many years later, one of his 431st squadron mates would remember him thus: "Tommy McGuire was a complete failure, socially. But he knew more about the P-38 and how to get the most out of it, of anyone. He could talk for hours about that airplane in great detail, to the point of driving everyone else nuts." Once in the 431st, McGuire got a reputation in the squadron as a "brown-noser," when his enthusiasm for the P-38 resulted in his appointment as squadron maintenance officer. This attitude quickly changed when aircraft availability moved up from 50 percent to over 80 percent with the ground crews' morale rising from the inspirational leadership of a young officer who didn't pay attention to military propriety and wasn't afraid to get his fingernails dirty working on the airplanes with them.

During training in the summer of 1943, the 475th adopted the group name "Satan's Angels." Training proceeded quickly and the unit was declared combat-ready at the end of July. On August 1, ground personnel went aboard a Liberty Ship for transport to Port Moresby, and by August 11, 1943, the 431st Squadron had arrived at 12-Mile 'Drome, while the 432nd made its home at Ward's 'Drome. Five days later, the 433rd Squadron arrived at Jackson 'Drome.

The group's first mission, an escort of C-47 transports to Tsili Tsili by the 431st Squadron, set for August 12, was canceled due to bad weather, but the weather cleared enough the next day to allow 15 432nd Squadron P-38s led by Danny Roberts to escort the C-47s to Bena Bene in an otherwise-uneventful mission. Two days later, the enemy was finally spotted over Lasanga Island but none of the pilots could make direct contact. On August 16, the 431st Squadron was finally blooded in combat. Escorting C-47s to Tsili Tsili, some 25 enemy fighters were spotted overhead as they dived to attack the transports. In the ensuing engagement 12 enemy aircraft were claimed shot down for a loss of two P-38s, with First Lieutenant Jack Mankin scoring a "Zeke" and an "Oscar." Both were most likely Ki.43 Oscars since the Imperial Navy had no fighters in New Guinea by now, since they were fully engaged in the Solomons. Pearl Harbor veteran Harry Brown shot down three Ki.43s which, combined with his victory over Pearl Harbor and his 9th Squadron victory with the 49ers, made him the first pilot in the group to become an ace.

The 345th Bomb Group had commenced combat operations in July 1943. Since their B-25s were not yet modified as gunships, their missions were the standard medium-altitude bombing missions the B-25 had been designed for. They experienced their first combat losses on July 13, when 36 B-25s from the 345th joined a squadron from the 38th Group on a mission to hit antiaircraft positions at Salamaua. After takeoff from Port Moresby, they were to pick up an escort from the 49ers over Dobodura before heading on to the target. The squadrons separated as they approached the Oro Peninsula. First Lieutenant Alden Thompson, leading the 499th Squadron, saw what was described by others as "a wall of flak" coming up from the positions around the airfield. Thompson executed a perfect bomb run, but just as the bombs began falling from his Mitchell, the gunners below got the range and the B-25 was hit in the wing between the right engine and the fuselage and caught fire, taking out the navigator's position. Wingmen Jack George and George Cooper escorted Thompson away from the target, despite the fact that George's bomber had also been hit. Thompson flew out over Huon Gulf and managed to make a successful ditching, but the Mitchell sank quickly. Bombardier John Yarborough, who had been wounded, was unable to get out, though the other five crewmen managed to exit the sinking bomber. Thompson and three of the crew managed after several hours of swimming to make it to shore, though they lost wounded navigator Lawrence Davis. Fortunately they came ashore near an Australian infantry unit and were able to return to the squadron by July 16.

Strangely, during these early missions, Japanese fighters seemed reluctant to attack the bombers. On a mission to Salamaua on July 5, the 501st Squadron reported they saw eight to ten enemy fighters identified as "Zeros" performing aerobatics at a lower altitude, which made no attempt to intercept the Mitchells. During July, the group flew more than a dozen missions to Salamaua. In August, they returned to Amberley Field in Australia, so the B-25s could be put through Pappy Gunn's modification center to become gunships.

The 475th Group flew their first mission to Wewak on August 17, flying with the B-25s of the 38th Group and completely surprising the enemy, who put up no aerial opposition. The next day saw a second mission to escort B-25s of the 38th Group on a strafing mission to hit Dagua airdrome outside Wewak. Lieutenant McGuire, who had missed engaging the enemy during the fight at Tsili Tsili, was among those assigned to the mission, flying a P-38H-1 he had named "Pudgy." When seven Ki.43 Oscars from the 24th Sentai, nine Oscars of the 59th Sentai, five Ki.61 Tony fighters of the 68th Sentai, and two Ki.45 Nick fighters from the 13th Sentai rose to contest the American attackers, McGuire demonstrated his flying and gunnery skills when he attacked five Ki.43s he mistakenly identified as Zeros, shooting down four. Back at base, his wingman Second Lieutenant Fran Lent also put in a claim for the fourth victory. There were no shared kills in the 475th; a coin-toss would determine who received full credit. McGuire lost, and was given credit for three, which was quite a way to lose one's "virginity." The mission also saw "Satan's Angels" record their first combat loss, when the 431st's Second Lieutenant Ralph Schmidt failed to return. Over the rest of the month, the 475th flew 16 missions to Wewak, during which they were credited with shooting down 41 enemy aircraft despite their relative inexperience. McGuire was in the forefront. On August 21, leading the 431st's Blue Flight in "Pudgy," with Fran Lent once again his wingman, he shot down two more Ki.43s and a twin-engine Ki.45, to become the first pilot to be credited as an ace completely within the group, while Lent was credited with the other Ki.45 they had encountered. During the same fight, Danny Roberts shot down two Ki.43s, which made him an ace when combined with his four victories scored in the 80th Squadron, while John Loisel opened his score with two Ki.61s. The 431st's squadron commander, Major Nichols, became an ace with his single Ki.43 claim. On August 29, on the group's 14th mission to Wewak, this time escorting B-24 bombers in a high-altitude attack, McGuire shot down a Ki.43 and a Ki.61 to bring his score to seven, tying him with First Lieutenant David Allen for leading ace of the group.

As he turned away from his second victory, McGuire came under fire from another enemy fighter and his left engine caught fire. He coolly shut down the engine and let the propeller windmill while he dropped to 9,000 feet, which put out the fire. Two enemy fighters followed him and he finally shook them by diving into clouds at 4,000 feet. With the engine out, he didn't feel able to make it back to Moresby and so landed at the forward airstrip at Marilinan, where he successfully landed single-engine. Future mayor of Los Angeles First Lieutenant Sam Yorty, at the time intelligence officer for the 41st Fighter Squadron of the 35th Fighter Group, took down McGuire's account of his fight with enemy pilots he termed "both experienced and eager." Yorty wrote a final remark in the report to describe McGuire: "this pilot remained calm in spite of the fire in his engine, and thereby successfully brought himself and his airplane safely to this base." McGuire caught a ride on a C-47 the next morning and returned to his squadron, where he was given a new P-38H-5, which he also named "Pudgy." On September 28, he christened the second "Pudgy" by shooting down two more Ki.43s over Wewak, to bring his score to nine and put him at the top of the group's list of aces.

The P-38s were not the only new fighter types sent to the Fifth Air Force. On June 14, the transport SS *Henry Gibbons* dropped anchor in Brisbane. Among the thousands of Americans who disembarked were the officers and men of the 348th Fighter Group's 340th, 341st, and 342nd squadrons. Their crated P-47D Thunderbolts were offloaded from one of the other ships in the convoy, and the men and their airplanes soon arrived at Amberley Field, where the big single-engine fighters were quickly assembled. General Kenney was not pleased by this turn of events, since he believed the P-47 wasn't a good fit with the operational conditions of the Southwest Pacific Theater, particularly since the fighter at this stage of its development had a notably short range in a combat theater where missions of 300–500 miles one-way were normal.

However, Kenney was impressed by the 348th's commander, 32-year-old Lieutenant Colonel Neel E. Kearby. Born and raised in Wichita Falls, Texas, Kearby had joined the Air Corps following his graduation from the North Texas Agricultural College in 1936. After flight training at Randolph and Kelly Fields, he was assigned to the 94th "Hat in the Ring" Pursuit Squadron of the 1st Pursuit Group at Selfridge Field outside Detroit, Michigan, just as the group began to replace its Boeing P-26 fighters with the brand-new Curtiss P-36A. Demonstrating excellent leadership abilities, he had been quickly promoted and assigned as commander of the 14th Pursuit Squadron in the Panama Canal Zone, where he oversaw the unit's transition to the Bell P-39 Airacobra in 1941. In October 1942, he received the assignment to stand up the new 348th Group at Westover Field, Massachusetts. The group was the second after the 56th Fighter Group to receive the new Republic P-47 Thunderbolt, and under Kearby's leadership they trained hard to master the big fighter.

The P-47s and their pilots were deemed ready for combat by the end of July, and flew up to Port Moresby at the same time the 475th took their P-38s to New Guinea. Kearby led the first mission, escort for C-47s to Tsili Tsili, on August 16. The P-47s then undertook escort for the B-25s of the 345th Bomb Group, which had not yet been modified as strafers, on bombing missions to Lae and Salamaua. By using the P-47's excellent high-altitude capability and the fact that it could dive faster than any other fighter in the theater, Kearby's pilots used the dive-and-zoom tactic to demonstrate that the P-47 with its heavy armament of eight .50-caliber machine guns was effective against Japanese fighters.

The fighting in New Guinea took an important turn with the invasion of Lae, which happened on September 3, 1943. In response to the Allied landing, three Ki.48 Lily twin-engine light bombers from Wewak damaged two landing craft in an attack shortly after dawn before being chased off. Seven hours later the Imperial Navy sent 12

Bettys and eight Val dive bombers, escorted by 61 Zeros, from Rabaul to attack the invasion fleet. Sixty P-38s and P-47s went after the enemy aircraft, but most managed to get past the defending fighters, though they missed the main invasion fleet and instead attacked six LSTs they discovered off Cape Ward Hunt. The Vals scored hits on one LST and near-missed an escorting destroyer, while a Betty put a torpedo into a second LST. American losses were 40 soldiers and sailors killed aboard the LSTs. Minutes later, Oscars from Wewak were intercepted by the defending American fighters. The P-38 pilots claimed 14 Zeros and Oscars, one Val, and two Bettys, while the 348th Group's Neel Kearby scored a Zero and a Betty for his first two victories. Ten days later, he put the P-47's high-altitude capability to good measure when he caught and shot down a Mitsubishi Ki.46 reconnaissance plane known as "Dinah," a notably difficult target due to its high speed at high altitude. In the fighting over Lae, the 25th Flotilla admitted the loss of three Bettys and four Zeros, with five Vals, seven Bettys, and three Zeros damaged. Crews returning to Rabaul made fantastic claims of sinking four transports and a cruiser and badly damaging two transports and two destroyers, while the Zero pilots claimed they had shot down 23 P-38s. In fact, only two P-38s were lost in the battle, with one damaged.

Captain Jay T. Robbins of the 8th Group's 80th "Headhunters" Squadron engaged in what he would later recall as his most memorable mission of the war in the air battle over Huon Gulf. Leading the third flight of four P-38s in a 16-plane formation led by squadron commander Major Edward Cragg that was tasked with maintaining a combat air patrol over the invasion fleet, Robbins and the others had taken off from 3-Mile 'Drome at Port Moresby just before dawn at 0515 hours and flown over the Owen Stanleys to Dobodura, where they refueled. They arrived over the invasion force shortly after noon for a two-hour patrol.

At 1345 hours, a pilot in the formation called out "Bandits!" Robbins led his flight toward the enemy, which were identified as Zeros. As they climbed toward the enemy fighters flying at 20,000 feet, the formation of Val dive bombers was spotted below. Robbins continued on toward the fighters as another flight dived on the Vals. Robbins and the other three pilots became involved in a swirling fight with the more numerous enemy. As he got onto the tail of a Zero, he glanced behind and saw several others closing on his tail. Hitting the Zero he was chasing, he set it afire as the right wing came off and the plane fluttered toward earth. Pulling out of his dive and realizing the other enemy fighters hadn't followed him, he spotted another P-38 in trouble, boxed in by several Zeros. Robbins turned toward the fight and two of the enemy spotted him and turned on the Lightning. In a head-on pass, the lead enemy fighter hit his P-38, but Robbins' fire set the Zero afire. Robbins watched his second victory head down a moment too long; moments later, he was hit by another Zero that he evaded by throwing the P-38 into a steep dive. Pulling out, he found another Zero and caught it with a deflection shot that holed it from nose to tail, setting it on fire. The enemy pilot bailed out just as the Zeros that had pursued him pulled out of their dives and turned toward the big P-38. Robbins realized he was low on fuel and likely low on ammo, but these new opponents were between him and the shore. He would have to fight them to get away. The fighters passed each other without scoring hits, and Robbins dived toward shore. As he passed through 4,000 feet, his right engine suddenly began misfiring. The enemy fighters turned for a second pass as a fourth Zero turned in on Robbins in a head-on pass. Waiting till they were too close to miss, Robbins fired a short burst and scored a fourth victory when the Zero nosed down toward the water below, trailing smoke.

Three other enemy fighters closed on Robbins' tail. He knew he must be nearly out of ammunition. Turning into the three pursuers, he initiated firing runs that made them turn away. Two of the enemy turned to attack again just as Robbins spotted a group of ships below. He dived toward them, followed by the enemy. The ships' AA batteries opened up, missing the P-38 but hitting his pursuers. Robbins flew on, crossing the shoreline. Now he had to nurse a plane with a bad engine over the mountains to return to Port Moresby. He made it through the pass with 500 feet to spare and was the last P-38 to return to 3-Mile 'Drome. He would never again score four in one fight, but his ultimate score of 22 would tie him for fourth place as top-scoring ace of the Southwest Pacific with Neel Kearby and Gerald Johnson. In the day's fight, Major Cragg scored two, as did Lieutenant Donald Hanover; Captain J.R. Wilson and Lieutenants M.T. Kasper and C.F. Homer all scored one each.

The next day, Kenney's fliers staged the first airborne operation in the Pacific, when 81 C-47s made a low-level drop of 1,700 paratroopers over the Nadzab plain in the Markham Valley under the watchful eye of General MacArthur in his personal B-17; the general was described as "jumping up and down in joy" as he watched the operation go off without a hitch.

The Air Apache's Mitchells, which had been turned into ground strafers during August, returned to New Guinea just in time to take part in the assault, in a combined strike with the B-25s of the 38th Group and the A-20s of the 3rd Group. The Mitchells led the way, strafing everything in sight. As they pulled away from the targets, the A-20s swept in, dispensing smoke from cannisters in their bomb bays intended to blind the defenders just before the C-47s arrived. The paratroopers found only scattered enemy resistance on the ground. Overnight, a dirt strip was hacked out of the grassy plain and the first C-47 landed after dawn carrying engineers who over the next two weeks turned the plain into a major Allied airfield. General Kenney reported the operation to Hap Arnold: "I truly don't believe that another air force in the world today could have put this over as perfectly as the 5th Air Force did."

Overwhelmed, the surviving Japanese evacuated Lae by September 15. Seven days later, on September 22, three Australian Army battalions landed just north of Finschafen. The ships were attacked by eight Bettys and 35 Zeros from Rabaul. The bomber crews returned to claim three cruisers and three destroyers that had not been present, when in fact the Allies suffered no losses. The 11th Air Fleet admitted losing six Bettys and eight Zeros, with two bombers and two fighters damaged by shipboard AA and defending Allied fighters. By September 29, Finschafen was declared secure. It would take another two months of hard fighting by Australian Army units before the entire Huon Peninsula was in Allied hands by early December.

Enemy fighters did finally come up to oppose the Air Apaches on September 17, when the 500th Squadron flew a mission to drop propaganda leaflets on Finschafen. The squadron was intercepted by eight enemy fighters identified as Zeros. Pilot Charles Howard spotted a fighter making a head-on attack and opened up with the eight guns of the new gunship package, which caused pieces of the cowling to fall off and the enemy fighter fell off on one wing, smoking heavily. An instant later, a second Zero attacked Howard's bomber from dead ahead, its fire blowing away the top turret's plastic dome and badly wounding gunner Sergeant Charles Brown. As he was pulled away from his guns, waist gunner Sergeant Fred Ellard manned the still-working top turret, but the other enemy fighters inexplicably turned away. Howard was able to nurse the B-25 back to Dobodura, where gunner Brown received first aid in time to survive.

At the end of the month, the 345th, along with the 38th and the 3rd groups, attacked Wewak on September 27. Operating from the secret Allied airfield at Tsili Tsili (later named Marilinan Airfield) that had become operational in mid-August, the bombers were able to reach Wewak, 300 miles to the northwest, in a surprise attack that was bigger than the other missions that had been flown against this major base. The 345th was led by their new leader, Clinton True, who had taken command ten days earlier.

The Air Apaches' four squadrons took off at 0800 hours, rendezvoused with the 38th and 3rd groups, then met up with their fighter escorts from the 49th and 475th groups over Bena Bena. As they headed toward the target, the Sundowners' Mitchells were in the lead, followed by the 3rd Group, with the Air Apaches bringing up the rear, each formation flying two minutes behind the one ahead. There would be no element of surprise to this strike, since Wewak was awakened shortly before dawn by B-24s of the 43rd Bomb Group when they struck all four airfields from high altitude.

Wewak was a burning, smoking collection of targets, some of which had been destroyed in previous raids, and some that had been blown apart minutes earlier as the B-25s of the 345th swept across their targets. Each bomber carried 36 23-pound parachute-retarded fragmentation bombs that were dropped in clusters of three. Colonel True led the 498th Squadron's first flight as they hit Boram airdrome. When the Falcons pulled off the target, over 30 enemy aircraft were counted afire. The other squadrons reported that results were difficult to see due to trees and camouflage, though the 501st hit Dagua airdrome hard, finding many targets on the ground and only light antiaircraft defenses. As the Mitchells swept across the field, an A6M2-N Rufe floatplane fighter flew in front of the formation. Jim Clark and Henry Knoll opened up with their nose guns, hitting the enemy fighter hard as it turned away toward the sea. Another enemy fighter dropped onto Clark's tail, unwittingly placing itself in front of the B-25 flown by Lieutenant Orby Moore, who lifted the nose and hit the fighter with all eight of his machine guns, shredding it as it fell away with a smoky trail.

The escorting P-38s tore into the enemy formations that attempted to intercept the attackers. The Air Apache's 500th Squadron was attacked by six defenders who pulled away without inflicting damage on the Mitchells when P-38s came after them. In less than ten minutes, the bombers of all three groups were heading away from the airfields, leaving fire and destruction in their wake. The Air Apaches had suffered no casualties, though George Cooper later remembered being "scared to death" by the tracers that flashed past his cockpit.

Lockheed F-5 photo Lightnings swept over Wewak in the wake of the attackers. The developed film revealed that there were extensive fuel and ammunition dumps that had not been hit due to their camouflage. On September 28, B-24s of the 43rd Bomb Group returned to Wewak. Their bombing was so accurate that when the main ammunition dump blew up, two B-24s 12,000 feet overhead were flipped over on their backs by the force of the explosion. The group reported that flames from the target could be seen from 50 miles away as they returned to base. Though Wewak would be hit again in later raids, the strikes in late September were so effective that the base never again posed a real threat to Allied operations.

By the end of September, General Kenney's offensive force included six veteran P-38 squadrons, two well-led heavy bomb groups, three groups of medium and light bombers modified for ground attack, and some RAAF squadrons, which could now all reach Rabaul. After more than a year of effort to build up an effective air force, his fliers were now in position to commence the direct attack on Rabaul itself. The next 90 days would see some of the greatest air battles that had happened in the Pacific War to that time.

13

THE SURPRISE WAS ABSOLUTE

With Rabaul now in range of Allied aircraft flying from bases on the northern side of the Owen Stanleys in New Guinea, it was time to implement Operation *Cartwheel*. The Allied Joint Chiefs had determined at the Quadrant Conference in August that Rabaul and New Ireland would not be invaded, though Allied ground forces would land at Cape Gloucester on New Britain. Thus, the main Japanese base would be neutralized through air power, and Admiral Nimitz was ordered to commence his plans for the Central Pacific campaign, with the seizure of the Gilbert Islands scheduled for mid-November and the Marshalls in January 1944. MacArthur was informed that the 2nd Marine Division, which had been committed for the invasion of Rabaul, was being transferred to Nimitz's command for the invasion of Tarawa.

On October 10, MacArthur's staff met with Admiral Halsey's staff in Brisbane to plan the coming campaign. Halsey had determined that he would not invade southern Bougainville and the surrounding islands of Ballale and Buin, where it had been discovered that the Japanese had 20,000 troops, but would land on the lightly defended northwest coast at Empress Augusta Bay on November 1 and take the airfields on the northern end of the island, leaving the enemy in the southern part of the island to be subjected to bombing for the rest of the war. He estimated that his forces would secure this part of Bougainville by the end of November, with airfields becoming operational in early to mid-December. Rabaul would then be in range of not only his long-range bombers but also the Dauntlesses and Avengers, while the entire Corsair force would be able to operate from the island to overwhelm the enemy air units at Rabaul.

It was agreed that the Fifth Air Force would commence an air campaign against Rabaul in mid-October to prevent the Japanese from interfering with the invasion of Bougainville. The 1st Marine Division would land at Cape Gloucester in western New Britain in late December. General Kenney announced that his airfield engineers had completed a new fighter airstrip on Kiriwina Island in the Bismarck Sea, which would allow P-38s to escort the bombers all the way to Rabaul.

Kenney had already withdrawn his six P-38 squadrons and the two groups of Mitchell strafers from further New Guinea operations after the attack on Wewak on September 27, and the 348th Fighter Group's P-47s took over primary responsibility for hitting the remaining JAAF airfields on New Guinea. On October 11, Neel Kearby led a flight of four P-47s toward Wewak. They were picked up on enemy radar, and the JAAF defenders launched 40 fighters. In the melee that followed, Kearby claimed six Oscars shot down, a record for Fifth Air Force fighter pilots. When General Kenney got word of Kearby's score, he brought the colonel to Government House in Brisbane, to brief MacArthur personally on the operation. When Kearby was finished, Kenney declared that, since the previous record for planes shot down in one mission had been Butch O'Hare's five in February 1942, for which he had been awarded the Medal of Honor, he was nominating Kearby for the same award. While the Japanese admitted only the loss of two airplanes that day, they did acknowledge the brave action of the four "foe craft" in the English language edition of the *Japan Times*. While no mention was made that these four were the only enemy aircraft involved in a fight with 40 of their own fighters, the acknowledgment of the enemy's bravery was unusual. No mention was made that Lieutenant Colonel Tamiji Teranishi, commander of the 14th Sentai, had been lost, likely one of Kearby's victims.

Several photo missions were flown to Rabaul by photo Lightnings of the 8th Photo Recon Squadron, with poor results due to bad weather. Finally, First Lieutenant Kay W. "Joe" Klages brought back useable photos on October 6. More bad weather kept the photo planes from getting more pictures until October 9. They "photoed hell" out of the base on October 10 and 11. On October 11, MacArthur's headquarters in Australia noted in their daily summary, "The mounting air strength at Rabaul, to which attention previously has been called, reached culmination yesterday. Photographs taken at 0915L showed a count of 294 planes, or as large a concentration as ever photographed at that base." Plans were laid on for the first major strike against Rabaul. General Kenney's Fifth Air Force, with the Royal Australian Air Force, would mount a maximum effort raid against the Japanese base with 349 aircraft on October 12.

To reinforce Rabaul, the Imperial Navy had stripped their carrier force at Truk Atoll of the planes and, more importantly, the aircrews who had been so carefully trained and their force rebuilt out of the losses that had happened at the Battle of Santa Cruz. While most of these men were, as Saburo Sakai put it in his memoirs later, "not as good as the men who washed out of my training class before the war," they were the best Japan had to offer. The carrier air groups from *Shōkaku*, *Zuikaku*, and *Zuihō* of the First Carrier Division flew down to Rabaul over the first weeks of October, in preparation to defend the base in the battle they knew was coming.

By the fall of 1943, most thinking Japanese officers at the front were aware of the vast superiority the Allied air forces had over the air forces of the Imperial Army and Navy. Commander Masatake Okumiya, who spent the summer and early fall of 1943 at Buin air base in the northern Solomons, recorded in his diary his impression of an Allied air strike:

The Zeros are fueled and armed, placed along the runway so the pilots have only to fly straight ahead to take off. The pilots wait near the personnel shack, listening to the radio reports from the distant ground watching stations… Now the outermost stations have sighted enemy planes… The fighter commander checks the reports of each station, estimating the enemy's time of arrival, waiting till the last possible moment before ordering the Zeros into the air.

The base is quiet now. Suddenly the lookout on our tower stiffens behind his binoculars, his voice carries to the ground. We see him pointing to the south. There they are! Enemy planes fast approaching. The siren screams its warning and the men on the field dash for cover, never too soon, as the enemy bombers close on the field with great speed.

Hundreds of men stare into the sky, seeing the bombers and searching for the Zeros which should even now be diving against the enemy planes. Here they come! But even before they reach the slower, heavier planes the escorting enemy fighters zoom up to intercept. No matter how determined our attacks, the bombers maintain their formations. Even as the fighter planes scatter over the sky in swirling dogfights, we can hear the rapidly increasing shriek of the falling bombs. The earth shakes and heaves; great blossoms of fire, steel, smoke and dirt erupt from the airfield as salvos of bombs walk across the revetments and runways... Planes on the field are burning fiercely, and wreckage is scattered across the runway, which now is cratered with great holes... Our men curse or only stare silently as we watch Zeros suddenly flare up in scarlet and orange flame, and then plunge from the sky like bizarre shooting stars, leaving behind them a long trail of angry flame and black, oily smoke.

Commander Okumiya concluded, "I must give credit where it is rightfully due. The American pilots who raided Buin were some of the bravest fliers I have ever seen. They flew at treetop level, racing at great speed over the field, their machine guns spraying lead and tracers into every possible target."

The 25th Flotilla's Captain Takahashi Miyazaki later stated that "In 1943, at any given time, only 50 percent of our planes were available, and on the day after an all-out operation, there would only be 30 percent availability. By the end of August, the flotilla's fighter units had 65 Zeros at Buin, but only 37 were operational. There were only 16 Bettys available, of an authorized strength of 48." In light of this situation, the Imperial Navy committed the air groups from the light carriers *Junyō* and *Ryūjō* of the Second Carrier Division to the central Solomons campaign, to operate from Buin. On September 1, the 25th Air Flotilla was so depleted of planes and crews that the unit was withdrawn to Truk to reorganize and re-equip.

By the end of September, Okumiya wrote:

The continual air battles against the savagely fighting Americans exacted a heavy and steady toll on our men. The constant interceptions and bombing missions meant that hardly a day passed without men dying or receiving serious wounds. The pilots and air crews did not honestly expect to survive their Buin duty tour, for the steady loss of men meant that no one could predict the time of his own passing.

He noted that, of the 150 aircrew who had arrived on Buin with him, 50 had been lost over the month. The ground crews suffered from tropical diseases for which there was no medication available and food became scarce as supplies dwindled. Okumiya recorded, "By mid-October the enemy air raids against Buin had become intolerable. With the base constantly subjected to enemy bombs and strafing attacks, with living facilities reduced to the lowest possible level, the navy pulled out, moving its air strength directly to Rabaul." The air groups of the Second Carrier Division were mere shadows of the forces that had flown south 120 days earlier.

In the 20 months that the Japanese had controlled Rabaul, they had made many improvements. The prewar Australian airfields at Lakunai and Vunakanau had been given all-weather surfaces, with Lakunai's runway made of sand and volcanic ash, while Vunakanau had a concrete runway, as did the fighter field at Rapopo, which also had extensive maintenance facilities. Tobera was completed in August 1943 with a concrete runway. Between them, the four airfields had protected revetments for 166 bombers and 265 fighters. The antiaircraft defenses were extensive, with 367 light, medium, and large guns. The Army operated 192 guns defending Rapopo airfield and the supply dumps and army installations, while 175 guns manned by the Imperial Navy guarded Simpson Harbor and Tobera, Lakunai, and Vunakanau airfields. A radar system provided coverage 90 miles from Rabaul, with the main early warning site at the promontory of Cape St. George, while additional radars on New Britain, New Ireland, and Buka gave 30–60 minutes' warning of an attack.

The 11th Air Fleet, composed of the 702nd and 705th air groups, operated G4M Betty bombers for long-range attack and patrol. The fighter units were equipped with the venerable A6M2 Model 21 and the A6M3 Model 32 known as "Hamp." The newly arrived carrier air groups were equipped with the new A6M5a Model 52 Zero, the latest version of the venerable Navy fighter, which was equipped with a more powerful engine; by this point in the Zero's development, the fighter had failed to keep up with the latest Allied types, and was outclassed technically, in addition to being flown by pilots who had few of the skills possessed by their predecessors. The dive and torpedo bomber squadrons of the carrier air groups were still equipped with the D3A Val and B5N Kate that had flown in the attack on Pearl Harbor two years before. A very few Yokosuka D4Y1 "Suisun" (Comet) dive bombers known to the Allies as "Jdy" arrived at Rabaul, in numbers too few to affect the outcome and were primarily used for reconnaissance.

In addition to the Imperial Naval Air Force units, the JAAF's Fourth Air Army was headquartered at Rabaul, with responsibility for operations in New Britain, New Ireland, and New Guinea. In addition to the units fighting in New Guinea, the 68th Hiko Sentai (68th Flying Regiment), equipped with the Kawasaki Ki.61 Hien ("Swallow") fighter known to the Americans as the "Tony," operated from Vunakanau airfield at Rabaul and Tuluvu airfield on Cape Gloucester in western New Britain, a dirt strip airfield built by the Australians before the war which had been improved with a second runway in 1942. The 13th Sentai operated Ki.45 Toryu ("Flying Dragon") twin-engine fighters known to the Americans as "Nick" from both fields. The 24th Sentai operated Ki.43-II Hayabusa ("Peregrine Falcon") fighters, a development of the fighter that was well known to the Allies as "Oscar," with its armament upgraded from two 7.62mm machine guns to two 13mm weapons. The 26th Sentai and the 83rd Dokuritsu Chutai (83rd Independent Air Chutai) operated the Mitsubishi Ki.51 Type 99 Assault Plane, a single-engine two-seat attack/dive bomber known to the Americans as "Sonia."

When the Japanese first arrived at Rabaul, they were impressed by its tropic beauty. *Kempeitai* (Japanese Army military police) Lieutenant Saiji Matsuda described his initial impression: "The first time I saw Rabaul, it was truly beautiful, like an oil painting in primary colors... I admired it all as what a battlefield should look like. Morale was high. The Southern Cross I saw in the sky that first night gleamed its silvery rays, giving one a feeling of mystery and romance." By the late summer of 1943, about one-quarter of the personnel at Rabaul suffered with tropical diseases. Most had malaria, but many others suffered from dengue fever, dysentery, and blood and respiratory infections. While the eight hospitals available had 4,000 beds between them, the sick lists averaged 20,000 at any given time. As the bombing increased over the months of October and November, the sick rate increased from 24 to 37 percent.

The attack force began to gather at the Dobodura airfield complex. The four squadrons of the 345th Group joined the 71st and 405th squadrons of the 38th Group and the 13th and 90th squadrons of the 3rd Group to provide a force of 115 B-25s and 12 A-20s, while the Beaufighters of the RAAF's 30th Squadron flew up to Dobodura from Goodenough Island. Though new to the theater, the 345th had demonstrated their capabilities in the September attacks on Wewak and were set to lead the attack force. The attacking bombers would be escorted by the three squadrons of the 475th Group and the 49ers' 9th Squadron, flying from Kiriwina. The objective was suppression of the enemy fighters prior to a high-altitude bombing mission by the B-24s of the 90th Group that would crater the airfields and bomb shipping and installations in Simpson Harbor. The B-25s and A-20s were set to hit the JAAF airfield at Rapopo and the Imperial Navy bomber field at Vunakanau, while the Beaufighters would hit the Imperial Navy fighter field at Tobera. There was no explanation why the main fighter field at Lakunai was left alone, other than perhaps it had been confused with Vunakanau, the main airfield at Rabaul where the bombers were based. This failure would ultimately have a major effect on the success of the mission.

The 3rd Group's 38 B-25s of the 8th (12 B-25s), 13th (14 B-25s), and 90th (12 B-25s) squadrons were set to strike Rapopo, with each formation following the one ahead separated by 30-second intervals. The 8th would be led by 26-year-old squadron commander Major Raymond Wilkins, one of the last of the original group pilots from the dark days of early 1942; Wilkins had already turned down two opportunities to return home and in the words of his executive officer, "believed he could personally influence the outcome of the war by his own commitment and example." Group commander Lieutenant Colonel Don Hall would lead the 13th Squadron, while squadron commander Major Henebry brought up the rear with the 90th Squadron. Well-known war correspondent Lee Van Atta, who had done much to publicize the work of Fifth Air Force in the papers back home, had received permission from General Kenney to fly in Henebry's "Notre Dame de Victoire" to provide a first-hand report of the raid.

The 345th would be led by recently promoted group commander Lieutenant Colonel Clinton True, flying the B-25D "Red Wrath" of the 498th Squadron followed by the 500th, 501st, and 499th squadrons, accompanied by the 38th Group's 71st and 405th squadrons. Their target was the bomber base at Vunakanau, which the squadrons would attack at one-minute intervals. Tobera would be strafed by 12 Beaufighters, each armed with four heavy 20mm cannon and six .303-caliber machine guns.

The men of the 345th Group were informed the night before that, the next morning, they would participate in the first major daylight attack against Rabaul. Vic Tatelman recalled later that no one got much sleep that night. At the morning briefing, the intelligence officer told them that "photo recon has spotted 89 fighters, 65 medium bombers and

21 light bombers on the fields around Rabaul. Your target is Rapopo airfield. There is light, medium and heavy flak surrounding the target." Tatelman particularly remembered that, "Our Australian Liason Officer said 'When you go down ... ahhh, *if* you go down – make your way to this location,' as he pointed to a map location on New Britain. Nobody laughed at his mistake."

The B-25s cranked engines at 0700 hours, and Colonel True lifted off the runway at 0731 hours, turning toward Oro Bay 12 miles south, where the group would rendezvous. Such a large number of aircraft had never been launched before from Dobodura's coral runways. The first bombers roared down the runway, creating a wall of coral dust behind them that the others would have to fly through. Each B-25 was to take off at ten-second intervals. The 498th's First Lieutenant John Bronson recalled, "When it was my turn, I lined up on the runway center, set my gyrocompass to zero, and hit full throttle." The airplane bucked as he fought to maintain the runway heading in the zero visibility created by the dust raised from the previous takeoffs. Bronson prayed the airplane ahead had gotten off, because if not he wouldn't see it until it was too late to avoid crashing into it. "As forward speed increased and the controls felt lighter, I lifted her off at 145mph and pulled back on the yoke." The airplane broke out of the dust cloud at an altitude of about 100 feet into completely clear air. Unfortunately, the visibility with the massive dust cloud was so bad after all the B-25s had taken off that the Australian Beaufighters were forced to wait until 0815 hours for the air to clear in order to take off, which forced them to miss the rendezvous and fly on to Rabaul alone, led by their squadron leader, Wing Commander William T.M. Boulton.

By 0830 hours, the bombers had joined up and Kiriwina Island hove into sight. The 72 bombers in the six-squadron formation flew a diamond-shaped formation of 12 Mitchells each. The 475th's P-38s were waiting overhead and joined the formation, with one squadron to either side of the bombers at the same altitude, while the third squadron flew S-turns overhead. The distance to Rabaul was 200 miles across the Bismarck Sea, but True took an indirect route to throw off any aerial patrols that spotted them, adding 50 miles. He held the formation at 1,000 feet, in order to stay under the Japanese radar. Two of the 345th's B-25s encountered mechanical difficulties and were forced to abort halfway to the target. After an hour flying over the ocean, the formation approached Warangoi

Bay on New Britain, and True dropped the formation's altitude to a few hundred feet above the ocean as he turned west toward Rabaul.

The formation crossed the beach and roared on over the jungle. In the bombers, the crewmen donned flak jackets and steel helmets. The co-pilots rested their left hands on the pilots' right hands as they grasped the throttles, ready to take control of the plane if the plane commander was hit. Gunners in their plastic bubbles and waist gunners at their windows pulled their triggers momentarily to fire a few shells and clear the weapons. Vic Tatelman recalled he had his eyes riveted on the plane just ahead to his left that led his three-ship formation. "The roar of the engines as we advanced to combat power made the planes, and all of us in them, vibrate."

Flying past Tobera airfield, the bombers made a final course correction and turned toward Vunakanau. The target airfield was 14 miles further inland than Rapopo, which meant that they would attack five minutes after the 3rd Group made their attack.

Meanwhile, Major Wilkins advanced his throttles; in moments his B-25 was flashing over the jungle below at an altitude of 50 feet, going at 250mph. The rest of the 8th Squadron followed, with the 13th and 90th squadrons minutes behind the leader. Ahead, Rapopo airfield became visible as open space in the surrounding jungle. The weather conditions were excellent, with unlimited visibility and scattered clouds at 3,000–5,000 feet above, while warm air from the jungle below set the attackers bouncing in the air currents as they roared toward the objective. The 12 B-25s broke out of their diamond formations and spread into a wide shallow "Vee" that would cover the target as they swept over it. A mile behind Wilkins, 3rd Group leader Don Hall signaled his wingmen to move out and the 13th Squadron prepared for the attack. Behind, the Mitchells of the 90th Squadron did the same. The attackers were shielded from the view of the enemy on the airfield ahead by a line of low hills that muffled the roar of their engines as they bored in from the south.

Wilkins bounced in the thermals as his bomber flew over the last ridge and the target spread before him. The runway was oriented north-south, and with only minor rudder pressure he was lined up exactly for the strafing run down its length. He pressed the trigger button on the left side of his control yoke and the plane shook from the fire of eight .50-caliber guns. The other 11 pilots also opened fire and 96 heavy machine guns began spitting a combined 57,600 bullets a minute into the airplanes, vehicles, gun emplacements, and running men.

Surprise was absolute. The antiaircraft guns ringing the field were unmanned, with the guns pointing in the wrong direction. Men on the field stood open-mouthed in shock as the raiders roared overhead. The pilots tapped their rudder pedals slightly, swinging their noses back and forth and spreading the damage wide. The bomb bay doors opened and parafrags dropped out, their white 'chutes blossoming as they drifted toward the field below. In 30 seconds, the firing stopped as the raiders zoomed over the jungle at the north end of the field, having spread 30,000 bullets into everything in the moment they were over the target.

Six Japanese aircraft were seen taxiing or rolling down the runway to take off as Wilkins' bombers flew overhead. These were six Ki.21 "Sally" bombers that had been scheduled to leave for patrol and had been rolling on the taxiways when the attackers first appeared. Four managed to get airborne just ahead of the Mitchells. Captain Teruo Kurano, the 2nd Chutai leader, was fifth to get off the ground. The Sally was mere feet above the runway when it was hit by so many bullets it was literally chewed up. Kurano was likely dead at the controls when a wing dipped and caught the tip on the runway. The bomber caught fire as it cartwheeled across the runway to explode in the jungle. The pilot of the sixth Sally aborted his takeoff and attempted to get across the field into the protective trees, but the airplane was hit multiple times before it collapsed mid-field.

The momentary silence was almost deafening as the 12 B-25s disappeared over the jungle to the north of the field. The silence was quickly replaced with the roar of engines and thunder of fire as Hall's 13th Squadron appeared over the southern ridge and commenced their attack. The 14 bombers roared low overhead as 693 parafrags blossomed from their bomb bays. The 30 seconds it took to make the run seemed like an eternity to both the men in the bombers and those on the ground as bullets whined across the field; then these attackers too became small in the distance as they departed the wrecked target.

A mile behind Hall's formation, correspondent Lee Van Atta looked out at the scene from Major Henebry's bomber while Hall's formation completed their attack. He later wrote, "In seconds, the whole path in front of us was a holocaust." By the time the 90th's planes made their attack, the ground gunners had gotten to their weapons and inaccurate tracers flashed past the speeding bombers. Explosions rippled across the field from the parafrags, adding to the terror and confusion of those who survived the attack.

In their wake, the attackers left six Ki.21 Sallys, eight Ki.48 Lilys, and two transports destroyed or badly damaged. Imperial Army doctor Tetsuo Aso later recalled taking cover in a bunker when the first attackers appeared, then trying to help the wounded before being driven back into cover by the succeeding waves of enemy bombers. He described the attack as "devastating."

As the 3rd Group's Mitchells roared over St. George's Channel to make their escape, Colonel True's force found the enemy at Vunakanau as unready as had been the case at Rapopo. While the bombers roared overhead, a few gun crews managed to swing their weapons to fire at the attackers, but the tracers were as inaccurate as they had been at Rapopo. Vunakanau's mile-long runway was 135 feet wide, with a taxiway equally wide alongside. One hundred and fifty revetments lined both sides. When the bombers arrived at 1037 hours, the airfield was still in normal operation, with mechanics and other personnel walking across the field or working on aircraft, while other planes taxied past the revetments toward the runway; several aircraft that had just landed taxied toward the revetments. Colonel True came up behind a Betty on final approach and blew it out of the sky with a burst from his eight guns. Flying past the falling bomber, True spotted a Zero that had just lifted off the runway and gave it the same treatment. As he pressed the attack, his co-pilot opened the bomb bay doors and dropped the 72 parafrags they carried. The bombs drifted down on six aircraft near the runway and set them afire with their explosions. True's wingman, Casey Dean, strafed a taxiing Ki.61 "Tony," then hit a "Dinah" and a Zero.

The ferocity of the attack and its speed stunned the enemy. A few pilots ran across the field toward their planes, only to be cut down by the spray of .50-caliber bullets. Gun crews were felled attempting to unlimber their weapons. Just as the 498th Squadron cleared the field, the 500th Squadron popped over the ridge and opened fire. The field before them was chaotic with burning aircraft, vehicles, and buildings. Pilot Robert Larsen was amazed when the control tower flashed a green light at him, the signal to land. Instead, he gave it a burst and set it afire.

The 500th flashed over the field and banked over the jungle on the far end 30 seconds before the "Bats Outta Hell" of the 498th Squadron roared down the ridge toward the field. First Lieutenant George Cooper in "Jayhawk" was forced to jink to the side when other planes turned to fire on a Ki.27 "Nate" that had incredibly managed to get airborne in the midst of the attack. Cooper recalled, "All I could remember was the ground seemed to be a blur, and the sound of the engines and the guns was overpowering." In less than a minute, the bombers were past the field and their propwash set the jungle 50 feet below to waving like the ocean.

The 501st Squadron and the two 38th Group squadrons had added to the carnage less than five minutes after Cooper had completed his run. The last of the Mitchells receded into the distance, the roar of their engines and chatter of their guns replaced by the crackling sound of the flames and the final explosions from several hundred parafrags that had drifted across the field, accompanied by the screams of the wounded. Vunakanau airfield was a shambles. Aircraft, vehicles, and buildings blazed. The field was littered with the bodies of dead and wounded.

Colonel True led the formation in a turn south for the coast, then turned left to the east when they crossed the beach. While the 498th, 499th, and 501st squadrons escaped unscathed, fighters from Tobera airfield caught the Mitchells of the 500th Squadron. Pilot Jim Nusbaum remembered that "at least a dozen" enemy fighters attempted to hit the bombers. The running fight lasted 15 minutes but the crewmen were unimpressed by the lack of tenacity of their opponents. The squadron's war diary recorded that "Our gunners shot down one Hamp and two Zekes for certain, and two Zekes probably."

As the Air Apaches raced for the sea, two squadrons came across the late-arriving Australian Beaufighters, head-on. Wing Leader Boulton recalled, "The leading B-25 squadron was at a height of approximately 80 feet and the second at approximately 150 feet." The Americans mistakenly identified the twin-engine Beaufighters as Japanese "Nick" fighters, and Mitchells in the lower squadron opened fire as they closed on the Australians. The P-38s flying above the bombers started to peel off to attack but Boulton managed to call them off over the radio. The Beaufighters flew on and made their strafing attack on Tobera, but most of the enemy fighters the others spotted there had already escaped. When the Beaufighters made their attack, 19 Zeros dived on them. Flight Lieutenant Errick R. "Dick" Stone, at the rear of the formation, was overwhelmed by the enemy fighters and crashed two miles short of the runway, his Beaufighter exploding on impact.

Back on Vunakanau, parafrags swayed from the trees in the wind where they had snagged on the branches, then fell to the ground where they exploded. After several men were killed attempting to recover the bomblets, the Japanese resorted to machine gun fire to clear the trees.

Two B-25s landed short of fuel and lightly damaged at Kiriwina Island, while the rest recovered at Dobodura. There were no losses, and everyone reported they had hit their targets hard. Intelligence experts examined gun camera film overnight and confirmed that the strikes had caused major damage to the enemy. Analysis credited the attackers with the destruction of 179 enemy aircraft, in the air and on the ground, which was higher than actual losses. While the claims of three destroyers and two transports sunk were over-optimistic, valuable port facilities had been set afire. Over the next week, correspondent Lee Van Atta's report was published across the United States. "The vanguard of raiding Mitchell medium bombers flew in so daringly low, and in such tight formations that the enemy's antiaircraft defenses were overwhelmed, bewildered, and in some cases abandoned. Such a demonstration of ability to dominate and demoralize Rabaul from the air very logically could hasten the end of the Solomons Campaign."

The attack by the gunships had been planned to knock out the enemy's defenses for the following attack by the 43rd and 90th groups' B-24s. The heavy bombers had taken off from the Port Moresby airdromes shortly after dawn, led by 90th Group commander Lieutenant Colonel Rogers. By 0800 hours, the seven squadrons' 87 Liberators had formed up and Rogers led them to the eastern tip of New Guinea before turning back over the Solomon Sea toward Rabaul, flying around rather than forcing the heavily loaded bombers – each loaded with six 1,000-pound bombs – to climb over the towering Owen Stanleys. Over Kiriwina, they were joined by 47 P-38s from the 35th Group's 39th Squadron and the 8th Group's 80th "Headhunters" Squadron. By the time they had crossed the Bismarck Sea and were approaching New Britain, 25 Liberators had aborted due to various problems. The 62 bombers closed their formations as Rogers turned toward the target, flying across the Gazelle Peninsula and over Wide Bay. Over the bay, the formation split up into six-plane formations and each banked away to hit their target. When the formation spread out, the 28 P-38s of the 80th Squadron above were hard-pressed to maintain cover after the 39th Squadron had broken off to take position south of Rabaul to cover the bombers' withdrawal.

Rogers' Liberator headed toward the shipping in Simpson Harbor. At 1205 hours, bombardier Captain George P. Dunsmore dropped the 6,000-pounders while the other five in the formation dropped on his signal. The 319th Squadron followed, while the 320th and 321st squadrons brought up the rear. The crews later claimed they had hit or sunk some ten ships. As Rogers turned away from the target, he was – as he later wrote – "amazed and flabbergasted to see just ahead the biggest formation of enemy fighters I had ever seen in the air at one time."

The 204th and 253rd Naval Air Groups had launched 34 Zeros from the unscathed Lakunai airdrome. The fighters formed up ahead of the Liberators to make head-on attacks against the bombers' weak forward defenses. However, in the month before the attack, many of the B-24Ds had been modified by Pappy Gunn's technicians, who replaced their glass noses with a structure mounting an Emerson rear turret, giving them good forward defense. Major Clarence R. "Kip" Chase, aide to General Kenney, was aboard Rogers' bomber and he counted 87 individual attacks on the right side of the bomber, while Rogers counted a similar number of attacks from the left as the fighters bored in, fired, then zoomed away to come around for repeated attacks. The gunners in the noses of the modified bombers opened fire with their twin .50-caliber weapons, and Rogers later reported seeing Zeros flying to pieces under the combined fire while the gunners in the top, tail, and belly turrets, as well as the waist gunners, fired repeated bursts at the attackers. The sky was filled with tracers and the smoke of bombers and fighters as they were hit.

Rogers' bomber took a hit in its left outboard wing fuel tank, immediately behind the number one engine. Nervous, he watched fuel splatter against the hot exhaust, but the wing didn't catch fire. All six of the lead B-24s were damaged by enemy attacks. Rogers called for fighter support, but none appeared. The P-38s waiting to support the bombers were too far away to get into the fight in time.

Behind Rogers, the 80th Squadron's Captain James R. Wilson led his flight of P-38s into a formation of Hamps diving on the bombers. He punched off his tanks, but one hung up. Undaunted, he continued his attack and shot down the only enemy defender the escorts would claim. The Zeros continued making determined attacks as the Liberators flew out to sea. Rogers wondered if any would survive to get home when the enemy followed and continued attacking them 75 miles away from Rabaul. Eventually, the 321st Squadron's "Pistol Packin' Mama" had three engines knocked out and pilot Lieutenant Hampton E. Rich was forced to ditch south of Wide Bay. When the crewmen tried to get out, Zeros strafed them, setting the floating bomber on fire. There were no survivors. Flight Officer Donald McNeff from the 400th Squadron was able to stick with the formation for 90 minutes after having an engine shot out, but the plane disappeared in the clouds and was never seen again.

While the 90th Group had received a hot reception from the enemy, the 43rd Group was left alone by the fighters, which allowed the group to successfully attack shipping in the harbor. Several ships tied up to wharves were hit and set afire, while the port area was also hit solidly. The group claimed "between six and a dozen ships" hit and destroyed, with an equal number damaged. Several of the bombers were forced by fuel shortage to land at Kiriwina Island to refuel before flying on to Port Moresby.

That night, General Kenney was happy to be able to count only two B-24s, two B-25s, and a Beaufighter lost in the mission. The next day, when the photo planes from the 8th Squadron returned with their post-strike photos, the over-optimism of the bombers' reports was revealed. The squadron reported in their war diary that, "According to the heavies, they sank everything in the harbor; according to the 8th Photo's pictures, they're damned lucky if they sank a total of five ships." Only six cargo and transport ships sank, the largest of which was the 5,800-ton *Keishu Maru*. Three were Army ships of less than 500 tons each. While the strafers claimed over 100 enemy airplanes destroyed on the ground, with 51 damaged and 24 shot down in air combat, the 204th and 205th naval air groups listed four Zeros shot down and nine others damaged beyond repair. General Kenney immediately ordered further missions.

With 108 Mitchells ready for further operations, along with 70 B-24s and 100 P-38s, General Kenney planned a "saturation" bombing mission for the next day. However, overnight the weather conditions deteriorated to such a state that the low-level strafing mission was called off. The heavy bombers still prepared to mount a second mission to Simpson Harbor, and B-24s from both the 43rd and 90th groups took off at 0800 hours on October 13, taking the same route around the Owen Stanleys they had the day before. At 1000 hours, they rendezvoused with 110 P-38s from all six squadrons over Kiriwina. When they headed across the Bismarck Sea, the formation encountered increasingly adverse weather. Halfway to the target, they came face to face with a massive squall line rising from 5,000 to 30,000 feet that was extremely turbulent, with heavy icing conditions above 15,000 feet. The formation broke apart when the B-24s attempted to penetrate the front with a squadron of P-38s following each formation. Whiteout conditions were encountered and Captain Gerald R. Johnson, leading the 9th Squadron's Lightnings, became increasingly concerned about the safety of his pilots as their flights became separated. Finally, at around noon, the mission was formally aborted when Colonel Rogers announced over the radio that there was no way through the storm. Turning back was almost as dangerous, with a B-24 and three P-38s failing to return to their bases, lost in the weather. The 43rd Group recorded that the lost B-24, which was from their group, had collided with one of the P-38s.

On October 15, the Japanese determined to strike back. Fifteen Val dive bombers of the 582nd Air Group, escorted by 39 Zeros, attempted to hit Allied shipping in the Oro Bay anchorage. The Japanese claimed five ships sunk or damaged, but the ships they attacked sustained little damage. The enemy formation was intercepted by 54 P-38s and eight P-40s; the Japanese admitted to the loss of 14 Vals and five Zeros in the air battle, while the Americans claimed 26 Vals and 18 Zeros.

Two days later, a fighter sweep of 56 Zeros was sent against Dobodura, but they were intercepted by 43 P-38s and three P-40s. Among the intercepting Lightning pilots was the 431st Squadron's Tommy McGuire, who tore into a formation of seven Zeros, shooting down three to bring his score to 12, but the other four turned on him. One got on his tail and shot up "Pudgy" so badly that McGuire was forced to bail out. Fortunately, as he descended, he was spotted by a PT boat that pulled him from the water minutes after he went in.

The morning of October 18, 36 Mitchell bombers of the 345th formed up at 1030 hours over Oro Bay. Once again, Group Commander Lieutenant Col. Clinton L. True was in the left seat of "Red Wrath," leading the Falcons of the 498th Squadron, followed by the "Black Panthers" of the 501st with the 499th's "Bats Outta Hell" in third place, and the 500th's "Rough Raiders" in trail. Once formed up, the bombers headed east-northeast over the Bismarck Sea, flying at 12,000 feet with each squadron in three "vee-of-vees" formations of nine aircraft, accompanied again by the 38th Group's 71st and 405th squadrons. This mission would differ from that of October 12 in that the 43rd and 90th groups' B-24s would simulate an attack on the town of Rabaul 30 minutes before the B-25 gunships arrived. Just before "bombs away," the heavies would turn and bomb Vunakanau and Lakunai, leaving Rapopo and Tobera fields, which the Mitchells would hit to catch the enemy fighters while they were refueling.

Vic Tatelman held "Dirty Dora" in close formation with flight leader and squadron commander Captain Julian C. Baird. In addition to their eight forward-firing guns, the bombers were carrying parafrags and "daisy-cutters," 500-pound bombs with a fuse on a length of iron pipe attached to the bomb's trigger, to ensure they exploded above round, showering shrapnel in a 100-yard circle each. In "Jayhawk," lead ship of the second flight on the right side of the formation, flight leader George L. Cooper maintained formation with the three bombers led by Captain Orin N. Loverin, while he checked his two wingmen, First Lieutenants William M. Parke to the right and William W. Cabell to the left. Ahead, a line of thunder clouds reared high above the ocean, directly across the track to Rabaul. The escorting P-38s from the 475th Group called in that they were aborting the mission due to weather. Cooper later remembered, "We had been briefed that it was likely we could find a squall line between New Guinea and New Britain. If we did, the B-24s would not penetrate the squall and the fighters would turn back."

At the head of the formation, Colonel True held "Red Wrath" on an unwavering course toward the huge line of thunderstorms stretching across the Bismarck Sea. The other Mitchells followed. In "Dirty Dora," Tatelman heard the radioed command from base to abort the mission and turn back. "I looked out, and Colonel True was penetrating the front as if nothing had been said. We all followed." True would later claim not to have heard the recall order. "I never believed that," recalled Cooper, "and neither did anyone else in the group. We all heard the order, but we were all young and tough. I liked Colonel True because he was aggressive and wanted to fight the war. I wouldn't have liked following someone who wasn't like that."

In moments, the Mitchells were flying through heavy rain and severe turbulence. Tatelman remembered, "Pilot tension in one airplane flying IFR [instrument flight rules] is tough enough, but to have 50 airplanes on instruments in the same area, with all the turbulence, that made it as tough as can be." Cooper couldn't see anything through his windshield, due to the heavy rain:

All I could see to either side were my wing men, tucked in as close as they could get without colliding. The turbulence was really heavy, and I was afraid of us flying into one of the other flights, so I took my flight down. I had to open the side window so I could see the ocean well enough to avoid flying into it. We went through the storm about 60 feet above the wave tops.

Once they emerged from the front, the crews found their flights widely separated. Pilots concentrated on closing up the formation while Colonel True headed for Kabanga Bay on New Britain, now visible in the distance. The B-25s followed their leader down till they were only 100 feet above the water. Tension rose in the individual aircraft with voices on the intercoms clipped, talk reduced to monosyllables. They crossed the beach and headed over the jungle, dropping to an altitude of 50 feet, the pilots concentrating on holding formation while the gunners test-fired their weapons. The Sundowners' Mitchells turned away to attack Tobera while the Air Apaches roared on toward Rapopo.

Cooper remembered:

Our strafing tactic was to approach the target at 500 feet, then begin our dive from the Initial Point, bringing the throttles up to METO (Maximum Except Take Off) power so that we came across at treetop height and doing about 310mph.

Going in as the third squadron, we knew the defenses would be waiting for us, so you wanted to fly the airplane as fast as you could, as low as you could, so they didn't have time to track you with any accuracy.

When we got to the initial point, Captain Loverin overflew it, so he had to make a tight left turn to get back. As the outside flight of the formation, we had to advance our throttles to full power to keep from lagging, while Baird's flight had to reduce power to keep with Loverin on the other side. When we rolled out on the Initial Point and commenced the run-in for the attack, I had full power and we leaped ahead of Loverin's flight. Baird's flight put their throttles to full as they came out of the turn, and they also passed Loverin.

In "Dirty Dora," co-pilot Second Lieutenant Willie Graham put his hands atop Tatelman's on the throttles so he could take control immediately should Tatelman be hit. The Mitchells dropped even lower as they flashed over the last ridge before the target. "There was no sound except the roar of the engines and an occasional word over the radio," Tatelman remembered.

I advanced the throttles to METO, with Willie's hand on mine to hold them. Black smoke poured out of the exhaust stacks and it felt like we were going a thousand miles an hour, down at 50 feet or less.

All of a sudden we were over the target and I was concentrating on keeping clear of Julian Baird so I wouldn't hit him as I pulled the trigger for the nose guns.

When Tatelman opened fire, Graham opened the bomb doors and hit the bomb release. "Smoke from the explosions obscured the targets, but they also made it harder for the gunners to hit us. I was surprised by the inaccuracy of the Japanese ack-ack," Tatelman recounted.

In "Jayhawk," Cooper had his hands full. He recalled:

When we came off the target, I looked over at my left wingman and he had a huge hole in his right wing. I slowed so he could maintain control and keep up. My flight separated from the other two, and we never did join up till we were out over the ocean. We were jumped by Zeros and my gunner shot down two of them.

When Tatelman's flight of three came off the target and crossed the shoreline of Simpson Harbor, he spotted what appeared to be a ferry boat directly in their line of flight. All three bombers opened fire together, scoring direct hits as troops jumped overboard to avoid their fire. "Off Cape Gazelle, we in the 499th were jumped by 15 Zeros. They made 21 passes, but mostly broke off before they got into range. Of the ten that came in close enough, our gunners shot down three. Once we were out to sea they left us alone."

While the first three squadrons of the 345th hit Rapopo field, the "Rough Raiders" of the 500th turned away and flew down the coast, hunting enemy shipping. They found more trouble than anyone else over Rabaul. Attacking a coastal cargo ship, Lieutenant Wallace's Mitchell, "Tondelayo," was hit and the left engine was set afire, just before he dropped his two 1,000-pounders. The bomber's speed dropped to just barely 150mph as he flew over the target, which allowed the gunners below to rake the Mitchell nose to tail. Wallace's wingmen, Lieutenants Peterson and Anaker, slowed down to cover him. Zeros swept in to attack and Peterson was shot down; the Mitchell exploded on impact with no survivors. Hit badly, Anaker turned back to New Britain and ditched on the coast. Two of his crew survived and were eventually rescued by coastwatchers.

Wallace flew on with a burning engine and took "Tondelayo" low over the waves while Captain Mortenson in "Snafu" attempted to give him cover. The two bombers took a course for Kiriwina, but the enemy fighters continued to attack them as they headed out to sea. The fight lasted nearly an hour, during which five enemy fighters flew into the water trying to shoot down the Mitchells as they stayed so low that their propwash created wakes in the water mere feet below them. Wallace's top turret gunner, Sergeant John A. Murphy, shot down several. Finally, halfway across the Bismarck Sea, the remaining enemy fighters turned back to Rabaul. With his co-pilot wounded in the stomach and still conscious, Wallace brought the wounded "Tondelayo" to a safe landing at 1510 hours on the emergency strip on Kiriwina Island.

Back at Dobodura, there was trouble. While the six squadrons claimed to have destroyed 41 enemy aircraft on the ground and 38 enemy fighters shot down with five probables as well as three ships sunk for a loss of only two Mitchells, Colonel Frederick Smith of the First Air Task Force didn't believe True's story that his radio operator had failed to receive the recall order, and was prepared to nail the mission commander for disobeying orders. Three days later, True reported to General Kenney in Brisbane, where he saw the headlines in the local papers: "MacArthur Using Daring New Tactics, Sends B-25s Over Rabaul Unescorted." He repeated his story about not receiving the order. Kenney didn't believe him any more than the pilots had, but in view of the overall success of the mission a court-martial was deemed inappropriate. Instead, True was awarded the Distinguished Service Cross for leading the daring mission, while 16 Silver Stars and seven Distinguished Flying Crosses were awarded to other crewmen. The Air Apaches received the first of an eventual four Distinguished Unit Citations they would earn by the end of the war.

Following the mission, several crews were able to take leave in Sydney. The group had a policy that when a bomber needed a 100-hour check, the crew was authorized to fly it to Australia and take a week's leave while the plane was worked on. Vic Tatelman remembered that the group pooled their finances and purchased a four-bedroom home on Rose Bay overlooking Sydney Harbor.

We even had our own taxi driver, George, who we supplied with 100 octane avgas drained from the planes so he could ply his trade. He knew where the best Aussie beer was sold and where to find the most luscious girls. If New Guinea was hell, Sydney was heaven! Clean clothes, hot showers, comfortable beds. Three girls made sure our house was always stocked with food, liquor and beer.

On October 20, armed with photos taken the day before that showed 200 enemy fighters on Rabaul's airfields, the 90th Group's B-24s were sent to hit Lakunai Field while the 43rd bombed Vunakanau, with a P-38 fighter sweep immediately before the bombers made their runs. Three other P-38 squadrons made up the escort. Arriving at Rabaul, the bombers found the targets socked in by thunder clouds rising to 20,000 feet. The leaders decided to hit Rapopo, which was in the clear. Despite poor bombing, the Japanese admitted to the loss of 11 aircraft destroyed and seven damaged. However, as they turned away the bombers were intercepted by 42 Zeros from three different naval air groups. The pilots of the 475th Group claimed 13 victories in the combat, while the 432nd Squadron, led by new commander Charles H. MacDonald, claimed another 12 destroyed in the fighter sweep. Gerald Johnson of the 9th Squadron scored one that blew up and damaged his P-38 when he flew through the explosion, while the bomber gunners claimed an additional four. Eighteen Zeros and Oscars were credited to the pilots, while the Japanese claimed 19 P-38s shot down though only the P-38 flown by the 431st Squadron's Edward Czarnecki was lost, with the pilot managing to make contact with the coastwatchers for later rescue.

The offensive continued on October 24, with the 3rd Group attacking Tobera and Rapopo while the 345th again hit Vunakanau. The attack was opposed by nearly 60 defending fighters. The 13th Squadron found few targets at Tobera while the 8th and 90th squadrons destroyed 21 at Rapopo. The Air Apaches claimed 27 destroyed at Vunakanau.

Among the escorting pilots was Dick Bong, whose 17 victories made him the leading Fifth Air Force ace. He and his wingman became involved in a fight over Tobera in which he fired at three different fighters but missed all. When he returned to the United States in the spring of 1944 as the top ace of the Pacific with a score of 27, his first request would be to take the gunnery training the USAAF had finally instituted for fighter pilots. On completion, he claimed, "If I had known what I know now when I was in New Guinea, my score would be double."

Jay T. Robbins and the other pilots of the Headhunters reported that the fight they found that day was "the hottest battle yet encountered by any of our pilots." Major Cragg was wounded in the fight, while Robbins added two to his score, reporting that the opposing pilots seemed "eager and experienced." The Lightning squadrons reported one of their best days, with a loss of one P-38 and pilot and slight damage to others, while the strafers lost a B-25 with its crew. The defenders suffered one of their worst days, losing a total of 12 Zeros, including Warrant Officer Shizo Ishii, who was credited with 29 victories during his time at Rabaul. The Japanese reported that every bomber attacking Vunakanau was hit with two destroyed, five "almost destroyed," and 27 suffering damage.

The next day, 61 B-24s joined 81 Lightnings over Kiriwina and headed toward Rabaul. The weather quickly deteriorated. Major MacDonald saw several B-24s turn back when the abort message was heard, but 50 bombers continued on. MacDonald led eight P-38s to cover them when the rest of the fighters turned back. He took his Lightnings to 27,000 feet, and they made it over the weather to provide cover to the bombers when they emerged from the storm just short of Rabaul. The Liberators were intercepted by 44 enemy fighters as they approached Lakunai Field. Over the harbor, the two heavy cruisers and six destroyers that had arrived from Truk the evening before opened fire at them. Despite the heavy AA, the group's bombardiers did well when they dropped their loads on Lakunai. The Japanese admitted the loss of 20 aircraft that were burned, including five Ki.46 Dinah recon planes; the airfield was temporarily out of use. Eight ships in Simpson Harbor were also hit. One B-24 went down, but the crew – other than the pilot and co-pilot who were killed in the ditching – were all rescued by a PBY Catalina after an hour in the water.

A fourth mission scheduled for the next day was canceled by bad weather. A final mission flown on October 29 saw the 43rd Group's B-24s drop 4,000 six-pound fragmentation bombs on Vunakanau, while the 90th Group followed up with over 400 500-pound high-explosive bombs. The Japanese scrambled 75 Zeros, of which 50 tangled with the bombers and their escorts. Dick Bong shot down three of the enemy fighters in a wild fight over the harbor.

During the October offensive, Fifth Air Force units claimed 350 enemy aircraft destroyed at Rabaul. The P-38s were credited with 53 enemy fighters shot down, while the air crews of the B-24s claimed 42 shot down and the B-25s claimed eight. The Japanese admitted far fewer losses, but they also reported that "enemy air raids became a great obstacle to the execution of operations."

14

BLOODY TUESDAY

Admiral Halsey's South Pacific forces invaded Bougainville on November 1 in a largely unopposed landing as planned. In the early morning hours of November 2, ships of the Japanese Eighth Fleet attempted to attack the invasion shipping but were beaten off by the US Navy in the Battle of Empress Augusta Bay. To support the invasion, Fifth Air Force sent a mission that day to strike the Japanese warships that had been spotted in Simpson Harbor in an attempt to keep them from interfering with the invasion further. Reconnaissance photographs taken on November 1 revealed seven destroyers, a tender, and 20 merchant vessels in the harbor. The 3rd and 345th groups were ordered to make the attack. Pilot Dick Walker of the 3rd Group's 13th Squadron remembered the morning briefing:

> The morning briefing conducted prior to takeoff was a very somber affair. Hearing the latest word on the extent of the Japanese defenses was pretty much a prediction that all of us would not be coming home. The 12 crews that were assigned to fly the mission sat gray faced and quiet during the briefing. The attack was to be carried out by waves of bombers attacking by squadrons in file with 12 airplanes per squadron flying in a line abreast sweeping across Simpson Harbor. My squadron was the second scheduled in.

Leading the 8th Squadron was the redoubtable Major Wilkins, who had just returned from leave in Australia with news that he and his Australian fiancée had set the date for their marriage. The 3rd, 38th, and 345th groups launched 75 B-25s for an afternoon attack, escorted by 70 P-38s from the six squadrons at Kiriwina. The plans called for two P-38 squadrons to sweep the airfields prior to the arrival of the strike aircraft, to suppress enemy fighters. This would be followed by the four Air Apache squadrons dropping a mixed load of parafrags and "Kenny Cocktails" – a 100-pound bomb filled with white phosphorus – on the antiaircraft positions ringing the harbor. Close on the heels of the 345th, the 71st and 405th squadrons of the 38th Group, and the 8th, 13th, and 90th squadrons of the 3rd Group, would make skip-bombing attacks on the shipping in Simpson Harbor with 1,000-pound bombs.

In a change from previous attacks, the five anti-shipping squadrons would approach over the volcanoes on Crater Peninsula, which would shield the bombers from antiaircraft fire while the Air Apaches went after the guns. The bombers would drop to low level as they flew between two volcanoes known as The Mother and The Northern Daughter. Coming from this unexpected direction, the prevailing tides would present the anchored ships broadside-on to the Mitchells. The overall mission would be led by the 3rd Group's Major Henebry, with the 90th Squadron in the lead, followed by the 13th with the 8th last as "clean-up batters." Coming in from the northwest, the force would be headed southeast, directly at the harbor mouth and their escape, before turning for home. Everyone involved in the mission planning believed they had come up with a knockout punch against Rabaul. No one considered that the bombers would have to fly between the two volcanoes in trail, presenting themselves as one long target to the AA gunners to either side as they came out of the mountains and then spread into their line-abreast formations.

Based on photos obtained on October 29, Fifth Air Force intelligence believed the enemy fighter strength had been reduced to approximately 50 fighters and perhaps 30 bombers. Unfortunately, additional photo missions after October 29 had been scrubbed due to adverse weather, and so it was unknown that Combined Fleet commander Admiral Koga, reacting to the losses incurred in the October missions, had managed to send 150 additional fighters from the carriers *Shōkaku*, *Zuikaku*, and *Zuihō* at Truk to Rabaul on November 1. The impenetrable front across the Solomon Sea had prevented nearly all New Guinea-based aircraft from flying a mission to Rabaul that could have discovered this unexpected reinforcement. However, late in the afternoon of

November 1, a single F-5 photo Lightning had managed to penetrate the weather and photograph the bases an hour after the arrival of Koga's reinforcements. Despite the knowledge that night that there were now some 300 enemy aircraft at Rabaul and a great increase in the defending fighter formations, the mission went forward as planned.

The morning of November 2, the bomber crews were awakened at 0400 hours to attend their briefings. The briefing officers sought to set aside foreboding about the number of aircraft seen the day before with reports of how many enemy planes had been shot down attacking the Bougainville invasion fleet. The bad weather that had canceled the strike the previous day – when the situation would have been close to what intelligence had forecast – was still around, and the crews manned their planes only to wait until word was received from an F-5 sent to Rabaul that weather over the target was acceptable.

The order to start engines was passed shortly before 1100 hours, and by 1130 hours all 75 B-25s had rendezvoused and were proceeding toward Kiriwina to pick up their fighter escort. The low number of strafers as compared with the 115 that had flown the first Rabaul mission on October 12 was indicative of the losses sustained in the following strikes that had yet to see replacements, as was the low number of 70 P-38s compared to the 125 that had flown the first mission.

After the fighters and bombers joined up, Major Henebry led the formation across the Bismarck Sea. The bombers flew at 1,000–2,000 feet, while the fighters maintained position above at approximately 3,000 feet beneath scattered rain squalls they flew around when encountered.

When they flew up St. George's Channel on the approach to Rabaul, the weather was good enough for Japanese spotters on New Britain and New Ireland to see and hear the approaching raid when the formation rounded Cape Gazelle. Rather than cutting across the Gazelle Peninsula as had been the case in the previous raids, Henebry turned northwest to take them over Crater Peninsula. The four Air Apache squadrons and the P-38s of the 475th's 431st and 432nd squadrons sped up to make their attack. The bombers rapidly approached the ingress point between The Mother and The Northern Daughter volcanoes.

At 1330 hours, the 16 P-38s of the 80th Headhunters Squadron, led by Major Cragg, turned toward Lakunai airdrome at low altitude. In a matter of minutes, they were involved in a fight later described in the unit history: "The Japs sent up the largest number of planes ever encountered by this squadron. A conservative estimate placed the number at 60 Zeros, but many pilots claimed there were over 100 enemy fighters in the air." As it turned out, the latter number was correct. The enemy fighters were from *Zuikaku*, and had been alerted in time by a lookout to get airborne just as the Headhunters arrived. The *Shōkaku* Zeros at Vunakanau airdrome were already airborne, making ready for a mission to Bougainville when the approaching Americans were spotted, as were the *Zuihō* Zeros that had taken off from Tobera. Combined with the 57 Zeros launched from the Rabaul-based 201st, 204th, and 253rd air groups, 115 defending fighters were airborne by the time the attackers began to fly through the pass between the volcanoes. The Headhunters were immediately in the fight of their lives. Flight Officer Willis F. Evers was quickly picked off, followed minutes later by Second Lieutenant Norman Shea. The other 14 Headhunters managed to maintain their formations and coordination and later claimed 14 victories. The 13 pilots of the 39th Squadron, flying high cover at 8,000–13,000 feet, never found any enemy fighters.

As the 345th's leading attackers came through the pass between the volcanoes and crested the high ground north of Rabaul, they separated into individual squadrons to go after their assigned targets. When they flew over Vunakanau, enemy fighters dived on the 498th Squadron just as the squadron flew over Rabaul town and dropped white phosphorus bombs to create a smoke screen to hide the ships in the harbor from the attackers. Flak hit several of the bombers, setting the aircraft on fire before they could drop their munitions.

Vic Tatelman remembered that the possibility of collision made the attack scary. "We were all flying in squadron line-abreast formations, which meant I had to keep glancing to the side to be sure I wasn't turning into that plane or it into me, which was hard to do while concentrating on firing the guns. It was dangerous to sway to either side for even a moment, which limited the field of fire." Most important, the squadron came close to a massed mid-air collision with the preceding bombers from the 500th, which crossed in front of them as that unit set themselves up for their attack. The 499th's nine bombers continued on over the town, firing at anything they saw, then flew over the harbor where flak from the ships below tore through the formation. "We bobbed and weaved," Tatelman remembered, "and managed to get through that without anyone being hit badly."

In the 499th Squadron, Jack George's bomber was hit by a fighter whose bullets inflicted leg wounds on the co-pilot and seriously wounded both the flight engineer in the upper turret and the radio operator. Despite his wounds, co-pilot Matt Simms crawled over the bomb bay to the rear of the plane, where he administered emergency first aid to the two men which likely saved their lives, while George concentrated on flying despite his windscreen being covered with hydraulic fluid from another hit they had taken.

A minute behind the 499th, Captain Mortensen's white phosphorus bombs were set afire when he took a hit in the bomb bay as he flew through the volcanic gap. Fortunately the bomb bay doors were already open and he was able to drop the load before the fire spread to the airplane. His wingman, Lieutenant Alfred R. Krasnickas, was not so lucky. Just before his co-pilot opened the bomb bay doors to drop the white phosphorus and parafrags, the Mitchell was hit in the bomb bay, igniting one of the phosphorus bombs. Crews in surrounding aircraft saw the bomber catch fire with flames quickly spreading down the fuselage and up into the cockpit. Mercifully, in less than a minute the B-25 rolled over and crashed into the jungle below, three miles short of their target at Tobera.

The 501st followed the 498th and 499th squadrons through the gap between the volcanoes and attacked Lakunai, dropping parafrags and white phosphorus as they raced across the field at an altitude of 100 feet. Lieutenant Marion Kirby, leading the 13 P-38s of the 431st Squadron, stayed with the bombers as the 432nd Squadron's Lightnings became involved in a fight with the defending Zeros. He later recalled:

> I saw a B-25 at this time with its right engine on fire. Three Zeros were attacking to finish him off. I attacked alone and definitely got one, then hit another one many times that I think I got. The third one got on my tail and Lieutenant Frederick Champlin got it off my tail. I saw him hit it and it started smoking, rolled over and hit the ground.

The rest of the 501st fought a running battle with 50 aggressive Zeros that closed to within 40–50 feet before breaking off. The Mitchells cut across Cape Gazelle and dropped to 50 feet over St. George's Channel, still pursued by the enemy until they were south of the Warangoi River, where Lieutenant Moore's burning B-25, which had been momentarily saved by Lieutenant Kirby, finally landed in the channel. Moore and his co-pilot went down with the bomber, while Sergeants John Barron, William Harris, and Michael Kicera got out only to be captured by the Japanese and become POWs.

The battered ships of the Eighth Fleet that had survived the night battle in Empress Augusta Bay, had only arrived back in Simpson Harbor some 20 minutes before the attack began. Captain Tameichi Hara, commander of Destroyer Division Two aboard the destroyer *Shigure*, later remembered the attack: "Previous attacks on Rabaul had all been made at high altitude, but the tactics were changed this day. The ensuing battle was the most spectacular action of my life."

The B-25s from the 3rd and 38th groups faced the hardest part of the fight. They had not expected the heavy cruisers *Haguro* and *Myoko*, each armed with eight 5-inch dual-purpose heavy antiaircraft guns and over 50 25mm rapid-fire cannon, to be in the harbor. The light cruiser *Agano* added another 60 25mm weapons. Having to come through the volcano gap a squadron at a time in trail, the 40 B-25s could not all attack at once, which might have enabled them to overwhelm the defenses.

First Lieutenant Frank M. Cecil led the 38th Group's 71st and 405th squadrons. After taking fire from gun positions above them as they flew between the volcanoes, they were faced with heavy smoke and drifting phosphorus clouds that rose to 400 feet, giving pilots only a few seconds to spot and line up on a target in the harbor to skip-bomb. Murderous fire from ships and shore batteries forced the pilots to jink and weave, which threw their aim off as they went after the ships with their 1,000-pound bombs. Despite everything thrown at them, the 38th's bombers scored what the squadron history later described as, "Two bombs were dropped on a 7,000–10,000-ton merchant vessel… causing it to explode and was left in a sinking condition." The ship was *Manko Maru* which must have seemed much larger to a B-25 pilot approaching at 200 miles an hour and an altitude of 50 feet, since she was only 1,500 tons displacement.

The 71st Squadron's First Lieutenant James Hungerpillar didn't make it out of the harbor. His B-25 was hit in the left engine and burst into flames. As flame spread through the bomber, he turned and attempted to skip-bomb the heavy cruiser whose AA fire had gotten him, but the bomb fell short. He flew low over the enemy ship and crashed into the harbor, exploding on impact. The bombers' race across the harbor took less than 60 seconds, but to those under enemy fire it seemed an eternity. The squadron history recorded, "The entire area was a mass of devastation and murder. Many enemy fighters were seen to leave a trail of flame behind them, then splashed into the water. A parachute with the charred but limp body of a flier was seen to float past one plane as he made his run."

The eight Mitchells of the 405th Squadron fell behind when they became separated in a heavy rain squall. Several Zeros intercepted the first four and the pilots dropped their bombs without effect as they attempted to evade the fighters. The second flight of four attacked from north to south across the harbor. Lieutenant Roger Fox's B-25 was shot down in flames over an enemy ship. By the time the other three cleared the harbor, they had all received moderate AA damage and one crewman was wounded.

Major Henebry led the 3rd Group into the cauldron of fire. Enemy warships fought with both their antiaircraft guns and their main batteries, which they fired into the water to create waterspouts in an attempt to knock the low-flying gunships into the water before they got into range. Two destroyers were anchored to the side of the approach path into the harbor, where their position made them difficult to attack. When they fired at the bombers as they flew past, the formation was forced to break up into single and two-plane elements. The air was filled with the black clouds of flak explosions from heavier weapons and tracers lashed the sky from the light weapons.

Major Henebry strafed and bombed a freighter before his Mitchell was hit by fire from one of the heavy cruisers. Captain Charles W. Howe managed to skip a bomb into another freighter, sinking it immediately. Henebry managed to fly his badly damaged airplane out of the harbor and was able to get back to Kiriwina Island. Howe followed and landed to give Henebry's crew a ride home.

Major Wilkins' 8th Squadron was the last in line as they headed into the harbor. He took a hit in the right wing but continued on and skip-bombed a 1,000-pounder into a destroyer that erupted in flames. One wingman, Lieutenant Joseph Meyers, turned away in the face of the fire, while his other, Lieutenant John Cunningham, was hit with an engine set afire. When Cunningham ditched in St. George's Channel, the bomber sank before anyone could get out.

With his left rudder damaged by flak, Wilkins continued on and slammed his second bomb into the side of a large transport. Turning away, his escape path was blocked by *Haguro*, the same enemy cruiser that had shot up Henebry. Her side lit up with flashes from the secondary batteries. Wilkins opened fire with his eight guns, whipping the yoke back and forth to spray the entire length of the ship. The sailors returned fire and Wilkins' left rudder was blown off as the Mitchell was raked by fire. When he turned left to evade and escape, he took a large-caliber hit that crumpled his left wing and the Mitchell smashed into the water, killing all aboard. For his actions, Wilkins was posthumously awarded the Medal of Honor on March 24, 1944.

Dick Walker remembered, "After I made my run through the harbor, the rest of my flight was uneventful and my only damage was a couple of bullet holes from small arms fire. We lost 45 airmen killed or missing. Eight B-25s and nine P-38s were shot down and several more suffered major damage."

Overhead, Gerald Johnson's 9th Squadron found their 11 P-38s engaged in an extended fight in which Johnson shot down two Zeros, while the rest shot down another four for the loss of Lieutenant Francis Lowe, who crashed at high speed in flames southeast of Tobera. First Lieutenant Carl Planck collided with a Zero and ditched his P-38 in the channel. Swimming ashore, he was fortunate to make contact with natives working with the coastwatchers.

Across the Gazelle Peninsula and down St. George's Channel, pilots and crews struggled to stay in the air with damaged flight controls, engines shot out, and wounded crewmen, with a sea crossing ahead before they would find safety. When Lieutenant Webster of the 8th Squadron finally landed back at Dobodura, he remembered, "I was so stiff and wrung out emotionally that I could barely get out of the plane."

The mission would be remembered ever after in the Fifth Air Force as "Black Tuesday."

Despite initial claims of success, the Japanese only lost the 3,000-ton *Shinko Maru* and the 1,500-ton *Manko Maru*. *Haguro* and *Myoko* were damaged by near misses. Twenty-four cargo ships, transports, and oilers suffered damage ranging from light to severe. General Kenney later wrote of the November 2 mission that it was Fifth Air Force's "toughest, hardest-fought engagement of the war."

Despite knowledge of the high losses in exchange for relatively little damage, MacArthur's headquarters in Brisbane issued Communique 572, which described a "desperate battle," with three destroyers sunk by masthead skip-bombing in addition to eight large merchant vessels, portraying Simpson Harbor as "a scene of utter wreckage and destruction" and claiming 90 enemy aircraft destroyed in the air and on the ground. General Kenney declared Rabaul "finished," a sentiment echoed later in November by a report from the US Strategic Bombing Survey team crediting Fifth Air Force with a decisive victory: "Heavy raids in October and a final strike on 2 November completely surprised the enemy and resulted in such heavy destruction that it was obvious that Rabaul was no longer a satisfactory base for any kind of operations."

In fact, the six P-38 squadrons would not return to their pre-October 12 strength until March 1944. The B-25 groups had taken nearly 30 percent casualties. Vic Tatelman would remember 60 years later that "the month of October and that mission in November were the most terrifying and memorable weeks of my entire life."

It was clear Rabaul remained a formidable fortress. The next day, a photo Lightning caught images of a new Japanese cruiser force in Simpson Harbor. Fifth Air Force would fly a bombing mission on November 5 to support a carrier raid on the base, but that would be the last one mounted by "Kenney's Boys." Responsibility for finishing the battle would become the task of Admiral Halsey.

15

THE JOLLY ROGERS

The F4U Corsair, meant to be the Navy's fleet defense fighter for the coming war when its development began in 1940, had proven itself so difficult to bring aboard a carrier that VF-12, the first squadron to equip with the new fighter, had turned it down and instead re-equipped with the Grumman F6F Hellcat, a fighter with far more docile handling in the shipboard environment.

The second Navy squadron to receive the Corsair found itself initially in a similarly difficult situation, with the captain of its carrier threatening to have them "put overboard" due to the high level of operational accidents that occurred during their carrier qualification; yet, by the time they deployed they had successfully dealt with every negative problem the airplane presented.

Fighting Squadron 17, VF-17, holds a very individual place in US Naval Aviation history. The unit was originally organized in January 1943 as the fighter squadron of Air Group 17, assigned to the newly commissioned USS *Bunker Hill* (CV-17), the fourth Essex-class fleet carrier to go to war, yet they made their combat reputation flying from land bases in the Solomons during the final offensive against Rabaul.

Squadron commander Lieutenant Commander John Thomas "Tommy" Blackburn, a member of the Annapolis class of 1933 who would provide much of the Navy's mid-level leadership in the Pacific War, was a third-generation naval officer, both his father and grandfather having made careers of the Navy. Following the mandatory two years of sea duty after graduation from the naval academy, his request for flight training was granted and he graduated from Pensacola with his Wings of Gold in 1937. By 1941, he was a flight instructor at Pensacola, when he was assigned as one of the officers who organized the new naval advanced training program at NAS Miami, Florida.

In July 1942, Blackburn was promoted to Lieutenant Commander and was ordered to organize and command Composite Squadron 29 (VGF-29), one of the first composite squadrons intended for service on the new escort carriers. Organized at NAS Corpus Christi, Texas, most of the squadron pilots were Ensigns recently graduated from flight school, with Lieutenant (jg) Henry "Brink" Bass providing a leavening of combat experience with VF-2 aboard USS *Lexington* (CV-2) at the Battle of the Coral Sea. When they were transferred to NAS Norfolk, Virginia, Blackburn discovered the auxiliary field at Pungo, Virginia, where he trained his young charges to be proficient in the F4F-4 Wildcat. The squadron went aboard the escort carrier USS *Santee* (ACV-29), the former tanker *Esso Sekay*, which had been commissioned after being converted to a carrier only on September 8, 1942. The air group, flying 18 F4F-4 Wildcats and eight SBD-4 Dauntless dive bombers, first landed aboard on September 24. Yard workmen were still aboard finishing the conversion while the ship made its shakedown cruise to the Bahamas that ended on October 25 when the carrier and her air group joined Task Group 34.2 to participate in Operation *Torch*, the invasion of North Africa, when VF-9 had flown Wildcats off the carrier *Ranger*.

Santee arrived off Morocco on November 6 and launched her first air strike on November 8 as the landings began. Due to poor weather and *Santee's* damaged homing equipment, most of the squadron was forced to ditch or force land in Morocco when they were unable to find their carrier after making their strike. Blackburn ended up ditching at sea and spent three days in a life raft before he was found by a destroyer. Due to the squadron's inauspicious combat debut, Blackburn imagined he faced professional ruin during the return voyage, but shortly after arriving at the Norfolk naval base on November 22, 1942, he was given orders to organize and command a new squadron, VF-17.

Fighting 17 "stood up" in a hangar at NAS Norfolk on January 1, 1943, when Blackburn read the commissioning order to ten newly graduated Ensigns and eight enlisted men. He was soon able to draft Lieutenant Commander Roger L. Hedrick, a 1936 graduate of the Aviation Cadet (AvCad) program, as the squadron executive officer. The two men had first worked together at the Miami Naval Aviation advanced training school in early 1942. Together, Blackburn and Hedrick would make VF-17 operate as a cohesive team. Originally equipped with North American SNJ trainers and F4F Wildcats, the squadron pilots flew every day to improve their skills while they awaited the arrival of their airplanes. The first F4U-1 Corsairs arrived in early February. Then-Ensign William L. "Country" Landreth, who was one of the ten "plank owners" in the squadron, remembered the arrival of the new fighters, which already had a bad reputation among the naval aviation community. "The airplane was difficult to fly and had about as much forward visibility when landing and taking off as Lindbergh's Spirit of St. Louis." Vought chief test pilot Boone Guyton, who had more experience flying the airplane than anyone else at the time, came down to Norfolk and gave the pilots the benefit of his experience, coaching them through their first flights in the big fighter. Blackburn remembered that "After six months working with the Corsair, we had a reasonable mastery and from there on it was relatively smooth sailing operating the airplane."

Soon after the squadron took a full complement of airplanes in late February, the pilots began engaging in "hot" flying, skimming the harbor waters and flying under bridges. Increasingly, Blackburn was fielding complaints from higher authority about his pilots' behavior in the air. For a while, the behavior abated as they concentrated on training for carrier landing qualification, which began aboard USS *Charger* in March. The pilots soon learned the hard way about the Corsair's tendency to stall without warning with the right wing dropping quickly. Once they began carrier training, several pilots were lost when their airplane stalled while on final approach to the carrier deck. The fighter's long nose meant that when they got the "cut" signal from the LSO, they were unable to see the carrier deck ahead. This was especially true with the F4U-1 "birdcage" Corsair with which they were equipped, in which the pilot was seated low in the cockpit, with a canopy that restricted visibility.

The squadron was fortunate that Blackburn chose Ensign Merl W. "Butch" Davenport as squadron engineering officer. The 24-year-old Davenport had been an engineering major at Wayne University when he left in his junior year to join the Navy AvCad program, receiving his Wings of Gold in May 1942. His engineering prowess quickly made itself known when he suggested using a stall warning strip on the right wing to give the pilot sufficient warning of an impending stall to avoid the dangerous wing drop. As a result, Blackburn had quickly promoted him to Lieutenant (jg) and formally appointed him engineering officer. Davenport worked closely with the Vought tech reps in coming up with solutions to the Corsair's often-deadly problems. The stall warning device was a triangular strip attached to the leading edge of the right wing, just outboard of the wing fold, which acted aerodynamically to provide stall warning by "shaking" the wing and the control stick about 5mph above the stalling speed. Boone Guyton took the invention back to the factory and eventually all Corsairs were fitted with it during production.

Another deadly design fault was the tail hook. If a plane landed heavily on the carrier deck, the hook could snap when it dropped and came into contact with the deck. When combined with the fighter's stiff landing gear that meant any landing but a perfect three-pointer would result in a bounce, during which the tail hook could also bounce up and fail to catch the arresting wire. The result was many Corsairs ending up on their nose, with the prop damaged and the engine in need of major repair work, while the wooden flight deck got chewed up by the turning propeller as the plane went over. This was solved by replacing the original tail hook with a newly designed heavier hook.

Davenport's most important contribution involved finding a solution to the "bounce" when the squadron nearly came a cropper once they went aboard their carrier on July 7, 1943, for the shakedown cruise to Trinidad. Not all the F4U-1s had been equipped with the stall warning plate on the wing, and the new tail hooks had not yet been produced. The big problem faced on the carrier was the airplane's stiff gear. Combined with the other problems, the stiff gear meant that the average Corsair landing was inevitably a crash unless the pilot was able to plant the airplane mid-deck with no side or forward motion on touchdown, something very few pilots could do with the airplane due to the lack of visibility over the long nose. By the time they arrived in Trinidad, *Bunker Hill's* Captain John J. Ballentine was ready to declare the Corsair unfit for service aboard an aircraft carrier. Once back at Norfolk in August, Davenport worked with the Vought service representatives and discovered that if the amount of fluid in the landing gear oleos was reduced, the airplane was "de-bounced." With the three modifications he developed, the Corsair was finally carrier-compatible. Vought service representative Ray DeLava said of Davenport and the squadron, "If it hadn't been for VF-17, we likely would never have gotten the Corsair modified to the point it could successfully operate at sea."

The squadron became known as a "problem" to the authorities due to the aeronautical hi-jinks of the pilots. One of the main culprits was Ensign Ira Cassius Kepford, who had been a star halfback at Northwestern University, where he joined the US Naval Reserve in 1941. He had earned his wings at Corpus Christi, Texas, on November 5, 1942, and was one of the ten original Ensigns assigned to VF-17 when the unit was commissioned. During their early training, Blackburn was forced to confine Kepford to quarters for ten days for mock dogfighting an Army pilot in a P-51 right above the city of Norfolk.

In answer to the "buzzing" complaints that were getting him in trouble with the Norfolk Naval Air Station authorities, Blackburn moved the squadron in April, first to Pungo and then to the even more isolated NAAS Manteo, located on one of the North Carolina offshore islands south of the Virginia border and north of Cape Hatteras, where he felt the pilots could fly as close as possible to real combat flying without running afoul of the authorities and their rules. He and Hedrick concentrated on training the pilots in teamwork. Hedrick explained their goal: "We were trying to meld a team of rugged individualists, to where we had a team that instinctively would react to the enemy. Certain conditions, positions even, so that each member of this team knew that he could count on the other one, knew what to expect of the other one."

Pilot Andrew "Andy" Jagger remembered:

We went through ten very intensive months of effort and the very tragic part of that was that we lost more people in training than the 12 we lost in combat. The word "safety" in war was unheard of. The expectation was that you were going to get killed, or somebody else was, and that was part of it. Really sad but so true.

Dan Cunningham remembered:

I think the big thing about our squadron was that we were good because Blackburn trained the hell out of us. We had the best fighter plane in World War II and we had the best skipper the Navy ever put out and he worked us, and that work paid off because we knew what the hell we were doing, what we were supposed to do.

The squadron soon became known as "Blackburn's Irregulars," sensing that such a name could lead to trouble with the more staid members of higher Navy command, particularly with the antics of pilots like Ensign Howard "Teeth" Buriss, who once flew his fighter inverted at an altitude of 50 feet and speed of 300mph down a two-lane North Carolina country road. Motorists pulled onto the shoulder to avoid what looked like an imminent crash, and one truck driver put his vehicle in the ditch trying to get out of the way. Blackburn recalled that "The admiral sure had me on the carpet for that one!" Wanting to keep the kind of squadron spirit the name implied without the name becoming a prior warning to authorities, Blackburn came up with the squadron insignia: the traditional pirate's flag with skull and crossed bones on a black background, known as the "Jolly Roger," which also fit with the airplane's name, "Corsair," which means pirate. Once the insignia was on the Corsairs, "Jolly Rogers" was adopted as the squadron name. Blackburn later remembered:

> I supposed I was pretty soft hearted or soft headed with my guys. The reason I condoned and encouraged overly aggressive behavior, was that this was going to be required in a combat situation. I was sorely pressed to keep ahead of these guys and turn in a good-enough performance so that I was leading them instead of them leading me.

By the time they finished training and went aboard *Bunker Hill*, each pilot had an average of 250 hours in the Corsair.

"Country" Landreth recalled Blackburn as a leader:

> He demanded top performance, he demanded you be there on time ready to fly, he expected you to be an expert formation flier, he didn't tolerate any lack of discipline in the air. He was inclined to be lenient about things on the ground until you crossed that invisible line. He was certainly a party man himself. I learned early that you don't go ashore with the skipper's group and try to stay up with him, because it was a useless task. He'd be the last one standing, and he'd be the guy that would be there first the next morning.

By the end of August, the squadron was re-equipped with what became known as the "F4U-1A" Corsair, though the Navy never officially used this designation. The main difference between it and the "birdcage" F4U-1 was a "bubble" canopy that allowed the pilot to sit six inches higher in the cockpit, vastly improving vision for takeoff and landing, as well as giving better visibility in combat. Now equipped with a fighter they were convinced was the best available, the "Jolly Rogers" went aboard *Bunker Hill* for the voyage to the Pacific. The carrier departed Norfolk on September 10, and after passing through the Panama Canal, arrived in Pearl Harbor on October 5, 1943.

By the time they arrived at Pearl Harbor, the Navy's Bureau of Aeronautics had decided to remove the Corsair from fleet carriers. The reason was that VF-17 was the only Navy Corsair squadron in the Pacific, which created a logistic difficulty since the supply line was filled with spare parts for the Grumman Hellcat that equipped all the other fleet carrier fighter squadrons. The squadron was given the option of remaining on board if they would transfer to the Hellcat. When Blackburn put this to the pilots, the "No" vote was unanimous. As "Country" Landreth remembered, "The Marines were operating Corsairs in the Solomons and they had all the parts down there, so when we got to Pearl the Navy decided they couldn't support us." After all the training, removal from the carrier air group was a blow to the squadron when they were replaced by the Hellcat-equipped VF-18.

On October 12, 1943, VF-17's 45 officers and 67 enlisted men went aboard the escort carrier USS *Prince William* (CVE-31) with their 36 Corsairs. The ship left Ford Island at 0730 hours the next morning, headed for Espiritu Santo. Arriving off the island on October 25, the Corsairs were launched to fly to Turtle Bay airfield while the carrier dropped anchor in the harbor and the rest of the squadron went ashore. Thirty-four Corsairs left Espiritu Santo at 1130 hours the next day, arriving at Henderson Field at 1515 hours. The next morning they departed Guadalcanal at 0600 hours and arrived at what would be their first operational base, Ondonga airfield on the island of Ondonga, off New Georgia, at 0730 hours. When they learned the name meant "place of death," it was taken as an omen of what was to come. There was no time spent becoming acclimated, since they flew their first three combat air patrols over the invasion of the Treasury Islands by dark. The rest of the squadron personnel were flown to Henderson, then on to Munda, arriving at Ondonga by boat from Munda at 2100 hours that evening. The squadron shared the airfield with fellow naval fighter squadron

VF-33's F6F-3 Hellcats and the P-40Ms of 15 and 18 squadrons of the RNZAF. Once in the forward area, Blackburn relaxed the rules about shaving and within a matter of weeks most of the pilots sported full beards that added to their reputation as pirates.

After a few more uneventful patrols, the Corsairs finally fired their guns in anger for the first time when Blackburn led 24 Corsairs to Tonolei Harbor on Bougainville, where they strafed shipping and harbor installations, sinking an 80-ton coastal steamer after setting it afire, as well as several landing barges before breaking off to return to Ondonga. Over the course of the next two days, the Jolly Rogers escorted Marine Avengers and Dauntlesses on missions to strike targets in Bougainville in preparation for the coming invasion.

Finally, the pilots found the opportunity to put their skills to the test against an airborne enemy on November 1, D-Day for Operation *Shoestring*, the invasion of Bougainville. Two divisions led by Tom Blackburn were orbiting over the invasion force when a formation of 40 Zeros and 16 Val dive bombers were spotted inbound over Mount Sugarloaf. Blackburn led the Corsairs in his F4U-1A named "Big Hog" as they dived on the enemy fighters, which didn't spot the approaching nemesis until the Navy fliers were some 2,000 feet away from the formation. Blackburn later described his first combat:

> I had a flight of eight Corsairs as part of the combat air patrol over Empress Augusta Bay. I spotted the enemy formation northeast from us at a distance of 25 miles. When we were about a mile away, the Japanese leader spotted us and honked around in as tight a turn as he could, to counter our attack. I fired at him and as far as I could tell I didn't hit him.
>
> I turned and went back into the mad scramble of airplanes and picked up a Zero and bored in on him to point-blank range. When he blew up I was close enough to get gasoline and hydraulic fluid on the windshield of my airplane. When I got that first flamer the sensation was almost identical to my first piece of ass.

Blackburn and his wingman, Lieutenant (jg) Danny Gutenkunst, then spotted a Corsair being pursued by a Zero. Blackburn managed to close on the enemy fighter and fire a burst that caused the pilot to turn away from the Corsair he was pursuing. Blackburn closed to 100 yards astern and fired again; the Zero caught fire, rolled over and crashed into the water of the bay below.

Ensign Frank Streig and Lieutenant (jg) Tom Killefer, the second section in Blackburn's division, spotted a Zero and made a run on it. Streig opened fire, hitting the enemy fighter in the wingroot. It caught fire and crashed. They then spotted another Zero over Mount Bagana that Killefer shot down. Lieutenant T.R. Bell and Lieutenant (jg) Ed May, the first element of the second division, spotted more enemy fighters and Bell shot down one.

Back at Ondonga, the pilots all remarked on how unaggressive the enemy pilots had been, only attacking Corsairs that had become separated from their wingmen. The total score for the squadron's first combat was two Zeros shot down and two damaged for Blackburn and one shot down for his wingman Gutenkunst, one each shot down for Streig, Killefer, Ensign Beacham, and a "damaged" for Lieutenant Bell.

That afternoon, a two-division CAP led by XO Roger Hedrick was vectored by the Fighter Direction Officer to intercept bogies spotted southeast of Cape Torokina. The bogies turned out to be nine Zeros flying at 23,000 feet. Hedrick closed on the enemy and opened fire on a Zero that caught fire and spun in, recalling that "I pressed the trigger maybe two seconds and he went up in a ball of fire." Hedrick's wingman, Lieutenant (jg) Mike Schanuel, fired at a Zero but missed, then spotted another formation of Vals that he attacked, damaging one. Other pilots engaged the Zeros, finding that this formation of enemy planes was more aggressive than those Blackburn had run across as they maintained their two-plane elements. Like those in the morning, the airplanes appeared brand new and, in fact, they were, being part of the Rabaul reinforcement from the Imperial Navy's carriers at Truk.

The day saw the Jolly Rogers' first combat loss, when Lieutenant Jim Halford led a two-division CAP over the invasion in the late afternoon. Spotting two enemy landing craft, the Corsairs dived to strafe them, bringing themselves under fire from AA positions on Poporang and Faisi islands. Lieutenant (jg) John H. Keith, leader of the second section in the second division, and his wingman and best friend "Country" Landreth, were in trail behind Halford's four Corsairs. Landreth remembered, "Boy, were they waiting for us! They saw us from I don't know how far out, but when we popped over the ridge I've never seen anything like it before or since. There were black 40mm explosions at our altitude like a flat black roof!" Landreth broke away to make a pass on a barge he spotted, then turned back to join up with Keith. "He was streaming white smoke, which is engine oil vapor – I knew right then that Johnny was not going home that day."

Two minutes later, Keith's engine failed. Landreth realized the ditching, 15 miles southeast of Faisi Island, wasn't going right when he noticed Keith unsuccessfully trying to lock his canopy open. "He wasn't a big guy, and he just couldn't get the canopy to lock, so when he landed it slid forward and slammed closed when he hit the water." Keith struggled to get out of the sinking Corsair and he unsnapped his parachute and life raft to squeeze out of the narrow opening. When he turned back to pull out his gear, the Corsair sank before he could do so. Landreth turned on his IFF and circled overhead while Halford called Barakoma airfield on Vella Lavella and requested a PBY "Dumbo" make a pickup, but it was too late for the flying boat to get there before dark. Landreth remembered, "I stayed until it was dark. The next morning we went out pre-dawn looking for Johnny – a whole bunch of airplanes flying all over the area. We never found him. So I lost my best friend the first day in combat. It was a little difficult to handle that."

When Imperial Navy headquarters at Rabaul received reports the Allies had landed at Empress Augusta Bay the morning of November 1, Eighth Fleet commander Vice Admiral Tomoshige Samejima immediately embarked 1,000 Special Naval Landing Force troops on five destroyers at Rabaul and ordered them to make a counter-landing on Cape Torokina. An escort force composed of the heavy cruisers *Myoko* and *Haguro*, the light cruiser *Agano* of the 10th Cruiser Squadron with the destroyers *Naganami*, *Hatsukaze*, and *Wakatsuki*, and the light cruiser *Sendai* with the destroyers *Shigure*, *Samidare*, and *Shiratsuyu* of the 3rd Destroyer Squadron, commanded by Vice Admiral Sentaro Omori, was hastily assembled; the units had never trained or fought together before. That night, the force was spotted by an American submarine and a search plane. Worried he had lost the element of surprise, Omori asked permission from Admiral Samejima to return the transport destroyers to Rabaul while he continued on to attack the Allied fleet still in Empress Augusta Bay. Samejima agreed and Omori pressed ahead.

At Bougainville, Rear Admiral A. Stanton "Tip" Merrill commanded Task Force 39, consisting of Cruiser Division (CruDiv) 12, with light cruisers USS *Montpelier* (CL-57), *Cleveland* (CL-55), *Columbia*

(CL-56), and *Denver* (CL-58), and two destroyer divisions – DesDiv 45 with USS *Charles Ausburne* (DD-570), *Dyson* (DD-572), *Stanley* (DD-478), and *Claxton* (DD-571), commanded by Captain Arleigh A. "31-Knot" Burke and known as "The Little Beavers." They were reinforced by DesDiv 46: USS *Spence* (DD-512), *Thatcher* (DD-514), *Converse* (DD-509), and *Foote* (DD-511).

Upon receiving the submarine report, the landing craft and troop transports were evacuated. TF 39 steamed slowly north from Empress Augusta Bay. Radar contact with the enemy happened at 0230 hours on November 2. With DesDiv 45 in the leading position, Commodore Burke ordered his destroyers to attack; at 0245 hours they fired a torpedo salvo at the enemy. Simultaneously, the Japanese 3rd Destroyer Division fired 18 torpedoes. Each side detected the other's attack and both sides successfully maneuvered away from the torpedoes. The Japanese formation was broken up when 3rd Destroyer Squadron turned into the path of the 10th Cruiser Division; in the confusion the fleet became separated into three groups: north, center, and south. At 0245 hours, the American light cruisers opened fire under radar control. The action became confused and the American radar was not as helpful as expected. Several Japanese ships collided with other ships in their force, while American ships narrowly missed collisions with ships of their force.

After an hour's exchange of fire, the Japanese cruisers were increasingly accurate and the American cruisers were forced to maneuver behind a smoke screen while taking hits that were not vital. Throughout, the US ships missed opportunities to attack the enemy out of fear they were attacking their own which had lost their IFF gear. At 0320 hours, Admiral Omori, worried about being caught in daylight by Allied aircraft, ordered a retreat. At daylight TF 39 broke off pursuit of the stragglers and all ships were ordered to rendezvous.

The day of November 2 was spent defending the landing beaches from strong Japanese air attacks. Poor fighter direction prevented VF-17 and the other Ondonga-based squadrons from successfully engaging these attacks. Fortunately, the attacks were not well-coordinated and no serious damage was inflicted. The next day, Admiral Halsey learned from a reconnaissance flight that four more cruisers and several more destroyers had arrived at Rabaul from Truk to reinforce the Eighth Fleet for a renewed attack on the Allied forces. He requested emergency help from Admiral Nimitz at Pearl Harbor, later stating that the threat the

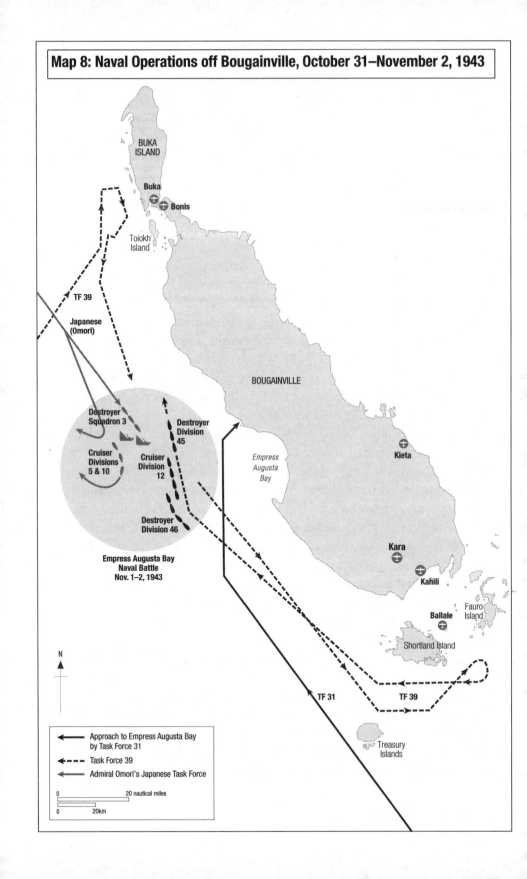

Map 8: Naval Operations off Bougainville, October 31–November 2, 1943

BUKA ISLAND

Buka

Bonis

Toiokh Island

TF 39

Japanese (Omori)

BOUGAINVILLE

Destroyer Squadron 3

Destroyer Division 45

Kieta

Cruiser Divisions 5 & 10

Cruiser Division 12

Empress Augusta Bay

Destroyer Division 46

Kara

Empress Augusta Bay Naval Battle Nov. 1–2, 1943

Kahili

Ballale

Fauro Island

Shortland Island

N

TF 31

TF 39

Treasury Islands

⟵ Approach to Empress Augusta Bay by Task Force 31

⟵--- Task Force 39

⟵ Admiral Omori's Japanese Task Force

0   20 nautical miles

0   20km

cruiser force at Rabaul posed to the Bougainville invasion was "the most desperate emergency that confronted me in my entire time as ComSoPac."

Halsey's emergency request caught Admiral Nimitz's Central Pacific Force committed to the coming invasion of the Gilbert Islands later that month, but he released Task Group 50.3, composed of *Essex* (CV-9), *Bunker Hill*, and *Independence* (CVL-22), commanded by Rear Admiral Alfred E. Montgomery, which left Pearl Harbor the morning of November 3.

The only carrier force immediately at hand in the South Pacific was Task Force 38, which had provided air cover for the Bougainville invasion. The force was composed of the veteran *Saratoga* and the new *Princeton* (CVL-23), commanded by Rear Admiral Frederick C. Sherman, who had commanded the first *Lexington* at the Battle of the Coral Sea. When Sherman received Halsey's order the evening of November 4 to strike Rabaul, the ships were refueling near Rennell Island. Other than Pearl Harbor, no other well-defended land target had ever been struck by carrier aircraft. The proposed strike was considered highly dangerous for the aircrews and placed the ships at risk. The fate of the invasion hung in the balance.

Racing north at 27 knots, Task Force 38 arrived at the launch point 57 miles northwest of Bougainville's Cape Torokina at 0900 hours on November 5. There was enough wind for an easy launch and enough cloud cover to confuse the enemy snoopers that spotted the force into reporting only cruisers were present. The two carriers launched all 97 aircraft – 52 F6F-3 Hellcats from *Saratoga*'s VF-12 and *Princeton*'s VF-23, 23 TBF-1C Avengers from VT-12 and VT-23, and 22 *Saratoga* VB-12 SBD-5 Dauntlesses, while two land-based fighter squadrons from Barakoma and Vella Lavella provided cover over the fleet.

Fortunately, the strike achieved almost complete surprise, since over 150 aircraft were present at Rabaul. A combat air patrol of 70 Zeros met the strike, but the defenders expected the Americans to split up before attacking, allowing them to attack smaller formations and overwhelm them. By the time they realized the attackers were holding formation right through the heavy flak, it was too late for an effective interception. In spite of heavy antiaircraft fire and waiting fighters, only five Hellcats and five Dauntlesses were lost. An hour later, 27 Fifth Air Force B-24 Liberators escorted by 58 P-38s bombed the harbor.

Six of the seven cruisers in Simpson Harbor were damaged, four heavily by the two attacks. *Atago* was near-missed by three bombs that caused severe damage and killed 22, including her captain. *Maya* was hit by one bomb above an engine room that killed 70 and caused heavy damage. *Mogami* was set afire by one 500-pound bomb, suffering heavy damage and 19 dead. *Takao* was hit by two 500-pound bombs that killed 23 and caused heavy damage. Several near misses slightly damaged *Chikuma*. The attacks ended the warship threat to the Allied landing forces at Bougainville when Admiral Koga was forced to order the damaged cruisers back to Truk for repair. That night, Halsey sent a message to Sherman: "My utmost admiration for your brilliant performance during recent operations. Your strike was another shot heard round the world. When the *Saratoga* is given a chance, she is deadly."

Task Group 50.3 dropped anchor at Espiritu Santo in the early evening of November 5 after three days at sea on a high-speed run from Pearl, where they learned of the strike by *Saratoga* and *Princeton*. The next day, the aircrews were informed they would make a second strike against Rabaul. VF-9 Hellcat pilot Lieutenant (jg) Hamilton "Mac" McWhorter remembered:

> We were very concerned when we heard we were going there. They lost ten or 11 airplanes in that strike. We were told we could expect to find 80–90 Zekes there. What no one knew was the Japanese had flown in more fighters from their carriers at Truk down to Rabaul the day after that raid. When we got there, we were up against approximately 160 Zeros.

In the next day's edition of *Essex's* shipboard newspaper, *The Buccaneer*, a cartoon showed the crew jumping overboard on being told they were headed for Rabaul.

On November 8, VF-17 demonstrated they possessed "the right stuff" on their third mission of the day, when the command ship radioed "Bogies!" to an eight-plane flight that had been reduced to six led by Executive Officer Roger Hedrick. The Corsairs swung southwest in a full-power climb. In minutes, Hedrick spotted 24 Zeros covering 15 Vals. He promptly gave chase with his four-plane division, ordering the two remaining Corsairs from the second division to provide high cover. He was astonished to see the more numerous Zeros respond to his attack by turning into a defensive Lufbery Circle, while the Vals retired to the north. With his initial altitude advantage, Hedrick decided to "dive and zoom" the Lufbery formation, making repeated firing runs. During the ensuing fight the three two-plane sections kept their integrity. While the official records only credited the flight with two kills and five "damaged," the battle removed Hedrick's remaining skepticism about the Corsair. This had been the first real test of the F4U in a maximum combat situation, and it made him a believer. He had experienced first-hand how the Corsair outclassed the Zero in all fighting qualities except horizontal maneuverability. Through the teamwork he and Blackburn had hammered into the squadron during training, the outnumbered Jolly Rogers came out of the fight without loss.

At Ondonga, Blackburn was told VF-17 would provide air cover for the carriers during the strikes on November 11, landing aboard to refuel and rearm. He later recalled:

> I was told two days beforehand that we would be flying out from Ondonga to land aboard the carriers in the Solomon Sea for their raid against Rabaul. We had taken the arresting hooks off the aircraft to lighten them and I had to tip my hand somewhat by telling the maintenance gang to install the hooks and insure they worked properly, but to keep their mouths shut.

Blackburn would lead 12 Corsairs that would land aboard *Bunker Hill* while Hedrick led 12 that would land aboard *Essex*.

Crew Chief George Mauhar recalled being told by engineering officer Butch Davenport that they had to put the tailhooks back on:

> We had taken off all the tailhooks three weeks earlier. When I found out we had to put them back on, I thought oh my God, what did we do with them? They were lying out there by the planes all rusting, lying in mud and water. We had to test them by putting the planes in flight attitude and then use a scale to test the pull on the hooks. We got them all on, and fortunately they all worked!

Sherman's Task Force 38 was under cover of a weather front near Green Island when they launched a dawn strike of 55 Hellcats, 25 Avengers, and 21 Dauntlesses on November 11. After flying through clouds most of the way, they found Simpson Harbor almost completely cloud-covered. The SBDs and TBFs concentrated on three cruisers visible in the rain and hit one. The defending force of 70 Zeros chased the raiders in and out of the clouds but only caught seven; five bombers returned to the carriers with battle damage while VF-12 scored one victory. Once the strike returned, TF 38 retired to the south, undetected by the enemy.

Shortly after dawn, the 24 Fighting 17 Corsairs, along with 12 Hellcats from VF-33, arrived over Task Group 50.3, which was in the Solomon Sea 165 miles southeast of Rabaul, and took up CAP. They were joined by Corsairs from VMF-212 and VMF-221, and P-40s of 15 Squadron, RNZAF. At 0945 hours, the three carriers launched a total of 185 aircraft, including 16 new SB2C-1 Helldivers of VB-17 on their combat debut. When it came time for the land-based squadrons to return to New Georgia, VF-17 lowered their recently reinstalled tailhooks and came aboard their old home, *Bunker Hill*, while VF-33 went aboard *Essex*. Hedrick remembered, "We were there to protect this task force from what was going to be a large raid coming in from Rabaul. So we knew that everything they could throw at us would be coming our way very shortly." Once aboard their old home, they were treated to a meal in the wardroom that beat the C-rations they had been getting used to ashore. Blackburn remembered, "We landed aboard, refueled and rearmed and had breakfast. After eating from an Army mess with spam, battery acid coffee and scrambled eggs made from powdered eggs, which was something less than superb, we had linen tablecloths, orange juice, corned beef hash and poached eggs." Blackburn was proud that, after having not operated from a carrier since September, all 24 Corsairs landed with no wave-offs. "Every approach was right the first time so that we got a cut and there were no blown tires and scraped wingtips. No damage whatsoever and the people on the ships couldn't believe that we could turn in such a smooth performance after a two-month lay-off."

While the Jolly Rogers were reacquainting themselves with civilization, the strike forces over Rabaul found an uneven reception from the enemy. Spotting a long line of warships leaving the harbor at high speed, VF-9's "Mac" McWhorter went after a heavy cruiser.

It seemed like every weapon on the cruiser and all the other warships were firing at me and I could actually see the eight-inch shells coming at me. I opened fire from about 2,500 feet out, and fired about a four-second burst at the open AA gun batteries, then zoomed over her. I thought that incredible flak barrage was going to get me for sure.

The heavy cruiser was *Atago*, which had remained at Rabaul after the November 5 strike; she was later torpedoed and damaged in this attack.

As he headed for the rendezvous point, McWhorter saw a huge World War I-style dogfight west of the harbor, involving some 24 Hellcats and about 50 Zeros.

I saw one Zero ahead that was scoring heavily on another Hellcat. I came in behind him and fired a short burst. I saw him explode, but couldn't tell if the Hellcat escaped. Then, all of a sudden, I heard a sound like when someone throws a handful of large rocks on a galvanized tin roof. It was the sound of bullets hitting my plane! I snapped into a split-S to get away from whoever was on my tail, and as I dove straight down there was another Zero passing right in front of me and he blew up when I fired a short burst and he flew into it. It seemed like I'd been in that fight for an hour, but all of a sudden I was alone and when I looked at my watch, the whole thing hadn't lasted a minute.

Fighting 9 claimed 14 Zeros, including one shot down by Lieutenant (jg) Hal Vita, putting him on the road to becoming the only Navy ace whose score included two Vichy French Curtiss Hawk-75s shot down over Morocco during Operation *Torch*.

Bunker Hill's VF-18, commanded by Lieutenant Commander Sam L. Silber, stayed close to the bombers but managed to score two Zeros. *Independence's* VF-22, supplemented by a 12-plane detachment from VF-6, scored four for the loss of three Hellcats. The Imperial Navy admitted an actual loss of six Zeros, as compared with claims from the three fighter squadrons for 30, though the enemy records also mentioned many fighters returning damaged. Overall, the strike was successful, with one destroyer sunk, another destroyer and light cruiser badly damaged, and three other ships lightly damaged, including *Atago*. The attacking squadrons lost only 11 aircraft.

Back in the Solomon Sea, *Essex's* radar spotted an incoming raid 119 miles distant that was following the returning strike. Most of the returning aircraft managed to get back aboard the carriers before the retaliatory strike arrived overhead. The Corsairs had been launched shortly after their "brunch," and ranged themselves for combat. The enemy strike was composed of 67 Zeros, 27 Val dive bombers, 14 Kate torpedo bombers, and a few G4M1 Betty twin-engine bombers. The 12 VF-33 Hellcats and 20 VF-17 Corsairs were vectored toward them. The Vals managed to evade the defending fighters but found the antiaircraft over the fleet accurate and deadly. No ships were hit, but Admiral Montgomery was compelled to cancel a second strike against Rabaul shortly after the launch began.

The *Independence* FDO vectored a VF-17 division toward the enemy at 1230 hours, which turned out to be a formation of JAAF Ki.61 Tony fighters. Ensign Streig got on the tail of one Tony and it exploded. He recalled:

> I was on a combat station at about 20,000 feet northeast of the carrier and the radar picked up a bogey coming in from the northeast. My division was sent out to investigate. We caught up with them and one immediately headed for the water and we took off after him down to about 500 feet. I made a run behind him and blew him up.

The division was later vectored to a large bogey that turned out to be 40–50 Vals and Kates at 18,000 feet and 50–60 Zeros between 20,000 and 25,000 feet. Division leader Lieutenant (jg) Cordray and his wingman Ensign Baker attacked one group of fighters while Streig and Ensign Cunningham attacked another. Streig described the fight:

> We were climbing, weaving in and out of the clouds and we looked to the left and we saw the whole Japanese force coming toward the carriers. I called the FDO and told him the shit was about to hit the fan. We got above them and dived on them. I got another flamer and two probables and started running out of fuel. They couldn't take me aboard so I headed back for the beach. I got as far as Vella Lavella and landed and as I turned down the taxiway my engine quit, out of fuel! We were airborne for about 3–4 hours, of which about two-and-a-half hours was hectic combat.

Cordray and Baker engaged the enemy and Cordray scored one he was certain was going down when it disappeared from the fight while Baker shot down a Zero that exploded. When they disengaged, they were too low on fuel to remain and were directed to return home. Baker's engine stopped, out of fuel, over Wilson Strait. He spotted a PBY Dumbo on the water and successfully ditched nearby shortly after 1500 hours, getting out of the Corsair just as it headed for the bottom. After five minutes in the water he was picked up by the PBY. Cordray was able to land at Barakoma at 1545 hours with his fuel gauge registering "zero."

Blackburn remembered:

> The melee was beyond description. The carriers had to land their airplanes while the enemy was pressing home their attack. Antiaircraft fire was not suppressed because there were friendlies around. They fired at anything that was in the air, including us. During the course of this action, Ike Kepford got four and I got one. We lost one airplane but the pilot was recovered.

Blackburn's victim was another JAAF Tony that spun into the water in flames after being hit in the wing root.

Blackburn had to duck into a cloud when he was chased by another flight of Tonys. When he came back out, he was right in front of Roger Hedrick and his wingman, Ensign Schanuel. As Hedrick recalled, "I spotted one Zero trying to get back to Rabaul and I took after him. Just as I got into firing position, he went into a big cloud. A moment later I thought I saw him coming back out. It was a full-deflection shot and I was squeezing the trigger when I realized it was a Corsair!" Blackburn remembered, "It was a beautiful shot – three bullets through the accessory section and three behind the armor plate at the back of the seat." Hedrick concluded, "Thank God I was a lousy shot." The three joined up and headed for home, landing at Barakoma at 1440 hours.

"Teeth" Buriss, who had flown inverted down back country roads during training, spotted a Betty being chased by several Hellcats. He dived on the bomber and shot it into the water with a long burst, then spotted a Kate that he nearly overshot before running up on it so fast that it exploded and he flew through the fireball. When he came out the other side he spotted a Kate making a run on the carriers and got behind it, shooting it down from an altitude of 1,000 feet to explode when it hit the water. Low on fuel and now alone, he turned for home and had enough fuel to land at Barakoma with ten gallons still aboard at 1430 hours.

Buriss's section leader, Lieutenant Kleinman, ran across eight Kates heading for the carriers at 500 feet. He hit the leader, which caught fire and crashed into the water. He flew over the destroyer screen through their antiaircraft fire and was going after a second Kate when he was hit in his cockpit by a 40mm shell fired by one of the ships that blew up his instrument panel and wounded him in his face. He managed to avoid two F6Fs that made a run on him and then navigated home by the sun, dropping onto the runway at Barakoma at 1445 hours.

Lieutenant (jg) Robert "Windy" Hill recalled the battle: "Suddenly the sky was filled with a mass of turning, twisting, diving aircraft. It was a fantastic sight. The air seemed to be filled with black puffs of bursting 5-inch AA shells. Japanese aircraft were exploding and hitting the ocean engulfed in flames. It was a wild free-for-all, a survival of the fittest." Hill plunged into the melee and spotted a Kate headed for *Bunker Hill.*

> I went into a high-speed dive, approaching from the left rear, ignoring the wall of antiaircraft fire from our ships that was exploding near the Kate. As I centered it in my gunsight and commenced firing, I could see tracer bullets coming at me from the rear seat gunner. My bullets were hitting now and suddenly it burst into a mass of flames, slowly turning upside down and crashing into the ocean.

He later explained how he felt on scoring his first victory: "There is nothing more exciting or thrilling than aerial combat, where you kill the enemy pilot before he can kill you. It's not like a ball game where if you lose you can play again tomorrow. If you lose in this arena, there is no tomorrow!"

Returning to base with his section leader, Lieutenant Pillsbury, Hill realized he didn't have enough gas to get there. He turned for the Treasury Islands, which he knew had just been taken from the enemy. A few miles offshore, he ran out of gas. Managing a successful ditching, he got out of the Corsair just before it went down. After ten minutes in the water, he saw a man in a small canoe put out from shore, who turned out to be a native who worked with the local coastwatcher. After radioing Hill's position, Pillsbury flew on to Barakoma where he landed at 1515 with 27 gallons, the last Jolly Roger to land there from the mission.

During the air battle, fighters on the carriers that were ready were launched to reinforce the CAP. Ensign C.T. Watts of VF-18 had only begun to retract his wheels from his launch when a Val appeared in front of him and he shot it down. Lieutenant (jg) Rube Denoff of VF-9 had a similar experience when he was launched from *Essex*. "I didn't have time to even retract my wheels before I had a Val in front of me." He shot it down, then found his wingman and shot down a Kate before he was hit by "friendly fire" and forced to make an emergency landing back aboard *Essex*. Radio control over the fleet broke down, forcing the defending fighters to fly toward flak bursts to engage the enemy.

Ensign Ike Kepford, who had scored his first four victories, three Vals and a Kate, during the battle found himself so low on fuel that he requested permission to land aboard *Bunker Hill* to refuel. During the 30 minutes the Corsair was being serviced, he managed a quick hot shower and was well-rested when he took off. He flew all the way back to Ondonga and landed at 1630 hours. In the air battles over Bougainville during the rest of November, Kepford went scoreless until the squadron returned for their second tour in mid-January 1944. In the swirling battles over Rabaul in what turned out to be the last Japanese aerial resistance in the South Pacific, he would shoot down 12 more Japanese aircraft to become VF-17's leading ace.

American claims for 90 shot down in the attack were as excessive as the claims over Rabaul, but the Japanese admitted losing eight Zeros and 31 Vals and Kates. VF-17 was credited with 18 shot down and seven damaged. Hedrick recalled, "Later we heard word from the task force commander that they were extremely pleased with the performance of Fighting 17." When asked to compare the Rabaul strike with later events in his career as the first Hellcat Ace, Hamilton McWhorter replied, "On a terror scale of 1–10, Rabaul was an 8. It was definitely my most memorable mission."

The damage inflicted on the Imperial Navy during the November 5 and 11 air strikes finally removed the Eighth Fleet as a threat. The fleet's ships had opposed the US Navy since the first battle off Savo Island on August 7, 1942, and had fought numerous sea battles through the American offensive in the Solomons, giving at least as good as they got over the 15-month struggle. Marine and naval air units would soon be able to use Bougainville as a base that was only 190 miles from their target and Rabaul would come under increasing attack. The evening of November 11, the Imperial Navy's Destroyer Division Two commander, Captain Hara, wrote, "The futility of our losses and the stupidity of our high command struck me forcibly, and I cursed aloud while wondering what Japan could do."

On November 16, the Jolly Rogers sent a two-division CAP over the invasion beaches led by Roger Hedrick that was vectored to enemy aircraft attempting to attack shipping. Hedrick's division went after a formation of three Kates and four Zeros, while the second division, led by Lieutenant Timmy Gile, attacked a formation identified as five Kates and five Tonys. Hedrick flamed one Zero while section leader Jack Chasnoff got a second. Hedrick circled, looking for other enemy aircraft, and saw a pilot parachuting, who was identified as Lieutenant (jg) Robert S. "Andy" Anderson, Chasnoff's wingman. He later remembered:

> I was following this guy down and the first thing I knew, I saw tracers going by my own airplane. I could feel hits and broke away to look for damage but couldn't see any. I saw another target and took off after him, but as I was firing I started to get smoke in the cockpit, so I broke off and saw a fire in my right wing. The cockpit was getting smoky. I started to bail out and I couldn't shake myself loose from my oxygen mask and my headphone cord. I got back in the airplane and disconnected them, and then I rolled the airplane over and dropped out. My 'chute opened just before I hit the water – Jack said I was below 800 feet when I went out. I got my raft out and climbed in and waved to the guys that I was okay.

Chasnoff got his first two kills in the fight, the first one being the Zero that shot up his wingman, which he shot down with a deflection shot as it turned away from shooting at Anderson. A Zero turned toward him and he then got involved in the dogfight that ended in his second victory. After the fight, he couldn't find Anderson, though he stayed and continued searching until low fuel forced him to break off and return to Ondonga.

Early the next morning, Butch Davenport took a division on a special pre-dawn flight to try to catch enemy aircraft that had been making dawn strafing attacks on the invasion beaches. This morning, they didn't appear. As the four Corsairs flew back into the rising sun, with the ocean below still dark, Davenport spotted what he took to be a flashing light on the water. Circling lower, he determined it might be a pilot in a raft. He called the rescue frequency and turned on his IFF so a radar fix could be taken, then led the division back toward Ondonga. Arriving back, he found nothing had been done to find the pilot he thought he had spotted, and so he went back with his wingman Chico Freeman to make a search. After about 20 minutes at low altitude flying at slow speed, he spotted a pilot in a life raft who turned out to be Anderson, and was able to call in a PBY to pick him up. Back at the hospital on Ondonga, Anderson was congratulated for being so lucky to have a flashlight and be spotted. He replied he had no flashlight. Davenport went back out in the late afternoon and spent an hour looking for the pilot whose flashlight he had spotted, but no one was ever found. As Davenport put it, "The irony is another pilot's efforts with his flashlight resulted in my finding Andy and saving him, while the other guy was lost. Fate is the hunter. You can't understand these things, why they occur the way they do."

Davenport's plan to catch the enemy by surprise when they attacked at dawn finally paid off on November 21. Leading a division with Chico Freeman as his wingman, with Lieutenant Ray Beacham and Ensign Andy Jagger as second section, the Corsairs were just west of Cape Torokina, which Davenport had decided was the direction from which the enemy planes were coming from studying previous reports of the strafings, when he noticed splashes in the water that turned out to be bombs. Turning toward the cape, he spotted six Zeros at low altitude, 500 yards to the division's right. As he turned the division toward them, the enemy pilots spotted the Corsairs and dropped their belly tanks, then four of them took up a Lufbery Circle while the other two disappeared into the darkness over the cape.

Davenport and Freeman made a flat side run on the four and he picked one off that caught fire. The pilot bailed out and was picked up and made prisoner by a PT boat. In the meantime, the two Zeros that had turned away came back into the fight and Beacham spotted them. He and Jagger attacked. As Beacham followed then down, Jagger suddenly discovered he had one on his tail. As he turned to make another pass, Davenport saw the Zero on Jagger's tail and closed to pick him off. A burst of fire sent the enemy pilot banking away, at which point Davenport latched onto a third Zero and shot it into the bay below. While he had done all this, Freeman had shot down the second Zero he'd attacked and missed. The two became momentarily separated and Freeman found another Zero that he chased for a minute before setting it afire. With the enemy off his tail, Jagger spotted the last Zero and shot it down in flames. The four pilots had shot down all six of the enemy fighters they had surprised.

By the end of their first month in combat, VF-17 was credited with shooting down 45 enemy aircraft. On December 2, the Jolly Rogers completed their first combat tour and flew down to Espiritu Santo, from where they flew out the next day for two weeks' R&R in Sydney. Fighting 17 was singular as the only Navy Corsair squadron in the Solomons, and thus "owned" their airplanes, unlike the Marines, a status that caused resentment among the Marine squadrons which were forced to share their aircraft among squadrons rotated in and out of theater on an operational tour. While most of the Marine squadrons were still flying F4U-1 "bird cage" Corsairs, VF-17's F4U-1As were the latest version; being their own airplanes meant they were kept in better condition than was possible for the Marine squadrons. When the pilots went to Sydney, their airplanes remained on the field at Espiritu Santo, unused by any other squadron while the ground crews took the opportunity to completely overhaul the well-used fighters.

On arrival back from Sydney just before Christmas, VF-17 remained on Espiritu Santo for the next five weeks while replacement pilots for those lost in combat came aboard and were absorbed into the squadron, receiving at least 50 hours each of accelerated advanced flight training so they would be up to speed with the veterans when they returned to combat. They returned to operations in late January, 1944. The front line had moved to Bougainville and they would fly from Bougainville's Piva Yoke fighter airfield in what would prove to be the final offensive against Rabaul.

The squadron's first mission of their second tour was escort for SBDs on a mission to Rabaul to hit Lakunai airdrome on January 26, 1944. The enemy defenders were airborne when they arrived and a fight broke out over the field. Blackburn scored first, hitting a Zero that flamed, while his wingman, Lieutenant (jg) Gutenkunst, got two. On return, claims were made for a total of eight destroyed, but it came at a high cost with two Corsairs shot down and four damaged.

Over the next four days from January 27 to 30, the rainy season weather cleared sufficiently for missions to be flown every day and the Jolly Rogers took full advantage. Blackburn came up with a strategy to send in two Corsairs at 30,000 feet ahead of the main formation, to hit the defenders as they were getting off the ground and organized. On January 29, Ike Kepford and "Teeth" Buriss proved the value of the idea on a mission escorting SBDs to Tobera, when the two of them spotted 12 Zeros 6,000 feet below. In the course of ten minutes, using the Corsair's dive-and-zoom capability, each knocked down four of the enemy, completely disrupting the planned enemy attack. The SBDs bombed with only AA to oppose them while the main escorts shot down two more defending fighters.

While the Jolly Rogers claimed 54.5 victories (sharing a score with VMF-215) over the four days, they paid a steep price, losing ten aircraft and six pilots – half the total losses of their entire South Pacific tour – including "Teeth" Buriss, who was last seen gliding out to sea streaming smoke after a fight near Tobera on January 31. During the first six days of their second tour, VF-17 claimed a total of 60 victories. The operational pace kept up and multiple kills became a norm, with Blackburn himself scoring four A6Ms on February 6. While the confirmed results were ultimately wildly out of correlation with enemy losses, the fact was that this period saw the largest and wildest air combats of the entire Pacific War, with American pilots scoring against progressively less-experienced and less-qualified opponents.

Butch Davenport had taken a while to get his "shooting eye," scoring only twice in the Jolly Rogers' first tour. Following the squadron's return for their second tour, he shot down two Zeros on February 16, which turned out to be the last "big day" over Rabaul. Then, on February 19, just before the Imperial Navy evacuated their surviving aircraft back to Truk, he scored four to become one of three pilots in the squadron to perform such a feat.

On February 18, Roger Hedrick took his division as high cover on a mission to hit Vunakanau. This time, the enemy was waiting for them and the four Corsairs found themselves fighting off eight Zeros. Hedrick led them in a climb to get above the enemy, then reversed and dived on the Zeros, setting two on fire and exploding a third, while the rest of the division knocked down four more, leaving one to tell the tale. The seven victories put VF-17 in the lead for the title of most successful Corsair squadron in the Solomons campaign.

Unknown to the Allies, February 19 would see the final large-scale air combat of the Rabaul campaign. AirSols sent 72 SBDs and Avengers, escorted by 20 Kiwi P-40s and 54 Corsairs and Hellcats, including 26 Jolly Rogers, to hit the main fighter field at Lakunai. Lieutenant Oscar Chenoweth and wingman Lieutenant (jg) Danny Cunningham got the high-cover assignment, arriving over the target at 30,000 feet, 20 minutes before the raid. Spiraling down to 24,000 feet in search of the enemy, they finally spotted a formation of enemy fighters, climbing to position themselves to hit the incoming raid. The two Corsairs hit the Zeros at 18,000 feet, scoring two each on their first pass. In a fight that ranged down to the deck, they became separated. Chenoweth shot down two more before he got into a turning fight with what he identified as an Imperial Army Air Force Ki.44 Tojo (which was impossible, since there were no Ki.44-equipped squadrons at Rabaul at this time), flying so low over Simpson Harbor that the enemy fighter caught a wingtip in the water attempting to out-turn him and went in before he could open fire. He had just become VF-17's last "ace in a day."

The enemy wasn't through. As they came off the target, the Jolly Rogers' two high-cover divisions were hit by a mixed formation of what they identified as 20 A6Ms and Ki.44s. Four of the enemy went down in the fight at no cost to the Jolly Rogers. The Corsairs turned for home, unaware they had seen their final combat.

The day also saw Ike Kepford's most memorable mission of his career. Butch Davenport led the division with Kepford, by then promoted to Lieutenant (jg), as element leader on what was originally planned as a strafing mission to Rabaul. Kepford's wingman soon developed engine trouble and was forced to return, which meant he was also ordered to turn back. Alone over the Solomon Sea, he spotted a lone A6M2-N Rufe seaplane fighter. Although he was alone and all the rules said to avoid combat, Kepford attacked the enemy plane. As he pulled out of his dive, he glanced back and saw the floatplane crash into the water. With an easy kill notched up, Kepford radioed, "Hog 29 here. Scratch one. Returning to base."

Minutes later he saw many, many dots high above, between him and Bougainville. Hoping to remain inconspicuous, he turned away and stayed low to go around them, but the enemy spotted him and four Zeros peeled off to intercept him. Unwilling to fight four-to-one odds, Kepford turned north to escape, but the four pursuers came on fast. As the lead fighter opened fire, Kepford decided to "go for broke," dropping flaps and landing gear, then nosing down until he was skimming the waves. As the Zero roared over him, he pulled the Corsair's nose up and opened fire. The enemy fighter flew into his fire and crashed into the waves. As he pulled up his gear and flaps, the three remaining enemies bracketed him. Now he faced three-to-one odds, low and slow, but he was heading in the direction of Rabaul.

The three spread out behind him, boxing him in, and continued to gain. Kepford's Corsair had recently been updated with a water injection system, "war emergency power," which provided a temporary boost to the Pratt & Whitney R-2800 engine. As the enemy planes stayed with him, getting closer and scoring some hits on his Corsair, it was time to find out how the new system worked, and he pushed the throttle "through the gate." Slowly, he began to pull away, but the high power was starting to overheat the engine; glancing over his shoulder, he saw the enemy fighters falling behind. Now out of range, he eased back on the throttle and the engine temperature gauge returned to the green arc.

If he was to get home, he had to make his move. As he cut across the path of the enemy fighter to his left, it dropped to his altitude at wavetop level and opened fire. The enemy pilot turned sharp, trying to turn inside Kepford. The Zero's left wingtip caught a wave, and it cartwheeled across the ocean, disintegrated, and sank. Kepford pushed the throttle into "war emergency" again and left the other two behind as he turned south and dashed for home. Looking back he saw them turn away and he reduced speed, climbing for altitude to minimize fuel consumption with what he had left. When he landed back at Piva Yoke, the Corsair's engine stopped when he turned off the runway, out of fuel. He struggled out of his plane, pale and exhausted, his flying suit and shoes soaked through with sweat. The three victories that turned out to have been scored "the hard way" made him the Jolly Rogers' leading ace, and the leading Navy ace of the moment, with a score of 16.

Poor weather closed in for several days. Finally, on February 29, 24 VF-17 Corsairs flew to Rabaul. Other than antiaircraft fire, the sky was empty. Three more missions were flown over the course of the week without opposition. It began to dawn on the Americans that the Rabaul campaign was over.

The Jolly Rogers appeared on the scene in the Solomons just at the outset of the final air campaign against Rabaul, and finished their deployment just at the point where final victory in the Solomons campaign was obtained with the Japanese withdrawal at the end of February, 1944. In 76 days of combat, the Jolly Rogers were credited with 154 enemy aircraft shot down. Over the five weeks they were in combat, they flew an amazing 7,192 hours, an average of 200 per pilot. When the squadron departed the combat zone, 13 pilots were aces, the record for a Navy squadron at the time. They had lost 20 planes and 12 pilots, an 8:1 victory record.

16

SIXTY-ONE DAYS

Following the B-24 mission flown on November 5 in support of the Task Force 38 strike against Rabaul, the Fifth Air Force flew no more missions to Rabaul as General Kenney concentrated his force on wiping out Wewak and supporting the New Guinea campaign, which came to an end in April 1944 with the invasion of Hollandia. The unplanned lull in attacks against Rabaul following these strikes came to an end in mid-December, when Admiral Halsey's AirSols took up the effort. No one knew at the time that the next 61 days would see Rabaul reduced to strategic and military irrelevance.

The 71st Construction Battalion had landed on Bougainville with the invasion on November 1, when 14 members led by battalion commander Lieutenant Commander Austin Brockenbough came ashore with the Marines, bringing ten International Harvester TD-9 bulldozers. By D-Plus-One, they were hard at work clearing roads and pads for supply dumps as the enemy failed to oppose the invasion and the Marines quickly moved inland. That day, the Seabees had identified the location for construction of the airstrip at Torokina Point, where the flat land allowed for a nearly 5,000-foot runway running to the tip of the point. The land was swampy, requiring construction of 50-foot drainage ditches that effectively turned Torokina into an island. The point was heavily forested with trees that were too large to knock down with the bulldozers. Each had to be cut down individually and the stump dynamited. Over the following days, the rest of the battalion and their heavy equipment arrived and construction of the most important airfield in the South Pacific continued despite enemy air attack and artillery shelling.

While this went on, events moved quickly. Combined Fleet commander Admiral Koga ordered the surviving aircraft of the 1st Carrier Division to return to Truk after losing 120 aircraft and over 60 aircrew in just two weeks. The 12 days since the invasion had seen the 1st Division's Vals and Kates, and the Betty bombers of the 11th Air Fleet, make night attacks on the American convoys bringing reinforcements to Bougainville. The missions were bally-hooed in Japan as "The Air Battles Off Bougainville," in which the aircrews made excessive claims of sinking ten aircraft carriers, five battleships, 19 cruisers and seven destroyers in Operation *Ro-Go*. The attacking crews were even praised in an Imperial Rescript issued by Emperor Hirohito. In fact, the light cruisers *Birmingham* and *Denver* had been torpedoed with repairable damage in the "second" and "fourth" Air Battles Off Bougainville; "Air Battle Three" was the November 11 attack on the three American carriers that had struck Rabaul.

The 11th Air Fleet that remained at Rabaul had a reported strength of 202 aircraft on November 12. However, of 113 A6M Zeros, 25 required major repair and 29 lesser maintenance, leaving 59 fighters operational. Of the 36 G4M Betty bombers present, only 17 were ready for operations. The situation was similar for the Vals, Kates, and the few Judy dive bombers, giving the Japanese only 100 operational aircraft in total. Aircraft readiness was also affected by the fact that approximately 34 percent of aircrews and ground crews were unavailable due to malaria and other tropical diseases.

Around 0400 hours on November 17, nine Bettys and five Kates attacked a convoy of LSTs and APDs which the Japanese reported as "a large carrier force." USS *McKean* (APD-5), an old World War I "four-piper" modified into a fast transport, was hit by a torpedo and sank in 15 minutes. This loss was turned into "eight warships sunk" in the "Fifth Air Battle Off Bougainville." Four Bettys and one of the Kates failed to return, shot down by the ship's defensive fire. Shortly after dawn that day, ten Vals escorted by 55 A6Ms attacked another convoy, claiming three transports sunk, a fourth beached, and a destroyer left on fire. In fact, there were no losses and the escorting combat air patrol intercepted the Japanese before they could attack, shooting down ten. The two attacks cost the enemy 14 aircraft and their crews, for no tangible result. This would be the last Japanese attack against invasion shipping.

At Rabaul, with the Fifth Air Force now employed elsewhere, the only air attacks were night raids made by the three RAAF Beaufort torpedo bomber squadrons based on Goodenough Island. The Beauforts alternated between torpedo attacks against Simpson Harbor shipping, and medium-altitude bombing attacks on the airfields and Rabaul town. In what was called by the Australian press "the heaviest all-RAAF raid on Rabaul" on the night of November 14–15, 32 Beauforts from all three squadrons made attacks. A crew from 6 Squadron reported sinking an 8,000-ton transport with skip-bombing. The 8th Squadron Beauforts carried torpedoes, but were unsuccessful in their attacks. The RAAF force continued these attacks through the rest of the month and early December, with equal lack of success.

Halsey's air arm was a multi-service affair, with RNZAF P-40s, US Navy land-based Hellcats, Corsairs, and PB4Y-1 Privateers (a modification of the USAAF B-24), and units of the First Marine Air Wing flying Corsairs, Dauntless dive bombers, and Avenger attack bombers. Additionally, the Thirteenth Air Force operated two bomb groups flying B-24s that were now based on Guadalcanal with advanced basing at Munda, in addition to two fighter groups equipped with P-38s. The force was under the operational direction of ComAirSols, a command that rotated among the services. Marine Major General Ralph J. Mitchell, commanding general of Marine Air South Pacific (MASP) and the First Marine Air Wing, assumed this position on November 20. He would command the force in the coming campaign against Rabaul, which was set to begin once the airfield at Torokina was operational.

At Torokina, 50 percent of the field had been cleared by D-Day-Plus-Twenty. Roads and aircraft revetments were surfaced with crushed coral, while the runway was surfaced with Pierced-Steel-Planking (PSP), also known as Marston Matting. Work on the field ran from dawn to dusk, seven days a week. On November 24, a Navy SBD Dauntless that had suffered an in-flight emergency was able to land safely and have its broken oil line fixed.

Two weeks later at sunset on December 8, the construction crews finishing the runway and taxiway were surprised to see three Corsairs drop into the landing pattern overhead and lower their gear and flaps. Construction equipment was hurriedly moved off the runway as it became apparent that they were committed to landing. The airplanes were flown by Black Sheep pilots who had recently moved up to Barakoma airstrip to commence their second combat tour. Led by Captain Cameron Dustin, these had been caught in weather over Bougainville while on combat air patrol over the island, and were in need of gas to return to Vella Lavella. A tropic downpour had swept the field only an hour before and the ground around the PSP was a muddy quagmire. The Seabees only had hand pumps with which to fuel the fighters, which meant the pilots ended up bunking with them overnight, but the next morning saw them on their way. Back at Barakoma, Boyington was dismayed when Lieutenant Edwin Oleander described Torokina as "a muddy mess."

Boyington had recently been advised by his friend and mentor, Brigadier General James T. "Nuts" Moore, who was General Mitchell's Chief of Staff, that the nomination for a Medal of Honor had been approved and sent on to Washington. Implicit in the news was the need for him to set a new scoring record and pass Foss, for the necessary approvals at higher levels for the award to happen. For a man who only a few years before had been on his way out of the Marines for personal failings, who had not achieved what he had hoped to do in joining the AVG, the acclaim he had received and the attention given by the correspondents during the Black Sheep's first tour had been heady indeed. With the tour he had flown with VMF-122, but this was his third Solomons tour and he was certain it was his last. To say he felt himself under pressure would be an understatement.

Boyington wasn't the only Marine ace who could set a new record. Marion Carl, who had scored 16.5 victories over Guadalcanal in the early days, had returned to the South Pacific as the commanding officer of VMF-223. There was already speculation among reporters as to which man would break the record, interest that Marine public relations officers fanned into an "ace race" as the best way to garner good publicity for the Corps back home.

Other Marine pilots looked forward to the coming air battles as personal opportunities. The "Fighting Corsairs" of VMF-215 were also returning for a new combat tour, led by former Executive Officer Major Robert G. Owens, who was as good a combat leader as Boyington, Carl, or Blackburn. Senior flight leader Captain Don Aldrich, who had joined the squadron the previous summer after transferring to the Marines from 18 months spent in the RCAF, had a score of 15 and all the makings of a great fighter leader and ace.

Unnoticed by all others at the time was 23-year-old First Lieutenant Robert M. Hanson. Born in 1920 in Lucknow, India, the son of missionaries, he became the heavyweight wrestling champion of the United Provinces before the war as a teenager. On vacation after his 18th birthday, he cycled with friends through Europe and arrived in Vienna the day of the Nazi *Anschluss*. Arriving in the United States that fall, he attended Hamline University in St. Paul, where he continued his wrestling career. Leaving college in his senior year in the aftermath of Pearl Harbor, he became a NavCad, graduating with his Wings of Gold in May 1943 and taking a Marine commission. Hanson had arrived on Guadalcanal in the summer of 1943 with VMF-214 during their "Swashbucklers" phase. Other pilots noted he was somewhat belligerent, someone who easily took a dislike to other fliers. However, he had an excellent eye for aerial gunnery. In his first combat mission on August 4, 1943, he flew as wingman to First Lieutenant Stanley "Chief" Synar. Returning from a strafing run in the Shortland Islands, the Swashbucklers were jumped by enemy fighters, with one pouncing on Lieutenant Synar, who was struck by gunfire and injured. Hanson got behind the attacker, and "shot his ass off," exploding the enemy fighter, only to get shot up himself moments later by another Zero, with his Corsair taking 20mm rounds between the guns in the right wing, the right flap, and the right stabilizer. In a case of mistaken identity, Hanson reported his victory as a Zero, though the more-experienced Synar described the white spinner, in-line engine, and rows of exhaust stacks of a JAAF Ki.61 Tony, which was new to the theater. Later that month, in a landing mix-up, Hanson stomped on his brakes, flipping over his Corsair and destroying it. On August 26, just before the end of the Swashbucklers' tour, Hanson scored his second victory while escorting PB4Y-1s. Lagging behind his division with his supercharger acting up, he was able to surprise a lone Zero that rashly attacked the Corsairs. His first shots had little effect, but he closed in, fired another burst, and the enemy fighter caught fire in the wing root and went down.

As one of the "Swashbucklers" who found themselves no longer part of their squadron after Boyington's organizational sleight-of-hand in September, Hanson transferred to VMF-215 just in time to fly a tour with the "Fighting Corsairs," promoted from wingman to element leader. In the air battles over Bougainville on D-Day, November 1, he intercepted an inbound enemy raid and shot down a Kate and two Zeros over Empress Augusta Bay at about 1345 hours to become an ace. Moments later, he was shot down himself and forced to bail out, but was fortunately picked up unhurt.

Even after the losses suffered in the Fifth Air Force campaign and by the withdrawal of the fleet carrier squadrons in early November, the Japanese forces on Rabaul still boasted some formidable pilots in their number.

Lieutenant (jg) Chitoshi Isozaki was unusual for being one of the very few Japanese enlisted pilots to become a commissioned officer. Entering flight training in 1932, he was later the advanced flying instructor for Saburo Sakai, the top-scoring surviving IJNAF ace of the Pacific War. He first saw combat during the war in China, flying from the carrier *Kaga* in 1937. At the outset of the Pacific War, he was assigned to the Tainan Air Group during the East Indies campaign. After more than ten years' service, he was promoted to Ensign in April 1943, a testament to his demonstrated leadership. He entered combat in the Solomons in 1943 during the invasion of New Georgia and scored against the RNZAF. That fall he was sent to Rabaul where he served as a squadron commander in the 204th Air Group of the 11th Air Fleet and fought in both the Fifth Air Force offensive and the final 61-day battle for the fortress, during which time he was credited with 12 victories. He survived the air battles, to be evacuated to Japan in March 1944 after being wounded in one of the final battles in February. He ended the war as a member of the 343rd Air Group "squadron of aces."

One of the youngest Japanese aces was Masajiro Kawato, who finished flight training in 1943 and reported to Rabaul at age 18. In air combat over Rabaul during November, he deliberately rammed his American opponents on two separate occasions, bailing out at the last moment to tell the tale. He survived a third mid-air collision on December 17, 1943 during the first Allied fighter sweep of the final Rabaul offensive when he accidentally collided with the P-40N flown by Flight Lieutenant John O. MacFarlane of 16 Squadron RNZAF, bailing out to be picked up by a boat in Simpson Harbor. By the end of the Rabaul campaign, Kawato was credited with 19 victories.

NAP 1/c Takeo Tanimizu arrived at Rabaul as a member of the *Shōkaku* air group and fought in the battles during November, shooting down two P-38s on November 2. He returned with the air group in mid-January to reinforce the two fighter groups of the 11th Air Fleet that were suffering heavy losses in air battles over Rabaul. Over the course of the war he was credited with 32 victories and was promoted to warrant officer in recognition of his accomplishments. Interviewed after the war, he stated he thought of the F6F Hellcat as his most dangerous opponent since it could successfully fight a Zero in a dogfight. He saw the P-38 and F4U as successful so long as the pilots fought in the vertical plane and used the dive-and-zoom tactic. Tanimizu was the first to use the "Ta-dan," a white phosphorus bomb that was dropped on enemy bomber formations. While only a few Allied bombers were lost to this weapon, the 345th's Vic Tatelman recalled that "it scared the hell out of everyone when one of those babies went off anywhere near the formation."

The leading Japanese ace in the fighting over Rabaul was Chief NAP Tetsuzō Iwamoto, who was also one of the few enlisted pilots to be later commissioned, being promoted to Ensign in November 1944 in view of his outstanding combat record and ending the war as a Lieutenant (jg). Iwamoto graduated one of 34 flight students in his class to survive the demanding prewar Imperial Navy flight training program in 1937, during which he was one of Chitoshi Isozaki's students during advanced fighter pilot training. Assigned after graduation to the elite 13th Flying Group known as the "Nango Flying Group" in honor of its former commander, Mochifumi Nango, he flew his first mission in a Mitsubishi A5M2 (later known to the Allies as "Claude") on February 25, 1938, over Nanchang, China. Flying escort for a group of G3M1 Type 96 Nell bombers, the formation was attacked by 16 Soviet-built I-15s and I-16s, which may have been flown by Soviet "volunteers." During the fight, squadron leader Lieutenant Takuma was lost.

Iwamoto demonstrated his outstanding ability as a fighter pilot by shooting down four of the enemy fighters. Closing to within 150 feet of an I-16, he opened fire and the enemy fighter caught fire after the third burst. Looking back, he saw another I-16 closing on his tail and split-essed to get away, coming out behind a third I-16 that he attacked from behind, setting the engine on fire. An I-153 then came at him and the two engaged in a close-in dogfight. When the enemy pilot tried to dive away, he got on the I-153's tail and shot it down to crash in the fields below. Turning away, he spotted a fourth enemy fighter, a damaged I-16 with its landing gear down. Chasing it, he caught up to the fighter at low altitude and opened fire. When the I-16 attempted to perform a split-S to escape, it crashed into the ground.

Assigned to the *Shōkaku* air group, Iwamoto took part in the Pearl Harbor attack and the Indian Ocean campaign in April 1942. At the Battle of the Coral Sea, he was credited with five F4F-3 Wildcats and six SBD-3s shot down. Iwamoto first arrived at Rabaul in September 1943 as part of the reinforcement sent from the carriers at Truk. He remained for the rest of the fighting, being evacuated to Japan in March 1944. During the Rabaul campaign, he was credited with shooting down four P-38s, 48 F4U Corsairs, 29 Hellcats, five TBF Avengers, an SB2C-1 Helldiver, and a P-40. The total seems amazing, but he was known to hang back during the air battles, watching for damaged airplanes and others departing for home, which he then attacked and shot down, so while the score might not be as high as claimed – a common situation on both sides during the Rabaul fighting – it was likely substantial. When he told Hiroyoshi Nishizawa, the other top Imperial Navy ace of the war who was there at the time, of his tactic, Nishizawa accused him of cowardice, to which Iwamoto replied that if he didn't shoot them down as he did, "they'd be back the next day." Iwamoto was one of the very few Imperial Navy pilots to survive the entire Pacific War, credited with 87 victories including 14 scored in China.

Several other Japanese aces fought over Rabaul, including Kazuo Sugino, who shot down a B-25 and a P-38 in the November 2 air battle and eventually scored 32 victories during the Pacific War. Warrant Officer Ryoji Ohara, called "the Killer of Rabaul" by his fellow pilots, fought with the 204th Air Group, where he was credited with shooting down and killing Major William Gise, the first commander of VMF-124. By the end of the war he was credited with 48 victories and was one of the group of Imperial Navy pilots, including Saburo Sakai, who attacked a pair of B-32 Dominators off Tokyo the day after the official surrender on August 16, 1945 in the last air battle of the Pacific War.

Since the Combined Chiefs had determined in August that Rabaul would be bypassed rather than invaded, the Allies continued to take bases in the region to surround and cut off the base and provide ever-closer airfields for attacking the enemy's main center of operations.

As part of the larger Operation *Cartwheel* to isolate and surround the enemy, Operation *Backhander* saw the 1st Marine Division return to combat for the first time since they had been finally withdrawn from Guadalcanal a year earlier. The target was the Cape Gloucester Peninsula in western New Britain, with the goal of capturing two Japanese airfields for further use by the Allies. The Marines went ashore the day after Christmas and found only light resistance at the outset. However, the swampy terrain of the peninsula forced the Marines to advance on the airfields along a narrow coastal trail. An enemy counterattack by units of the Imperial Army's 17th Division slowed them temporarily, but the airfields were under Allied control by the end of the month. Fighting continued until January 16, 1944, when the perimeter was extended to Borgen Bay. US Army engineers had determined on inspecting the airfields that the Japanese had made no move to develop them, and that the best of the two was Airfield No. 2, The kunai grass that had overgrown the field was cut down and grading began in early January. By the end of the month, a 4,000-foot runway covered with PSP was available for use. Fifth Air Force units were able to operate from the field by the end of January. Eventually the P-40Ns of the RAAF's 78th Wing were permanently based there in March 1944. Ultimately, Cape Gloucester never became an important base, with plans to base Thirteenth Air Force units there canceled in August 1944 as the war moved toward the Philippines earlier than expected.

Major General Ralph J. Mitchell, who commanded the Allied force in the final battle, was a member of the Annapolis class of 1915, who had become a Marine aviator in 1921. During the interwar period, he was a student at the Army Air Service Tactical School and graduated from the Army's Command and General Staff School at Fort Leavenworth before attending the Naval War College following service in Nicaragua in 1929–30 during the campaign against the Sandino Rebellion as commander of VO-7M. Mitchell was awarded the Distinguished Flying Cross for leading a mission on June 19, 1930, in which six Marine O2 Corsairs found and attacked a large force of Sandinistas near the town of Jinotega, forcing them to retreat after inflicting heavy casualties. At the time he had recommended Boyington not be allowed to return to active service, Mitchell was Director of Aviation in the corps headquarters where he was responsible for the organization of Marine aviation into the form in which it would operate in the Pacific War. He relieved Major

General Roy S. Geiger as commander of the First Marine Air Wing in April 1943, when he was promoted to Major General. Mitchell and his staff had been planning the coming Rabaul campaign since before the Bougainville invasion. Their plan, simply, was an all-out attack on the enemy base on every day the weather in the coming rainy season would allow, flown relentlessly until the enemy quit.

Mitchell saw promoting morale in the fighter squadrons as essential to success. Among his orders for the coming campaign was a directive to squadron intelligence officers that they were to accept the claims of their pilots for enemy aircraft shot down, whether the claim was confirmed by other members of the squadron or not. When it was pointed out that this would lead to over-claiming and the possibility that operational decisions would be made on the basis of these unconfirmed claims which were inaccurate, Mitchell replied that they would know the enemy was defeated when they quit.

Over-claiming by fighter pilots was not a new phenomenon. It had happened in every air battle since 1915. In most cases, claims were made in all sincerity by individual pilots. The nature of air combat, in which a pilot had only a few seconds to aim and shoot at an enemy plane and little opportunity to stick around to observe the final result if the plane didn't explode or catch fire immediately in front of him, without putting himself in danger of attack by another enemy plane, meant that the majority of claims were in reality guesses and hopes on the part of the claimant.

There was also the fact that the pilots did not know all the technical characteristics of their opponent's mount, and that normal operation of that airplane might be seen as evidence of destruction when in fact it wasn't. During World War II, this was frequently the case in combat against the Luftwaffe's Bf-109 fighter. Because it was equipped with direct fuel injection for the engine, a pilot could push over straight down in a negative-g maneuver without affecting engine performance as was the case with an engine equipped with a float carburetor. A side-effect of this maneuver was that when the pilot pushed over, the negative-g built up pressure in the exhaust system, and a cloud of smoke was emitted. For a pursuing pilot unaware of this technicality, the simultaneous dive of the plane accompanied by a cloud of smoke was often seen as evidence the enemy fighter had been hit in its engine and was headed down for a crash. Turning away, the "victor" wouldn't see his opponent pull out below, and would return to base confident he had been successful. The Japanese Zero also emitted a cloud of smoke from its exhaust if the pilot suddenly increased the engine boost, with the advance of the throttle resulting in a backfire and a momentary flash of flame from the exhaust, which could be mistaken by a pilot firing on the Zero as evidence of fatal hits. This "dirty" exhaust was exacerbated by the 87-octane fuel in use and declining maintenance standards. In the case of air combat in the Solomons and New Guinea, the fact that American fighters were not equipped with gun cameras which could provide evidence to support a pilot's claim led to even more over-claiming than happened in other theaters of operations.

Over-claiming was not merely an American failing. Japanese aircrew regularly made claims that were impossible regarding the success of their attacks against Allied ships and aircraft. In the 61 days of the final Rabaul offensive, both sides would overclaim by as much as 4:1. In the end, however, the individual claims didn't matter to the outcome.

At the outset of the final campaign, the Allied air forces in the Solomons totaled 270 fighters. Sixty-nine were P-39s suited only to provide ground support. The fighters available for combat over Rabaul included 71 Corsairs and 58 Hellcats, 39 P-40s and 31 P-38s. The F4U still suffered from a low in-commission rate, with 47 Corsairs ready for the first mission on December 17, as compared with 53 F6Fs and 36 P-40s. The complex P-38s could only supply 13 fighters.

Eighty Allied fighters were scheduled to participate in the first mission. Newly operational Torokina Airfield, 100 feet wide and 4,900 feet long, with an equally wide and long taxiway, was crowded with fighters that morning. Boyington, who would lead the fighter sweep, had led two divisions of Black Sheep up to Torokina from Barakoma at dawn, to bring the total of participating Marine Corsairs to 32, with 24 Navy F-6Fs and 24 RNZAF Kittyhawks from 14 and 16 squadrons. The field was crowded to capacity.

Boyington lifted off at 0900 hours. Over the next 60 minutes, the rest took off and formed up for the sweep. The Kiwis, led by Wing Commander Trevor O. Freeman, were low at 15,000 feet, assigned to be first over Rabaul to bring up the defenders. The rest of the squadrons were at medium and high altitude, attempting to simulate what would look like a bomber mission to Japanese radar. At 1000 hours, the P-40s turned northwest, with 140 miles of the Solomon and Bismarck seas ahead of them. Having assembled first, the New Zealanders departed early and soon left the rest of the formation behind. The Corsairs and Hellcats were forced to fly around a large storm front halfway to Rabaul, which put them even further behind the Kittyhawks.

Shortly after dawn, 50 Zeros and 12 Kates had attacked an Allied convoy off New Britain carrying troops destined to reinforce those that had landed at Arawe on Cape Gloucester on December 15. Many of these fighters were still airborne, returning to Lakunai, as the New Zealanders' formation arrived over the harbor. An additional 27 Zeros from the 201st and 204th air groups at Lakunai were launched when radar spotted the incoming Allied formations, while another 20 from the 253rd Air Group at Tobera were also airborne. Altogether, some 70 enemy fighters were in the sky over the harbor. The P-40s spotted the Lakunai defenders still climbing for altitude and dived on them. Several Zeros went down in the first pass, but after that the Kittyhawks were at low altitude, fighting the enemy on the horizontal plane rather than climbing and diving to get an advantage. Wing Commander Freeman, who shot down the first Zero, was hit in the subsequent fight and attempted to get across the Bismarck Sea to New Ireland, where a coastwatcher named Boski was prepared to rescue downed pilots. Enemy fighters drove off the two P-40s escorting their commander, who was never seen again.

Teenage fighter pilot Masajiro Kawato collided with a P-40 he was chasing. As the damaged airplanes headed for the water below, both pilots were able to bail out. Kawato was rescued, while the Kiwi pilot was captured. Altogether the RNZAF pilots claimed five Zeros for a loss of three, though the Japanese admitted only the loss of Kawato's plane and the one shot down by Freeman.

While the Kittyhawks and Zeros fought it out over the harbor, Boyington's Corsairs and Hellcats found no action as they cruised over Simpson Harbor at 20,000 feet. Frustrated as he orbited over Lakunai airdrome, Boyington cranked his radio to the Japanese ground control frequency of 6050 kilocycles and called to the fighters below to "come on up and fight!" Below, in 11th Air Fleet HQ, several Nisei Americans who had returned to Japan before the war and were now translators, listened to Boyington's call. Chikaki "Edward" Honda, who had left Hawaii to return to Japan back in 1931 and had forfeited his citizenship in 1941 when he joined the Imperial Navy, keyed his microphone and called back, "Come on down, sucker." The American-accented voice surprised Boyington when he heard it.

While Boyington was so engaged, Black Sheep First Lieutenant D.J. Moore spotted enemy fighters below and left the formation to go after them. Diving on them unseen, he came up behind four and shot down two before turning away. These were the only victories scored by the main sweep. On return to Vella Lavella, Boyington reported the lack of success, which he ascribed to having sent too many fighters on the sweep, which resulted in the enemy avoiding combat.

The next day, weather forced cancelation of the planned sweep, while the Thirteenth Air Force was able to launch 48 B-24s of the 5th and 307th groups from Guadalcanal, but only 16 reached the target, escorted by 50 P-38s, P-40s, and F4Us. The defenders at Rabaul had been reinforced with 18 A6M3 Hamps flown in from Truk behind the front that prevented the Allied sweep, and 90 enemy fighters were airborne when the Liberators arrived. Fortunately, the poor weather limited combat to only some 40 fighters that made limited attacks on the bombers. VMF-222's First Lieutenant Carl McLean and his wingman, Second Lieutenant Charles Jones, managed to flame one enemy fighter each, while two Corsairs from VMF-216 failed to return, including Captain Lawrence M. Faulkner, one of only two experienced pilots in the squadron.

Overall, the mission was very costly, with ten fighters and five pilots lost – most in ditching or landing accidents due to the poor weather. For one of the few times in the campaign, the Allied claims for five defenders shot down and the Japanese admission of five fighters lost were in agreement. The rainy season meant there would be more impenetrable weather fronts rising above the warm seas and creating a condition almost as dangerous to the Allied fliers as the enemy.

After two more days of bad weather, Boyington was scheduled to lead a sweep on December 21, which was canceled at the last moment when a patrolling Catalina radioed a weather report from the Rabaul region that the weather there was worse. Boyington was upset by the cancelation. The Black Sheep deployment was half over and he was still scoreless. Two days later the weather cleared enough to fly a sweep. Major Pierre Carnagey, the newly assigned Black Sheep XO, led the close escort force, while Boyington led two divisions in the formation of 48 Corsairs in the sweep, which was led by Marion Carl. The fighters topped off fuel at Torokina and rendezvoused with B-24s of the 5th and 307th groups up from Guadalcanal. The formation was picked up by the Japanese radar station on Cape St. George, providing the defending fighters enough time to get into the air. The 201st Air Group launched 30, the 204th sent up 38, and the 253rd added 31. Sixty defenders made contact with the inbound Allied formation. Several Zeros penetrated the Black Sheep formation in the escort screen; Carnagey and his wingman, First Lieutenant Jim Brubaker, were among the three Corsairs that failed to return to Barakoma. Two 44th squadron P-38 pilots and three VF-33 Hellcat pilots each claimed an enemy fighter shot down. The two formations of Liberators bombed Lakunai airdrome with great accuracy, badly damaging ground installations on the field. The bombers faced air-to-air bombing by 30 fighters dropping white phosphorus bombs, which scared the airmen while mostly missing the formation.

Carl and the other Corsairs appeared over Simpson Harbor 15 minutes after the bombers and their escorts departed, and found many enemy fighters returning to their fields after the interception. Boyington's two divisions at the bottom of the formation were ideally placed to engage the enemy. Carl later described the ensuing battle: "We made contact over Cape St. George and I stalked a Tony through the clouds. I splashed him between Rabaul and New Ireland while the rest of the squadron claimed three confirmed and three probables. Boyington and the rest of the formation added 15 more."

In fact, the Black Sheep claimed 12 of the 15 other defenders shot down in the melee. The four credited to Boyington suddenly put him within two victories of the record. The 201st and 204th air groups involved in the battle admitted the loss of six, including the commanding officer of the 201st group. The Allied fighter pilots and the gunners aboard the B-24s claimed 30. The award of credit demonstrated the problem of over-claiming by pilots and the acceptance of these claims by the intelligence officers interviewing them after the mission. Boyington was the only pilot to claim more than two victories, with his descriptions of the fights the only evidence presented; his wingman, First Lieutenant Robert McClurg, was unable to support Boyington's claims because he had gone off on his own and claimed two Zeros shot down himself.

Boyington's claims are hard to reconcile on two grounds. The first is that he never made any bones throughout his life about being an inveterate liar; he used the term "pathological" to describe his lies in his memoir *Baa Baa Black Sheep*. The second is that there were only six enemy fighters actually lost that day. If his four were accurate, then the claims of 23 other pilots and gunners are impossible. While the Japanese admitted the loss of six, an unknown number of other planes returned to Lakunai and Vunakanau with moderate to severe damage, which supports the reports of close combat. The Japanese were lucky throughout the campaign that they were primarily fighting directly over or close to their own airfields, which meant that airplanes that might have been lost in other circumstances did make it back. As with almost all other air forces, any plane that made it home – regardless of whether or not it ever flew again – stayed off the combat loss records. As for the squadron intelligence officers, they were under intense pressure from their unit leadership and the authorities above to award credit liberally. Thus, if a pilot or gunner presented a plausible account of his claim, it was credited.

Black Sheep squadron intelligence officer Captain Frank E. Walton admitted after the war:

> The records were way, way inflated; all of our claims were inflated. We shot down about four times as many planes as the Japanese ever produced, according to the records. We never had any verification on a lot of the claims. We trusted, in many cases, just the guy's word: "Yes, I did this and I did that." The way he detailed it was what we put down.

Black Sheep pilot Bruce J. Matheson, who retired from the Marines as a Brigadier General after a 30-year career, admitted in his retirement:

> Frank would tend to sort this out. He'd say "Now, wait a minute, you said this," and somebody else would say "Yeah, but I was over here and I'm sure I shot it." Frank would say "Is there a possibility you two guys were shooting at the same airplane?" Hell yes! There may have been three or four of us shooting at this poor sucker before he finally blew up!

The air battle see-sawed throughout the early period. On December 24, a sweep by 50 Hellcats and Corsairs was sent to Rabaul before the arrival of the bombers, which were escorted by P-40s. However, a delay on the part of the bombers due to weather meant that the defenders were able to meet both raids, with 94 fighters scrambled against the sweep, and 81 against the bombers. The 11th Air Fleet's fighters claimed to have shot down 55 fighters in the sweep – five more than the total force. The New Zealanders claimed 12 for a loss of six, while the Hellcat pilots of VF-33 and VF-40 claimed six. One of those was claimed by VF-33 pilot Lieutenant (jg) David A. Scott, who followed his victim down till it crashed in St. George's Channel. Unfortunately, he was so fascinated by the fate of his enemy that he failed to see the attacking Zero that hit him from behind and disabled his engine. Scott glided as far out over the water as he could and successfully ditched ten miles from the cape. Despite the Dumbos being notified, he wasn't found, but in the end managed to survive in his raft for a week before he was sighted by a PV-1 Ventura and rescued by a Catalina on New Year's Day 1944.

The weather held for a third mission on Christmas Day. Fifteen Liberators escorted by 50 P-38s, P-40s, F6Fs, and F4Us dropped 40 tons of bombs on Vunakanau and Tobera, despite being intercepted by 88 Zeros. In the rugged fighting, VMF-214 and 223 claimed eight of the 14 Allied victory claims, while the 11th Air Fleet claimed four B-24s and 20 fighters. The B-24s suffered no losses though three escorts – two P-38s and a Corsair – failed to return. The Japanese admitted the loss of six, with many others returning to their airfields damaged.

By this point, Boyington was deep into problematic drinking in after-action parties that turned into binges; his hangover cure, plunging his head into a rain barrel the next morning, was becoming less effective. Scheduled to lead a mission on December 27, he found he needed several repeats, later writing, "I repeated the dunking several times… until I was able to steady myself down. This little aid had become standard procedure with me by then, for the pressure was really on me." Flying to Torokina to top off fuel, he led 60 Hellcats and Corsairs that headed for Rabaul at 1000 hours. Just before they took off, the Japanese at Rabaul had launched a strike of 78 Zeros and 15 Vals to hit the invasion force on Cape Gloucester. These planes were just returning to their airfields when Boyington's sweep arrived overhead. Spotting 50 Zeros, he led the formation on a sweeping turn that brought them 1,000 feet higher and behind 12 Zeros. The Allied fighters claimed 16, including one splashed and a probable by Marion Carl. Boyington only claimed one; this time his wingman was First Lieutenant Edwin Harper, who stuck with his leader, unlike McClurg who so often went off freelancing on his own, and did so while managing to score one of his own. Harper was thus able to confirm this claim by Boyington to Captain Walton after return. The Japanese recorded seven losses.

Now one victory away from tying the record, Boyington learned that a dawn strike was on the schedule for the next day. Within 90 minutes of landing, he lifted off for Torokina at 1745 hours at the head of three divisions. The pilots spent the night on Bougainville. The next morning VMF-216's CO, Major Rivers, led 18 Corsairs from his squadron, 12 Black Sheep, and eight each from Marion Carl's VMF-223 and newly arrived VMF-321. The VMF-321 pilots had only arrived at Vella Lavella four days earlier, and Rivers had never led a sweep.

Once over St. George's Channel, Rivers led the Corsairs in a wide sweep around to the west side of the harbor. He saw enemy fighters climbing from Lakunai and led the formation toward them, unaware of a large gaggle of enemy fighters circling above the Corsairs. The enemy planes disappeared into the sun, then fell on the Corsairs. Black Sheep "tail-end Charlie" Second Lieutenant Donald J. Moore, who was lagging behind his element leader, went down in the first pass. Captain Cameron Dustin turned the third division to face the enemy and then made the mistake of climbing into the sun and losing sight of the Zeros. His wingman, Captain Ed Olander, and element leader Bruce Matheson, rolled into a dive to escape the Zeros. Dustin and Matheson's wingman, Second Lieutenant Harry Bartl, were not seen again. Matheson flew into a cloud with several Zeros behind him. Popping back out, he found himself behind the enemy and blasted tail-end Charlie, then split-essed and firewalled his throttle till he was well out to sea, after which he flew back home. The Zero chasing Olander overshot him and paid the price, with Olander taking his survival as an order to high-tail it for Vella Lavella. While the other three squadrons in the sweep claimed 22 victories, the Black Sheep only claimed four. Boyington was only able to claim a probable, leaving him still one off tying the record. Rather than face the reporters back at Barakoma, he landed at Torokina and spent the night. The 22 claims from the sweep were far more than the three fighters the Japanese listed lost with their pilots and two heavily damaged that returned to base.

The mission planned for December 29 was canceled for weather. On December 30, Boyington was disappointed when the fighter sweep he was scheduled to lead was canceled. He sent new XO Major Henry

S. Miller to lead two divisions of Black Sheep Corsairs with 20 other Corsairs and an equal number of Hellcats as escorts for the bombing mission flown by 20 B-24s of the 5th Bomb Group led by group commander Colonel Marion D. Unruh. The poor weather delayed the full join-up of bombers and fighters, and the bombers were only escorted by VF-33's Hellcats when they made their run over St. George's Channel into Rabaul. The B-24s bombed through the clouds from 22,000 feet. Heavy AA fire exploding through the clouds appeared to miss the Liberators, but on withdrawal, Colonel Unruh handed over mission leadership to 71st Squadron commander Major Charles Pierce, informing him, "We're going down." Unruh headed for New Ireland, hoping for rescue by the coastwatcher there, and ditched off the island successfully, losing only two crewmen. Rescued by natives, they were captured a few days later and taken to Rabaul.

While a POW at Rabaul, Unruh managed to convince his interrogators that he had in fact been flying the first B-29 Superfortress to arrive in the Pacific. He filled their notebooks with fantastic tales of the bomber's capabilities, none of which had any connection to reality and were pure invention on his part. The Japanese took him so seriously that after several months he and the interrogators were sent to Japan, where the "information" spread through the Imperial defense units that expected attack from the new super-bomber any day.

New Year's Eve brought steady rain to the northern Solomons. Boyington grew more morose as he watched the days of the squadron's tour tick away, and with them his chance for fame. He later wrote, "I came to see the record meant absolutely nothing; it would be broken again and again, in spite of anything I did. I was worried only about what others might think of me." During this time, Associated Press correspondent Fred Hampson filed a story about Boyington in which he used the nickname "Pappy," lifting it from a song about "Our Pappy" penned by squadron pilot "Moon" Mullen. Black Sheep pilots called their commander "Greg," or "Gramps." Hampson's report appeared in the stateside newspapers a week later, timing that led to the creation of an entirely new myth about Gregory Boyington.

New Year's Day 1944 saw the weather clear sufficiently for AirSols to run another mission like the one in which Colonel Unruh was lost. Again, Black Sheep XO Miller led the Corsair escort of 68 fighters to escort 15 307th Group Liberators. The mission turned into the blackest day of the campaign for the heavy bombers, as more than 40 defending fighters mauled the B-24s, shooting one down in flames over St. George's Channel and sending two others limping home with heavy damage. As this fight happened, bombers from *Bunker Hill* and USS *Monterey* (CVL-27) struck Kavieng Harbor on New Ireland for their second strike on shipping there in a week, with their Hellcat escorts knocking down seven defending Zeros. Following the departure of the Liberators from Rabaul, 40 Zeros arrived from Truk to reinforce the defenders.

Boyington's run of bad luck continued on January 2, when the engine of the F4U-1 Corsair he was scheduled to fly began acting up on the flight to Torokina. A junior pilot flew F4U-1A "883" up as a replacement. Having scored his last victory in this plane six days earlier, Boyington took it as a sign of good luck and soon departed, leading 28 Corsairs and 20 Hellcats on his fifth sweep to Rabaul. Near Rabaul, the engine sprang an oil leak that soon covered his windshield. He was so determined to make the mission that he surprised the other pilots by slowing nearly to stalling speed, at which point he opened his canopy and stood up in the slipstream, in a futile attempt to try to wipe the windshield clean enough to continue. He continued the mission regardless. The sweep was met over Rabaul by the 201st Air Group's 19 Zeros, along with 31 from the 204th and 30 from the 253rd. A massive air battle broke out, but Boyington couldn't see well enough to shoot. Disgusted, he aborted with his wingman and returned to Vella Lavella. His mood was not raised by reports of success by other Black Sheep when they returned.

That afternoon, Boyington visited the operations office and found there was no sweep to Rabaul scheduled for the next day. Desperate for an opportunity to beat the record, he managed to convince the planners to lay on an additional mission, a dawn sweep of Rabaul. With the operation approved, he took off at 1730 hours to fly to Torokina. Rather than take the pilots he had been flying with in his division, he substituted Captain George Ashmun as his wingman, with lieutenants James Hill and Alfred Johnson as the second element; none of the three had so far scored in combat. Ed Olander led the second division.

The morning of January 3, 1944, Boyington led a sweep of 28 Corsairs and 16 Hellcats that departed Torokina at 0630 hours. During the flight across the Solomon Sea, half the Black Sheep Corsairs aborted for various mechanical difficulties. Boyington continued on, exchanging Bruce Matheson and Lieutenant Rufus "Mack" Chatham from Olander's division as his second section. The sun was still low in the east as he led the reduced formation in a counter-clockwise sweep over the harbor at 20,000 feet. A layer of haze obscured the harbor and the surrounding airfields.

The enemy had plenty of advance warning, and 30 Zeros from the 204th Air Group had taken off from Lakunai and climbed to altitude while 37 253rd Group fighters had taken off from Tobera. Halfway through his circle, Boyington spotted enemy fighters below at 15,000 feet. Pushing over, he aimed at tail-end Charlie. His anxiety to score led him to open fire out of range, but the enemy pilot continued on unaware of the tracers that shot past him. He closed to 300 feet and opened fire again; immediately, the pilot pulled open the canopy and took to his parachute seconds before the Zero caught fire and exploded. Boyington had now tied the record. Matheson and Chatham both shouted confirmation of the victory. An instant later, Matheson went after another enemy fighter and Chatham discovered his guns wouldn't fire due to an electrical short. Neither pilot noticed where Boyington and his wingman Ashmun went.

Unsatisfied with merely tying the record, Boyington spotted another group of Zeros 3,000 feet below him and descended into the haze layer in search of another victory. As he closed on the enemy fighters, the two Corsairs were hit by another formation of A6Ms that fell on them from out of the sun. Rather than use the Corsair's superior dive capability to escape, Boyington and Ashmun set up a defensive weave. They were quickly swarmed by 20–30 enemy fighters. Each shot a Zero off the other's tail, but a few turns later Ashmun was hit. He headed down, trailing smoke, but several of the Zeros closed in and soon the Corsair was on fire. Seconds later the big blue fighter slammed into the waters of St. George's Channel, taking Ashmun down with it.

Alone now, Boyington turned as tight as he could, pulling the stick back in his gut and bringing the wings vertical. Vapor trails spiraled from the wingtips. Enemy fire hit the Corsair but the engine still put out power. The next burst of enemy fire saw a 20mm shell enter the plane's belly and explode in the "hell hole" beneath Boyington's seat – shrapnel cut his left calf and ankle. A large piece of shell casing entered his left thigh and blood sprayed over the controls. Another piece missed his legs and slashed his right forearm, while smaller pieces peppered his head. Dazed and bleeding, he broke the turn and put the Corsair's nose down in a desperate bid to get away.

Boyington fled down the St. George's Channel, relentlessly pursued by the enemy fighters. Finally, hit in the engine, he banked toward New Ireland, hoping to ditch and make contact with the coastwatcher Bolski. The enemy fighters continued the pursuit, taking turns making firing runs on the smoking Corsair. Boyington called for a Dumbo, stating he was going to ditch in the channel, but since he was at low altitude the message didn't get through. Finally, abreast of Cape St. George and five miles from shore, just before the Corsair ran out of flying speed, he kicked the rudder and fired indiscriminately, hitting a final Zero that overshot him and exploded, then the Corsair hit the water. The plane sank immediately and Boyington managed to push the canopy open and swim to the surface. For the next 15 minutes, he watched the enemy fighters take turns strafing him, diving under the water as bullets zipped past. Finally they ran out of ammunition and flew off. Satisfied after two hours that he was finally alone, he deployed his raft and climbed in. He was weak from loss of blood and temporarily passed out.

Boyington came to shortly before dusk, when he heard the sound of a submarine surfacing. For a moment, he thought he was saved, then he saw the rising sun insignia on the conning tower. Realizing there was no escape, he threw his .38 pistol into the water – the soft lead bullets in it were a direct violation of the Geneva Convention and could have led the enemy to execute him on capture had they been discovered. He was surprised when the crew of the submarine gave him tea, cookies, and cigarettes while they took him to Simpson Harbor.

No word was ever given by the Japanese that they had captured Boyington. In March 1944, his wife accepted his "posthumous" Medal of Honor. The Black Sheep completed their tour on January 8. Under Boyington's leadership, the squadron was credited with 97 confirmed victories, 32 probables, and 21 destroyed on the ground, for a loss of 12 pilots dead and six wounded during 84 days in combat. The squadron name would remain a legend in Marine aviation ever after. A month later, Marion Carl was unexpectedly pulled from combat and sent to the staff of Marine Air Group 12. He would never again fly combat.

Two weeks after Boyington's loss, the two most important airfields of the campaign opened for business on Bougainville. Piva Uncle, the shorter, would become the main operating base for AirSols fighters, while the longer runway of Piva Yoke would serve the SBD Dauntlesses and TBF Avengers that would finally enter the campaign and bring with them the destructive capability that had eluded the high-altitude bombers of the Fifth and Thirteenth Air Forces.

With Boyington out of the race and the Black Sheep departed, the competition for top honors shifted. The end of January saw the "Fighting Corsairs" of VMF-215, still under the leadership of Major Robert Owens, move up to Piva Yoke. There were several pilots in the squadron now who were in contention to move to the top position. The career of one would illuminate all the problems of an air campaign that played fast and loose with the acclaim of individual effort, and what a man willing to take advantage of the limitations in that system could achieve. By mid-January, the Liberator groups had moved up from Guadalcanal to Munda, allowing them to exchange fuel for bomb load. The Treasury Islands had been successfully invaded, with an airfield newly operational where fighters could be refueled on Stirling Island less than 100 miles from Rabaul.

According to the record books, the most successful Corsair pilot in the Navy or Marine Corps during World War II was VMF-215's First Lieutenant Robert Murray Hanson, officially credited with 25 victories between August 1943 and February 1944, with 20 scored in a 17-day period. Hanson was different from other pilots in that he made no bones whatsoever about his plans to become a leading ace and make the most of that. When the squadron was notified in early December that they would soon return to combat, he declared he would be "on the cover of *Life* magazine" by the end of the tour. Such naked ambition was generally not considered socially acceptable, even among the egoists who populated fighter squadrons. He particularly rubbed his senior division leader, Captain Aldrich, the wrong way. Like Boyington, Hanson was extremely ambitious and, as it would turn out, he would prove not averse to doctoring his record as Boyington had regarding his AVG "victories."

The first attempt to send Dauntless dive bombers to hit an airfield at Rabaul on January 5 was scrubbed by rain. Poor weather the next day saw less than a third of a sweep of P-38s and Corsairs make it to Rabaul, where they confronted 33 defenders. The 44th Fighter Squadron lost two of 16 P-38s while the Japanese recorded two Zeros lost. The next day a Dauntless strike against Tobera got to Rabaul to find the target closed in by weather – they took out their frustration dive bombing the Cape St. George radar station. The mission was expensive, with the loss of three escorting F6Fs and four Navy and Marine SBDs. Success was finally achieved on January 9 when 16 TBFs were able to drop a 2,000-pound bomb each on the runway at Tobera, while the defending AA positions were struck by 24 SBDs. For a loss of one SBD and three fighter escorts, the more accurate low-level strike by the Avengers put the Tobera runway out of commission for the several days it took the enemy to repair the extensive damage.

On January 11, Solomons-based B-25s of the 42nd Bomb Group made a low-level attack on Vunakanau. General Mitchell continued to send his light and medium bomber units against the enemy, hitting Lakunai on January 14. Escorted by 80 fighters, 36 Navy and Marine Dauntlesses, each carrying a 1,000-pound bomb, and 16 Avengers, each toting a 2,000-pound bomb, forced their way through a defending force of 84 enemy fighters that first intercepted them over New Ireland. Despite the enemy's attempts to draw off the Kiwi P-40s providing close escort to the bombers, the Kittyhawks of 17 Squadron refused to take the bait and maintained their position protecting their charges. Despite this, two SBDs went down before the strike arrived over Lakunai, which they found was clouded over. The bombers then hit shipping in Simpson Harbor and shore installations, with the TBFs causing major damage to the 15,000-ton tanker *Naruto Maru*, leaving it sitting on the bottom, partially sunk in the shallow water near shore. The mission resulted in major over-claiming, with the gunners in the bombers and the escorting fighters credited with 27 fighters against an actual loss of three (with many landing damaged). This overclaim was matched by the Japanese, who claimed 34 fighters and 13 bombers shot down, against an actual loss of two SBDs and one TBF.

Robert Hanson returned to Bougainville claiming to have shot down five Zeros, doubling his score. Flying low escort to the Avengers, Hanson and his wingman, Second Lieutenant Richard Bowman, stuck with the bombers until they reached the rally point at Cape Gazelle. With Bowman on his wing, Hanson lined up a pair of A6Ms and both pilots fired simultaneously, each scoring when the enemy planes went down. Hanson then became separated from Bowman. On return, he reported he had engaged in a 30-minute running combat, shooting down enemy fighters he caught trying to get back to their airfields. There was no confirmation, since his wingman had become separated in the fight, but his claims were credited by the squadron in accordance with the AirSols policy. The rest of the squadron submitted claims for an additional 13 enemy fighters shot down. Given that only three Zeros were actually lost, the claims of Hanson and his squadron mates were impossible.

Even with eyewitness confirmation, many claims were mistaken. On January 9, Yasushi Shimbo of the 253rd Air Group was attacked by a Corsair flown by Lieutenant Robert See of VMF-321, who reported that when he fired he saw a "flash of fire" from the enemy fighter's wing tank; the claim was confirmed by Captain Marion McCown who saw the fighter go down "billowing black smoke." In reality, Shimbo's fighter had been hit in the wing, but he was able to bring the damaged plane down safely at Tobera, where the fire was put out and the damaged plane was later repaired.

While losses on both sides were approximately at parity in the first half of January, with the Japanese admitting the loss of 27 fighters while the Allied command recorded the loss of 17 fighters and seven bombers – a 1.1:1 Allied advantage – the situation began to change in the latter half of the month, as the number of available Allied fighters increased. New squadrons had arrived at Turtle Bay and been given their advanced theater operational training and now moved up to Bougainville. Finally, the Allies could put more fighters into the battle than the Japanese could with reinforcements flown in from Truk. Weather permitting, the Allies staged raids every day in late January.

At the same time, the liberal claims credit policy of the Americans gave rise to a large increase in credited victories, with the leading pilots in the fighter squadrons submitting claims for multiple victories in every mission that resulted in a battle. Regardless of imaginary victories, Rabaul was still dangerous, with one bad day on January 17 resulting in the loss of eight P-38s, one Hellcat, one Corsair, a Dauntless, and an Avenger.

Hanson's record continued to grow. He claimed one on January 20, three on January 23, four and a probable on January 24, three and a probable on January 26, and four on January 30 for a phenomenal total of 15 shot down in five missions and a total score of 25, putting him one off the record. Doubt began to grow among his fellow pilots about the truth of his claims. He would return after the rest of the squadron had landed to report his claims, while his regular wingman, Second

Lieutenant Samuel Sampler, returned with the others. Sampler always seemed to lose his element leader just after they brought the bombers to the rally point. Asked point blank by squadron pilot George Brewer what was the secret of his success, Hanson claimed that he would fly south of Rabaul where he would duck in and out of the cumulus clouds built up over the volcanoes, to shoot down fighters that were returning to land. Brewer thought it sounded like a great strategy.

Bad weather forced cancelation of all missions until February 3, when the scheduled mission was an attack on Tobera by dive-bombing SBDs and glide-bombing TBFs, escorted by 60 fighters including three divisions from VMF-215. By then, Hanson's division leader, Captain Don Aldrich, who was closing in on a final score of 20 himself, decided to put his doubts of the young ace's veracity to the test on the upcoming mission. He rearranged flight assignments for the division, ordering his normal wingman George Brewer to fly Hanson's wing and telling him personally that his assignment was to stick to his element leader like glue from takeoff to landing.

Hanson was not happy with Sampler's reassignment and gave Brewer the "silent treatment" throughout the pre-mission preparations. When Brewer asked if Hanson had any special instructions as element leader, the ace told him to fly like he always did, then told him that once the bombers arrived at the post-strike rally point, he might drop down and strafe the lighthouse on Cape St. George as they left the target.

After takeoff, Hanson maintained a strict radio silence, unlike most of the rest of the pilots, and never acknowledged Brewer's presence off his wing. Once the bombers had struck Tobera, Hanson turned toward the towering clouds to the south. Realizing Hanson intended to enter the clouds, Brewer closed up as tight as possible in order to keep his leader in sight once they were inside. Moments after they entered, Hanson wrapped up into a nearly vertical left bank. The cloud was so dense Brewer almost lost sight of him. Without warning, Hanson reversed his bank to the right, forcing Brewer to tuck under him quickly to avoid a collision. Brewer now anticipated the next reversal and kept his position below and behind Hanson, matching every movement as Hanson reversed his bank four more times in what was now an obvious attempt to lose his wingman. Brewer now knew Hanson's secret, and the knowledge made him angry as he realized he had respected a man who deserved none.

Finally, unable to shake Brewer, Hanson flew out of the cloud and headed toward Bougainville. Brewer concentrated on flying wing so close that Hanson couldn't miss his presence out of the corner of his eye no matter what he did. Minutes later, Brewer spotted a Zero below with two Corsairs pursuing it, but Hanson made no move to help, despite the fact it would have been an easy victory. Brewer fumed at this, but remembered his promise to Aldrich and maintained his position.

Suddenly, tracers flashed past Brewer's cockpit and he instinctively pushed over into a maximum-performance dive to lose his pursuer, but the Corsair had been badly hit and the engine caught fire. Flames leaped back as far as his cockpit. He leveled off, jettisoned his canopy and prepared to bail out. Looking down he realized he was still over the Gazelle Peninsula. He decided to make for St. George's Channel and ditch, where he had a prospect of being picked up.

Retarding his throttle, the flames suddenly went out and the engine ran smoother. Trailing a stream of smoke, he set course for home, determined to publicly expose Hanson for the fraud that he now knew the young ace was. Two Hellcats that spotted his damaged plane joined up and escorted him back to Barakoma.

Once on the ground, Brewer went to the operations tent to make his report to the squadron leaders. When he arrived, he learned that, after they had become separated, Hanson had joined up with the squadron. When they passed the lighthouse on Cape St. George that was known as an enemy flak tower and observation post, Hanson dived and strafed it as he had assured Brewer he might. The rest of the squadron watched from above as the Corsair ran at the tower, peppering the structure with machine gun fire. They were horrified to suddenly see the aircraft shudder as its wing disintegrated from flak hits. Hanson tried to ditch, but his Corsair hit the water, cartwheeled, and sank, leaving only scattered debris.

Brewer made his report of the mission and what he had observed to the squadron intelligence officer, who only seemed to take interest in his comment about seeing the Corsairs pursuing the Zero. Two days later, Brewer saw the intelligence report, which credited Hanson with diving to the rescue of two Corsairs being chased by Zeros. The report was used as the basis for a recommendation of Hanson for the Medal of Honor as the top-scoring Marine Corsair pilot.

Brewer fumed at the hypocrisy and thought about going public with his accusations regarding Hanson's real behavior. However, when he read of Hanson's missionary parents receiving the posthumous award at the White House from President Roosevelt, he decided telling the truth would do more harm than good. Robert Hanson was the third and last Marine Corsair pilot to receive the Medal of Honor and the youngest. His death occurred the day before his 24th birthday.

At Rabaul, 11th Air Division commander Admiral Kusaka decided to relieve the Sixth Air Attack force that included the 204th Air Group in light of the losses the unit had incurred over the month of January and requested reinforcement from Combined Fleet commander Admiral Koga at Truk. By now, the Central Pacific campaign was in full swing. The Gilbert Islands had been taken in November and December, and American troops had landed at Kwajalein in the Marshalls during January. Admiral Koga now saw even the main base at Truk as a potential target of the enemy fleet. Before he withdrew the carriers to Palau, out of range of the fast carriers of Task Force 58, he sent 62 Zeros from the carriers *Junyō*, *Hiyo*, and *Ryūjō* to Rabaul. The Sixth Air Attack force withdrew to Truk, leaving behind 20 fighters and transferring 20 pilots – including Tetsuo Iwamoto and Sadamu Komachi – to the 253rd Group at Tobera. Commander Okumiya accompanied the reinforcements, and found himself dismayed when he landed at Rabaul to realize that his friends there had come to the point of giving up under the pressure of the unrelenting Allied attacks.

The Allied campaign continued unabated during the first three weeks of February, with the weather relenting sufficiently to allow frequent missions. The 62 Zeros sent from Truk sustained losses without replacement. On February 10, 150 Allied bombers struck Rabaul's airfields in multiple strikes. The first strike of the day involved 59 Dauntlesses and 24 Avengers, escorted by 99 P-38s, P-40s, F4Us, and F6Fs, which struck Vunakanau airfield. With fewer than 15 defending fighters seen in the air, the Avengers scored 11 direct hits on the concrete runway with 2,000-pound bombs, which left the field unserviceable, while the SBDs knocked out most of the AA positions, losing one bomber to flak along with a Marine Avenger that also went down. This strike was followed an hour later by a low-level strafing and bombing mission against the field by 24 B-25s escorted by 20 P-38s. Shortly after that, 21 Liberators bombed Tobera airdrome.

Similar-sized raids hit Rabaul on February 12 and 13. Okumiya later wrote, "We repeated ambush after ambush, day in and day out... It seemed that no matter how many enemy planes were shot down, they reinforced their units even more."

On February 14, the 3rd New Zealand Division landed on Nissan Island in the Green Islands, 45 miles north of Buka and only 75 miles from Kavieng on New Ireland. A Japanese attack against the invasion forces resulted in five Vals, a Kate, and a Betty bomber shot down, with no damage to the invaders. Resistance ended with a suicidal banzai charge by the defenders on February 19. A new airfield would be ready by early April.

On February 15, Nisei intelligence agent Chikaki Honda took six high-value POWs, including Boyington, aboard a Betty bomber at Vunakanau to fly them to Japan for further interrogation. Before they could take off, 23 B-25s struck the field and the flight was delayed until the night of February 17 when the Betty took off, headed for the airfield on Moden Island at Truk.

The Betty arrived in the middle of Operation *Hailstone*, the full-scale attack on the Imperial Navy's main Pacific base by the carriers of Task Force 58. Somehow, the bomber avoided being shot down by the marauding Hellcats and touched down at Moden in the midst of a strafing attack. Boyington and the other prisoners were quickly hustled off the plane. Boyington later wrote of the event in his memoir, *Baa Baa Black Sheep*: "A Hellcat screamed over low, spraying .50-calibers all through the Nip aircraft standing there in front of us. The piece of transportation we had just crawled out of went up before our eyes in flame and smoke, and so did nearly every other plane we could see around there."

The prisoners scrambled into a slit trench beside the runway as a bomb hit the remains of the Betty and blew it up. Up and down the field, Japanese aircraft burned furiously and their ammunition exploded, filling the air with bullets and shrapnel. As the attacker flew off, a surviving Japanese pilot landed and ran for cover, only to discover the six Americans in the trench. Boyington later described what happened. "He was wearing one of those fuzzy helmets with the ear flaps turned up, and he looked in at us, as surprised as we were, then composed himself and said in English: 'I am a Japanese pilot. You bomb here, you die,' and patted the gun on his hip." Boyington burst out laughing at the preposterous moment, stopping long enough to say, "With all the God damned trouble we got, ain't you the cheerful son of a bitch, though."

Before the pilot could make good on his threat, another formation of Hellcats arrived overhead and he took off running. "The last we saw of him, his short legs were busy hopping over obstructions, the ear flaps of his fur helmet wobbling up and down so that he gave the appearance of a jackrabbit getting off the highway."

Boyington would "return from the dead" at the end of the war to discover he had been posthumously awarded the Medal of Honor. The Marines accepted his unconfirmed account of shooting down two final enemy planes and listed him as their top ace of the war, crediting him with a score of 28, including the six non-existent AVG "victories."

With Truk destroyed as a base for reinforcement, the Allied air force struck Rabaul again two days after Operation *Hailstone*, on February 19, 1944. A force of 48 SBDs and 23 TBFs were sent to attack shipping in Simpson Harbor, but found nothing there and instead bombed Lakunai airdrome. An hour after they departed, 20 B-24s bombed Lakunai and Tobera, knocking out their runways. Tetsuo Iwamoto led 36 Zeros that intercepted the Liberators, claiming one escorting Corsair for the loss of eight of their own number. It was the last air battle fought over Rabaul.

Eleven of the surviving Betty bombers had been sent to Guam the day before the raid, while several of the remaining Kates returned to Truk. Over the course of February 19–20, 40 Zeros, 21 Vals, 13 Bettys, four Judys, and seven freshly repaired Kates departed Rabaul's airfields headed for Truk and then on to Palau. Over the remaining 18 months of the Pacific War, Rabaul would receive no reinforcement while Marine and RNZAF bombers pounded the base, "bouncing the rubble" in the words of one airman, until Japan finally accepted the inevitable result that had been obvious since at least the day the Imperial Navy's air force failed to rise in defense of their main position in the South Pacific.

17

FINALE IN THE SOUTH PACIFIC

Outside of the epic Marine battle at Guadalcanal, the campaign against Rabaul is little-remembered, with the years dimming public memory and the final departures of the participants leaving no one to tell the tale first-hand. Rabaul town itself is close to non-existent in the wake of the September 19, 1994 eruption of the Tarvur crater, which destroyed 80 percent of the town's buildings, though in the years immediately after the war it had been rebuilt and became a popular tourist destination due to the opportunities to dive on the sunken ships in Simpson Harbor. The airfields that were once the most important targets in the South Pacific returned to jungle, though wreck enthusiasts managed to pull out sufficient aircraft remains that two of the five surviving A6M Zeros that fly today have been partially rebuilt with those parts.

The South Pacific campaign was the cornerstone of Allied victory in the Pacific War. It began with American forces stretched to their thinnest, with inexperienced units often outfought by their more-experienced opponents. It ended with the best Japan had to offer in terms of its warriors and their equipment lying blasted in the depths of the Coral Sea and Ironbottom Sound, or rotting in the unforgiving jungles on islands that only became important as the result of their geography.

By the time the Central Pacific campaign, which would result in complete victory, began in the fall of 1943, a new American Navy had been built, replacing the fleet that fought the opening battles and held the line against further Japanese expansion. The battles in the South Pacific were won by that older navy, which gave its all in so doing.

Admiral Halsey departed his headquarters at Nouméa in March 1944, promoted to command the Navy's Third Fleet, sharing command of the fast carrier task forces with Fifth Fleet commander Admiral Raymond Spruance over the final 17 months of the Pacific War. The Marine fighter and dive bomber units left the Solomons and moved to atoll airfields in the Marshalls and Carolines of the Central Pacific, where they honed their bombing skills against bypassed enemy-held islands for most of the rest of 1944. When they went into action again in the Philippines and at Okinawa, the Marine aviators were universally acclaimed the best at delivering close air support to the ground forces fighting the final battles of the war. The Corsair squadrons also finally went aboard the fleet carriers, providing the margin of victory to the air groups during the battles against the dreaded kamikazes.

Four months after the Imperial Navy evacuated its surviving air units from Rabaul, they fought their last battle in the Philippine Sea west of the Mariana islands. The air groups launched by the carriers that were chewed up, in what became known to their American opponents as the Marianas Turkey Shoot, were a shadow of the force that had spread across the South Pacific two years earlier. A handful of the experienced fliers, who had been part of the best naval air force in the world on December 7, 1941, still remained, but the planes that fought in June 1944 were flown by men who had difficulty getting airborne from the ships, men described bitterly by Saburo Sakai as "not as good as the worst of those who failed our training course in 1938." As a result of the Rabaul campaign, the Imperial Navy was left unable to meet its opponent on any sort of equal terms when the final battles came. The experienced fliers who still survived were too few to stem the American tide.

The victory proclaimed in Tokyo Bay in September 1945 was only possible because of the battles against the odds fought three years earlier in the waters and islands beneath the Southern Cross. There would never again be massed air battles between forces of near equal capability like those seen over Rabaul between October 1943 and February 1944. In the end, it didn't matter who scored how many individual victories. It rather mattered that, in their combined force, the Allied fliers stopped their enemy. The campaign against Rabaul was both the end of the beginning and the beginning of the end of the Pacific War.

BIBLIOGRAPHY

Anderson, Charles R., "Guadalcanal: The US Army Campaigns of World War II," United States Army Center of Military History, CMH Pub 72-8, 1993

Bell, Frederick Jackson, *Condition Red: Destroyer Action in the South Pacific* (New York: Longmans, Green & Co., 1943)

Bergerud, Eric M., *Fire in the Sky: The Air War in the South Pacific* (Boulder, CO: Westview Press, 2000)

Birdsall, Steve, *Log of the Liberators: An Illustrated History of the B-24* (New York: Doubleday, 1973)

Cleaver, Thomas McKelvey, "Raid on Rabaul," *Flight Journal*, October 2002

Cleaver, Thomas McKelvey, "One-Slug McWhorter," *Flight Journal*, November 2002

Cleaver, Thomas McKelvey, *Aces of the 78th Fighter Group* (Oxford: Osprey Publishing, 2012)

Cleaver, Thomas McKelvey, *F4F and F6F Aces of VF-2* (Oxford: Osprey Publishing, 2014)

Cleaver, Thomas McKelvey, *Fabled Fifteen: The Pacific War Saga of Carrier Air Group 15* (Havertown, PA: Casemate Publishers, 2014)

Cleaver, Thomas McKelvey, *Pacific Thunder: The US Navy's Central Pacific Campaign, August 1943–October 1944* (Oxford: Osprey Publishing, 2017)

Clubb, Timothy L., "Cactus Air Power at Guadalcanal" (pdf) Master's thesis, Leavenworth: United States Army Command and General Staff College, 1996

Coggins, Jack, *The Campaign for Guadalcanal: A Battle that Made History* (New York: Doubleday, 1972)

Cook, Charles O., *The Battle of Cape Esperance: Encounter at Guadalcanal* (Annapolis, MD: US Naval Institute Press, 1992)

Cook, Lee, *The Skull and Crossbones Squadron: VF-17 in World War II* (Atglen, PA: Schiffer Aviation History, 1998)

Davis, Donald A., *Lightning Strike: The Secret Mission to Kill Admiral Yamamoto and Avenge Pearl Harbor* (New York: St. Martin's Press, 2005)

Domagalski, John J., *Sunk in Kula Gulf: The Final Voyage of the USS* Helena *and the Incredible Story of Her Survivors in World War II* (Washington, DC: Potomac Books, 2012)

Drury, Bob and Tom Clavin, *Lucky 666: The Impossible Mission* (New York: Simon & Schuster, Inc., 2016)

Dull, Paul S., *A Battle History of the Imperial Japanese Navy, 1941–1945* (Annapolis, MD: US Naval Institute Press, 1998)

Frank, Richard, *Guadalcanal: The Definitive Account of the Landmark Battle* (New York: Random House, 1990)

Gailey, Harry A., *Bougainville, 1943–1945: The Forgotten Campaign* (Lexington, KY: University Press of Kentucky, 1995)

Gamble, Bruce, *Target: Rabaul: The Allied Siege of Japan's Most Infamous Stronghold, March 1943–August 1945* (New York: Zenith Press, 2013)

Grace, James W., *Naval Battle of Guadalcanal: Night Action, 13 November 1942* (Annapolis, MD: Naval Institute Press, 1999)

Hammel, Eric, *Guadalcanal: Decision at Sea: The Naval Battle of Guadalcanal, Nov. 13–15, 1942* (Pacifica, CA: Pacifica Press, 1988)

Hammel, Eric, *Carrier Clash: The Invasion of Guadalcanal and The Battle of the Eastern Solomons August 1942* (Pacifica, CA: Pacifica Press, 1997)

Hammel, Eric, *Carrier Strike: The Battle of the Santa Cruz Islands, October 1942* (Pacifica, CA: Pacifica Press, 1999)

Henebry, John P., *The Grim Reapers at Work in the Pacific Theater: The Third Attack Group of the US Fifth Air Force* (Missoula, MT: Pictorial Histories Publishing Company, 2002)

Hess, William N., *49th Fighter Group: Aces of the Pacific* (Oxford: Osprey Publishing, 2004)

Hornfischer, James D., *Neptune's Inferno: The US Navy at Guadalcanal* (New York: Bantam, 2011)

Ichimura, Hiroshi, *Ki-43 "Oscar" Aces of World War 2* (Oxford: Osprey Publishing, 2009)

Kenney, George C., *The Saga of Pappy Gunn* (New York: Duell, Sloan and Pierce, 1959)

Kurzman, Dan, *Left to Die: The Tragedy of the USS* Juneau (New York: Pocket Books, 1994)

Lardas, Mark, *Rabaul 1943–44: Reducing Japan's Great Island Fortress* (Oxford: Osprey Publishing, 2018)

Lundstrom, John B., *The First Team and the Guadalcanal Campaign: Naval Fighter Combat from August to November 1942* (reprint) (Annapolis, MD: US Naval Institute Press, 2005)

Molesworth, Carl, *P-40 Warhawk Aces of the Pacific* (Oxford: Osprey Publishing, 2003)

Morison, Samuel E., *The Struggle for Guadalcanal, August 1942–February 1943*, Volume 5 of *History of United States Naval Operations in World War II* (Boston: Little, Brown, 1949)

Morison, Samuel E., *Breaking the Bismarcks Barrier*, Volume 6 of *History of United States Naval Operations in World War II* (Castle Books, 1958)

Okumiya, Masatake, Jiro Horikoshi and Martin Caidin, *Zero: The Story of Japan's Air War in the Pacific* (New York: Ballantine, 1956)

Prados, John, *Combined Fleet Decoded: The Secret History of American Intelligence and the Japanese Navy in World War II* (New York: Random House, 1995)

Sakaida, Henry, *The Siege of Rabaul* (St. Paul, MN: Phalanx, 1996)

Sakaida, Henry, *Imperial Japanese Navy Aces of World War 2* (Oxford: Osprey Publishing, 1999)

Salecker, Gene Eric, *Fortress Against the Sun: The B-17 Flying Fortress in the Pacific* (New York: Da Capo Press, 2001)

Sherrod, Robert, *History of Marine Corps Aviation in World War II* (Washington DC: Combat Forces Press, 1952)

Sims, Edward H., *American Aces* (New York: Harper & Brothers, 1958)

Spector, Ronald H., *Eagle Against the Sun: The American War with Japan* (New York: The Free Press, 1985)

Stanaway, John, *475th Fighter Group* (Oxford: Osprey Publishing, 2007)

Stille, Mark, *Guadalcanal 1942–43: America's First Victory on the Road to Tokyo* (Oxford: Osprey Publishing, 2015)

Stille, Mark, *The Solomons 1943–44: The Struggle for New Georgia and Bougainville* (Oxford: Osprey Publishing, 2018)

Tillman, Barrett, *The Dauntless Dive Bomber in World War II* (Annapolis, MD: US Naval Institute Press, 1976)

Tillman, Barrett, *Corsair: The F4U in World War II and Korea* (Annapolis, MD: US Naval Institute Press, 1979)

Tillman, Barrett, *Wildcat: The F4F in WWII* (Annapolis, MD: US Naval Institute Press, 1990)

Tillman, Barrett, *TBF/TBM Avenger Units of World War 2* (Oxford: Osprey Publishing, 1999)

Tillman, Barrett and Henk Van der Lugt, *VF11/111 Sundowners, 1942–45* (Oxford: Osprey Publishing, 2010)

Toll, Ian W., *The Conquering Tide: War in the Pacific Islands, 1942–1944* (New York: W.W. Norton, 2015)

Zimmerman, John L., *The Guadalcanal Campaign*, Marines in World War II Historical Monograph (Quantico: USMC, 1949)

INDEX

References to maps are in **bold**.